War and

War and Revolution
Rethinking the Twentieth Century

DOMENICO LOSURDO
TRANSLATED BY GREGORY ELLIOTT

VERSO
London • New York

This paperback edition published by Verso 2020
First published in English by Verso 2015
Translation © Gregory Elliott 2015, 2020

Chapters 1–5 first published, in Italian, as *Il revisionism storico. Problemi e miti*
© Laterza 1996
Chapter 7 first published, in Italian, as *Il peccato originale del Novecento*
© Laterza 1998

1 3 5 7 9 10 8 6 4 2

Verso
UK: 6 Meard Street, London W1F 0EG
US: 20 Jay Street, Suite 1010, Brooklyn, NY 11201
versobooks.com

Verso is the imprint of New Left Books

ISBN-13: 978-1-78873-666-4
ISBN-13: 978-1-78168-617-1 (US EBK)
ISBN-13: 978-1-78168-724-6 (UK EBK)

British Library Cataloguing in Publication Data
A catalogue record for this book is available from the British Library

The Library of Congress Has Cataloged the Hardback Edition as Follows:

Losurdo, Domenico.
War and revolution : rethinking the twentieth century / Domenico Losurdo ;
translated by Gregory Elliott.
    pages cm
An amplification and revision of three works: chapters 1–5 reproduce Il
revisionismo storico : problemi e miti (Laterza, 1996. 5th edition, 2002); chapter
6 was written especially for the English edition; and chapter 7 is a translation of Il
peccato originale del Novecento (Laterza, 1998. 3rd edition, 2007).
    Includes bibliographical references and index.
    ISBN 978-1-78168-616-4 (hardback) – ISBN 978-1-78168-724-6 (electronic)
    – ISBN 978-1-78168-617-1 (electronic)
1. History, Modern–20th century–Historiography. 2. History, Modern–20th
century. 3. Historiography–Philosophy. 4. World politics–20th century.
5. Military history, Modern–20th century. 6. Revolutions–History–20th century.
7. Civil war–History–20th century. 8. Genocide–History–20th century.
9. Communism–History–20th century. 10. Fascism–History–20th century. I.
Losurdo, Domenico. Revisionismo storico. English. II. Losurdo, Domenico.
Peccato originale del Novecento. English. III. Title.
    D413.5.L67 2014
    909.82072–dc23

                                                2014029117

Typeset in Perpetua by Hewer Text UK Ltd, Edinburgh, Scotland
Printed and bound by CPI Group (UK) Ltd, Croydon, CR0 4YY

Contents

Authorial Note

The text that follows is an amplification and revision of three works. Chapters 1–5 reproduce *Il revisionismo storico. Problemi e miti* (Rome/Bari: Laterza, 1996; 5th edition, 2002). Chapter 6 was written especially for the English edition, while Chapter 7 is a translation of *Il peccato originale del Novecento* (Rome/Bari: Laterza, 1998; 3rd edition, 2007). The idea for the book derived from an intense and fruitful exchange of ideas with Sebastian Budgen, to whom I express my warm gratitude.

In revising the text, I have had the help of Dr Giorgio Grimaldi, to whom many thanks.

CHAPTER ONE

Two Centuries Under Discussion: Historical Revisionism

Historical Revisionism and the Liquidation of the Revolutionary Tradition

Is there a thread to guide us in the labyrinth of rereadings, re-examinations and reinterpretations known as 'historical revisionism'? According to one of its most eminent representatives – Ernst Nolte – Hitler, in exterminating the Jews, regarded the 'Asiatic' barbarism of the Bolsheviks, and the class genocide carried out by them, both as a model and as a danger to be averted at any cost.[1] The Nazis' actions amounted to a policy of 'counter-annihilation' – a response to the challenge of the policy of 'annihilation' implemented by the regime deriving from October 1917. Not only was the horror of the Third Reich a derivative phenomenon, but its crimes – 'until 1941' – 'were incomparably less massive than those perpetrated in the name of the proletarian revolution in the Soviet Union'.[2] The author of this appraisal is another prominent figure in historical revisionism, François Furet, who does not confine himself to incriminating the 'Stalinist phenomenon', but reverts to the 'Jacobin tradition' behind it. With its pitiless revelations,

Solzhenitsyn's work has become the basic historical reference for the Soviet experience, ineluctably locating the issue of the Gulag at the very core of the revolutionary endeavour. Once that happened, the Russian example

---

1 Ernst Nolte, 'The Past That Will Not Pass: A Speech That Could Be Written but Not Delivered', in *Forever in the Shadow of Hitler?: Original Documents of the Historikerstreit, the Controversy Concerning the Singularity of the Holocaust*, trans. James Knowlton and Truett Cates, New Jersey: Humanities Press, 1993, p. 22.

2 François Furet, *The Passing of an Illusion: The Idea of Communism in the Twentieth Century*, trans. Deborah Furet, Chicago and London: University of Chicago Press, 1999, pp. 357–8.

was bound to turn around, to strike its French 'origin' . . . the two revolutions . . . are today . . . accused of being, consubstantially, systems of meticulous constraint over men's bodies and minds.[3]

And there is no point invoking alleged 'circumstances' – 'external phenomena that had nothing to do with' the revolutionary project and ideology. In fact, the latter generated horrors exclusively out of its own internal logic or insanity. Furet draws attention to Tocqueville's diagnosis of the incessant revolutionary upheavals in France between the seventeenth and eighteenth centuries. We are dealing with an 'illness', 'a virus of a new and unknown kind',[4] which has continued to rage with redoubled violence in the twentieth century.

From the capital of the former Soviet Union arrives news of a process of rehabilitation – in fact, a veritable 'canonization of the last Czar and of his family' ('Nicolas II's sister-in-law, Princess Elizabeth, has already been proclaimed a saint').[5] Once again we are led back to the French Revolution, when the Bourbon king, a descendent of St Louis, was compared by the monarchist press to the son of God, so that the punishment inflicted on Louis XVI by the Jacobins could be depicted as a replica of Golgotha.[6] In the collective mentality, as in revisionist historiography, the prevalent negative judgement tends to equate Jacobinism and Bolshevism.

The homage paid to the Romanovs involves a tendency to de-legitimize the whole movement that issued in the fall of Czarism. Let us attend to Nolte once again: 'The diary of an attaché at the French embassy, Louis de Robien, confirms the conviction of other observers of the time that the February Revolution was already marked by the kind of atrocity that was labelled "Bolshevik".'[7]

The American historian Richard Pipes goes even further. On the basis of Furet's (and Tocqueville's) diagnosis of the revolutionary disease, he impeaches

---

3   François Furet, *Interpreting the French Revolution*, trans. Elborg Forster, Cambridge: Cambridge University Press, 1981, p. 12.

4   Ibid., p. 163 n. 26. Cf. Alexis de Tocqueville, *Oeuvres complètes*, Paris: Gallimard, 1951–, Vol. XIII, pt. 2, p. 337.

5   'Per Nicola II si prepara una corona di santo. Parte la canonizzazione della famiglia dello zar', *Corriere della sera*, 8 April 1992.

6   Jean-Paul Bertaud, 'La presse royaliste parisienne, l'idée de guerre and la guerre, 1789–1792', in F. Lubrun and R. Dupuy, eds, *Les Résistances à la Révolution*, Paris: Imago, 1987, p. 206.

7   Ernst Nolte, *Gli anni della violenza. Un secolo di guerra civile ideologica, europea e mondiale*, trans. P. Azzaro and S. Azzaro, Milan: Rizzoli, 1995, p. 45.

the whole cycle from 1905 to 1917 in Russia.[8] It cannot be explained solely by objective conditions. In the early twentieth century, and at any rate during the First World War, a new political and constitutional reality was in fact developing, comparable to 'the vigorous growth of saplings in the shade of an old and decaying forest' (the Czarist autocracy), which was set to disappear without any need for painful external intervention. On the one hand, 'a silent revolution' was underway, 'the more effective in that it was accomplished to meet actual needs rather than to realize utopian visions'.[9] On the other, the incessant agitation of a 'militant minority' asserted itself ever more vociferously, engaging in 'physical coercion' in 1905,[10] and unleashing bloody violence as early as February 1917. Police barracks were 'attacked and demolished', policemen caught in uniform 'beaten and killed', and anyone who dared to oppose those who had mutinied was threatened with 'lynching'.[11]

Such were the disastrous manifestations of the 'revolutionary psychosis' gripping 'an unusually large and fanatical body of professional revolutionaries', who were consumed by 'an intensely felt, irrational desire to pull down the entire edifice of monarchic Russia'.[12] The symptoms of this disease can be described drawing on Taine as well as Tocqueville. What prevents people seeing 'men as they really are' are 'a few simple ideas', 'political geometry', abstract constructs.[13] Equally valuable is the lesson of another major critic of the French Revolution: 'Cochin's description of the atmosphere in the French *sociétés de pensée* of the late eighteenth century perfectly fits that prevailing in intelligentsia circles in Russia a century later.' In each case, the 'arid terror' of the *Encyclopédie* or the anti-Czarist intelligentsia paved the way for the subsequent 'bloody terror'.[14]

There was no justification for the latter. 'In the first half of November 1916', Nicholas II had already 'capitulated to revolutionary demands'. Yet the opposition, 'smelling blood', demanded more.[15] It was not only the Bolsheviks. With his 'hysterical speech' against the 'ruling classes' responsible

---

8   Richard Pipes, *The Russian Revolution*, New York: Vintage Books, 1990, pp. 132–3 and 129 n.

9   Ibid., p. 232.

10   Ibid., pp. 36, 41.

11   Ibid., p. 280.

12   Ibid., pp. 255, 122.

13   Ibid., p. 681.

14   Ibid., pp. 130, 353; Auguste Cochin, *Les Sociétés de pensée et la démocratie moderne. Études d'histoire révolutionnaire*, Paris: Copernic, 1978, p. 13.

15   Pipes, *The Russian Revolution*, p. 257.

for having pushed Russia into war, Kerensky scarcely differed from Lenin.[16] In conclusion, 'had he lived into the twentieth century, Tocqueville might have found it easier to identify the "virus", because its peculiar blend of ideas and group interests has become commonplace since his day'.[17]

To explain the ravages of the revolutionary disease in the twentieth century, Pipes thus goes back to the French Revolution and the Enlightenment, which he interprets with the aid of Furet. The latter, having started out from a critique of the French Revolution and condemnation of Jacobinism, subsequently felt compelled to subject the experience initiated with October 1917 to a pitiless analysis. In radicalizing his denunciation of Bolshevism, Nolte in turn felt obliged to work backwards, condemning the French Revolution in its entirety. The main target of historical revisionism thus becomes clear: the whole historical cycle running from 1789 to 1917.

Its assault has a series of knock-on effects. Without the French Revolution, the Italian Risorgimento is unintelligible, for behind it were 1848, the Napoleonic experience and, even earlier, the Neapolitan revolution of 1799. In his time, Lincoln was accused by contemporaries and opponents of having resorted to ruthless measures of a Jacobin kind. And, in our day, we find a substantial literature engaged in condemning the 'catastrophe' of the American Civil War, provoked (according to a prominent representative of US revisionism) by 'hotheads' on both sides.[18] In fact, others argue, it was a bloody, senseless 'revolution' unleashed by the North,[19] with which is to be contrasted the 'Southern epic'.[20] In its turn, the collapse of the 'myth' of the Bolshevik October inevitably casts a shadow over the worldwide anti-fascist Resistance, in which a leading role was played by political and social forces explicitly identified with Bolshevism. And an even more eerie shadow falls over the anti-colonial revolutionary movement, stimulated and strongly influenced from the outset by Communist agitation and participation. Authors who do not explicitly profess revisionism, even if they can be included in its ambit, salute the 'revival of colonialism'. Along with the country born of the October Revolution have collapsed its 'ideological

---

16   Ibid., pp. 252, 228.

17   Ibid., p. 133.

18   Harry E. Barnes, *Entlarvete Heuchelei (Ewig Krieg um ewigen Frieden). Revision der amerikanischen Geschichtsschreibung*, Wiesbaden: Priester, 1961, p. 3.

19   Richard M. Weaver, *The Southern Essays*, ed. G.M. Curtiss, III and J.J. Thompson Jr., Indianapolis: Liberty Press, 1987, p. 213.

20   See Dominique Venner, *Le blanc soleil des vaincus. L'épopée sudiste et la guerre de Sécession 1607–1865*, Paris: La Table Ronde, 1975.

beliefs' and 'sacred canon', an integral part of which was Lenin's pamphlet denouncing imperialism.[21] The disastrous influence of October 1917 sometimes seems to be closely bound up with that of the 1789 revolution: in the years of the Resistance, 'France was shaken by much worse explosions of hatred than during the French Revolution.'[22]

The main theme of this comprehensive reinterpretation of the contemporary world thus becomes even clearer: it involves the liquidation of the revolutionary tradition from 1789 to the present. At this point, the term 'revisionism' becomes intelligible. In the debate within the political movements inspired by Marxism, the 'revisionists' were those like Bernstein who sought to expunge the 'Blanquist or Babouvist' legacy,[23] the Jacobin spirit they detected in Marx and Engels' theory and, *a fortiori*, in the theory and practice of the Bolshevik Party.

The Second Thirty Years' War as a World Revolution

The cultural and political tendency in question represents a historiographical and cultural turn of great significance, a turn that is in a sense epochal. To account for it, we must take a step back and briefly reconstruct the prevalent ideological and political climate during the so-called Second Thirty Years' War, to employ a term often used by historians to characterize the massive upheavals of 1914–45. During the First World War, a substantial literature in Germany sang the praises of the German army and people's unanimous commitment and revolt against the 'ideas of 1789'. On the other side, the Entente justified and celebrated the war it was waging as a decisive contribution to the cause of the triumph of democracy and peace over despotism and militarism – as an international democratic revolution set to destroy the stronghold of the *ancien régime* represented by the Central Powers and, in particular, Prussia. Above all, the latter had committed the error of rejecting the 'noble ideas' hailing 'from eighteenth-century and revolutionary France'.[24] Positive judgements of this key historical episode did not

---

21   Paul Johnson, 'Colonialism's Back – and Not a Moment Too Soon', *New York Times Magazine*, 18 April 1993.

22   Barnes, *Entlarvete Heuchelei*, p. 12.

23   Eduard Bernstein, *The Preconditions of Socialism*, ed. and trans. Henry Tudor, Cambridge: Cambridge University Press, 1993, p. 38.

24   Henri Bergson, *Mélanges*, ed. A. Robinet, Paris: Presses Universitaires de France, 1972, p. 1106.

discriminate against Jacobinism. The French prime minister Clémenceau did not shy away from posing as the head of a kind of new Committee of Public Safety saving the country from the intervention of counter-revolutionary powers – once again, as ever, Germany and Austria. After February 1917, Kerensky behaved in similar fashion, seeking to relaunch the war and summoning the Russian people to mass mobilization in defence of both nation and revolution. Even across the Atlantic, intervention was sometimes called for and celebrated with reference to the French Revolution. Like that of 1789, the 'stupendous revolution' of the First World War was set to usher in 'a new world'.[25]

This way of depicting things was consolidated with the subsequent development of the Second Thirty Years' War. Even setting aside the USSR's ideological platform, we might recall Roosevelt himself declaring that, in order to destroy the 'seeds of Hitlerism', it was necessary to take the changes that had occurred after the First World War (in Germany, the end of the Hohenzollerns and the advent of a democratic republic) much further and achieve 'freedom from want', thereby impacting radically on socio-economic relations. Where Wilson had promoted the USA's entry into the war in the name of democracy, Roosevelt's slogan seemed to foreshadow a project of social-democracy, which (as has been noted) went far beyond the prior US political tradition.[26] These are slogans that refer to the French Revolution's radicalization in a social direction. They end up casting an objectively favourable light even on October 1917. It is no coincidence if, some decades later, Hayek was to detect the disastrous influence of 'the Marxist Russian Revolution' in the theorization of 'freedom from want'.[27]

Let us turn to the First World War and the indictment of Germany tabled in the literature of the Entente. Along with the ideas of 1789, Germany had also rejected the notion of equality between different peoples and races, as was attested by German culture's enthusiasm for an author like Gobineau, who (according to Bergson) did not merit any attention.[28] A few decades later, the leaders of the Third Reich were condemned at Nuremburg for having formulated from the foundation of the Nazi Party a programme of colonial conquest in the name of the superior rights of the 'master race',

---

25   Stuart I. Rochester, *American Liberal Disillusionment in the Wake of World War I*, University Park: Pennsylvania State University Press, 1977, pp. 44, 65.

26   Henry Kissinger, *Democracy*, New York: Simon & Schuster, 1994, pp. 389–90.

27   F.A. Hayek, *Law, Legislation and Liberty: A New Statement of the Liberal Principles of Justice and Political Economy*, Abingdon: Routledge, 2013, p. 264.

28   Bergson, *Mélanges*, p. 1113.

and for having developed a massive system for siphoning and exploiting forced labour during the Second World War, as 'in the darkest days of the slave trade'.[29] The Third Reich was represented as a fearsome counter-revolutionary wave against the abolitionist revolution initiated with the decree of the Jacobin Convention that ended slavery in French colonies. And such a representation ends up casting an at least objectively favourable light on the Bolshevik October and Lenin's appeal to the 'colonial slaves' to break their chains.

We thus see the Second Thirty Years' War gradually assume the shape of a democratic and social revolution on a global scale. Naturally, this ideological process did not develop without profound, acute contradictions. Lenin ironized about interpretations of the war by some Entente countries in a revolutionary, even Jacobin, key. Condemning the First World War as imperialist on both sides, he challenged the right of 'social-chauvinists, both French and Russian' to evoke 'the spirit of 1793' and raise the banner of the revolutionary defence of the nation.[30] The Bolsheviks began to invoke Jacobinism not to celebrate the mass mobilization of the nation against despotic Prussian invaders, but to legitimate the Terror of the new Soviet power in its desperate struggle against the revolution's external and internal enemies. The continuity thus established also ended up prevailing in the opposite camp for a while, albeit with a radically negative value judgement. These were the years when, in order to explain the French Revolution but with a view to the October Revolution, conspiracy theory was dusted off and refurbished in Britain. The author of a book tending in that direction had the honour of being immediately cited by Winston Churchill, who seems to have regarded the upheavals in Russia as new evidence for this theory.[31]

However, with the advent of the Third Reich and the outbreak of the Second World War, contentions within the anti-German front seemed to vanish, so that Germany reverted to being an *ancien régime* or Vendée of international dimensions – an image which, having emerged in 1914, only now became genuinely unanimous, without divisions and contradictions. This interpretation of the war seemed all the more convincing in that Nazism, adopting and radicalizing the slogan of the Wilhelmine empire,

---

29   Quoted in Joe J. Heydecker and Johannes Leeb, *Der Nürnberger Prozess*, Köln: Kiepenheuer & Witsch, 1985, Vol. II, pp. 531, 543.

30   V.I. Lenin, *Collected Works*, London: Lawrence and Wishart, 1960–, Vol. 25, pp. 86–7. See also Vol. 24, pp. 401–2.

31   Léon Poliakov, *The History of Anti-Semitism*, trans. Richard Howard et al., Philadelphia: University of Pennsylvania Press, 2003, Vol. 4, p. 207.

launched a crusade against the 'ideas of 1789', alleged source of all the disastrous upheavals in the contemporary world, including the most subversive and barbaric revolution of them all: the Bolshevik Revolution. As early as 1920, Hitler regarded Wilson as a repulsive, fanatical 'apostle who wants to save the world', negating the natural order of things, and hence similar to that 'Jew who wants to save the world', as Lenin was defined at the time by 'Hitler's best friend and advisor'.[32] In other words, the American president was depicted with those features which the conservative, reactionary tradition was fond of attributing to revolutionary intellectuals. This is the essential meaning of the accusations subsequently directed against Franklin Delano Roosevelt: 'Jewish blood' circulated in his veins and the woman married by him had a 'completely negroid appearance' (the British Minister of War, for his part, was 'that Moroccan Jew').[33] For the leaders of the Third Reich, the American (and British) administration seemed to contain echoes of the anti-colonial revolutions, the revolt of peoples of colour. On the other hand, precisely because the war of Germany's enemies was explicitly represented as a democratic revolution, behind this subversion, like previous ones, there could only lie a Jewish conspiracy, which had to be scotched once and for all.

Germany and the *Ancien Régime*

For all these reasons, the unanimous mobilization against the Third Reich ended up involving a legitimation of the revolutionary tradition as a whole. This was a mental climate that temporarily survived the outbreak of the Cold War in some respects. So much is clear from two books which, although deriving from the opposed alliances, nevertheless exhibit significant common ground. Lukács' balance sheet of the catastrophe of Germany stresses the absence of a revolutionary tradition in that country, whose tragic 'fate', having already begun to be foreshadowed in 1525 – year of the defeat of the peasants who had risen up to abolish serfdom[34] – assumed ever clearer

---

32   Reginald H. Phelps, 'Hitler als Parteiredner im Jahre 1920', *Vierteljahreshefte zür Zeitgeschichte*, Vol. XI, 1963, p. 305; Ernst Nolte, *La Crisi dei regime liberali e i movimenti fascisti*, trans. C. Gamaleri and A. Caiani, Bologna: Il Mulino, 1970, p. 72.

33   Adolf Hitler, *Hitler's Table Talk 1941–44*, London: Weidenfeld & Nicolson, 1973, pp. 545, 202 (conversations of 1 July, midday and night of 12–13 January 1942).

34   Georg Lukács, *The Destruction of Reason*, trans. Peter Palmer, London: Merlin Press, 1980, p. 40.

contours as Germany evinced its foreignness or active hostility to the revolutions of the modern age. At virtually the same time Hannah Arendt intervened. A few years had passed since the end of the war, whose 'revolutionary significance' she had underscored and which had witnessed '*la levée en masse*' of Warsaw's Jews against their oppressors and exterminators.[35] On the one hand, Arendt subsumes Stalin's USSR together with Hitler's regime under the category of 'totalitarianism'. On the other, she reconstructs the parabola leading to Auschwitz, starting like Lukács with reactionary critics of Enlightenment and the French Revolution – Boulainvilliers, Burke and Gobineau. Her harsh assessment of the British Whig is especially significant: his view of liberty as a hereditarily transmitted privilege, and his rejection of the rights of man, were imbued with a sentiment of inequality that would later inspire the imperial metropolis in its relationship with the colonies. In this sense, the first great indictment of the French Revolution already contained the 'seeds of racist ideology'. A direct line runs from Burke to Disraeli and the most virulent forms of imperialism, inherited by the Third Reich. Like Lukács in the case of Social Darwinism, Arendt pointed the finger at 'naturalistic conceptions' which, starting with the liquidation of the ideal of equality, were above all diffused in Britain and Germany. The country that experienced the ominous triumph of the Third Reich was one where Burke had enjoyed 'considerable influence'. The 'affinities between German and British racist ideologies' were apparent. The country at the head of the anti-French coalitions was obsessed 'by theories of heredity and their modern equivalent, eugenics'. It was no accident if the hopes of the anti-democrat and racist Gobineau were initially focused on Britain and then, after 1871, on Germany.

By contrast, the ideas of the theoretician of natural racial inequality met with little response in post-revolutionary France, which was in the vanguard in achieving 'political equality' (it was the 'only country' not to discriminate against blacks). A positive judgement of the French Revolution also seems to apply to Robespierre, who is approvingly cited several times for standing firm on the unity of the human race and for his hostility to colonial conquests. This is all the more significant because it was precisely in the colonies that the *univers concentrationnaire* made its first appearance (Arendt takes the example of Egypt under British domination), and large-scale massacres and genocides were perpetrated (with the collapse of 'the peaceful Congo

---

35   Hannah Arendt, *Essays und Kommentare*, ed. E. Geisel and K. Bittermann, Berlin: Tiamat, 1989, Vol. II, p. 191 and Vol. I, pp. 157–8.

population – from 20 to 40 million in 1890 to 8 million in 1911'[36]), anticipating the horrors of the twentieth century.

As opposed to the Anglo-German conservative and reactionary tradition,
the positive term of the antithesis comprises the American and French
revolutionary tradition. At this point in time, the two revolutions were
not contrasted: the two declarations of rights were equated and analysed
conjointly. Hence condemnation of the 'totalitarian' USSR did not as yet
involve denunciation of 1789 and 1793. In fact, strictly speaking it did not
even involve condemnation of October 1917, given that, at this stage of
her development, Arendt was concerned to distinguish between Lenin's
revolutionary dictatorship and Stalin's totalitarianism. Immediately after
the Bolshevik Revolution, Soviet Russia presented itself as a society which,
albeit within the limits imposed by a dramatic state of emergency, had a
richly articulated internal life. Whereas Czarism had harshly oppressed the
various nationalities, Lenin, by contrast, strove to accommodate them to
the maximum. There was broad support from ethnic groups, which were
able to express themselves as autonomous cultural and national entities
for the first time. They represented an antidote to the totalitarian regime:
between the amorphous mass and the charismatic head stood a whole
series of organisms that impeded and frustrated the latter's immediate
volition. In addition to various nationalities, this also applied to other
forms of expression of social and political reality. For example, trade unions
achieved an organizational autonomy unknown in Czarist Russia. The rich
articulation of the society born of the revolution was completely dismantled
by Stalin, who, in order to impose the totalitarian regime, had to artificially
create an atomized, amorphous mass, which then became the object or
base of the charismatic, unchallenged power of the infallible leader.[37]
Moreover, according to the Arendt of the early 1950s, the transition from
one phase of the Soviet Union's history to the next was punctuated not
by the inexorable logic of Bolshevik ideology, but by the 'outbreak of the
civil war'.

---

36   Hannah Arendt, *The Origins of Totalitarianism*, New York: Harcourt, Brace & World,
1951, p. 185 n. 2.
37   Ibid., pp. 318–19.

From the Denunciation of Bolshevism to the Liquidation of Jacobinism and the French Revolution

We are far removed from the cultural and political climate of revisionism. It is therefore appropriate to take a quick look at the stages via which it was created. A few years after *The Origins of Totalitarianism*, an American historian undertook to reconstruct as a unitary phenomenon the revolutionary cycle that developed on both sides of the Atlantic and, in particular, in America and France. While its key moment was the revolt of the British colonies (of which the upheavals in France were to be regarded as a mere 'consequence'), this 'Western revolution', which created 'Western' and 'Atlantic civilization',[38] excluded neither Rousseau nor Robespierre, who were the first to confer a positive meaning on the term 'democracy' and to theorize a 'democratic state' based on the principle of political equality.[39] Likewise essentially positive was Palmer's assessment of Toussaint L'Ouverture, the black Jacobin who led the great slave revolt in San Domingo, which was also to be situated in the ambit of the 'Western revolution':

> Struggling against chaos, against breakdown in labor, production, and government, in a turmoil of strife between rivals, and between mulattoes and Negroes, with threats of Spanish and British intervention, and in fear of a reimposition of slavery, Toussaint managed to maintain a regime whose stated ideals at least were those of the European revolution, at the cost of atrocities that were worse than those of the Vendée or Ireland.[40]

From this rapid comparative overview it emerges that violence and terror are not attributable exclusively to Jacobinism. In fact, Britain was no stranger to the phenomenon. Conventional representations of the revolution across the Atlantic likewise involve excluding the struggle with the 'loyalists' from the historical picture. It was so bitter that in 1776 America seemed to presage 'something of the *gouvernement révolutionnaire* and even the Terror of France in 1793'. Certainly, there were 'differences of scale and intensity', which are not *a priori* deducible from ideology. The greater or lesser bitterness of the struggle primarily derived from the concrete situation: while the 'French

---

38 Robert R. Palmer, *The Age of Democratic Revolution: A Political History of Europe and America, 1760–1800*, Princeton: Princeton University Press, 1959–64, Vol. I, pp. 185–6, 4.

39 Ibid., Vol. I, pp. 314, 17.

40 Ibid., Vol. II, p. 514.

émigrés' returned home, their American counterparts 'peopled the Canadian wilderness'.[41]

As with the author of *The Origins of Totalitarianism*, Britain remained synonymous with reaction in Palmer. There the aristocracy, which controlled both Houses of Parliament, severely repressed 'agitation for parliamentary reform' and 'movements for democracy'.[42] While it conjoined America and France, the 'Western revolution' thus found Burke's native land and Burke himself in opposition. Compared with Arendt, Palmer's novelty consists in his dichotomy between 'the revolution of the Western world', which occurred in the eighteenth century in advanced countries, and 'that of the non-Western world', which occurred in the twentieth century in as yet backward countries: where the former had occurred, there was little or no room for the latter. Having broken out in the eighteenth century, the French Revolution was bound up with 'other movements of its own time within the area of Western Civilization', not 'modern Communism'.[43] Constructed thus, the dichotomy abolishes the distinction between Lenin's revolutionary dictatorship and Stalin's totalitarianism and condemns the October Revolution, totally excluded from the West, from the outset.

However, reference to the theme of slavery ends up problematizing the configuration and confines of the Western revolution. The black Jacobin Toussaint L'Ouverture sought to found a free republic that might prove acceptable to some European republicans in these years, but not to their American counterparts. By contrast, the white colonists appealed to the example of the USA and the southern states. They regarded their liberal or democratic professions of faith and defence of the institution of slavery as perfectly compatible and, in their dispute with the abolitionists, threatened secession from France and adhesion to the North American republic. Around 1790, San Domingo was the site of 'the first great shock between the ideals of white supremacy and race equality'.[44] In asserting this, Palmer cites a text of 1914 by T. Lothrop Stoddard, theoretician of white supremacy, who a few years later denounced the October Revolution as a further stage in the revolt of 'peoples of color' against civilization. With the pre-eminence he accorded to the revolt of the British colonies, Palmer provoked critical reactions from Marxist- and Jacobin-inspired historiography. Even more

---

41   Ibid., Vol. I, pp. 189–90, 199.
42   Ibid., Vol. I, pp. 149, 9, 23.
43   Ibid., Vol. I, pp. 11–13.
44   Ibid., Vol. II, p. 338.

serious, however, are the reservations elicited on the other side by a category like 'Western revolution'. It excludes Burke's aristocratic England; it casts a rather problematic light on America itself, in some of its sectors and at a point in its history when it was strongly opposed to revolutionary France, which was engaged in abolishing slavery in the colonies; it ends up creating an opening for the October Revolution, which, with its appeals to the 'slaves' of the colonies to rebel, seems to be aligned with the black Jacobin who was the protagonist of the San Domingo revolution.

These were the years when Sartre characterized Lumumba as 'a black Robespierre' and urged renovation and radicalization of the 'Jacobinism' of Third World revolutionary movements in a socialist direction;[45] the years when the Cuban revolution drew attention to the revolution that had occurred almost two centuries earlier a short distance away, in San Domingo, so that the figure of Fidel Castro summoned up that of Toussaint L'Ouverture. Numerous links seemed to connect Robespierre, Toussaint L'Ouverture, Lenin, and anti-colonial movements, which sometimes referred both to the revolution led by the black Jacobin and to the Bolshevik Revolution. They ended up identifying with these two revolutions that had occurred on the margins, or outside, of the West – in San Domingo and Russia – and the first inevitably referred back to France. In a sense, the expulsion of the Bolshevik Revolution from the West also required the expulsion of Jacobinism and the French Revolution as a whole. Arendt registered this, now lamenting the regrettable fact that 'even revolutions on the American continent speak and act as though they knew by heart the texts of revolutions in France, in Russia, and in China, but had never heard of such a thing as an American Revolution'.[46] Her 1963 book *On Revolution* proposed to remedy this situation. It was not enough to assert the primacy of the Founding Fathers in the 'Western revolution'. The very category now seemed dubious or an encumbrance. According to Arendt, an 'Atlantic civilization' did indeed exist in the eighteenth century (the 'glorious example' of America had certainly influenced and encouraged the anti-feudal movement in Europe). At the very latest, however, it was shattered by the 'disastrous course' of the French Revolution – that is, the emergence of Jacobinism. Certainly, 'one is tempted to hope that the rift which occurred at the end of the eighteenth century is

---

45 Jean-Paul Sartre, 'The Political Thought of Patrice Lumumba', in Sartre, *Colonialism and Neocolonialism*, trans. Azzedine Hadour, Steve Brewer and Terry McWilliams, Abingdon and New York: Routledge, 2006, p. 196.

46 Hannah Arendt, *On Revolution*, London: Faber & Faber, 1963, p. 218.

about to heal in the middle of the twentieth century, when it has become rather obvious that Western civilization has its last chance of survival in an Atlantic community'.[47] Such a community was in fact being reconstructed on an entirely different basis from that envisaged by Palmer: celebration of the American Revolution was now matched by utter condemnation of the French Revolution, regarded as the first stage in a disastrous process leading to the October Revolution and the Third World revolutions, which threatened the very bases of 'Western civilization'. Whereas, in *The Origins of Totalitarianism*, the parabola leading to the Third Reich's barbarism was reconstructed from the prominence of counter-revolutionary literature and culture in Germany, and hence from the weakness of that country's revolutionary tradition, *On Revolution* claimed that 'freedom has been better preserved in countries where no revolution ever broke out' (in the wake or on the model of the French), or where it had been defeated.[48] Only now did a negative assessment of the October Revolution involve condemnation of the French Revolution as well. Liquidation of the thesis of the 'Western revolution' implied the expulsion from 'Atlantic civilization' of a revolution that formed the start of a tradition issuing in the Bolshevik October and the other disastrous upheavals pervasive in the Third World at the time.

The good revolution/bad revolution dichotomy no longer strictly coincided, as in Palmer, with the Western revolution/Eastern revolution dichotomy. It now involved contrasting the American Revolution (little space was devoted to Britain) with the revolutionary cycle from 1789 to 1917 and the ensuing anti-colonial movements, it being understood that the authentic West continued to coincide with the first term of the antithesis. At this point, Arendt's view did not differ significantly from that of Hayek or Talmon, who well before her celebrated the excellence of 'English ideas', which were not only contrasted with the French Revolution (and, *a fortiori*, the Bolshevik), but stood out in splendid isolation in the liberal Western firmament.[49]

We have attended at some length to Arendt. An anti-fascist Jew exiled in the USA, she had looked with respect and sympathy on the USSR, which in 1942 she credited with having 'patently eliminated anti-Semitism' in the context of a 'just and very modern solution of the national question'.[50] Only

---

47   Ibid., pp. 217–18.
48   Ibid., p. 111.
49   F.A. Hayek, *The Road to Serfdom*, London: Ark Paperbacks, 1986, pp. 16–17; Jacob L. Talmon, *The Origins of Totalitarian Democracy*, London: Secker & Warburg, 1952, Part II, Chapter 2.
50   Arendt, *Essays und Kommentare*, Vol. II, p. 193.

via subsequent, laborious stages did she arrive at wholesale condemnation of the October Revolution and the French Revolution. Hers is an evolution that illuminates with especial clarity the radical mutation in the *Zeitgeist*, with the transition from the anti-fascist grand alliance to the outbreak of the Cold War and the consequent development of a 'Western' ideology commensurate with the new situation. This is a transition which, for chronological and biographical reasons, cannot be tracked with such clarity in any of the individual representatives of historical revisionism.

When Alfred Cobban, the author who initiated historical revisionism as regards the French Revolution, published *Dictatorship* in 1939, the anti-fascist coalition was not yet in existence (the Non-Aggression Pact between Hitler and Stalin still obtained). And while he stressed that 'in a sense all European dictators of the present day are children of the *Communist Manifesto*', the British historian was concerned to formulate a balanced judgement of Robespierre, explaining the Terror on the basis of the concrete situation imposed by the war and sometimes providing a respectful, if not sympathetic, image of the Jacobin leader: 'he fell, not because he was a tyrant, but because he was not sufficiently tyrannical'. Instead, it was Marat who was 'potentially the first dictator of modern Europe'; and 'Marx and Engels were the political heirs, not of Robespierre, but of Marat.'[51] As we can see, condemnation of the Bolshevik October and Marxism did not as yet involve liquidation of Jacobinism as such.

Subsequently, we witness a hardening of judgements. But this is not the key point. The isolation of the Bolshevik Revolution was accentuated by a different strategy – that is, by highlighting the weak points in the Marxist interpretation of the French Revolution as a bourgeois revolution, so as to radically challenge it. In Cobban's view, it involved a teleological type of interpretation which, in terms of the philosophy of history, seemed to contain implicit justification of the Bolshevik Revolution as a proletarian revolution.[52] But while it de-legitimizes October 1917, liquidation of the category of bourgeois revolution suspends the French Revolution itself in a vacuum. For it now lacks an objective, material basis and is in fact all the more inexplicable given that supersession of the *ancien régime* had already been accomplished prior to 1789, or was at an advanced stage at any rate. Jacobin radicalism

---

51   Alfred Cobban, *Dictatorship: Its History and Theory*, New York: Haskell, 1971, pp. 112, 71, 63.

52   Alfred Cobban, 'The Myth of the French Revolution', in *Aspects of the French Revolution*, London: Jonathan Cape, 1968.

was no longer – could no longer be – (in Marx's terms) the plebeian mode in which the revolutionary bourgeoisie dealt with its enemies. Instead, according to Furet, it was an example of *dérapage* – derailment from the normal reformist logic peculiar to the English and American revolutions. In France, ideology had battened on to itself, losing any contact with reality. It was ideological delirium that had generated the Terror and, more than a century later, the Gulag. Albeit in a different sequence and a different way, in European historiography and culture, as in its American counterpart, the isolation of the Bolshevik Revolution resulted in the liquidation of Jacobinism and the French Revolution as a whole.

In analysing the Gulag, Furet frequently refers to *The Origins of Totalitarianism*, but without noticing that it contains a positive evaluation of Jacobinism and, at least in part, of the October Revolution. Likewise ignored or repressed is the fact that the parabola culminating in totalitarianism commences with the negation of the concept of man as such formulated by Burke, to whom Furet constantly refers. The latter takes no account of Arendt's indictment of colonial domination, perceived in her work as the laboratory in which the constitutive elements of the *univers concentrationnaire* were assembled. The triumph of historical revisionism yields a compact, unnuanced ideology that places Jacobinism and Bolshevism exclusively in the dock.

Liquidation of the Revolutionary Tradition and Re-transcription of the Second Thirty Years' War

The liquidation of the revolutionary tradition in turn stimulated or dictated reinterpretation of the struggle between the great powers during the Second Thirty Years' War. It is clear, for example, that outright condemnation of the experience which began in October 1917, and indictment of the Bolsheviks for having unleashed international civil war, ends up casting a less inclement, if not exactly favourable, light on the 'parties of the civil counter-war, Fascism and National Socialism'.[53] The latter must be assigned at least one merit: they were 'historically right to counter' the attempt by 'millenarian, violent communism' to destroy the system based on the 'world market economy'.

---

53   Ernst Nolte, 'Weltbürgerkrieg 1917–1989?', Italian trans. in Nolte, *Dramma dialettico o tragedia? La guerra civile mondiale e altri saggi*, ed. F. Coppellotti, Perugia: Settimo Sigillo/ Perugia University Press, 1990, p. 41.

Mussolini and Hitler objectively played a vanguard role: 'the United States long kept itself outside this civil war . . ., which it too readily underestimated, notwithstanding its rank as "principal capitalist power"'.[54] Furthermore, identification of the French Revolution as the main culprit in the emergence of the *univers concentrationnaire* was bound to have a positive influence on the international image of a country like Germany, long engaged in the struggle against the 'ideas of 1789'. Assimilated during the Second Thirty Years' War to a kind of international stronghold of the *ancien régime* or Vendée, Germany benefited from the more favourable light cast on both by historical revisionism. The Arendt of *The Origins of Totalitarianism* had emphasized Burke's major influence in the country that subsequently produced Nazism. But now a massive literature and journalism celebrated the merits of the British Whig for his far-sighted denunciation of the 'totalitarianism' secreted in the revolutionary tradition. In any event, de-legitimation of the latter undermined the war ideology employed by Germany's enemies.

Herewith emerges the second key aspect of historical revisionism: a critical rereading of the two world wars. With the Versailles Treaty, Germany was forced to acknowledge its 'guilt' in unleashing aggression in violation of 'international morality' (articles 231 and 227). The victors thus posed as champions of legality and morality, as well as democracy and peace. This prompted bitter reactions – and not only on the part of Germany. Powers variously interested in challenging a historical verdict which, while it put Germany in the dock, also de-legitimized the Soviet Union – the country deriving from desertion of the crusade – appeared 'revisionist'. On the other hand, the war had from the outset been condemned as imperialist on both sides by Lenin, who subsequently pointed an accusing finger at the victors, responsible for having imposed a peace treaty that was even more rapacious than Brest-Litovsk. In this sense, among the most radical revisionists was precisely the Bolshevik leader.

The third front from which the revisionist offensive unfolded was the USA. This is easily explained. The country had intervened belatedly in the gigantic global struggle, when, hopes or predictions of a *Blitzkrieg* or rapid showdown having faded, the unprecedented scale of the carnage became evident. Unlike the other great powers, the USA could not claim that it had fatally slid into war; nor could it argue that its integrity or very existence

---

54 Ernst Nolte, 'Der europäische Bürgerkrieg 1917–1945', Italian trans. by P. Sorge, in *Dopo il comunismo. Contributi all'interpretazione della storia del XX secolo*, Florence: Sansoni, 1992, p. 45; 'Weltbürgerkrieg 1917–1989?', p. 40.

as a nation was at stake. This is also why US participation in the war was presented by Wilson as a purely idealistic crusade, as a disinterested, self-sacrificial contribution to the cause of peace and democracy, to the international democratic revolution. The ensuing wave of disillusionment proved all the more powerful. It was further swelled by Soviet publication of the secret treaties exposing the existence in the Entente of an imperial appetite scarcely less strong than that of the Central Powers.[55] Something similar occurred in the USA on the morrow of the Second World War. What was the sense in presenting the struggle with the Third Reich and imperial Japan as a democratic crusade or revolution, if their collapse meant the expansion of a power that was equally totalitarian, if not more so? Was Stalin's Soviet Union perhaps even more of a slave state than Hitler's Germany? Thus argued an American revisionist historian, who liked to cite the political line suggested by the then Senator Truman immediately after the start of Operation Barbarossa: 'If we see that Germany is winning we ought to help Russia and if Russia is winning we ought to help Germany, and that way let them kill as many as possible, although I don't want to see Hitler victorious under any circumstances.'[56] This shrewd stance had been disregarded and replaced by demands on the powers regarded as the embodiment of despotism and militarism for 'unconditional surrender'. But this ideology, which made the Soviet Union part of the democratic crusade, proved to be in sharp contradiction with the ideology consolidated once the Cold War broke out: the crusade was no sooner over than it was de-legitimized.

That is not the only reason for the strong roots of historical revisionism in the USA. Total liquidation of the revolutionary tradition was impeded by the fact that hanging over the country consistently engaged in the struggle against the ideas of 1789 was the shadow of Auschwitz. The Jews exterminated by the Third Reich had been emancipated by the French Revolution and, in Russia, by the upheavals from February–October 1917. On the other hand, the influence on Nazism of the intellectual tradition of 'white supremacy', already imbued with 'Aryan' pathos, was now confirmed. Referring to this intellectual tradition (in particular, Lothrop Stoddard and another American author of the same persuasion, Madison Grant), in 1937 Alfred Rosenberg expressed his admiration for the United States, that 'magnificent land of the

---

55   See Arno J. Mayer, *Political Origins of the New Diplomacy, 1917–1918*, New York: Vintage Books, 1959, pp. 14–22.

56   Quoted in William H. Chamberlin, *America's Second Crusade*, Chicago: Regnery, 1950, pp. 136–7.

future' whose merit it was to have invented the inspired 'new idea of the racial state' – an idea which was now to be applied in practice, with 'youthful strength', by expelling and deporting 'the Blacks and the Yellow men'.[57]

The ideology of 'white supremacy' remained alive and well in post-war America, tenaciously defending racial segregation and laws against miscegenation (mixed-race sexual relations and marriages), which still survived in some southern states in the 1950s and '60s. In this context, a revisionism developed that historically condemned the American Civil War and subsequent Reconstruction (the years until 1877, when the Union army sought to impose racial equality) as senseless and superfluous, while in more immediately political terms it condemned the federal authorities' renewed commitment to abolish black segregation as an assault on the 'standards of white civilization'.[58] The most radical exponents of this revisionism bemoaned the fact that the 'myth' of Auschwitz made it impossible 'constructively' to confront the 'racial problem', since any attempts to do so were at once accused of 'racism' – an unbearable accusation in the light of the catastrophic results attributed to it.[59] The defence or rehabilitation of 'anti-Hamitism' presupposed if not the trivialization, then the relativization, of the malign consequences of anti-Semitism.

Such relativization was all the more necessary because the horrors caused by the cult of the Aryan race risked re-legitimizing historical movements and figures who had opposed such discrimination. They risked showing in a favourable light the tradition which from Toussaint L'Ouverture, via the abolitionist revolution (the Civil War and subsequent Reconstruction), to Lenin remained the target of those nostalgic for 'white supremacy'. We can now understand the centrality of the debate over the extermination of Jewry. We can also understand why, along with a Germany desirous of extricating itself from the infamy imputed by Versailles and Nuremburg, the USA formed one of the most important centres of historical revisionism, which, amid contradictions and internal divisions, reopened discussion of two centuries of history, starting with the French Revolution against which Edmund Burke had acted as prosecuting counsel.

It might be said that historical revisionism was born out of a compound of critique of the revolutionary tradition and critique of interpretations of

---

57 Alfred Rosenberg, *The Myth of the Twentieth Century: An Evaluation of the Spiritual-Intellectual Confrontations of Our Age*, Newport Beach, CA: Noontide Press, 1993, p. 419.

58 Weaver, *The Southern Essays*, p. 253.

59 Cf. Deborah E. Lipstadt, *Denying the Holocaust: The Growing Assault on Truth and Memory*, New York and Toronto: Free Press/Macmillan, 1993, pp. 107, 146–52.

the Second Thirty Years' War as a democratic crusade and revolution. If this is so, the father of the cultural and political current is doubtless Carl Schmitt (who on at least one occasion made explicit laudatory reference to the revisionist literature proper).[60] The oeuvre of the German political theorist (and his school) is an extended indictment of revolution, which, along with the classics of counter-revolution, draws on Cochin, to whom Furet later drew attention for his denunciation of the 'delirium' of revolutionary ideology. But as early as the 1930s Schmitt was referring to Cochin, whom he later included in his 'calendar of saints' for his merit in analysing the *sociétés de pensée*, or 'political-criminal associations', or which become such by dint of the ideological cult of 'abstract thought in opposition to reality'.[61] Cochin has likewise been precious to a whole school that utilizes him to inculpate the French Revolution *ab initio*, if not from its prelude, starting with *sociétés de pensée* created in the wake of the Enlightenment – a philosophy which, appearances to the contrary notwithstanding, was 'expressly aggressive' and violent, already harbouring the Terror.[62]

But let us examine the main counts in Schmitt's indictment. The revolutionary project – in particular, Jacobinism and Bolshevism – is responsible for constructing the figure of the 'absolute enemy', on whom a war without rules or limits is declared, ending in massacre. It is responsible for having replaced war-as-duel, whose *dramatis personae* were states and their armies, by international civil war that cuts through and across the countries involved in the conflict, rendering any distinction between combatants and the civilian population impossible. The ideal of perpetual peace deriving from the French Revolution has produced the exact opposite of what it promised: branding the enemy as aggressor and warmonger, it has deprived him of the status of *justus hostis*, protected by international law, and equated him with an outlaw consigned to the vendetta of a victor who claims to be the interpreter of

---

60   See Carl Schmitt, *Theory of the Partisan: Intermediate Commentary on the Concept of the Political*, trans. G.L. Ulmen, New York: Telos Press, 2007, p. 37 n. 51, which refers, *inter alia*, to the 'extraordinary book' of Frederick J.P. Veale, *Advance to Barbarism: The Development of Total Warfare* (1948). Not coincidentally, it was reprinted in 1979 by the Institute for Historical Review, engaged in the front line of the revisionist struggle.

61   Carl Schmitt, *Positionen und Begriffe im Kampf mit Weimar-Genf-Versailles 1932–1939*, Berlin: Duncker & Humblot, 1988, p. 229; *Glossarium. Aufzeichnungen der Jahre 1947–1951*, ed. E. Freiherr von Medem, Berlin: Duncker & Humblot, 1991, p. 91.

62   Hanno Kesting, *Geschichtsphilosophie und Weltbürgerkrieg*, Heidelberg: Winter, 1959, p. ix. On Cochin, see also Roman Schnur, *Revolution und Weltbürgerkrieg. Studien zur Ouvertüre nach 1789*, Berlin: Duncker & Humblot, 1983, pp. 17, 30, and Reinhart Koselleck, *Critique and Crisis: The Pathogenesis of Modern Society*, Cambridge, MA: MIT Press, 1988, p. 110.

humanity and the moral law. In conclusion, the tradition that runs from 1789 to 1917 has impressed a character of missionary fanaticism on war which, at the same time, produces universal interventionism and total war. However, this relentless requisitory also implicates the countries that from 1914 onwards conducted a war-revolution against Germany, equated by them with the *ancien régime* or Vendée. The critique of 1789 and 1917 is thus intimately bound up with the critique of Versailles and Nuremburg. An identical philosophy of history governs revolution and war-revolution. Starting with the Enlightenment and the French Revolution, the inevitability of progress and democracy (and, subsequently, socialism) becomes self-evident for intellectuals reared in *sociétés de pensée* or similar organizations. History is configured as 'the triumphal march of democracy', in whose favour a precise 'dispensation of providence' seems to weigh.[63] By reference to this philosophy of history, the minority in possession of such privileged knowledge legitimizes the use of violence and its 'educational despotism'.[64] But a kind of 'educational despotism' is also what the victors sought to impose on Germany. With the war-revolution and democratic revolution launched against it, they interfered in the merits of its domestic order, condemning it as an *ancien régime* contrary to the course of history. Following victory, with the Versailles Treaty and the Nuremburg Trial they summoned or compelled the defeated country to engage in political and moral re-education and expiate its guilt. The political and military leaders of Germany (and Japan) were tried and condemned on the basis not of existing international law, and respecting the principle of *nullum crimen, nulla poena sine lege*, but of a principle of 'revolutionary legitimacy'. This allowed the victors, heedless of 'legality', to apply retroactively the crime of war of aggression, cancelling the *jus ad bellum* hitherto possessed by each individual state. Not even mentioning Stalin, 'Churchill appears as the Clémenceau of the Second World War'[65] – that is, as the heir of the 'Jacobin' statesman who was an architect of Versailles. What went into operation at Nuremburg and Tokyo were in fact revolutionary tribunals or committees of public safety that left the accused little or no chance to defend themselves.

---

63   Carl Schmitt, *The Crisis of Parliamentary Democracy*, trans. Ellen Kennedy, Cambridge, MA: MIT Press, 1985, pp. 22–3.

64   Carl Schmitt, *Dictatorship: From the Origin of the Modern Concept of Sovereignty to Proletarian Class Struggle*, trans. Michael Hoelzl and Graham Ward, Cambridge: Polity Press, 2014, p. 278 n. 22.

65   Schmitt, *Glossarium*, pp. 184, 237; 'The International Crime of the War of Aggression and the Principle "*Nullum crimen, nulla poena sine lege*"', in Carl Schmitt, *Writings on War*, ed. and trans. Timothy Nunan, Cambridge: Polity Press, 2011.

Historical Revisionism, Neo-Liberalism
and the Clash of Revisionisms

To identify the character of the revolutionary virus more clearly, in addition to Tocqueville and Furet, Pipes refers to Mises, whom he credits with having clarified a decisive issue for understanding contemporary history: 'intellectuals gravitate to anti-capitalist philosophies "in order to render inaudible the inner voice that tells them that their failure is entirely their own fault"'.[66] According to Furet, the insanity of the revolutionary project manifests itself in reveries of social engineering. Although not explicitly cited, what lies behind this diagnosis is clearly the teaching of Hayek. The convergence between historical revisionism and neo-liberalism is patent. In reality, it comprises two facets – one more directly political, the other more specifically historiographical – of the same movement. As Hayek explicitly acknowledges, the negation of economic and social rights assumes liquidating the revolutionary tradition or, at any rate, a tradition which even before the Bolshevik October had begun with Robespierre to theorize the 'right to life' as the first of 'the imprescriptible rights of man'.[67]

Mises is harshly critical of the French Revolution, with which he contrasts the wisdom and realism not only of Burke, but also, to a certain extent, of Bonald, Maistre and Haller.[68] Under the banner of the reactionary critique of modernity, a direct line leads from Rousseau to Marx and Engels, as well as the 'various sects of fanatics' inspired by them,[69] to the upheavals in Russia and the revolution from which the Weimar Republic emerged: 'It is not a uniform Marxian sect that attacks capitalism, but a host of Marxian groups. These groups – for example, Stalinists, Trotskyists, Mensheviks, supporters of the Second International, and so on – fight one another with the utmost brutality and inhumanity.'[70]

Not only is the liquidation of the revolutionary tradition post-1789 already clearly present in neo-liberalism, but some of the key themes of contemporary historical revisionism emerge. One thinks in particular of Mises, according to whom the horrors of the twentieth century start with the

---

66   Pipes, *The Russian Revolution*, p. 134.
67   Maximilien Robespierre, *Oeuvres*, Paris: Presses Universitaires de France, 1912–, Vol. IX, p. 112.
68   Ludwig von Mises, *Human Action: A Treatise on Economics*, Chicago: Contemporary Books, 1966, p. 864.
69   Ibid., pp. 165, 83.
70   Ibid., p. 152.

arrival in power of the Communists – in fact, with the emergence on the political scene of the 'Marxist Social Democrats' or the most radical currents of that movement, which demand the annihilation of the bourgeoisie: 'The frank espousal of a policy of annihilating opponents (*Vernichtung*) and the murders committed in the pursuance of it have given rise to an opposition movement (*Gegenbewegung*). All at once the scales fell from the eyes of the non-Communist enemies of liberalism.' The schema of (Communist) 'annihilation' and (Fascist) 'counter-annihilation' – the one sponsored by Nolte – is already present in 1927 in Mises. And as for the German historian, so for the patriarch of neo-liberalism, this counter-annihilation or 'opposition movement' aimed to save the West from Asiatic barbarism. The Russian Bolsheviks were barbarians on two counts. As a political movement, they were to be included among 'the arch-enemies of civilization'. Furthermore, they represented 'barbarian peoples on both sides of the Urals, whose relationship to civilization has never been any other than that of marauding denizens of forest and desert accustomed to engage, from time to time, in predatory raids on civilized lands in the hunt for booty'. Perhaps going further than Nolte, or at any rate speaking more candidly, Mises regarded Mussolini's *squadristi* as 'an emergency makeshift' appropriate for the task of saving 'European civilization': 'The merit that Fascism has thereby won for itself will live on eternally in history.'[71]

Nevertheless, the differences and divergences (political and methodological) between neo-liberalism and historical revisionism are clear. We have noted the widespread recourse to Cochin. But the latter referred back, via Taine, to the great reactionary tradition and the rejection of modernity. The 'revolutionary enigma' (or disease) could only be unravelled by reference to the 'sociology of the democratic phenomenon'.[72] In and through the *sociétés de pensée*, Cochin was intent on criticizing modern political parties and trade unions, which (following the work of Ostrogorsky and Bryce) he denounced with his focus principally on the USA. The Cochin taken up by Furet (or Pipes) is not only diminished, but even distorted, in that he is invoked in defence of democracy against Jacobinism and Bolshevism. By an extraordinary paradox, observes another judge of the student of the *sociétés de pensée*, 'while Cochin perfectly understood Bolshevism, which he never

---

71   Ludwig von Mises, *Liberalism: The Classical Tradition*, ed. Bettina Bien Greaves, trans. Ralph Raico, Indianapolis: Liberty Fund, 2005, pp. 26–30, and Mises, *Omnipotent Government: The Rise of the Total State and Total War*, Spring Mills: Libertarian Press, 1985, p. 194.

72   Augustin Cochin, *La Révolution et la libre pensée*, Paris: Copernic, 1979, p. 14.

experienced, he understood nothing of liberal democracy, which he had right in front of him'.[73] 'Jacobin fanaticism' is the result, and one possible manifestation, of 'corporate fanaticism',[74] or 'sociologized man', who loses all contact with reality in an existence that revolves around the narrow, abstract circle of a party.[75] The 'sociology of the democratic phenomenon' employed by Cochin to explain the revolutionary clubs is constructed by him on the basis of observing the political parties and organizations of his time, which evince 'an astonishing similarity' to the 'revolutionary societies' that produced the Terror.[76] It is not clear how an analysis, a main presupposition of which is negated, can be regarded as wholly valid, even if we confine our attention to the eighteenth century; it is not clear why denunciation of the *sociétés de pensée* and Masonic clubs should apply exclusively to France, and not to Britain and America as well. While Cochin sought to demonstrate that 'the major historical event' was not 1792, and not even 1789,[77] his putative followers strive to deduce the catastrophe of the West from Jacobinism (and Bolshevism).

The operation whereby the French author is twisted to the needs of contemporary neo-liberalism and historical revisionism proves instrumental and problematic. But it is not enough to resolve all the contradictions. In the critique of the revolutionary tradition, neo-liberalism halts half-way, stopping short of challenging the major revolution against the German *ancien régime* which the Western great powers gloried in having conducted from 1914. In Mises' view, the Wilhelmine Germany against which the Entente fought was dominated by a 'caste system' and a militarism that infected the whole population without exception.[78] Prussia as a stronghold of international reaction: such is the depiction favoured by democratic interventionism and theoreticians of war-revolution. The patriarch of neo-liberalism turns out to be one of the most ardent democratic interventionists, calling for the ejection of governments hostile to *laissez-faire* — governments that are also those fatally inclined to despotism and militarism.[79]

---

73 Jean Baechler, 'Introduction' to Augustin Cochin, *Lo spirito del giacobinismo*, Milan: Bompiani, 1989, p. 37.

74 Cochin, *Les Sociétés de pensée et la démocratie moderne*, pp. 83, 89.

75 Cochin, *La Révolution et la libre pensée*, p. 200.

76 Ibid., p. 81.

77 Cochin, *Les Sociétés de pensée et la démocratie moderne*, p. 88.

78 Mises, *Omnipotent Government*, pp. 161, 167.

79 Ludwig von Mises, *Socialism: An Economic and Sociological Analysis*, trans. Jacques Kahane, Indianapolis: Liberty Fund, 1981, p. 208.

The conflict between neo-liberalism and historical revisionism is a contradiction within historical revisionism and a conflict between different revisionisms. Cochin was an implacable critic of the revolutionary ideology and 'socialized man'. The culmination of this new, odious figure is to be found in the decree on the *levée en masse*, which 'placed all French people in a state of permanent requisition, body and goods alike, for the common salvation'. By a tragic twist of fate, the scholar himself died fighting bravely, and identifying profoundly, with a war that led even more radically to total mobilization – a war that was presented as an international democratic revolution and which, in the mouth of Prime Minister Clémenceau, had no hesitation in France in referring to Jacobinism. The irony of fate becomes a glaring contradiction in Furet. On the one hand, he incriminates revolutionary ideology, while on the other he transfigures the Second Thirty Years' War into a revolution against a Germany 'imbued with the idea that it was the chosen nation' and with 'racist theory'; against a power which with Wilhelm II was already an enemy of 'Western-style liberal democracy', and which with Hitler 'had sworn death to democracy'.[80] The war against the Second Reich is depicted by Furet as a war in which the 'democratic nations', the 'two great democratic universalisms' of France and America – the two countries that were protagonists of the 'two revolutions in the late eighteenth century' – embarked on a 'democratic crusade'. The French historian draws on Burke to criticize the French Revolution and, *a fortiori*, the Bolshevik Revolution. At the same time, however, he celebrates the democratic crusade as if the main count in the British Whig's indictment of revolutionary France were not its missionary spirit, the idea of exporting revolution. While, as we shall see, he criticizes those who base themselves on 'fidelity to the revolutionary consciousness and experience of the nineteenth and twentieth centuries' when reconstructing the history of the French or Bolshevik revolutions,[81] Furet is incapable of applying this appropriate methodological consideration to the Second Thirty Years' War. He seems to be wholly identified with the experience of the war-revolution or 'democratic crusade' proclaimed by Wilson against 'Prussian autocracy'.[82] The French historian condemns the potential violence contained in the philosophy of history, but applies this critique to revolution (French or Bolshevik), not to war-revolution. He seems unaware of the philosophical debate that occurred over

---

80   Furet, *The Passing of an Illusion*, pp. 129, 46, 44, 35.
81   Furet, *Interpreting the French Revolution*, p. 14.
82   Furet, *The Passing of an Illusion*, p. 57.

the First World War. Prior to US intervention, Dewey criticized as 'absurdly sentimental' the thesis that 'force can never be used to change men's minds'. Indeed, the war was precisely called on to put an end to 'Germany's desire for a spiritual and political monopoly'. A few years later, however, US 'revisionists' reproved the philosopher (and Wilson) for having sought to export democracy and the democratic revolution on the point of bayonets, celebrating 'creative force' and fostering the senseless dream of creating a kind of new man through military victory.[83] Furet underlines the devastating impact of social engineering. However, he does not register the fact that, for the great conservative and reactionary culture of Germany, the most ambitious and devastating social engineering was that which, claiming to abolish conflict and war between states, ended up prompting exterminist crusades. The French historian denounces the ultimate inversion of utopia into dystopia, but ignores the fact that according to Schmitt precisely such a dialectic characterized the anti-German international crusade or revolution, proclaimed with the promise of eradicating militarism and war, but issuing in unprecedented horror.

It is worth noting the judgement on the fate of Hiroshima and Nagasaki expressed by Paul Johnson. The neo-liberal author, who counts among the most fervent 'revisionists' when it comes to liquidating the revolutionary tradition, does not seem particularly interested in reinterpreting the Second Thirty Years' War. He entertains so few doubts about the 'wisdom or morality' of employing the atom bomb as to claim that not to have used it 'would have been illogical, indeed irresponsible'. A massacre of the civilian population certainly ensued, but 'those who died in Hiroshima and Nagasaki were the victims not so much of Anglo-American technology as of a paralysed system of government made possible by an evil ideology which had expelled not only absolute moral values but reason itself'.[84] Having devoted so much of his work to describing the horrors produced by the ideological fanaticism of revolutionaries, here we find the British historian justifying the destruction of the civilian population, attributing it to a perverse 'government' and 'ideology' which democratic America's war-revolution was set to sweep away. Unanimous in liquidating the revolutionary tradition, neo-liberalism and the various revisionist schools otherwise diverge. Not all of them share

---

83   Warren I. Cohen, *The American Revisionists: The Lessons of Intervention in World War I*, Chicago and London: University of Chicago Press, 1967, pp. 8, 19–21.

84   Paul Johnson, *Modern Times: The World from the Twenties to the Nineties*, New York: Harper Collins, 1991, pp. 425, 427.

the attempt, hailing above all from Germany, to reopen discussion of Versailles and Nuremburg (and, as regards Asia, Tokyo).

Burke is invoked by Mises and Hayek, Johnson and Pipes, Furet and Nolte. But the Burke of the twentieth century is Schmitt, and not only because he developed certain arguments earlier and more rigorously than others. Only in him do we find a general critique of revolutionary ideology in all its guises. In the name of 'the standard of life of all mankind', 'peaceful cooperation', and 'collaboration in work' and the division of labour, Mises calls for the ejection of governments hostile to liberalism and for them to be viewed like 'a dangerous animal'.[85] We have seen Johnson justifying – in fact, celebrating – Hiroshima and Nagasaki in the name of 'absolute moral values' and 'reason'. In Schmitt's view, such views give quintessential expression to revolutionary ideology and its homicidal logic: 'When the word "humanity" rings out, the élite remove the safety-catch from their bombs and the masses seek the air raid shelters.'[86] And all this in the name of the 'rights of man', which, by dint of their universality, are not obliged to respect either state boundaries or existing legality.

A conjoint denunciation of the revolutionary tradition and of the ideology fashioned by the enemies of the Second and Third Reichs is widely diffused in the twentieth-century German culture. It attains an acme of generalization and 'metaphysicalization' in Heidegger. Albeit in different accents at different times over the course of his tortured development, he deconstructed the universalistic ideology (proclaimed by the revolution and inherited by the Entente) as a declaration of war on 'historicity' and the particular traditions of a specific people; as an instrument of homogenization and massification, suppression and domination. To those who invited him to clearly distance himself from a regime that had produced the Holocaust, the philosopher replied in 1948 that the tragic experience of Jewry was not substantially different from that reserved by the Allies for the 'eastern Germans' or Japanese, or that which the USSR visited (or sought to visit) on the population of Berlin by blockading the city.[87] It is no coincidence if Nolte is a pupil of Heidegger . . .

---

85   Mises, *Socialism*, pp. 208, 284.

86   Schmitt, *Glossarium*, p. 283.

87   See Domenico Losurdo, *Heidegger and the Ideology of War: Community, Death and the West*, trans. Marella and Jon Morris, Amherst, NY: Humanity Books, 2001, Chapter 6, §6.

Reinterpretations and Rereadings, Historical Revisionism, and Comparativism

In the US cultural tradition, reference is sometimes made to revisionism in a purely formal sense, with paradoxical results. Revisionists are defined as those who de-legitimize the American Civil War and Lincoln's 'Jacobinism', proceeding to a kind of rehabilitation of the Confederacy.[88] But revisionism is sometimes also referred to in connection with historians reinterpreting Reconstruction, which is traditionally depicted in rather sombre colours, as an initial, difficult stage in multi-ethnic and inter-racial democracy.[89] However, the cycle extending from 1861 to 1877 – from the Civil War and the abolition of slavery to attempts to terminate the regime of white supremacy, defended by the squadist violence of the Ku Klux Klan and other organizations, which sought to preserve the Confederacy's memory and political legacy – is clearly uniform. We should therefore refer to revisionism as being synonymous with the liquidation of the revolutionary tradition (and, in this case, of the abolitionist revolution) and of the war-revolutions of the twentieth century.

According to one of its most prominent representatives, the American Harry Elmer Barnes, revisionism 'means no more than the establishment of historical truth', which 'court historians' seek by any and all means to keep concealed.[90] There is no question that historical research involves incessant revision of the results of previous research. Indeed, this is a tautological statement. However, to stick to such a tautology is to fail to grasp the specificity of a cultural and political phenomenon that emerges in a very precise context and in connection with determinate events and a determinate historical cycle. When not referring to this specific movement, we shall refer in this book to rereadings and reinterpretations, rather than revisions, of history.

Our approach will be comparative in cast. Historical revisionism adopts an oscillating, contradictory attitude to this method. In tackling the history of the twentieth century, it has ample recourse to it. Relativization of the horror of the Third Reich occurs through a comparison with the horrors of

---

88   In Kenneth M. Stampp, ed., *The Causes of the Civil War*, New York: Simon & Schuster, 1991, pp. 107–8, 112, 159.

89   See Eric Foner, *Reconstruction: America's Unfinished Revolution 1863–1877*, New York: Harper & Row, 1989, p. xxii.

90   Harry E. Barnes, ed., *Perpetual War for Perpetual Peace*, Idaho: Caldwell, 1953, pp. 629, 638.

Stalinist Russia. Thus proceed Nolte, Furet and the American revisionist Chamberlin. Things are very different when it comes to denouncing Jacobin or Bolshevik ideological 'delirium'. The French historian has devoted many pages to this theme, but we shall search them in vain for a comparative analysis of the intellectual classes and policies of different revolutions. As regards the twentieth century, historical revisionism's comparative analysis finds it hard to go beyond a comparison of Hitler's Germany with the country that emerged from the Bolshevik Revolution – that is, one of the revolutions which is to be liquidated. In this essay, by contrast, a comparative approach will be a constant.

Such a method may elicit reservations, even indignant rejection, especially in connection with an event like the Holocaust, whose absolute uniqueness and incommensurability is underlined by a vast committed literature. But our starting-point here is a methodological presupposition that it is appropriate to set out in brief: *omnis determinatio est negatio*. In so far as it requires a demarcation of its boundaries, understanding a historical phenomenon always involves an element of comparative analysis. The significance of a crisis or revolution is revealed when it is compared with others, and the same applies to violence, terror, massacres and genocides. On the other hand, comparing does not mean equating and putting everything on a par. The negative judgement implicit in any determination can also be of a different kind. Drawing on Hegelian logic, we might say that a simple form of negative judgement exists, which is limited to negating the species, or one of its characteristics, without calling into question the genus: this rose is not red, but is nevertheless subsumed under the genus of rose; a revolution possesses particular features that distinguish it from another revolution, even though both must be subsumed under the category of revolution. But there is also a form of infinite negative judgement, which negates the genus as such: this is not a rose; this is not a revolution but a coup d'état; this is not a case of genocide but something different, to be determined subsequently through further negations and hence through further comparisons. At all events, the element of comparativism proves unavoidable. The only alternative is silence in the face of the ineffable. If it is to be articulated, described and understood, a historical event, however horrific, must be compared.

But does not comparison contain the danger of justifying one instance of violence by another, one terror by another, one massacre by another? Does comparativism not risk taking the form of a negation or evasion of moral judgement? The danger is real. But let us reflect on the converse case. Although formulated differently, we find a theorization of slavery for 'barbarians' in Aristotle and Hitler alike. Yet it would be demented to seek to conjoin two theories separated by thousands of years of history in a single moral judgement. The utterly repugnant character of the second precisely consists in its seeking to negate or repel a massive historical process of emancipation and also of the development of moral consciousness. In other words, a moral judgement that does not take the form of a Pharisaic celebration of one's own excellence with respect to the whole of the past, to the history of humanity, presupposes historical contextualization, and this in turn cannot avoid a comparative moment.

CHAPTER TWO

The Revolutionary Cycle and Terror: Britain, France, America

Ideological Intoxication, Ignorance and Venality

We have identified the central theme in the liquidation of the French Revolution undertaken by historical revisionism: the denunciation of ideological abstraction and fanaticism. It is important to dwell on diagnoses of this disease. In France, leadership of political life was assumed by 'intellectuals' and 'men of letters', 'make-believe substitutes for a ruling class'. This was 'the social group most lacking in political experience'[1] – in fact, exhibiting 'frenzy' or 'collective frenzy' and behaving like 'drug addicts'.[2] The author of these statements is Furet, who invites us to dispense with a historiography based on 'fidelity to the revolutionary consciousness and experience of the nineteenth and twentieth centuries', on sympathetic identification with Robespierre or Lenin. 'There was a gulf between the Revolution's true outcome and the revolutionaries' intentions.' Hence its history cannot continue to be written on the basis of the subjective consciousness of its protagonists: 'revolutionary times are precisely the most difficult to understand, since they are often periods when the veil of ideology hides most completely the real meaning of the events from the protagonists'.[3] Admirers of the Great Revolution to the last, Marx and Engels nevertheless on many occasions revelled in highlighting the contrast between the intentions of its leaders – especially the Jacobins – and objective outcomes. Consequently, fierce resistance on the part of a 'Marxist'-inspired

---

1 François Furet, *Interpreting the French Revolution*, trans. Elborg Foster, Cambridge: Cambridge University Press, 1981, p. 157.

2 Ibid., pp. 54, 48, 70 (trans. modified).

3 Ibid., pp. 14, 16, 159.

historiography to the methodological point that 'no consciousness is more "ideological" (in the Marxist sense of the term) than that of the revolutionaries' is paradoxical.[4]

In historical revisionism, the critique of the revolutionary consciousness of the protagonists of revolution in fact takes the form of an indictment of intellectuals. In the course of it, Furet adopts themes and arguments from opponents of Jacobinism and the French revolutionary cycle. One thinks in the first instance of Burke, remorseless in his polemic against 'mechanick philosophy', bereft of any sense of reality and incapable of escaping the magical, accursed circle of 'abstract principle' and 'Chimera' – in fact, prey to a permanent state of 'intoxication'.[5] With particular reference to the Jacobins, Constant refers to 'delirium'.[6] Across the Atlantic, Hamilton was in no doubt that the *enragés* were 'madmen'.[7] This diagnosis was revived at each stage of the French revolutionary cycle. In the years following the 1848 revolution and its failure, Tocqueville warned against a 'virus of a new and unknown kind';[8] while, after the Paris Commune, it was Taine's turn to denounce the 'disturbed mental balance' of the Jacobins, as well as the contagion (similar to the 'mysterious disease usually found in poor quarters') rampant in revolutionary France, which was 'inebriated on the strong liquor of the *Social Contract*'.[9] This is a topos which, with successive variations and modifications, comes down to Cochin and Furet. In addition to citing the student of the *sociétés de pensée*, Furet refers with especial warmth to Tocqueville, concerned about the spread of the revolutionary virus in France, and makes constant reference to Burke, who was the first to diagnose mental 'intoxication' as the original evil of the French Revolution. Another great admirer of the British Whig is Talmon, who in turn denounces the 'paranoiac streak' characteristic of Rousseau, Robespierre, Saint-Just and Babeuf.[10] Diagnosis of the revolutionary disease links historical revisionism and neo-liberalism.

---

4   Ibid., p. 142.

5   Edmund Burke, *The Works: A New Edition*, London: Rivington, 1826, Vol. V, p. 152; Vol. IX, pp. 281, 94–5; Vol. VII, p. 135.

6   Benjamin Constant, *Oeuvres*, ed. A. Roulin, Paris: Gallimard, 1957, p. 1094.

7   Quoted in Stanley Elkins and Eric McKitrick, *The Age of Federalism: The Early American Republic, 1788–1800*, New York and Oxford: Oxford University Press, 1993, p. 319.

8   Alexis de Tocqueville, *Oeuvres complètes*, ed. Jacob-Peter Mayer, Paris: Gallimard, 1951–, Vol. XIII, pt. 2, p. 337.

9   Hippolyte Taine, *Les Origines de la France contemporaine*, Paris: Hachette, 1899, Vol. V, p. 21ff. and Vol. IV, pp. 261–2.

10   Jacob Talmon, *The Origins of Totalitarian Democracy*, London: Secker & Warburn, 1952, p. 81.

In the course of the debate – in fact, the fierce ideological struggle that exploded after 1789 – we witness a remarkable exchange of accusations. Branded as madmen, Robespierre and Marat stigmatized their enemies as servile and venal, as the 'kept men of despots' and authors of 'mercenary rhapsodies' or 'hired sophists'.[11] Even before the outbreak of the revolution, Rousseau, today dismissed as a paranoiac, scorned jurists intent on proving the legitimacy of slavery and tyranny as 'sold to tyranny' and 'mercenaries'.[12] Across the Rhine, addressing the opponents of revolutionary France, Fichte exclaimed: 'On our side stand the most lucid heads and most noble hearts of the various nations and on your side nothing but simpletons, hypocrites and corrupt intellectuals.'[13] In his turn, however, the idealist philosopher was included by Constant among the 'lunatics' with more or less Jacobin ideas.[14] The attitude of both parties is readily intelligible. The bitterness of the struggle, and the unprecedented character of the constant upheavals, left little alternative. Impelled by their pathos of reason and morality to challenge an order that in their view was irrational and immoral, the revolutionaries were led to attribute the resistance and obstacles they encountered to ignorance or subjective bad faith. On the other side, the frenzy of negation and destruction of age-old arrangements and relations was bound to appear as a deviation from the natural order of things – hence lunacy – in the eyes of those who were bound to such institutions and relations by multiple ties. It might be said to be a clash between rational and moral self-evidence (appealed to by intellectuals furthest removed from the centres of power) and sociological self-evidence (referred to by the social classes closest to wealth and power). It involved two forms of self-evident truth, both of which were illusory and yet deeply felt by the protagonists in the struggle, who were incapable of developing an analysis of objective contradictions (or were rendered such).

---

11   Maximilien Robespierre, *Oeuvres*, Paris: Presses Universitaires de France, 1912–, Vol. X, pp. 455–6. For Marat, cf. Christine Fauré, ed., *Les Déclarations des droits de l'homme de 1789*, Paris: Payot, 1988, p. 272.

12   Jean-Jacques Rousseau, *Oeuvres complètes*, ed. B. Gagnebin and P. Raymond, Paris: Gallimard, 1959–, Vol. III, p. 616.

13   J.G. Fichte, *Werke*, ed. I.H. Fichte, Berlin: de Gruyter, 1971, Vol. VI, p. 17. The text published by the philosopher in 1793 refers to *feile Schriftsteller*. In editing the new edition, his son corrected it to *feige*. This is clearly a *lectio facilior* (cf. Vittorio Enzo Alfieri, Introduction and notes to Fichte, *Sulla rivoluzione francese*, Bari: Laterza, 1974, p. 19 n. 5). However, the meaning is not changed substantially: only intellectuals who are corrupt or craven can be against the revolution.

14   Benjamin Constant, *Journal intime, précédé du Le cahier rouge et de Adolphe (1767–1787)*, ed. Jean Mistler, Monaco: Éditions du Rocher, 1945, p. 183.

In their exchange of accusations, the two parties sometimes employed categories that *prima facie* were identical, but whose meaning was profoundly different in each instance. The fanaticism denounced by the supporters of Enlightenment and revolutionary leaders, with their focus on the mass social base of the *ancien régime*, was synonymous with superstition, ignorance, lack of enlightenment, and unthinking attachment to what exists. The fanaticism pointed to by opponents of the revolution involved condemnation of 'abstraction', the destructive frenzy of the enlightened, reason that dissects living things conceptually rather existentially. It is the 'tremendous power of the negative' referred to by Hegel,[15] which, in the modern era, is embodied in an intelligentsia enjoying a dangerous degree of independence from power and the dominant classes. Intellectuals organically linked to the existing political and social system appear servile and corrupt to intellectuals who are *freischwebend* (in Mannheim's celebrated expression). The latter, by virtue of apparently floating free of constraints in a space remote from existing politico-social 'concreteness', cannot but seem insane to their opponents.

At this point we can draw an initial conclusion. Furet correctly stresses 'the discrepancy between the role objectively played by revolutions in historical change and the perception of that role by contemporaries'.[16] But he fails to live up to his own methodological criterion: genuine distantiation from the lived experience of the protagonists of revolutionary upheavals is matched by substantial identification with the experience of their antagonists. Thus is explained the re-emergence of the category or metaphor of the revolutionary disease, which not by chance triumphed in the years of the Restoration. In such a way (objects Hegel), rather than regarding the upheavals as the expression of objective 'contradictions', everything is explained by recourse to 'an anomaly and a transient pathological paroxysm'.[17] This type of explanation is reiterated by historical revisionism. Diagnosis of the malady undergoes subsequent development and refinement: an attempt is made to take account of developments in psychology, psychoanalysis or sociology, so as to clarify the genesis of the ideological 'intoxication' already denounced by Burke. But it is basically faithful to the formulation of the British Whig, who (according to Nolte) is to be credited with having foreseen

---

15   G.W.F. Hegel, *Werke in zwanzig Bänden*, ed. E. Moldenhauer and K.M. Michel, Frankfurt am Main: Suhrkamp, 1969–79, Vol. III, p. 36.

16   Furet, *Interpreting the French Revolution*, p. 159.

17   Hegel, *Werke*, Vol. VI, pp. 75–6.

the catastrophic results of the 'ideological fanaticism' diffused even before 1789 'among the authors of the *Encyclopédie*'.[18]

To appreciate the one-sidedness of this approach, it suffices to compare it with that of Burckhardt, who summarized the explosions produced by great historical crises thus: 'the fierceness of these struggles, the unleashing of passion on both sides. Each side defends "what it holds most sacred" – on the one hand, an abstract loyalty and a religion; on the other, a new "world order".' The fury of the struggle prompts an 'indifference as to methods' on both sides, resulting in 'general massacres', which, however, do not seem to arouse particular indignation.[19]

Abstract and Concrete

What does the ideological 'intoxication' consuming the French Revolution consist in? For Burke, there is no doubt: it is universalism, theorization of the 'supposed rights of man' and the 'absolute equality of the human race'; it is recourse to 'abstract principle', 'general principles' and 'vague speculative right'. Contrasted with all of this is the 'practical wisdom' of the authors of the Glorious Revolution, with its consecration of the rights of Englishmen hereditarily transmitted like a legacy.[20] We are familiar with Burke's great success in Germany, where we find Justus Möser, one of the most intelligent theorists of conservatism, who not by chance was regarded as a kind of German Burke,[21] polemicize as early as 1772 against 'the tendency to universal [*allgemein*] rules and laws', which he reproved for proceeding 'despotically' against all particular 'privileges and liberties'.[22] As Karl Mannheim justly observed, such a rejection of the category of universality was a peculiarity of 'caste [*ständisch*] thinking'.[23] This was also the opinion

18   Ernst Nolte, 'Weltbürgerkrieg 1917–1989?', Italian trans. in *Dramma dialettico o tragedia? La guerra civile mondiale e altri saggi*, ed. F. Coppellotti, Perugia: Settimo Sigillo/ Perugia University Press, 1994, p. 33.

19   Jacob Burckhardt, *Reflections on History*, trans. M.D.H., London: George Allen & Unwin, 1943, pp. 149–50.

20   Burke, *The Works*, Vol. IX, p. 281; Vol. VII, p. 129; Vol. V, pp. 76–7.

21   Friedrich Meinecke connects the two in *Die Entstehung des Historismus*, Munich: Oldenbourg, 1965, pp. 323, 342, 347 and passim.

22   Justus Möser, *Sämmtliche Werke*, ed. B.R. Abeken and J.W.J. von Voigts, Berlin: Nicolaische Buchhandlung, 1842, Vol. II, pp. 22–3.

23   Karl Mannheim, 'Der konservative Denken', in *Wissenssoziologie. Auswahl aus dem Werk*, ed. K.H. Wolff, Berlin and Neuwied: Luchterhand, 1964, pp. 477–8.

of Tocqueville, according to whom 'truly general ideas' were not to be found in aristocratic society.[24] By contrast, the socio-political dimension of the debate is dissolved in the context of historical revisionism, which uncritically subscribes to the polemic against abstraction. Where Burke inveighed against 'political metaphysics',[25] and Louis XVI himself, at the moment of the flight to Varennes, reproached the Constituent Assembly for its projects of 'metaphysical government',[26] Furet reprehends the 'metaphysics of the subject' and the 'metaphysics of the French Constituents'.[27] To appreciate how total and unconditional is the identification with the lived experience of the French Revolution's opponents, we must proceed to a new comparison with Burckhardt, whom we have seen define the duty of 'loyalty' peculiar to defenders of the *ancien régime* as 'abstract', because it disregards concrete content and appeals exclusively to respect for continuity and historical tradition (as in Burke).

At this point it is appropriate to introduce two philosophers who, if only by dint of geographical and social location, were far removed from the 'intoxicated' Jacobins of Paris. Kant not only criticized the theory/practice dichotomy, but also felt obliged to take on the defence of the 'metaphysicians' and their 'sanguine hopes of improving the world'.[28] Even more interesting is the position of Hegel, author of a memorable critical analysis of the Terror, who nevertheless celebrated the development of the 'abstract, universal' concept of man, possessor as such of inalienable rights, as an epochal event.[29] Obviously, the term in question can also assume a negative connotation in the philosopher's pages. A contemptuous attitude towards servants, fashionable in still feudal Prussia, is a form of 'abstract' thinking, in as much as it ignores the concrete reality of the human being and fixes her or him in a single 'abstract determination' – that of wealth or social rank. Referring to post-revolutionary France, Hegel contrasts such behaviour with the cordial and even amicable relations, ultimately based on the 'concreteness' of equal human worth, linking the domestic

24   See Alexis de Tocqueville, *Democracy in America*, London: Everyman, 1994, Vol. II, Bk. 1, Chapter 3.

25   Burke, *The Works*, Vol. V, p. 120.

26   Quoted in Walter Markov, ed., *Revolution im Zeugenstand. Frankreich 1789–1799*, Leipzig: Reclam, 1982, Vol. II, p. 175.

27   François Furet, 'Burke ou la fin d'une seule histoire de l'Europe', in F. Lebrun and R. Dupuy, eds, *Les Résistances à la Révolution*, Paris: Imago, 1987, pp. 354, 358.

28   Immanuel Kant, *Gesammelte Schriften*, Berlin: Academy of Sciences, 1900–, Vol. XXIII, pp. 127, 155.

29   G.W.F. Hegel, *Vorlesungen über die Philosophie der Weltgeschichte*, ed. G. Lasson, Leipzig: Meiner, 1919–20, p. 611.

to his or her master.[30] Assessment of an 'abstract' concept first of all involves examining what one is abstracting from. According to Furet, one of the few representatives of the French regime to engage in a struggle against 'abstract reason', or the 'abstract mind', was Barnave.[31] Yet the latter was allied with white colonists in defending the institution of slavery and, for that reason, would have seemed frighteningly abstract to the German philosopher.

It is now necessary to investigate the accusation of abstraction levelled at the French revolutionaries by Burke in more strictly historical terms. Their error was not to be linked to the theory that presided over William of Orange's arrival on the throne of the Stuarts and hence the birth of the British constitutional monarchy. This is a critique based on a massive historical repression: it is as if the American Revolution had never happened. During the latter, the crisis of the theory that Burke sought to revive on French soil was consummated. The American colonists began their rebellion invoking the rights of Englishmen and, on that basis, demanded autonomous representation in the legislative body as a precondition of taxes being levied on them. But this ideological platform immediately turned out to be rather fragile, given that the principle of representation on an individual basis was alien to the British legal and political tradition. Important, heavily populated areas like Sheffield, Birmingham and Leeds were completely without representatives at the time. The British Crown relied on this to discredit the claims of the colonists, who were thus led to base their demands no longer on 'old parchments or musty records', on 'immunity' and 'parchments or seals', in the words of Hamilton and Dickinson, but on appeals to 'the sacred rights of mankind': 'They are written as with a sunbeam in the whole volume of human nature, by the hand of the Divinity itself and can never be erased or obscured by mortal power.' The polemic against parchments and seals exposed the crisis of the ideological platform peculiar to the Glorious Revolution cherished by Burke. The right to representation and political rights now began to assume the shape on American soil of inalienable rights possessed by man as such, not only Englishmen. Explicit polemics against 'English liberties', which (declared Adams) 'are but certain rights of nature reserved to the citizen by the English constitution', were not wanting.[32]

---

30   Hegel, *Werke*, Vol. II, p. 580.

31   François Furet, 'Barnave', in Furet and Mona Ozouf, eds, *A Critical Dictionary of the French Revolution*, trans. Arthur Goldhammer, Cambridge, MA: Belknap Press of Harvard University Press, 1989, p. 190.

32   Quoted in Charles E. Merriam, *A History of American Political Theories*, New York: Kelley, 1969, pp. 44–51.

Such reverence for natural law and universalism informed the French Revolution from the outset. In fact, it developed even further given that the presence of black slavery no longer served to check it. It goes without saying that fairly similar ideological platforms yielded very different results either side of the Atlantic because of the radically different objective conditions. This fact is underlined by Furet, who notes how it was only in America that egalitarian theories proved 'in harmony with the social state', because the former colonies were 'peopled by minor landowners with democratic customs, who from the start had cultivated the spirit of equality, unhampered by external enemies or a feudal or aristocratic heritage'.[33] Initially expelled as irrelevant when it comes to assessing the revolutionary process and project, the despised 'circumstances' make their reappearance here. Hence it might be concluded that what explains the particularly tormented character of its revolution was France's different geopolitical and social configuration. But this is not the conclusion of Furet, who does not wish to renounce the thesis that the Terror is deducible *a priori* from ideology. Circumstances are introduced to demonstrate that an identical or similar ideological platform can have a concrete or abstract significance, depending on whether it is mobilized in America or France. Consequently, it is no longer the theorization of the rights of man as such that defines the abstractness of the French revolutionaries, but their theorization in a country marked by profound, deeply rooted inequalities. But then an analogous judgement is called for in the case of the American abolitionists who, some decades later, aimed to apply the idea of equality to relations between the races, in a country vast regions of which had for centuries been accustomed to regard black slavery as a 'positive good'. The consequences of such 'abstraction' could only be a terrible civil war. By contrast, 'concreteness', with which one avoids discussing the successive deportations inflicted on Native Americans, spared the white community other conflicts, even as it sealed the tragedy of an ill-fated 'race'.

In reality, Burke's (and Furet's) criticism of the French Revolutionaries is based on a colossal abstraction from historical time, as if it were possible to ignore the ideological results of the American Revolution and regress to a political and cultural platform now challenged even in Britain by large sections of public opinion, which, well before 1789, demanded an extension of the suffrage and demanded it on the basis of individual representation, thus coming into conflict with the inflexible Edmund Burke.

---

33   François Furet, *Revolutionary France, 1770–1880*, trans. Antonia Nevill, Oxford and Cambridge, MA: Blackwell, 1992, p. 73.

The Advent of Democracy and Historical
Cycles: France, Britain, USA

Added to this first arbitrary abstraction is another. Furet recognizes that, in staging a comparison between France and Britain, the British Whig passed over 'the civil war of the 1640s' in 'complete silence'.[34] Yet this is the kind of comparativism that has triumphed today, and which enables revisionist or neo-liberal literature to contrast other revolutions with the French Revolution, liquidated as abstract and productive of the Terror and the Vendéan 'genocide'. But is separating the Glorious Revolution of 1688 from the English revolutionary process as a whole a sign of historical concreteness? What would we say of an author who, in order to demonstrate the sanguinary character of the English Revolution, compared it (starting with the Civil War) with the July Revolution? To freeze in a particular phase one, and only one, of the two revolutionary cycles being compared involves an arbitrary abstraction. Constant and the pre-1848 Guizot made a comparison between the French Revolution and the English Revolution as a whole, 'from 1640 to 1688'.[35] With reference to England, Ranke refers in analogous terms to a single revolutionary process extending from the Great Rebellion to the Glorious Revolution.[36] As regards the history of the USA, numerous historians, of very different orientations, regard the Civil War as a second revolution or a second stage of the American Revolution.

By contrast, Furet applies the category of historical cycle solely to France, whose revolution encompasses a period of time stretching from 1770 to 1880 — that is, from the crisis of the *ancien régime* to the advent and consolidation of the Third Republic.[37] Because of its tortured development, the French Revolution is distinguished

> from the American Revolution to such an extent that one hesitates to apply the same word to the two events. Both, nonetheless, were animated by the same ideas and comparable passions; they can almost be said to have founded modern democratic civilization simultaneously. Yet the American Revolution concluded in the development and ratification of a

---

34 Furet, 'Burke ou la fin d'une seule histoire de l'Europe', p. 353.

35 François Guizot, 'Avertissement de l'auteur pour le deuxième édition', in *Histoire de la révolution d'Angleterre*, Brussels: Société Typographique Belge, 1850, pp. 123–4.

36 Leopold von Ranke, *Über die Epochen der neueren Geschichte*, Darmstadt: Wissenschaftliche Buchgesellschaft, 1980, p. 121.

37 See Furet, *Revolutionary France*.

constitution that has lasted to this day and has become the sacred ark of American citizenship. The French Revolution produced a multiplicity of constitutions and regimes and gave the world its first look at egalitarian despotism.[38]

In reality, if its objective was the emergence of 'a society of citizens equal before the law', and the realization of 'a society composed of equal individuals, in contrast to the old society of corps',[39] the democratic revolution cannot be regarded as having been concluded in the USA prior to the abolition of the institution of slavery, prior to the disappearance of an order which in the South, by the express declaration of its theoreticians and apologists, was articulated in 'three *castes* – of free white, free colored, and slave colored population'.[40]

The presuppositions of the war that occurred between 1861 and 1865 were already implicit in a Constitution which on the one hand proclaimed the natural right of every man to liberty, while on the other sanctioning the reduction of a fifth of the population to slavery. In 1790, a motion presented by the abolitionists of Pennsylvania, and also signed by Benjamin Franklin, expressed the wish that Congress assert its powers for the purposes of 'restoration of liberty to those unhappy men, who alone, in this land of freedom, are degraded into perpetual bondage'. Thomas Tucker of South Carolina immediately replied: 'Do these men expect a general emancipation of slaves by law? This would never be submitted to by the Southern States without a civil war.'[41] Several decades later, Calhoun, the most acute and brilliant theoretician of the beneficent character of the institution of slavery, reiterated the point: 'Abolition and the Union cannot co-exist.'[42] But this warning in turn elicited a prompt response from Henry Clay: 'War and dissolution of the Union are identical and inevitable.'[43]

---

38   François Furet, *The Passing of an Illusion: The Idea of Communism in the Twentieth Century*, trans. Deborah Furet, Chicago and London: University of Chicago Press, 1999, p. 9.

39   François Furet, 'Mirabeau', in Furet and Ozouf, eds, *Critical Dictionary of the French Revolution*, p. 270.

40   Richard Hofstadter and Beatrice K. Hofstadter, *Great Issues in American History*, New York: Vintage Books, 1982, Vol. II, p. 319.

41   David B. Davis, *The Problem of Slavery in the Age of Revolution 1770–1823*, Ithaca and London: Cornell University Press, 1975, p. 132.

42   John C. Calhoun, *Union and Liberty*, ed. R.M. Lence, Indianapolis: Liberty Classics, 1992, p. 472.

43   Hofstadter and Hofstadter, *Great Issues in American History*, Vol. II, p. 347.

The advent of the Third Republic in France was virtually contemporaneous with the end of the Civil War in the USA and the passage in Britain of the two electoral reform bills of 1867 and 1884, whereby the suffrage was substantially extended. In the first country, we witness the collapse of the Bonapartist regime; in the second, the abolition of slavery; and in the third, not only the conquest of political rights by large sectors of the popular masses, but also the end of the discrimination that prevented Catholics, Jews and 'non-conformists' in general from sitting in representative bodies, sometimes from holding public office and, in certain cases, even entering universities.[44] We can therefore say that in the late nineteenth century the three countries had a political regime which, at a first approximation, was fairly similar, based as it was on the possession of civil rights and parliamentary institutions with universal or well-nigh universal male suffrage. It is now time to examine the historical processes and upheavals, and the train of sorrows and suffering, involved in arriving at this outcome. That is, we must proceed to a comparative analysis of what, from various standpoints, has been defined as the democratic revolution or the bourgeois revolution in the three countries under comparison.

The Three Stages of the British Revolution

To be more precise, we should refer to the three stages of the British revolutionary process, the first of which comprised the Anglican Reformation. This involved 'massive transfers of wealth', 'the successive dissolution of the monasteries and the transfer of their enormous landed property to the crown', the creation of 'a whole vast class of new rural property owners, indissolubly linked to the crown and the Anglican ecclesiastical regime', the emergence of 'a vast single economic market', and the development of the 'wool industry' thanks to the 'enclosure of open fields'.[45] Henry VIII availed himself of the collaboration of Thomas Cromwell, a follower of Marsilius of Padua committed to the construction of 'a national monarchy, liberated from papal power and limited only by the vote of Parliament'. We can therefore

44   G.M. Trevelyan, *History of England*, London: Longman, 1977, pp. 564–5 and Part VI, Chapter 4; *British History in the Nineteenth Century and After (1782–1919)*, Harmondsworth: Penguin, 1979, Chapter 22. As regards Jews, in particular, see Michael C.N. Salbstein, *The Emancipation of the Jews in Britain: The Question of the Admission of the Jews to Parliament 1828–1860*, London and Toronto: Associated University Presses, 1982.

45   Giorgio Spini, *Storia dell'età moderna*, Turin: Einaudi, 1982, pp. 184, 251–2, 257.

conclude that the Anglican schism was a 'major anti-clerical and nationalist revolution'.[46]

None of the three stages of the British revolutionary process was bloodless. In the case of the first two, this is self-evident. Let us examine the third. Trevelyan describes the situation created after the deposition of James II as follows: 'civil war in Scotland remained endemic until 1746'. Repression of the Jacobite rebellions was extremely harsh and sometimes took the form of appalling massacres. To say nothing of Ireland: 'the Revolution Settlement was a racial and religious re-conquest of the most brutal kind'.[47] Nor can events in Ireland (and Scotland) be disconnected from the Glorious Revolution, given that the victory of English troops in rebel areas was essential 'to prevent a Jacobite restoration in England'. Yet, following this highly dramatic picture, Trevelyan arrives at a conclusion that has something extraordinary about it: 'The true "glory" of the British Revolution lay in the fact that it was bloodless, that there was no civil war, no massacre, no proscription', with everything proceeding under the banner of tolerance.[48]

The author we have cited was something of an official historian: he always speaks in the first person plural, as if identifying himself with the options of Britain's rulers in past centuries. We must now attend to historians of a different persuasion, if only because bound by ties of sympathy to the peoples subject to racial and/or religious conquest by London. In truth, the Scottish rebellion continued well beyond the date indicated by Trevelyan. Nonetheless, let us look at what occurred in 1746, this time giving the floor to Scottish historians:

> The English, led by the Duke of Cumberland, defeated the Scots and began one of the worst persecutions of a nation known to history, earning the title 'Butcher' Cumberland for their leader. The Scottish survivors were chased from the field of battle and slaughtered. For two days the wounded and dead of the Scottish army lay where they had fallen, guarded by English soldiers so that no medical or burial parties could get to them. Looting was officially organised and £5 was paid for the head of every 'rebel' brought to Major-General John Huske, the English Commander at Fort Augustus. Towns and villages were razed to the ground, people

---

46   Ibid., p. 257.
47   G.M. Trevelyan, *The English Revolution 1688–1689*, London, Oxford and New York: Oxford University Press, 1968, p. 6 n.1.
48   Trevelyan, *History of England*, pp. 575, 563.

slaughtered wholesale and those that managed to escape massacre were imprisoned, executed or transported.

The historians quoted here go so far as to speak of a tendency or aspiration to a 'final solution' of the Scottish question.[49]

Even more tragic was the fate of Ireland in all three phases of the revolution. From the sixteenth century, England conducted a 'policy of extermination'; 'the English cared much more for the suppression of the Irish race than for the suppression of its religion'.[50] The author of these words was a staunchly Unionist Anglo-Irish historian, according to whom the suffering visited on the Irish population can be compared only to the treatment meted out to the Native Americans by the white colonists in America. Almost a century after the Anglican Reformation, and nearly two decades before the outbreak of the Puritan revolution, in 1622, in the context of a discourse on natural science, Bacon referred in passing to the moss growing in the island 'upon slain bodies, laid in heaps unburied'.[51] As the aforementioned Unionist historian remarks, the conduct of the English

was literally a war of extermination. The slaughter of Irishmen was looked upon as literally the slaughter of wild beasts. Not only the men, but even the women and children who fell into the hands of the English, were deliberately and systematically butchered. Bands of soldiers traversed great tracts of the country, slaying every living thing they met. The sword was not found sufficiently expeditious, but another method proved much more efficacious. Year after year, over a great part of Ireland, all means of human subsistence were destroyed, no quarter was given to prisoners who surrendered, and the whole population was skilfully and steadily starved to death.[52]

This was a tragedy that continued for centuries. After the 1798 uprising, Camden, Viceroy in Ireland, observed that the British colonists, 'mad with fury', were 'scarcely to be satisfied with anything short of extirpation' of

49   Peter Berresford Ellis and Seumas Mac a'Globhaim, *The Scottish Insurrection of 1820*, London: Pluto Press, 1989, p. 49.

50   William E.H. Lecky, *A History of England in the Eighteenth Century*, London: Longmans, Green & Co., 1883–8, Vol. II, p. 99.

51   Francis Bacon, *The Works*, Stuttgart-Bad Cannstatt: Frommann-Holzboog, 1963, Vol. II, p. 670.

52   Lecky, *A History of England in the Eighteenth Century*, Vol. II, pp. 95–6.

the Irish population. A similar picture was drawn shortly afterwards by the new Viceroy, Cornwallis, who referred to 'the ferocity of our troops who delight in murder' and 'butchering without discrimination'.[53] We could go on at length with details and quotations. Writing in the late nineteenth century, Lecky was in no doubt that what had been imposed on the Irish population was the worst of 'all tyrannies'.[54] The judgement of the liberal historian coincides with that of Marx, according to whom British policy in the unhappy island was so ruthless and terroristic that it was 'unprecedented in Europe' and could only be compared with the 'mongols'.[55]

As we can see, the charge of genocide has not been pressed solely in connection with the French Revolution. At the time of the 1798 rebellion, notwithstanding all the massacres that had already occurred, Ireland numbered 4,500,000 inhabitants – one-third of the total population of the British Isles.[56] Hence we are dealing with a 'genocide' of much greater extent and duration than that denounced by historical revisionism in connection with the Vendée.

From the First to the Second American Revolution

Trevelyan, who offers such a heart-warming assessment of the British Revolution, adopts a more realistic tone when analysing the rebellion of the British colonists in the New World. At the start of their estrangement from the mother country, the American revolutionaries did not hesitate to 'terrorize, or expel, [their] opponents'. Once the separation of the colonies had been achieved, the 'United Kingdom loyalists' were compelled to flee en masse from 'the intolerance and injustice of the victorious Republicans of the United States, who made life impossible for their late political opponents' after the War of Independence.[57] Perhaps we detect a hint of nostalgia for the empire on the English historian's part. Yet this picture has the merit of rendering the conventional image of the American Revolution, based on repression of the bitter civil war that occurred, all the more problematic. It suffices to think of the massive emigration that occurred following Britain's

---

53 Thomas Pakenham, *The Year of Liberty: The History of the Great Irish Rebellion of 1798*, New York: Random House, 1969, pp. 164, 265–6.

54 Lecky, *A History of England in the Eighteenth Century*, Vol. I, p. 285.

55 Karl Marx and Friedrich Engels, *Werke*, Berlin: Dietz, 1955–, Vol. XVI, p. 552.

56 Pakenham, *The Year of Liberty*, p. 30.

57 Trevelyan, *History of England*, pp. 654, 699–701.

defeat. More than 60,000 refugees moved to Canada and the maritime provinces. Thousands more emigrated to the West Indies, while a crowd of wretches poured into England: 'There will scarcely be a village in England without some American dust.'[58]

An American historian to whom we have already referred – Palmer – has ventured a comparison with the French Revolution: 'There were about 2,500,000 people in America in 1776, of whom a fifth were slaves . . . There were about 25,000,000 people in France at the time of the French Revolution. There were, therefore, 24 émigrés per thousand of population in the American Revolution, and only 5 émigrés per thousand of population in the French Revolution.'[59] Even more dramatic is the picture sketched by descendants of the opponents of the Declaration of Independence, which had been imposed by an activist minority: 'From the beginning the Loyalists were deprived of freedom of the press, freedom of assemblage, and under an espionage universal, sleepless, [and] malignant.' Then there was the sequestration of goods and collective punitive measures against those suspected of loyalty to the Crown; life was made impossible even for 'neutrals'. The Convention of the state of New York decreed that 'any person being an adherent to the King of Great Britain should be guilty of treason and suffer death'. The new authorities' terror from above was combined with terror from below: loyalists were 'hunted and killed at pleasure'. The historian we are following reports John Adams' urgent exhortation 'to fine, imprison, and hang all inimical to the cause, without favour or affection . . . I would have hanged my own brother had he taken a part with our enemy in the contest.'[60] While it can also invoke the authority of a historian like Furet, the habitual Manichaean counter-position of the American Revolution to the French Revolution is manifestly the result of a method that is the acme of a-critical thinking. In the case of the American Revolution, what counts are the oleographic images of the victors; when it comes to the French Revolution, the bitter denunciations of its enemies alone are to be trusted.

So persistent are the echoes of the struggle accompanying the American Revolution that, during the war between the USA and Britain in 1812–15, the US attempt to seize Canada was prompted not only by old expansionist

58 Quoted in Allan Nevis and Henry S. Commager, *America: Story of a Free People*, Oxford: Oxford University Press, 1943, p. 92.

59 Robert R. Palmer, *The Age of Democratic Revolution: A Political History of Europe and America, 1760–1800*, Princeton: Princeton University Press, 1959–64, Vol. I, p. 188.

60 Egerton Ryerson, *The Loyalists of America and Their Times: From 1620 to 1816*, New York: Haskell, 1970, Vol. II, pp. 5, 30, 123–8, 183.

ambitions, but also by a desire for a final settlement of accounts with the ex-loyalists, who were opposed to the revolution and who continued to regard and conduct themselves as loyal subjects of the British Crown. Published in Toronto in 1879, the extended documentary history of the loyalists we have used was, significantly enough, dedicated to the British Queen. We are dealing with a first example of historical revisionism regarding the American Revolution, which (it was stressed) could not continue to be written exclusively by the victors, or the 'enemies and spoilers' of loyalists and Native Americans.[61]

That last allusion draws our attention to a completely repressed tragic experience. Yet one of the most serious charges levelled at George III by the Declaration of Independence was that of having 'endeavoured to bring on the inhabitants of our frontiers, the merciless Indian Savages whose known rule of warfare is an undistinguished destruction of all ages, sexes and conditions'. In this indictment, the Native Americans were depicted as a kind of barbarian Vendée. And, in fact, the majority of them sided with the British Crown, having experienced first-hand that they had much less to fear from the remote rulers and traders of London than from the white colonists in their immediate vicinity, who aspired to seize their land by any means. Repression of this Vendée was not only ruthless, but often marked by sheer sadism. The systematic destruction of crops and villages; the deliberate diffusion of smallpox; women and children 'butchered in cold blood and burned alive'; 'they put to death all the Women and Children, excepting some of the Young Women, whom they carried away for the use of their soldiers & were afterwards put to death in a more shameful manner' – such are but some of the details of the picture that emerges from witnesses.[62] It is a picture that casts a dark shadow over Washington, Jefferson and the Founding Fathers in general, who were directly involved in the exterminatory crusade.

The War of Independence against Britain became intertwined with civil and social war within the white community. Historians from various countries, and of different political and ethical persuasions, agree that what rendered the anti-British struggle

> longer and often cruel [was] the civil war between the Americans themselves, a section of whom adopted the royalist cause rather than the

61   Ibid., Vol. I, p. iii.
62   Colin G. Calloway, *The American Revolution in Indian Country: Crisis and Diversity in Native American Communities*, Cambridge: Cambridge University Press, 1995, pp. 5, 50–3.

revolutionary one. Obviously, the royalists or Tories frequently, if not exclusively, came from among the better-off . . . it was not unusual for the struggle between the two sides also to take on the features of social conflict.[63]

The loyalist property-owners became the targets of a policy of asset seizure and property redistribution on a massive scale. Judging from the compensation subsequently paid out to those affected, 'revolutionary France, ten times as large as revolutionary America, confiscated only twelve times as much property from its émigrés . . . The difference, even allowing for margins of error, is less great than is commonly supposed.'[64]

But let us move on to the second stage of the democratic revolution. As we have seen, Furet emphasizes that the Constitution promulgated at Philadelphia 'has lasted to this day and become the sacred ark of American citizenship'. Alas, the introduction of a handful of amendments required an extremely bloody civil war, with a casualty figure higher than that suffered by the USA in the two world wars put together. In the wake of the Civil War and the state of emergency, terror even made its appearance across the Atlantic. It is enough to read some 'democratic' – i.e. pro-slavery – pamphlets of the time to appreciate the vigour of the condemnation of Lincoln's Jacobin methods. He was denounced for having imposed 'military government' and 'military commissions', and for having interpreted 'the word "law"' as 'the will of the President' and *habeas corpus* as the 'power of the President to imprison whom he pleases, as long as he pleases'.[65]

During the Civil War, the Union was compelled to employ an iron fist not only against the secessionist South, but also internally. When compulsory conscription was introduced in the North, 'the mass of poor immigrants of New York – especially the Irish' – rebelled. An army corps marched on the city to put down the revolt.[66]

63　Giorgio Spini, *Disegno storico della civiltà*, Rome: Cremonese, 1963, Vol. II, p. 385.

64　Palmer, *The Age of Democratic Revolution*, Vol. I, p. 188.

65　Arthur M. Schlesinger Jr., ed., *History of United States Political Parties*, New York and London: Chelsea House and Bawker, 1973, pp. 915–21.

66　Raimondo Luraghi, *Introduzione a La guerra civile americana*, Bologna: Il Mulino, 1978, p. 53.

Saturn and the Dynamic of 'Historical Crises'

There is perhaps a point where Furet registers the unsustainability of the black-and-white contrast between the history of France and the history of the Anglo-American world. Here once again is the French historian, this time referring to Quinet's polemic against Louis Blanc:

> The behaviour of the British in India has been compared with the regime of '93. But where is the analogy? The world is full of violence and war. Who can doubt it? But that is not the point. Did the British generals in India kill one another? Things would have to stand thus for the comparison to be sustainable. Can we not see that one of the peculiar features of the French Revolution is that revolutionaries were put to death by revolutionaries, Jacobins by Jacobins, Montagnards by Montagnards? Why did this occur?

And Furet piles it on, inveighing against 'the inability to clarify the characteristics of the social violence that has had such a long career in left-wing ideology'.[67] This is a theme dear to a massive literature and also to Arendt, for whom the French Revolution is to be regarded as a failure because it placed everything 'under the sign of Saturn'.[68]

In truth, there is no revolutionary cycle that cannot be interpreted in accordance with this schema. Let us see what happened in the British colonies in America. The united camp that fought against the 'despotism' of the mother country, demanding the right to independent representation, subsequently split over the issue of independence. And it is enough to glance at the loyalist literature to observe the heartbreak with which they saw repression rain down on them. It was experienced and denounced as ferocious, and of a ferocity that was all the more inexplicable in that it was inflicted by former allies. These were the years when 'a ferocious saying came to be current in America, that though we are commanded to forgive our enemies, we are nowhere commanded to forgive our friends'.[69] The operative dialectic did not end with the attainment of independence. The Federal Constitution subsequently promulgated at Philadelphia was

---

67   François Furet, *La Gauche et la révolution au milieu du XIXe siècle. Edgar Quinet et la question du jacobinisme*, Paris: Hachette, 1986, pp. 95–6.

68   Hannah Arendt, *On Revolution*, London: Faber & Faber, 1963, p. 42.

69   Ryerson, *The Loyalists of America and Their Times*, Vol. II, p. 128.

invoked for the purposes of confronting with adequate executive power the 'factional violence' and 'civil war' started by Daniel Shays, a retired colonel in the army that had fought and defeated the British, who now put himself at the head of a revolt by poor farmers and debtors in Massachusetts.[70]

This was the second division in the front that had challenged the power of George III. Obviously, however, the more profound and bloody split is the one that occurred some decades later. The forces that had defeated the Tories and loyalists, on the one hand, and the poor farmers, on the other, promulgated the new Federal Constitution in a kind of 'coup d'état'. It was marked by a compromise that allowed the southern states to continue to enjoy black slavery undisturbed. A few decades later, the same forces confronted one another in a fight to the finish, when the contradictions that had previously been smoothed over or masked by a compromise that proved unstable matured to breaking-point. We can now understand why both abolitionists and supporters of slavery alike referred to the anti-British War of Independence, and the declarations and constitutional texts deriving from it, during the Civil War. Lincoln's followers invoked the Philadelphia Constitution, with its solemn opening in which 'the People of the United States' declared that they wished 'to form a more perfect Union'. The literature of the Confederacy, on the other hand, laid claim to the legacy of the patriotic struggle against an oppressive central power, underscored the centrality of the rights of each single state in the process of the country's foundation and its legal tradition, and reminded the abolitionists that Washington, Jefferson and Monroe were all slave-owners. Both sides declared that they were following in the tracks laid down by the Founding Fathers. Saturn does indeed devour his children. Initiated with the anti-British rebellion, the democratic revolution went beyond the old constitutional compromise, no longer recognized it, could no longer recognize itself in it.

The struggle was so bitter that it continued beyond the end of the Civil War. While the iron fist of the military occupation regime imposed by the Union made itself felt in the South, a counter-offensive for the restoration of white supremacy began, with the squads of the Ku Klux Klan, violence, and even a form of guerrilla warfare. In the words of a distinguished American historian, 'as surely as the struggle between 1861 and 1865 was civil war,

---

70   See Domenico Losurdo, *Democrazia o bonapartismo*, Turin: Bollati Boringhieri, 1993, pp. 89–90.

so was the conflict from 1865 to 1877, with as much bitterness and hatred but less bloodshed'.[71]

Denouncing the French Revolution as a Saturn that devoured its children, Furet refers to Quinet, ignoring the fact that for the latter the relevant dialectic implicated not so much Jacobin ideology as France's enduring Catholic legacy.[72] But we have seen how fashionable the depiction of the historical development of Protestant countries implied by this claim is. On the subject of Saturn we may turn to Burckhardt. Examining the phenomenology of major 'historical crises' from antiquity onwards, he summarized their general characteristics as follows:

> Any man who flags for an instant, or can no longer keep pace with the increasing momentum of the movement, is replaced with astonishing rapidity. In the shortest space of time, a second generation of leaders has found time to mature, and is already representative of the crisis alone, and of its essential, specific spirit. They feel their bond with the former state of things far less strongly than the men who came first . . . Whenever a man – or a party – wearies, another is waiting to take his place, and though he may, in his turn, be extremely inadequate to his moment, the whole movement may crystallize round him for just that moment . . . *La révolution dévore ses enfants*. Every stage of the crisis . . . devours the representatives of the preceding stage as 'moderates'.

We can view the dialectic of Saturn with 'foolish amazement'. However, far from being specific to Catholicism or Jacobinism, it also emerges in sharp relief in the Puritan revolution:

> In the first stage of the crisis, when old oppressions have to be swept away and their representatives persecuted, we already find the phenomenon which causes so much foolish amazement, namely that the initiators of the movement are ousted and replaced. *Either* they had been the agents of very diverse forces, while from now on *one* force stands revealed as the real leader, annihilating the others or carrying them with it; this, for instance, was the case in the Civil War in England, which was set in motion by the Cavaliers but carried through by the Roundheads alone, a proof

---

71   John H. Franklin, *From Slavery to Freedom: A History of Negro Americans*, New York: Knopf, 2000, pp. 276–7.

72   Edgar Quinet, *Le Christianisme et la Révolution française*, Paris: Fayard, 1984, pp. 240–1.

that the essential impulse was not the defence of the constitution but the Independent movement.[73]

Not only Burckhardt, but also distinguished contemporary historians stress that a 'process of division within the original opposition' characterized the Puritan revolution throughout.[74] It will suffice here to refer to its final phase. In 1646, the royalist armies had been completely defeated and Charles I was a prisoner of the revolutionary forces. But this did not mean the end of the Civil War. A struggle between Presbyterians and Congregationalists or independents, to whom Cromwell adhered, ensued. Having secured victory, Cromwell struck out at the more radical current of the Levellers.

Thus, successive waves of division are not a peculiar feature of the French Revolution. Significantly, even before its outbreak, Herder affirmed that, given the constant upheavals in the history of 'governments', 'the greater part of our Earth merits not such a name, but that of Mars or child-devouring Saturn'.[75] Even more interesting is the fact that one of the first denunciations of this dialectic is attributable to the *philosophes*, who ideologically paved the way for the French Revolution. Examining the Reformation and its development, they charged clerical fanaticism with reproducing in practice 'the abominable cult of Saturn and Moloch'.[76] In fact, the schema of Saturn is readily applicable to the decades or centuries of politico-religious struggles that arose out of the Protestant Reformation and continued until the Glorious Revolution or even the American Revolution. Müntzer started off as a follower of Luther, appreciated and loved by his teacher, who was subsequently prominent and implacable in demanding his physical elimination. It is a dialectic that assumes international dimensions, first with the Reformation and its sequels in Britain, and then with the American Revolution led by descendants of the Puritan exiles. It is no coincidence that Tucker in England characterized the rebels as 'the Dissidence of Dissent, and the Protestantism of the Protestant Religion'.[77]

---

73   Burckhardt, *Reflections on History*, pp. 147–51.

74   Hans Christoph Schröder, *Die Revolutionen Englands im 17. Jahrhundert*, Frankfurt am Main: Suhrkamp, 1986, p. 83.

75   Johann G. Herder, *Outlines of a Philosophy of the History of Man*, trans. T. Churchill, New York: Bergman Publishers, 1966, p. 444.

76   *Encyclopédie ou Dictionnaire raisonné des sciences, des arts et des metiers*, new edn, Geneva: Pellet, 1778, Vol. XXXIII, p. 596, entry on 'Tolérance'.

77   Quoted in J.G. Pocock, *Virtue, Commerce and History*, Cambridge: Cambridge University Press, 1988, p. 164. This is a polemical inversion of the defence Burke had mounted of the American rebels: see *The Works*, Vol. III, p. 53.

The 'Triumph' and 'Failure' of Revolutions

We have said that, on an initial estimate, the three countries under comparison present a fairly similar political picture in the late nineteenth century.
But this was precisely an initial estimate. With the advent of the Third
Republic and a parliamentary democracy based on (male) universal suffrage
in France, the *ancien régime* may be regarded as definitively transcended. In
Britain, on the other hand, it remained alive with the persistence of censitary
restrictions on the suffrage and the role of the House of Lords, which was
monopolized by the aristocracy. Furthermore, the question of Ireland was
unresolved. There rebellion continued to simmer, flame up, or even explode,
and in that eventuality was met with a state of emergency or martial law.

Even more bleak, albeit different, was the scene in the USA. After 1877,
the Union, abandoning the iron fist and military dictatorship, reached a
compromise with the whites of the South. The ex-slaves lost not only the
political rights won immediately after the Civil War, but also some of their
civil rights, through legislation that sanctioned racial segregation in schools,
public places, means of transport and lifts, and through a legal system
monopolized by whites which discriminated against blacks. For this reason,
distinguished American historians speak of the Civil War and Reconstruction
as a second revolution, but one that must be regarded as unfinished or a
failure.[78] Even more tragic, the fate of the Native Americans was sealed by
the slaughter at Wounded Knee in 1890, which indiscriminately targeted
adult males, the elderly, women and children.

At this point, the result of the comparison between the three countries
seems to be reversed – an inversion we find in Arendt herself. In the assessment she made in 1970, when black protest was spreading and assuming
radical forms, it was not (as in 1963) the French Revolution that had proved
a failure, but the American Revolution. This put a serious question mark
over the responsibility of the Founding Fathers themselves. An 'original
crime' weighed on the history of the USA. It was the 'simple and frightening
fact' that blacks and Native Americans

> had never been included in the original *consensus universalis* of the Amer-
> ican republic. There was nothing in the Constitution or the intent of the

---

78   See Eric Foner, *Reconstruction: America's Unfinished Revolution 1863–1877*, New York:
Harper & Row, 1989. Cf. Harold J. Laski, *The American Democracy: A Commentary and an
Interpretation*, Fairfield: Kelley, 1977, p. 462.

framers that could be so construed as to include the slave people in the original compact. Even those who pleaded eventual emancipation thought in terms of segregation of Negroes or, preferably, of deportation.

It was true that the end of the Civil War saw passage of the Fifteenth Amendment. But it did not in fact substantially alter the terms of what was at stake: 'on the contrary, the *tacit* exclusion from the *tacit* consensus was made more conspicuous by the inability or unwillingness of the federal government to enforce its own laws'.[79] Not only were 'the provisions for racial equality . . . not enforced for roughly a hundred years', but the changes that did subsequently occur were the result not of a painless process, but of pressure from below which challenged authority and institutions: 'Not the law, but civil disobedience brought into the open the "American dilemma" and, perhaps for the first time, forced upon the nation the recognition of the enormity of the crime, not just of slavery, but of chattel slavery.'[80] The 'original crime' continued to cast a dark shadow over the present. Perhaps an 'explicit constitutional amendment, addressed specifically to the Negro people of America' could be introduced, with a specific commitment to remedy the bloody injustices suffered by former slaves. Yet this necessary measure had not been taken and, as a result, the black protest movement was assuming ever more radical forms that no longer respected 'the rules of nonviolence'. Attempts at integration were bound to fail as long as the nation as a whole did not engage in a profound, genuine self-criticism.[81]

How are we to explain the reversal in the result of the comparison between the three countries? For now, we should bear in mind the various modalities of the revolutionary process. In Britain, following the failure of the Puritan popular revolution, that of 1688–9 took the form of a revolution from above, with little or no popular participation. The role of the English aristocracy was decisive or significant from the outset. Consequently, it was long able to retain control in Ireland and its social role and privileges in Britain. Similar considerations apply to the USA. Although involving significant participation by blacks (who in the closing stages of the Civil War rushed to enrol *en masse* in the federal army's ranks and participated in a widespread network of informers and sympathizers),[82] the second American revolution unfolded

---

79   Hannah Arendt, *Crises of the Republic*, San Diego, New York and London: Harcourt Brace Jovanovich, 1972, pp. 90–1.

80   Ibid., p. 81.

81   Ibid., pp. 91–2.

82   See Foner, *Reconstruction*, pp. 3–4, 8; William E.B. Du Bois, *Black Reconstruction in*

mainly as a revolution from above. When federal troops withdrew from the South in 1877, terminating Reconstruction, the descendants of the slave-owners were able to exploit the North's consent or benevolent neutrality to restore 'white supremacy', curbing blacks through the Ku Klux Klan and squadist violence.

That is why some historians believe the second American revolution to have been a failure. The 1960s and '70s saw the federal government, spurred on by a powerful black movement, intervene energetically to break the resistance of the southern states and impose recognition of black political citizenship, the end of racial segregation, and the abolition of laws prohibiting mixed sexual relations and marriages. This period is sometimes viewed as a second Reconstruction and, in this sense, constitutes the third stage of the American democratic revolution. However, as can be inferred from Arendt's bitter judgement, the shadow of failure even looms over this. Important results were unquestionably achieved. Overall, the regime of 'white supremacy' was ended. But the gap between the two races in terms of education, employment, income and participation in public office and political life has not only not been made good, but has grown once again – conspicuously so. In more specifically cultural and ideological terms, while texts demonstrating the incorrigible mediocrity of blacks' IQ (and hence the futility of the first and second reconstructions) enjoy success once more, black separatist movements are developing on the other side. The watchword of secession, advanced by slave-owners during the second stage of the American Revolution, has been adopted by descendants of slaves. Regarding the two reconstructions, or the last two stages of the American Revolution, as a failure, some of them seem to aspire to a problematic territorial separation. Meanwhile, religious separation is a reality, with some blacks opting for a different religion from whites and presenting themselves as the Nation of Islam.

It is clear that French society today is comparatively more homogeneous than American or British society. If we stage a comparison between the different revolutionary cycles under the sign of the *longue durée*, it is the French one that exhibits a greater degree of success.

America 1860–1880, ed. D.L. Lewis, New York: Atheneum, 1992, pp. 94, 104–5.

Two Forms of 'De-Specification'

But it would be an error to invert historical revisionism's formulations, neglecting the different objective situations of the three countries under comparison. We must not lose sight of the inter-meshing of objective situation, ideology and political movement. Here we might start from the remote past – to be precise, a popular revolt in Brittany in 1675, repressed with 'unparalleled atrocity'. The phrase is from Tocqueville, who draws attention to the serene, almost amused tone with which a noblewoman – Madame de Sévigné – refers to the 'horrors' of which she was the 'witness':

> Your letter from Aix, my daughter, is droll enough . . . Do you wish to hear the news from Rennes? A tax of a hundred thousand crowns has been imposed upon the citizens; and if this sum is not produced within four-and-twenty hours, it is to be doubled, and collected by the soldiers. They have cleared the houses and sent away the occupants of one of the great streets and forbidden anybody to receive them on pain of death; so that the poor wretches (old men, women near their confinement, and children included) may be seen wandering around and crying on their departure from this city, without knowing where to go, and without food or a place to lie in. Day before yesterday a fiddler was broken on the wheel for getting up a dance and stealing some stamped paper. He was quartered after death, and his limbs exposed at the four corners of the city. Sixty citizens have been thrown into prison, and the business of punishing them is to begin tomorrow. This province sets a fine example to the others . . .

And in another letter: 'You talk very pleasantly about our miseries, but we are no longer so jaded with capital punishments; only one a week now, just to keep up appearances. It is true that hanging now seems to me quite a cooling entertainment.' Must we (asks Tocqueville) adjudge Madame de Sévigné 'a terrible, barbaric creature'? That is not the point: the fact is that the noble lady 'had no clear notion of suffering in anyone who was not a person of quality'. In a rigidly hierarchical society, not even feelings can transcend class or caste barriers. It might be said that, just as 'truly general ideas' do not emerge, nor does a general compassion applicable to humanity in its 'abstractness'. Only in a democratic society, where the idea of equality is predominant, does 'general compassion for members of the human race' begin to emerge.[83]

---

83 Alexis de Tocqueville, *Democracy in America*, Vol. II, pp. 164–5.

This process must not be regarded as universally and definitively completed. In democratic America, rather than their disappearance, we observe a different emplacement of the emotional barriers that characterize the society of the *ancien régime*. In fact, 'slaves still endure frightful misery . . . and are constantly exposed to very cruel punishments', without this disturbing the serenity and good conscience of their masters, who have attained a feeling of 'general compassion', but exclusively for the white community.[84] Even within the restricted community, new divisions can develop. The 'general compassion' fostered by a sense of the unity of the human race is an obstacle to the most brutal forms of violence. For such violence to be deployed during conflicts of great bitterness, without too many impediments or inhibitions, 'general compassion' must be neutralized, undermining the unity of the species once again. In this sense, total conflicts presuppose a 'de-specification' of the enemy. They involve the exclusion or expulsion of particular ethnic, social or political groups from the valued community, the properly civilized group, even the human race.

De-specification can develop in very different ways. We may distinguish two ideal-typical attitudes. In the eyes of defenders of the existing social order, revolutionary intellectuals are madmen, while the popular masses that burst onto the scene of history with their unprecedented demands and their plebeian, vulgar ways seem like barbarians, even in the literal sense of the term. For they belong to an alien community, people and ethnic group, which is different and lower on the scale of civilization. Referring to the process of radicalization of the French Revolution, Mallet du Pan launched the cry of alarm 'the Huns . . . are in our midst'. Four decades later, following the revolt of the Lyon silk workers, Saint-Marc Girardin denounced a 'new barbarian invasion'.[85] After the workers' uprising of June 1848, Tocqueville, describing the collective feelings of the time, evoked the spectre of 'the Vandals and the Goths'.[86] With particular reference to the Paris Commune, Nietzsche dreaded the irruption of a 'barbaric class of slaves'.[87] This was the sense in which Burke branded the Jacobins

---

84 Ibid., p. 166.
85 Quoted in Volker Hunecke, 'Tendenze anticapitalistiche nella rivoluzione francese', *Società e storia*, Vol. 1, No. 1, 1978, p. 164.
86 Tocqueville, *Oeuvres complètes*, Vol. XII, p. 93.
87 Friedrich Nietzsche, *Sämtliche Werke, Kritische Studienausgabe*, ed. G. Colli and M. Montinari, Munich: DTV, 1980, Vol. I, p. 17.

as 'savages', 'Turks' or, worse, cannibals.[88] Such they appeared to Constant – members of a 'detestable race' whose 'extirpation' was to be desired.[89] The campaign against the Bolsheviks resorted to similar formulations and categories. Churchill branded them as synonymous with 'barbarism' and even accused them of having 'driven man from the civilization of the twentieth century into a condition of barbarism worse than the Stone Age'.[90] With the arrival of the Bolsheviks in power, wrote Spengler, Russia had cast off 'its "white" mask', 'again becom[ing] an Asiatic, "Mongolian" State'; it was now an integral part of 'the whole of the earth's coloured population' full of hatred of 'white humanity'.[91] The theme was subsequently obsessively repeated by Nazism.

Starting leastwise from the French Revolution and the universalism characteristic of it, revolutionaries mostly practised de-specification of the enemy on a politico-moral basis. Morality was the sole foundation of a society worthy of the name, asserted Robespierre, who criminalized all other political orders accordingly:

> Vice and virtue decide the fate of the earth: they are the two opposed spirits that fight it out. The source of both lies in the passions of man . . . The sole foundation of civil society is morality. All the societies waging war against us are based on crime. In truth, they are but hordes of uncivilized savages and disciplined outlaws.

> So what does all this mysterious science of politics and legislation boil down to? To implementing in legislation and administration the moral truths that are consigned to philosophy books, and applying to people's behaviour the elementary notions of probity which everyone is obliged to adopt in their private conduct . . . What impudence for them [kings and their accomplices] to make laws against theft when it is they who are invading the public fortune! Murderers are condemned in their name, while they murder millions of men through war and poverty.[92]

88 Edmund Burke, *Correspondence*, ed. Th. W. Copeland and J.A. Woods, Cambridge: Cambridge University Press, 1958–, Vol. VII, p. 382; Burke, *The Works*, Vol. V, p. 146 n.

89 See Henri Guillemin, *Benjamin Constant muscadin 1795–1799*, Paris: Gallimard, 1958, pp. 13–14.

90 Winston Churchill, *His Complete Speeches 1897–1963*, Vol. II, New York and London: Chelsea House, 1974, Vol. II, p. 2920.

91 Oswald Spengler, *The Hour of Decision*, trans. Charles Francis Atkinson, London: George Allen & Unwin, 1934, pp. 208–9.

92 Robespierre, *Oeuvres*, Vol. X, p. 446.

Robespierre likewise equates his enemies with barbarian hordes, but employing politico-moral categories, rather than anthropological or ethnic ones. It would be wrong to think that such attitudes pertain exclusively to Jacobin 'delirium'. In England, the black slaves' revolt in San Domingo was greeted thus by Percival Stockdale: '*We* are the savages, the Africans act like *men*; like beings endowed with rational and immortal minds; with warm and generous sentiments . . . [Their] cries . . . against their tyrants, is the *Voice* – their revenge, is the *Act* – of NATURE and of GOD.' Not content with ardent support for a rebellion deemed atrocious by much of public opinion, the British abolitionist included in his pamphlet a poem published in 1773 appealing to the slaves 'to rush with resistless fury on their foes' and 'exterminate the race of pale fiends'.[93]

We register a paradox. At the very moment when de-specification on a naturalistic basis is indignantly rejected, moral sentiment can result in a different type of de-specification, with the expulsion from the moral (and human) community of a social stratum (in this instance, slave-owners). According to Condorcet, 'either morality does not exist' or the institution of slavery, and the conduct of states that tolerate or legally sanction it, must be regarded as scandalous and criminal. Addressing black slaves, and bitterly criticising their masters, the French philosopher wrote:

Dear friends, although I am not the same colour as you, I have always regarded you as my brothers. Nature has fashioned you to have the same spirit, the same reason and the same virtues as whites. I am only speaking here of whites in Europe, for when it to comes to whites in the colonies, I shall not insult you by comparing them to you . . . Were one to set off in search of a man in the islands of America, he would certainly not be found among the populations with white flesh.[94]

The most radical representatives of American abolitionism seem to argue in similar fashion. Having condemned the institution of slavery as a 'combination of death and hell', and having branded the US Constitution as a 'covenant with death and an agreement with hell', in 1841 Garrison demanded that slaveholders should be stripped of their seats in Congress:

---

93   Quoted in David Geggus, 'British Opinion and the Emergence of Haiti, 1791–1805', James Walvin, ed., *Slavery and British Society 1776–1846*, London: Macmillan, 1982, p. 127.

94   Marie-Jean-Antoine Condorcet, *Oeuvres*, ed. A. Condorcet O'Connor and M.F. Arago, Stuttgart and Bad Canstatt: Formmann-Holzboog, 1968, Vol. VII, pp. 69, 63.

No political, no religious copartnership should be had with them, for they are the meanest of thieves and the worst of robbers. We should as soon think of entering into a compact with the convicts at Botany Bay and New Zealand . . . We do not acknowledge them to be within the pale of Christianity, of republicanism, of humanity.[95]

Reconstructed via the rejection of racial prejudice, the unity of the human race is once again undermined by moral or politico-moral sentiment or fanaticism.

This dialectic can be found even in revolutionaries who are radically different from those previously cited, and who were deadly enemies. Stalin credited Lenin with the merit of having 'laid bare' a 'crying incongruity' and 'broke[n] down the wall between whites and blacks, between Europeans and Asiatics', thereby targeting the 'national oppression in its most savage and cruel form' suffered by 'scores and hundreds of millions of Asiatic and African peoples' – the 'slaves of imperialism' who were regarded as alien to civilization.[96] On the other hand, in launching the collectivization of agriculture, Stalin took up Lenin's terrible requisitory against the kulaks. They were 'the most brutal, callous and savage exploiters', 'bloodsuckers [who] have grown rich on the want suffered by the people in the war', 'leeches [who] have sucked the blood of the toilers', 'vampires'.[97] Once again in 1928, to increase their profits, they preferred to feed their cereals to their livestock, rather than sell them at reasonable prices to urban workers, even though the latter were stalked by the threat of hunger and famine.[98] In a tragic irony, the millions of victims of the ruthless 'revolution from above' that was collectivization mainly came from the USSR's Asiatic populations, discrimination against whom on naturalistic and tendentially racist criteria had aroused such eloquent moral indignation. To accusations that Communists were inspired by the 'morality of the kaffirs' and 'Hottentot morality', Trotsky proudly responded invoking the close solidarity and unity between 'revolutionaries' and 'colored races' struggling not only against the 'biological and zoological standards' applied by Nazism and Fascism, but also against the 'white

---

95 Quoted in Charles E. Merriam, *A History of American Political Theories*, New York: Kelley, 1969, p. 209.

96 J.V. Stalin, *Problems of Leninism*, Moscow: Foreign Languages Publishing House, 1953, p. 71.

97 Ibid., p. 444.

98 See J.V. Stalin, *Works*, Moscow: Foreign Languages Publishing House, 1952–, Vol. 11, pp. 1–2.

slave-owners' in general – those despicable individuals who 'husband the workers' blood for the next imperialist war'.[99] Having vigorously denounced the idea of the 'German chosen race', and the pogroms and massacres committed by Hitler's troops, Stalin branded them as 'men with the morals of beasts', who in their 'moral degradation' had lost any semblance of humanity, becoming 'non-human'.[100]

Only philistinism reduces the revolutionary tradition to a cult of *Realpolitik* utterly deaf to moral arguments. Once again, this reveals Schmitt's superiority to contemporary exponents of historical revisionism (and neo-liberalism). He was well aware of the moral sentiment that can inspire the revolutionary project, but at the same time stressed the charge of violence it can detonate. The German political thinker credited Donoso Cortès with having been able to look into the 'abyss of the forces that use the idea of absolute humanity to brand any adversary as a beast'; the concept of man as such can be used to expel the enemy as alien to humanity, as 'non-human'.[101] Yet politico-moral de-specification is only one form of the phenomenon. About the other, Schmitt, like the various representatives of historical revisionism, is silent.

The two forms of de-specification are two different forms of ideological fanaticism. However, in a further example of identification with the experience of the French Revolution's opponents, we find Furet denouncing the Manichaean 'credo', viewed exclusively as a consequence of 'eschatological ideology', solely in connection with the Jacobins.[102] Nolte proceeds similarly. In his view, Burke's merit is to have clarified that what the French revolutionaries governed was not, strictly speaking, a state, but 'an association of armed fanatics, comparable to Islam in the era of Mohammed'.[103] As we can see, although starting from different premises, the British Whig arrives at the same conclusion as Robespierre: the enemy is denied the status of a state; he is nothing but an outlaw. But for the German historian, fanaticism only exists on one side. As was once again made clear by Burke, it is the incurable disease of 'zealous atheists who want to strip the world of its

99   L.D. Trotsky, *Their Morals and Ours*, trans. Max Eastman, New York: Pioneer Publishers, 1942, pp. 36–7, 43, 52, 63.

100   J.V. Stalin, *On the Great Patriotic War of the Soviet Union*, London, New York and Melbourne: Hutchinson, n.d. [1944], pp. 17–18; *Über den Grossen Vaterländischen Krieg der Sowjetunion*, Frankfurt am Main: Dokumente der Kommunistichen Weltbewegung, 1972, p. 154.

101   Carl Schmitt, *Donoso Cortés in gesamteuropäischer Interpretation*, Köln: Greven, 1950, pp. 110–11.

102   Furet, *Interpreting the French Revolution*, pp. 53, 163.

103   Nolte, 'Weltbürgerkrieg, 1917–1989?', p. 33.

foundations with their slogan of the natural equality of human beings, which is utterly contrary to reality'.[104] We might compare Burke's attitude towards the Jacobin threat with the attitude to the Bolshevik menace of Hitler,[105] who thus likewise seems to be absolved from the charge of fanaticism. Branding Bolshevism as purely synonymous with 'Asiatic' barbarism, Nolte ends up fundamentally identifying with the type of de-specification peculiar to opponents of the October Revolution.

Clearly, we are dealing not with a geographical referent, but with a process of de-specification. It suffices to reflect on the fact that Lenin, reader of Hegel and Marx, had nothing to do with the Slavophiles (he ridiculed those who anticipated 'light' from 'the mystic, religious East'). In his work, the condemnation of colonialism and imperialism was intimately linked to celebration of the 'European spirit' and 'European culture' breaking into the colonies, which, enthused by 'ideas of liberation', were beginning to rebel against their masters (who were often the major Western powers or recipients of their support).[106] To their opponents, the Bolsheviks were Asiatics and coloured people, just as the Jacobins were Turks. Both pertained to Islam for the same reasons that, turning now to America, the Communards and socialists or communists (or even mere strikers) were equated with 'redskins' or, once again, 'Turks',[107] while abolitionists were branded as advocates of miscegenation and the bastardization of the race, if not blacks.[108]

Vendeans, Irish, Blacks and 'Redskins'

At times of acute conflict, we witness a kind of mutual excommunication from civilization (this is the essence of the process of de-specification). The friend/enemy dichotomy tends to coincide with the civilization/ barbarism dichotomy. However, the two forms of de-specification are not equivalent. One of them establishes a politico-moral distance between the self and the enemy, while the other establishes a distance more charged

---

104   Ibid., p. 34.

105   Ernst Nolte, *Der europäische Bürgerkrieg 1917–1945. Nationalsozialismus und Bolschewismus*, Frankfurt am Main: Ullstein, 1987, p. 543.

106   V.I. Lenin, *Collected Works*, London: Lawrence & Wishart, 1960–, Vol. 5, p. 82 and Vol. 18, pp. 165–6.

107   Richard Slotkin, *The Fatal Environment: The Myth of the Frontier in the Age of Industrialization 1800–1890*, New York: Harper Perennial, 1994, pp. 443–4, 450–51, 463, 484.

108   Ibid., p. 149.

with naturalistic elements, because it identifies the enemy as foreigner and barbarian or, with reference predominantly to revolutionary leaders, as a lunatic, who is likewise alien to a community within which conflict arises not because of internal contradictions, but because of an external pathogenic or ethnic cause. The first type of de-specification refers to a form of conduct which, by definition, is particular and mutable. Going beyond conduct, the second ends up referring to characteristics that tend to assume a naturalistic fixity. We have seen revolutionaries and rebels being compared to Turks, Huns, blacks and 'redskins'. Comparison is not an assertion of identity. The equation of two heterogeneous entities – one of them definable on the basis of history and politics, the other on the basis of 'nature' – cannot be complete. Revolutionaries and rebels can be menacingly compared with blacks and 'redskins', but it is on the latter that naturalistic de-specification weighs most heavily, to the point of becoming inexorable and irrevocable.

A 'natural' curse also seems to pursue the Irish, victims of British conquest and domination. Even more revealing than ruthless repression are the measures whereby Britain's rulers sought to prevent mixed marriages (one thinks of the laws in America outlawing miscegenation with blacks).[109] According to a law of 1725, a priest guilty of secretly performing a mixed marriage could be condemned to death.[110] Even more significant is a draft law of 1719 from the British colonists in Ireland (subsequently rejected by the London government) intended to replace the existing penalty – branding of unregistered priests – by castration ('the most effectual method that can be found out, to clear this nation of those disturbers of the peace and quiet of the kingdom').[111] This measure likewise refers to the history of racial discrimination. It is further to be noted that the Irish were deprived of education.[112] We are taken back to the America described by Tocqueville, where teaching slaves to read and write was strictly prohibited in the southern states. The Anglo-Irish author we are following here concludes that British legislation aimed to despoil the Irish of their 'property' and 'industry', aimed 'to make them poor and to keep them poor, to crush in them every germ of enterprise, to degrade them into a servile caste who could never hope to rise to the level of their oppressors'.[113]

---

109   Lecky, *A History of England in the Eighteenth Century*, Vol. II, p. 371ff.
110   Ibid., Vol. II, p. 373. Cf. also Vol. I, p. 289.
111   Ibid., Vol. I, pp. 296–7.
112   Ibid., Vol. I, p. 287.
113   Ibid., Vol. I, p. 288.

In conclusion, like the blacks and Native Americans in the USA, the Irish were a colonial population, a race inferior in every way. The British oppressors were uncertain whether to assimilate this inferior race to blacks, and so exploit their forced labour, or to Native Americans, and so expropriate their land and reduce their numbers by castration or other, more drastic measures. This is an oscillation we find in Cromwell, who boosted the colonization of Ireland, bringing carnage and selling numerous rebels as slaves in America. Significantly, when in the late nineteenth century the historian we have cited called on the London government to implement a policy of conciliation of the Irish, he recommended it on the basis that, after all, the Irish too formed part of the 'great Aryan race'![114]

Obviously, naturalistic de-specification is not absent from the history of France; it manifests itself in the colonies. While, according to Tocqueville, the whites in America refused to recognize 'the general features of humanity' in blacks (as well as Native Americans), degrading them almost to the status of 'animals', in Algeria 'the Arabs are like vicious beasts' for French officers.[115] However, Jacobinism was not implicated in the history of colonialism. At key points it challenged it, just as, sanctioning the abolition of slavery in the colonies, it proved capable of undermining naturalistic and racial de-specification. It is illuminating to compare two declarations: 'No man, whether born red, black or white, can be the property of his fellow', proclaimed Toussaint L'Ouverture, the black Jacobin who, taking the Declaration of the Rights of Man at its word, led the slave revolution in San Domingo. 'I am for the whites because I am white; not for any other reason – but that is a good one', replied Napoleon Bonaparte, engaged in restoring the slavery in the colonies abolished by the Jacobin Convention.[116] And according to some historians at least, during the attempt to reconquer San Domingo, the French troops, led by Napoleon's son-in-law Lederc, waged a 'war of extermination' involving gratuitous sadism.[117]

Does this mean that naturalistic de-specification never emerged in the course of the Great Revolution and within Jacobinism? It would be rash to venture such a conclusion: the two forms of de-specification are not equivalent, but this does not mean that they are separated by an insurmountable

---

114   Ibid., Vol. II, p. 380.

115   Tocqueville, *Oeuvres complètes*, Vol. I, pt. 1, pp. 357, 332; Vol. XV, pt. 1, p. 224.

116   Quoted in Florence Gauthier, *Triomphe et mort du droit naturel en Révolution*, Paris: Presses Universitaires de France, 1992, p. 282.

117   Aimé Césaire, *Toussaint Louverture. La révolution française et le problème colonial*, Paris: Présence africaine, 1961, pp. 302–4.

barrier. Let us see what occurred during the ruthless repression of the Vendée. The rebels suffered politico-moral de-specification, which stigmatized them as abject slaves to despotism. The logic of total war against a guerrilla then came into operation. It impacted on the whole civilian population, with an infernal spiral of massacres and reprisals on both sides. Carrier explained: 'All the inhabitants of this region have more or less actively participated in the war.' And once again: 'Children of thirteen or fourteen take up weapons against us and even younger ones act as the outlaws' spies.'[118] But the repression went far beyond the ruthless requirements of total war. The fact is that politico-moral de-specification gradually ceded to the more specifically naturalistic variety: 'the ferocious Vendeans' became a 'horde of outlaws' – in fact, a 'race of outlaws', the 'race of men in the Vendée', to be regarded as 'evil' in its entirety. It was an 'accursed race'.[119] It is true that in the late eighteenth century the term race did not yet possess the meaning it has assumed in our day. Yet the tendency to interpret the conflict in naturalistic terms is manifest. According to General Turreau, the revolt was to be explained by 'the ignorance, habits and superstition of this people', who were always the 'scene and cradle' of 'wars of religion', but also by 'the very nature of the land', which rendered it utterly inaccessible to civilization. This is a representation of the Vendée long predating the revolution[120] – a representation encouraged by the fact that the population in the rebel region was seen as an 'ethnic minority' with respect to the French population.[121]

The transition to de-specification of the naturalistic variety, which was opposed at the most tragic stage of the civil war by generals who refused to participate in indiscriminate massacres, proved precarious and unstable. The logic of politico-moral de-specification ended up prevailing. At the end of the revolutionary cycle, the Vendeans, unlike the Native Americans and blacks in the USA and the Irish in the United Kingdom, enjoyed full citizenship rights.

---

118   Reynald Secher, *Le Génocide franco-français. LeVendée-Vengé*, Paris: Presses Universitaires de France, 1986, p. 297.

119   Ibid., pp. 296, 158–9, 336 n. 26, 296.

120   Alan Forrest, 'La guerre de l'Ouest vue par les soldats républicains', in J.-C. Martin, ed., *La Guerre civile entre Histoire et Mémoire*, Nantes: Ouest Editions, 1995, pp. 92–3.

121   Antonio Gramsci, *Quaderni del carcere*, ed. Valentino Gerratana, Turin: Einaudi, 1976, p. 2029.

Ideological Approaches and Concrete Historical Analysis

Certainly, this conclusion is open to challenge on the grounds that the specific characteristics of Great Britain and, above all, the USA (continental dimensions, racial melting-pot, etc.) must be taken into account. For the comparison between the three different countries to be accurate, we must not lose sight of the fact that the French Third Republic likewise discriminated against 'inferior races' and oppressed them, albeit outside the metropolitan territory. However, with this necessary caveat the purely ideological contrast between good revolutions and bad revolutions collapses.

To demonstrate that Terror and dictatorship are an exclusively French creation, and the immanent result of a determinate ideology, historical revisionism – here in full agreement with the neo-liberal vulgate – proceeds to a double or triple arbitrary abstraction. The first erases circumstances; the second isolates a single stage (the most relatively painless) of the British and American revolutionary cycles, triumphantly contrasting it with the French revolutionary cycle as a whole. At the same time, isolation of this single stage (the Glorious Revolution and the War of Independence) involves abstracting the experience of the truly civilized community from the experience of the barbarians and savages (Irish and Scottish in the one case, blacks and Native Americans in the other). This is the foundation on which what we might call Talmon's sophism, after one of the authors who has most distinguished himself in offering a black-and-white contrast between different political traditions, to the greater glory of Anglo-American liberalism, is erected. The sophism consists in comparing utterly heterogeneous magnitudes: a political tradition judged on the basis of a state of emergency in a situation of acute danger is contrasted with another political tradition judged exclusively on the basis of periods of normality, albeit that they are fully enjoyed only by a privileged fraction of the total population. On this basis, Talmon (but Furet's thinking is substantially similar) can celebrate the Anglo-American liberal tradition as synonymous from the outset with liberty for all and rejection of any form of 'coercion' and 'violence'![122] Obviously, with such hosannas we abandon the terrain of historiography to soar into the firmament of hagiography.

While the abstractions analysed above are intent on glorifying the liberal tradition by contrast with the French Revolution, it must be acknowledged

---

122   Jacob L. Talmon, Introduction to *The Origins of Totalitarian Democracy*, London: Secker & Warburg, 1952.

that that tradition, in its best representatives and moments, has proved capable of a much more lucid, realistic analysis. In 1787, on the eve of the promulgation of the new federal Constitution, Hamilton explained that the limitation of power and establishment of the rule of law had succeeded in two countries of an insular kind, guarded against the threats of rival powers and competitors by the sea. Were the Union project to fail, and a system of states analogous to that on the European mainland to emerge on its ruins, the phenomena of a standing army, a strong central power, and even absolutism would make their appearance in America as well.[123] Tending in the same direction is an observation by Tocqueville, who noted that the Americans were favoured in the War of Independence by the fact that they were 'separated by 1300 leagues of sea from their enemies', while revolutionary France was 'exposed to the attacks of the whole of Europe, penniless, without credit, without allies', and also forced to face 'the blaze' consuming it within.[124] Contemporary historians have confirmed the importance of geopolitical location, also as regards developments in the struggle between patriots and loyalists. Obliged to flee, the latter took refuge in Canada and even Britain, from which they did not return, thus contributing significantly to the stabilization of the new state entity.[125]

Furthermore, the plebeian turbulence of the French revolutionary tradition was absent or reduced in the USA, because the institution of slavery made it possible to maintain an iron grip on the 'dangerous classes' at the point of production. The politico-social geography of the USA was rooted in a very precise material context. The protagonists of the American Revolution were well aware of the radical difference between the 'European states and kingdoms' (in the first instance, France) and America. The latter was an intensely rural country with very low population density, where 'nine-tenths of the population were landowners' and where, thanks to a still open frontier, it was possible to restrict the number of 'mechanics and manufacturers'. That is, moderation of politico-social conflict was the flip side of a policy of expansion and colonial oppression, even of annihilation of the excluded (an analogous function to the Far West was played in the history of Britain by Ireland and other colonial territories).[126]

123   Alexander Hamilton et al., *The Federalist: A Commentary on the Constitution of the United States*, ed. Robert Scigliano, New York: Modern Library, 2000, pp. 41–6 (article no. 8).

124   Tocqueville, *Oeuvres complètes*, Vol. I, pt. 1, p. 114.

125   Trevelyan, *History of England*, p. 699; Palmer, *The Age of Democratic Revolution*, Vol. I, pp. 189–90.

126   Losurdo, *Democrazia o bonapartismo*, pp. 112–13.

In his own way, the author particularly dear to historical revisionism clarifies this point. Presenting his 'motion of conciliation' with the American colonies in 1775, Burke justified it on the grounds that liberty could not be denied to those belonging to a nation 'in whose veins the blood of freedom circulates'. Every member of 'the chosen race and sons of England' venerated 'liberty'; and it seemed all the more 'noble' and 'liberal' to slave-owners:

> these people of the Southern Colonies are much more strongly, and with an higher and more stubborn spirit, attached to liberty, than those to the Northward . . . and such will be all masters of slaves who are not slaves themselves. In such a people, the haughtiness of domination combines with the spirit of freedom, fortifies it, and renders it invincible.

In other words, naturalistic de-specification of blacks and Native Americans rendered the white, European community more homogeneous, united as it was by a sense of common worth peculiar to 'Englishmen', and them alone, to whom the right to liberty could in no wise by refused. It was a matter of 'pedigree', in the face of which 'human art' was powerless.[127] Referring to Burke's analysis, in 1832 a Virginian politician lauded 'the perfect spirit of equality so prevalent among the whites of all the slaveholding States', which could thus claim superiority. In the North, there was not that familiarity between men of different social conditions which characterized the South, where the 'menial and low offices being all performed by the blacks' – i.e. slaves – 'all who are white are equal in spite of the variety of occupation'; 'color alone is here the badge of distinction'.[128]

Thus is explained both the triumph of the American Revolution (i.e. the War of Independence), celebrated by Arendt in 1963, and the failure of the American revolutionary cycle as a whole, deplored by the same author in 1972. The relative moderation of conflict within the civilized, free 'race' is the obverse of the extreme difficulty in fully including members of 'inferior' races in the category of human being and citizen. Corresponding to the relative homogeneity of the community of 'Englishmen' is the total alterity of blacks and Native Americans, excluded from civilization and even the dignity of human beings. When naturalistic de-specification of blacks fell into crisis with the Civil War, North and South not only confronted one another on the battlefield, but mutually excommunicated each other from

---

127 Burke, *The Works*, Vol. III, pp. 54, 66, 124.
128 Hofstadter and Hofstadter, eds, *Great Issues in American History*, Vol. II, p. 320.

civilization, branding each other as barbarians – something that rendered the conflict even more bloody and cruel.

The debate that has developed in the USA is conclusive proof of the sterility of a purely ideological approach. During the abolitionist revolution, who represented the cause of spontaneous social development and who that of oppressive social engineering and the philosophy of history? For theorists of slavery, there was no doubt. It was sufficient to eschew abstract speculation and take a glance at history: slavery 'has been more universal than marriage and more permanent than liberty'. By contrast, generalized liberty consti- tuted 'a small and recent experiment', but 'we want no new world'. As has been observed, for such ideologues slavery was a kind of 'common law' that abolitionists sought to abolish through the 'positive action of the state', and hence through interventions which presumed to compress reality in rigid, oppressive schemas.[129]

This is a debate which, albeit in different ways, remains alive to this day. Invariably appealing to the authority of Burke, American historical revisionism continues to insist upon a crucial point. Unleashing a bloody and possibly even superfluous 'revolution' (the South's 'peculiar institution' was supposedly already in the process of gradual humanization or extinc- tion), and waging a total or totalitarian war, the Union ended up creating a regime with totalitarian tendencies in the South, which disappeared after 1877 only to be reintroduced during the second Reconstruction. What, according to revisionist historiography and literature, was the guiding thread of the Union's and the North's policy in these two historical peri- ods? It was an attempt to impose racial equality from above, abolishing or drastically curtailing states' autonomy, through a pedagogical dictatorship intended to erase racial 'prejudices' in the people of the South, through an experiment in social engineering which, breaking with a secular tradi- tion and trampling over the established values and customs of the overwhelming majority of the (white) population, claimed to realize racial equality and integration from above by means of despotic measures. This policy of violence and oppression, which had inflicted on the American people the greatest tragedy in their history with the Civil War, ensured itself a good conscience and acquired fanatical self-certainty by calling on

---

129 See Eugene Genovese, *The Southern Front: History and Politics in the Cultural War*, Columbia and London: University of Missouri Press, 1995, p. 105; Genovese, *The Slaveholders' Dilemma: Freedom and Progress in Southern Conservative Thought, 1820–1860*, Columbia: University of South Carolina Press, 1995, p. 13.

a philosophy of history that proclaimed the inevitability of emancipation and black equality, branding the South as an *ancien régime* condemned by historical progress.

The arguments – all the arguments – employed by historical revisionism in its diatribe against Jacobinism and Bolshevism make their reappearance. And the rejoinder, especially from Afro-American historians, is readily imaginable. Does totalitarianism consist in the nightmare of Reconstruction (whether the first or the second)? Or is it represented by the absolute, unlimited power exercised in the antebellum South by white masters over their slaves? What should be reprehended as social engineering? Attempts to impose a society based on racial equality and integration from above? Or the institution of slavery and, later, apartheid and laws against miscegenation? Is proclamation of the inevitable end of the institution of slavery the sole philosophy of history? Or is legitimation of the institution of slavery, and then white supremacy, in the name of the 'burden' imposed by Providence on the 'white man' one too?[130]

This is a debate that is not cast in the same terms in connection with the French Revolution, simply because of the distance separating France from San Domingo. If totalitarianism is a new form of 'serfdom' in Hayek's definition,[131] it is not clear why it should be attributed to the black and white Jacobins, protagonists of the abolition of slavery, rather than their opponents who restored it, or sought to, after Thermidor. Exclusive resort to the dichotomies of freedom/despotism, friends/enemies of the open society, is schematic, because it represses the conflict between different forms of liberty. Meanwhile, the categories of philosophy of history and social engineering, employed by historical revisionism to liquidate the revolutionary tradition, turn out to be completely formal, capable of subsuming completely different contents. And it is pointless seeking to deduce terror or totalitarianism *a priori* from them, or to resort to them as a substitute for a concrete historical assessment.

---

130   See Richard M. Weaver, *The Southern Essays*, ed. G.M. Curtis, III and J.J. Thompson Jr., Indianapolis: Liberty Press, pp. 211, 213, 250, 253; John H. Franklin, *Race and History: Selected Essays 1938–1988*, Baton Rouge and London: Louisiana State University Press, pp. 38–9; Kenneth M. Stamp, ed., *The Causes of the Civil War*, New York: Simon & Schuster, 1991.

131   See F.A. Hayek, *The Road to Serfdom*, London: Ark Paperbacks, 1986.

Puritans, Jacobins, Abolitionists and Bolsheviks

The crying lack of a comparative analysis of the different revolutions is also felt when it comes to another fundamental theme of revisionist historiography and literature: the identification of the carrier of the revolutionary disease as the 'abstract', 'fanatical' intellectual – *homo ideologicus*. Notwithstanding constant mobilization of this theme, readers will search this historiography and literature in vain for a comparative analysis of the intellectual strata thrown up by the major revolutions or, at any rate, revolutions that have had to confront bitter political and social conflicts. We must turn elsewhere for such an analysis. A now famous study stages an interesting contrast between Puritans, Jacobins and Bolsheviks. Some key shared features emerge: fanatical hatred of the sinful or unjust existing order; confident engagement in creating a new society and even a 'new man'; and a sense of election and mission through which obstacles are surmounted, and direction maintained, amid the earthquake causing the collapse of hitherto dominant institutions and values.[132] The analogy between Puritans and Bolsheviks is particularly illuminating and persuasive (reference to theological or historical Providence does not seem to play a significant role in Jacobinism).

However, to the three intellectual and political strata compared by the US historian cited here (Michael Walzer), we should add a fourth. What best embodies the ideal type of 'fanatic' are the intellectuals who emerged during the abolitionist agitation and revolution. In the early decades of the nineteenth century, representatives of the (albeit moderate) British abolitionist movement seemed manifestly affected by 'fanaticism', 'madness' and 'metaphysical madness' in the eyes of the American John Randolph.[133] This is the theme of ideological intoxication we have noted in Burke, to whom the eminent conservative southern politician explicitly refers. The psychopathological diagnosis seems to gain in precision with Calhoun. According to him, the abolitionists, at least the most 'fanatical' among them, those most fanatically engaged in the 'crusade', so intensely 'consider[ed] themselves under the most sacred obligation' to fight sin that they felt immune from it only if

132   See Michael Walzer, *The Revolution of the Saints: A Study in the Origins of Radical Politics*, Cambridge, MA and London: Harvard University Press, 1965; Schröder, *Die Revolutionen Englands im 17. Jahrundert*, pp. 80–1.

133   Quoted in Russel Kirk, *John Randolph of Roanoke: A Study in American Politics*, Indianapolis: Liberty Press, 1978, pp. 66, 176–7.

they employed 'all and every means' to destroy it.[134] What is described here is a form of paranoia.

As the storm of the Civil War brewed, Calhoun's requisitory became more merciless, inveighing against the 'incendiary spirit', the 'spirit of fanaticism', the 'rabid fanatics', the 'blind fanatics' who threatened war on the South, towards which they evinced 'a hatred more deadly than one hostile nation ever entertained towards another'.[135] These 'ferocious zealots'[136] made it 'an obligation of conscience' to proclaim 'a general crusade against us and our institutions'.[137]

Such denunciations capture an essential aspect of the reality. Having violently stigmatized not only slaveholders and defenders of the South, but also (and possibly with even greater ardour) those in the North who displayed 'apathy' or indifference to the 'standard of emancipation' raised by him; having rejected 'the popular but pernicious doctrine of *gradual* abolition'; and having branded appeals to moderation as largely philistine or hypocritical, Garrison proclaimed: 'Let southern oppressors tremble — let their secret abettors tremble — let their Northern apologists tremble — let all the enemies of the persecuted blacks tremble . . . I *will be* as harsh as truth, and as uncompromising as justice. On this subject, I do not wish to think, or speak, or write, with moderation.'[138] Such rhetoric was no different from that of the French Jacobins or subsequent generations of revolutionaries. If anything, we can discern additional pathos here. In condemning slavery as a 'heinous crime in the sight of God',[139] abolitionist campaigners proceeded not only to the criminalization, but also to a veritable excommunication, of their opponents, who were considered guilty of violating every law, human and divine, of cohabitation and hence expelled from any possible civilized community. The potential for exclusion contained in moral de-specification is at its maximum here. Nor was the abolitionists' fanaticism restricted to this. From the outset, their campaign assumed explicitly eschatological accents: it involved achieving man's 'universal emancipation' from the

134   John C. Calhoun, *Union and Liberty*, ed. R.M. Lence, Indianapolis: Liberty Classics, 1992, pp. 529, 582–3.

135   Ibid., pp. 465, 471, 466, 529, 474, 472.

136   Quoted in David B. Davis, *The Slave Power Conspiracy and the Paranoid Style*, Baton Rouge and London: Louisiana State University Press, 1982, p. 37.

137   Calhoun, *Union and Liberty*, pp. 471, 469.

138   Quoted in Hofstadter and Hofstadter, *Great Issues in American History*, Vol. II, pp. 321–2.

139   Garrison, quoted in Aileen S. Kraditor, *Means and Ends in American Abolitionism: Garrison and his Critics on Strategy and Tactics, 1834–1850*, Chicago: I.R. Dee, 1989, p. 5.

dominion of man and the power of brute force; and it also involved promoting liberation from the 'slavery' of sin and egotism, which found their most concentrated, despicable form in the shackling of other human beings and other Christians or potential Christians.[140] In this sense, not inappropriately, the Civil War has sometimes been described as a clash between 'the law and the prophets';[141] and among the latter is to be numbered one of the most successful leaders of the Union's military campaign — Sherman, the 'fighting prophet',[142] protagonist of total war.

It goes without saying that such fanaticism was not answered by a more lucid or secular view of things on the other side. With the dissolution of the objective character of the underlying contradictions that ran through slave society, the latter was regarded by its ideologues as a healthy organism under attack from without by the kind of black and barbarian in disguise — in fact, the kind of Biblical serpent — represented by the agitator suffering from abolitionist frenzy or fanaticism.[143] In this instance too, the contemporary student cannot identify with the experience of either of the antagonists. However, historical revisionism not only underwrites the denunciation of fanaticism by defenders of the established order, but underwrites it in some cases more than others, without explaining the reasons for its options. And that is not all. When Burke contemptuously referred to the French 'levellers', or the 'principles of French levelling',[144] he made an indirect comparison between the radicals of the French Revolution and the radicals of the Puritan revolution. And Constant alluded to both when he condemned ideological 'delirium'.[145] However, historical revisionism drops even this hint of comparativism, denouncing the ruinous presence of *homo ideologicus* only in the French and Bolshevik revolutions.

A germ of comparative sociology of the different intellectual strata can be found in Burke's denunciation of French revolutionary intellectuals as beggars of the pen, or *gueux plumés*, using the lower classes as 'a body of Janizaries' to attack property.[146] Constant evinces a certain sociological concreteness, when, precisely on the basis of an appraisal of the French

---

140   See Davis, *The Slave Power Conspiracy and the Paranoid Style*, p. 44; Merriam, *A History of Political Theories*, pp. 216–17.

141   Weaver, *The Southern Essays*, p. 245.

142   Ibid., p. 170.

143   See Kirk, *John Randolph of Roanoke*, p. 167; Hofstadter and Hofstadter, *Great Issues in American History*, Vol. II, p. 319.

144   Burke, *The Works*, Vol. V, p. 104; *Correspondence*, Vol. VI, p. 451.

145   Constant, *Oeuvres*, p. 1094.

146   Burke, *The Works*, Vol. IX, p. 49 and Vol. VII, p. 135.

Revolution, he proposes the exclusion from political rights of non-property-owning intellectuals, who, as a result of their social condition, tend 'to reason like visionaries about society' and to develop 'chimerical theories'.[147] Likewise Maistre, who from a St Petersburg still shaken by a peasant revolt suppressed but a few decades earlier expresses his anxiety about the possible outbreak of a new 'European' revolution, led this time by a 'Pugachev of the University'.[148] For all these authors, the novel, scandalous fact is the emergence of a layer of intellectuals not organically bound to the property-owning classes, but open to the influence of the popular masses. Such elements of realistic analysis are largely lost in historical revisionism, which simplistically interprets the contrast between property owners-intellectuals and 'beggars of the pen' as one between concrete intellectuals and abstract intellectuals suffering from delirium. In the heat of the struggle against Manichaeism and ideological fanaticism, the struggle between different social classes becomes a clash between sanity and madness; key moments in modern and contemporary history risk being reduced to mere chapters of psychopathology.

Furet denounces the Jacobin and Bolshevik obsession that detects machinating aristocrats or class enemies everywhere.[149] But what role does fear of conspiracies play in Burke and opponents of the French Revolution and what role does it play outside France and Russia? There is no point looking to historical revisionism for an answer; the very question is missing. We must turn to other historians, who stress how an obsession with plots assumed 'paranoid characteristics' during the first English Revolution, and how it played an absolutely decisive role in the first and second American Revolution – in fact, throughout the history of the USA, so that the latter is marked by a peculiar 'paranoid style'.[150] All this is ignored by historical revisionism, which only by so doing can offer a black-and-white contrast between the American (and English) Revolution and the French Revolution.

147   Benjamin Constant, *Cours de politique constitutionelle*, ed. J.P. Pagès, Brussels: Société Belge de Librairie, 1837, pp. 106–7 and *Oeuvres*, pp. 1050–1.

148   Joseph de Maistre, *Oeuvres complètes*, Hildesheim, Zurich and New York: Olms, 1984, Vol. XII, pp. 59–60.

149   See Furet, *The Passing of an Illusion*, pp. 45, 144.

150   See Schröder, *Die Revolutionen Englands im 17. Jahrhundert*, p. 67, and Davis, *The Slave Power Conspiracy and the Paranoid Style*.

Historical Balance Sheets and Genealogical Myths

To those who criticize the oleography that traditionally transfigures the American Revolution and draw attention to the fate of the blacks and Native Americans; to those who note that the latter's ordeal began, and underwent a qualitative leap, with the formation of the United States, an eminent American historian replies as follows:

> America's Enlightenment project was not realized at the time, nor has it been fully realized now. The miracle, in view of the everyday realities of the eighteenth century, is that it existed at all, that it had any kind of practical expression, however limited, in a world as brutal and exploitative as the *ancien régime*, and that it established ideals to which, in our better moments, we still aspire. Colloway shows just how grim the reality of racial exploitation was, and how incompletely realized the Revolution's ideals proved to be in the Founders' generation. The 'huge tapestry' of the 'full meaning' of the Revolution that he refers to at the start will have to include the 'patches' he presents in this comprehensive account of the devastation of the Indian country; but it will also have to include the basic fabric and bright coloration of the enlightened aspirations that defined the purposes and ideals of the new nation.[151]

In reality, the whites' autonomy and expansion developed *pari passu* with increased oppression of the Native Americans (as well as continuing slavery for blacks). But the conflicts between the various liberties are smoothed out here into a gradualist schema that cancels objective contradictions. The historical balance sheet is drawn up predominantly on the basis of the good intentions of the protagonists of the American Revolution – good intentions that in other cases are read as an expression of ideological consciousness. In any event, with such arguments one could defend the French Revolution and even the October Revolution. But it is significant that they are employed exclusively on behalf of the American Revolution, an object of hagiography that historical revisionism is very careful not to query. Its reading of the revolutionary tradition is radical and pitiless. But there is in fact an inviolable *terminus a quo*: one may not go back before 1789. Despite its iconoclastic appearance, today's revisionist wave also stops short before certain taboos

---

151   Bernard Bailyn, 'An American Tragedy', *New York Review of Books*, 5 October 1995, p. 16.

or *topoi* of the dominant ideology. 'Talmon's sophism' – the black-and-white contrast between different political traditions – has in fact given rise to one of those genealogical myths with which different countries, especially great powers, always seek to transfigure their origins and images.[152] If we examine the development of the contemporary world, we can see that there are three gigantic conflicts at the centre of the last two centuries of history, each of which lasted for years and even decades, developing at an ideological level as well as a politico-military one. The first began with the French Revolution and ended with the Restoration. The second comprised the period of the two world wars. The third, having begun to emerge with the outbreak of the October Revolution, experienced its decisive stage in the years from the Cold War to the dissolution of the Soviet Union. The sole politico-ideological entity to emerge regularly victorious from all three conflicts was the Anglo-American world. The transfiguration of the Anglo-American political tradition and, in particular, of the USA is the consecration of this fact.

---

152 Léon Poliakov, *Le Mythe aryen. Essai sur les sources du racisme et des nationalismes*, Brussels: Complexe, 1987, p. 15.

CHAPTER THREE

The Bolshevik October, International Civil War and the Colonial Question

The Bolshevik October: Revolution or Coup d'État?

With the transfiguration of the history of Britain and America by way of successive repressions and arbitrary abstractions, and with the isolation of the Jacobin Terror from its historical context, the latter assumes the appearance of a frenzy set to rage at length. In this purely ideological history, along with other events and 'circumstances', scant attention is paid to the First World War. The starting-point of the catastrophe of the twentieth century is Bolshevism, an extension and paroxysmal intensification of Jacobinism. It might be said that ideological intoxication is present in the pure state this time, since October 1917 was not even a revolution, but a mere coup d'état – one that felled not the *ancien régime* or its residues, but democracy.

This is a thesis that ultimately goes back to Churchill, who on 3 January 1920 accused the Bolsheviks of having overthrown not Czarist autocracy, but the 'Russian republic' and 'Russian Parliament'.[1] The source of this accusation is remarkable: the statesman and the country most implicated in attempts to overthrow the regime deriving from the February Revolution. Having initially hoped that the fall of Czarism might revive Russian participation in the 'democratic' war against the Central Powers, the Entente viewed the new situation and the 'disorder' it was fostering with profound disquiet, and engaged in a frantic search for a strong man. In his memoirs, Kerensky denounces the support of every kind provided by the 'allies' for military plots aimed at 'reestablishing a strong "national" regime in Russia'.

---

1 See Alex P. Schmid, *Churchills privater Krieg. Intervention und Konterrevolution im russischen Bürgerkrief, November 1918 –März 1920*, Zurich: Atlantis, 1974, p. 293.

Churchill explicitly declared himself in favour and British tanks participated in General Kornilov's attempt in September 1917 to march on Petrograd and eject the soviets and Provisional Government.[2] In fact, 'British soldiers in Russian uniforms were among the few not to desert.'[3]

To support the thesis of a coup d'état, reference is frequently made to the dissolution of the Constituent Assembly – for example, by Furet, who does not mention the fact that, amid the wave of violence and terror occasioned by the war, even in the USA representative bodies were purged of undesirable elements in violation of existing laws. In Wisconsin, a socialist duly elected to the House of Representatives was deprived of the seat to which he was entitled. A similar phenomenon occurred in the State of New York on a larger scale.[4] In Italy, a minister – Bissolati – even threatened parliament with a physical purge, when, addressing pacifist or insufficiently bellicose deputies, he shouted: 'To defend the country, I would be ready to open fire on all of you!'[5] As for Russia, the Bolsheviks who dissolved the Constituent Assembly had experienced the deportation of their anti-war deputies to Siberia.

Obviously, a purge is not the same thing as dissolution, any more than constitutional normality and revolution and civil war (and a situation of dual power with tense or antagonistic relations between the Constituent Assembly and the soviets) are the same thing. Nor can it be said that the Bolshevik October interrupted Russia's democratic development, and not only because (as Furet himself observes) guns were now doing the talking, given the habituation to 'absolute violence' occasioned by the war.[6] Let us examine the state of the country on the eve of the revolution or coup d'état:

> If Lenin had failed in the autumn of 1917, Russia would have become a scene of terrible anarchical chaos and not the theatre of a peaceful democratic development. For the vast Russian nation was now in movement. The peasants no longer tolerated the estate-owners; the soldiers refused obedience to their officers; the workmen wished to abolish capitalists. No

---

2 Alexander F. Kerensky, *The Kerensky Memoirs: Russia and History's Turning Point*, London: Cassell, 1966, pp. 395–8.

3 Schmid, *Churchills privater Krieg*, p. 15.

4 Oscar Handlin and Lilian Handlin, *Liberty in Peril 1850–1920*, New York: Harper Collins, 1986, p. 17.

5 Quoted in Antonio Gramsci, *La Città future 1917–1918*, ed. Sergio Caprioglio, Turin: Einaudi, 1982, p. 409 (editorial note).

6 François Furet, *The Passing of an Illusion*, trans. Deborah Furet, Chicago and London: University of Chicago Press, 1999, p. 75.

power on earth could have restrained them in their blind fury once the
traditional authority of the Social Revolutionaries had been destroyed.
This frenzied chaos would have ended in the break-up of Russia, in
pogroms, and in a 'White' Terror. The Bolsheviks rescued the Russian
nation from this danger and in doing so saved the Revolution in Russia,
notwithstanding their many experiments and failures. The Russian Revolution was not the work of the Bolsheviks. Their service lies in the
recognition by Lenin and Trotsky that at midnight a great anarchical revolt
would occur. Five minutes before midnight Lenin and Trotsky gave the
order for a Bolshevik rebellion and in doing so created the impression
that the tremendous occurrence at midnight was their work. It was in
this manner that they won for themselves the authority necessary to enable
them to govern Russia.[7]

But this is also Furet's view: 'From February to October, the prevailing
anarchy was uncontrollable by any one person or party. From crisis to crisis,
power moved increasingly to the left until the Bolsheviks gathered it up from
the streets of Saint Petersburg.'[8]

The revisionist thesis of a coup d'état now seems all the more problematic.
If a coup d'état is the overthrow of a government and institutions enjoying
democratic legitimacy, it is clear that, if anything should be subsumed under
this category, it is the events that signalled the end of the monarchy in
Germany and Austria. In his memoirs Scheidemann recalls that, faced with
the rise of an impetuous mass movement, he felt compelled to proclaim the
republic on 9 November 1918 to block its further radicalization. Immediately
afterwards, Ebert, who became Chancellor not following appointment by
the Emperor or election by the Reichstag, but on a revolutionary wave,
accosted his party comrade 'flushed with anger': 'You have no right to
proclaim the republic! What Germany will be, a republic or whatever else,
must be decided by a constituent assembly.'[9] Thus we have a further example
of elimination of the constituent assembly at a decisive moment! If we follow
the logic of revisionist historiography, we must define as attempted coups
d'état the Paris Commune and the workers' revolt of June 1848 and, essentially, the February days themselves in Paris, which likewise put an end to

---

7   Arthur Rosenberg, *A History of Bolshevism: From Marx to the First Five Years' Plan*, trans.
Ian F.D. Morrow, New York: Anchor Books, 1967, pp. 110–11.

8   Furet, *The Passing of an Illusion*, p. 60.

9   Quoted in Gerhard A. Ritter and Susan Miller, eds, *Die deutsche Revolution 1918–1919*,
Frankfurt am Main: Fischer, 1968, p. 73.

a government enjoying a degree of democratic legitimacy (at least on the 'minimal' definition of democracy formulated by Bobbio). On the other hand, the proclamation of the republic in Germany brings to mind what occurred some decades earlier in France, without the authorization of a constituent assembly. Contemporary history as a whole thus ends up taking the form of a succession of coups d'état.

That of October 1917 is distinguished by its decidedly singular character. Far from being prepared in great secrecy, it was repeatedly announced in a public discussion that found the Bolshevik leaders themselves on different sides (Kamenev and Zinoviev vigorously challenged Lenin's line and did not hesitate to appeal to the party's base). In a sense, even prior to 1914 this 'coup d'état' was threatened by the working-class and socialist movement in response to a potential war. On the other side, some months before the outbreak of the world war, Pyotr Durnovo, ex-Interior Minister and director of the police department,

submitted to Nicholas II a memorandum on the dangers of war for Russia. This document, discovered and published after the Revolution, so accurately foretold the course of events that if its credentials were not impeccable one might well suspect it to be a post-1917 forgery. In Durnovo's estimate, if the war went badly 'a social revolution in its most extreme form will be unavoidable in Russia.'

Our attention is drawn to this document by the American historian Pipes,[10] who has excelled in refusing to characterize the Bolshevik October as a revolution. We are therefore dealing with a coup d'état that on the one hand was announced, while on the other it was dreaded some years before its execution. It has to be said that this is an event unique in world history!

Does the category of coup d'état stand by virtue of pointing to the fact that its success was solely attributable to violence? Not only was recourse to violence not exclusive to the Bolsheviks, but the latter conquered political power in the first instance by dint of the hegemony they succeeded in exercising within a mass movement that was now irrepressible:

the network of soviets, as they became more radical, was starting to constitute a sort of parallel state that as yet had no head (in October the Bolshevik Party would step into that role), while the state itself,

---

10   Richard Pipes, *The Russian Revolution*, New York: Vintage Books, 1990, p. 211.

contrariwise, certainly had a head, the Provisional Government, but its organs no longer carried out its orders, because the soviets controlled the country's life. In Petrograd, in some other towns as well and in the army, the Bolsheviks now held the majority in soviets of all kinds. They were thus able to take power and consolidate their position through an armed insurrection that set their seal on mastery of the country.[11]

Once again, this analysis is confirmed by Furet, who underlines how the Leninist formula calling for a transition 'from war to revolution . . . coincided with the hopes of millions of surviving soldiers'.[12] But it is above all Nolte who lets slip an almost admiring description of the agitational and propagandistic impact of the party that carried out the 'coup d'état'. Here is how, some months earlier, Kornilov's select troops were confronted by the Bolsheviks:

> They opposed an army of agitators to the supreme commander's advancing troops, to convince them that, in obeying their officers, they were acting against their true interests, prolonging the war and paving the way for the restoration of Czarism. And so, in the march on Petrograd, and already earlier in various parts of the country, the troops yielded to the persuasive force of arguments that simply articulated their own deepest desires and anxieties, of which they were not fully conscious. None of the officers present can have been able to forget how their soldiers slipped away from them not under grenade fire, but under a storm of words.[13]

When, after October, Kerensky attempted a counter-offensive, the troops assembled by him dispersed 'under the impact of agitation', as had Kornilov's troops.[14] As we can see, the facts adduced by the historian are a precise negation of the revisionist ideologue's *parti pris*. Not only the conquest, but also the retention, of power by the Bolsheviks is inexplicable in the absence of their ability to exercise political hegemony. In 1919, while the offensive against Soviet power launched by Kolchak was underway, Churchill opposed the idea of a military ceasefire (which would have facilitated food aid for an

---

11   Marc Ferro, *Nicholas II: Last of the Tsars*, trans. Brian Pearce, New York: Oxford University Press, 1993, p. 224.

12   Furet, *The Passing of an Illusion*, p. 75.

13   Ernst Nolte, *Der europäische Bürgerkrieg 1917–1945. Nationalsozialismus und Bolschewismus*, Frankfurt am Main and Berlin: Ullstein, 1987, p. 55.

14   Ibid., p. 58.

exhausted civilian population) with an argument that merits reflection: a ceasefire would only damage Kolchak's troops, who would end up dissolving under the impact of 'Bolshevik propaganda', which was even more powerful than Bolshevik arms.[15]

We might therefore conclude with the Nolte of 1969, who had not yet arrived at revisionism, that those who 'deny it any basis out of sheer visceral anti-Marxism' will not understand the 'Russian revolution'.[16] The coup d'état thesis becomes intelligible on the basis not of Russia in 1917, but of the history behind this topos. We may start with the American Revolution. Even a century later, loyalist historians basically depicted the Declaration of Independence as a coup d'état whereby an activist, overbearing minority sealed the rupture with the mother country, shattering the vast united front that had hitherto limited itself to demanding incisive reforms.[17] And we might arrive at the February Revolution in Russia, which (according to Pipes) should be defined more accurately as a military 'mutiny'.[18] There has never been a revolution that its opponents have not sought to de-legitimize by downgrading it to a coup d'état or conspiracy. And Pipes refers interchangeably to coup d'état or conspiracy in connection with the Bolshevik October.[19]

At all events, the fact of the enormous enthusiasm it elicited far beyond Russia's borders remains. Paradoxically, the exponents of historical revisionism do not deny it, cannot deny it, precisely because they derive the international civil war that was destined to rage on a global scale for decades from the enormous resonance of October.

From International Civil War to the Bolshevik October

With Lenin's appeal to transform the imperialist war into a revolutionary civil war, an ideological crusade and war of religion once again burst upon Europe. In its theological fury against heretics, it did not admit of distinctions between combatants and the civilian population. Following the cycle generated by the French Revolution, it initiated or resumed 'a global civil war of

---

15   See Schmid, *Churchills privater Krieg*, p. 156.

16   Ernst Nolte, *La crisi dei regime liberali e i movimenti fascisti*, trans. E. Gamaleri and A. Caiani, Bologna: Il Mulino, 1970, p. 38.

17   See Egerton Ryerson, *The Loyalists of America and Their Times: From 1620 to 1816*, New York: Haskell, 1970, Vol. II, pp. 57, 137 n. 147.

18   Pipes, *The Russian Revolution*, p. 278.

19   Ibid., p. xxiii.

revolutionary class enmity', aiming to destroy what it hated and fought as the class enemy, the 'absolute enemy', who was to be treated like a criminal.[20] Thus Schmitt. In his wake, Nolte likewise identifies and denounces the disastrous turn of the twentieth century in October 1917, when the First World War ceased to be 'exclusively a war between states', or 'a conventional state war of European international law', becoming a global civil war that was ruthless and without rules.[21] In fact, three years prior to the Bolshevik Revolution, Salvemini in Italy characterized the conflict that had just broken out thus: 'Rather than a war between nations, we are witnessing a global civil war',[22] destined to signal 'the end of German imperialism — that is, the liquidation of the Hohenzollerns and Hapsburgs and their feudal clientele — and the democratization of Austria and Germany'; to lay the bases for the establishment of 'juridical society between nations' and permanent peace between them. This 'war for peace'[23] was a veritable revolution, developing on a European and global scale: 'We wish the democratic principle to emerge victorious from this severe ordeal: to sever the knot of conservative forces in the German empire against whom the efforts of the socialist party have hitherto always proved unavailing.'[24]

The task the German labour movement had not succeeded in acquitting was now entrusted to the armies of the Entente. The elements of 'international civil war' contained in the ideology of the anti-German alliance are patent, as was subsequently confirmed by the recurrent theme of the contrast between Weimar and Potsdam, by the attempt to insert a wedge between militaristic, despotic Prussia, on the one hand, and the fundamentally pacific regions of the Wilhelmine state, on the other. These tendencies found their fullest expression in the speech in which Wilson announced the USA's intervention. To pave the way for the triumph of the cause of 'democracy', 'peace' and the 'universal dominion of right', the Second Reich had to be defeated. The war launched by it was a 'challenge to all mankind'. It must be met and victoriously confronted, so as to proceed to the 'liberation' of all the peoples of the world, 'the German people included'. The latter were

---

20   Carl Schmitt, *Theory of the Partisan: Intermediate Commentary on the Concept of the Political*, trans. G.L. Ulmen, New York: Telos Press, 2007, pp. 95, 52.

21   Ibid., p. 95; Ernst Nolte, 'Weltbürgerkrieg 1917–1989?', Italian trans. in F. Coppellotti, ed., *Dramma dialettico o tragedia? La guerra civile mondiale e altri saggi*, Perugia: Settimo Sigillo/Perugia University Press, 1994, p. 36.

22   Gaetano Salvemini, *Opere*, Milan: Feltrinelli, 1964–78, Vol. III, pt. 1, p. 366.

23   Ibid., pp. 360–1.

24   Ibid., p. 349.

implicitly summoned to make their contribution to the crusade thus proclaimed, to what the US president's followers defined as 'a holy war, the holiest in all history'[25] – a crusade and holy war that at the same time were a 'stupendous revolution' of a democratic kind.

Albeit comparatively late on, the Germans appreciated the purchase of this ideology, which, if it did not succeed in provoking civil war in the enemy's ranks, proved capable to a certain extent of disrupting its ideological mobilization, which was now an integral part of total war. We must start from here – the pathologically inflated perception of a modest factual datum – to understand the myth of the 'stab in the back'. We should not only think of the most enthusiastic chauvinists. While the war was still on-going, Thomas Mann denounced the radical intellectual of his country as a traitor: 'from the outset' he was aligned 'with the enemy' and had 'automatically adopted the standpoint of the Entente', to which he belonged 'body and soul'. Was the betrayal to be imputed, if not to the October Revolution (which had not occurred when *Reflections of an Unpolitical Man* were being written), then at least to the political movement informed by Marxism? This was not the view of the great writer, who instead observed that, in choosing his camp, the German radical intellectual was certainly not influenced by social-democracy, whose patriotic loyalism it viewed with the contempt reserved for 'philistines'. No, 'the structure of his mind' was in fact 'anti-national' (*unnational*) – more precisely, 'French-national'.[26] This is something not to be lost sight of: Mann believed that, in the final analysis, Germany had been defeated in the course of a kind of international civil war orchestrated by the Entente, which in waging a campaign or crusade against Germany had availed itself of the work of the 'international sect of the Enlightened', the 'world lodge of masons'.[27]

Although committed to identifying October 1917 as the disastrous start of the international civil war, Schmitt objectively ended up suggesting a different periodization and implicating culprits other than the Bolsheviks. He attributed the crisis of the *jus publicum europaeum* to the Versailles Treaty (likewise hateful to Lenin) and the League of Nations (which in its early

---

25   Quoted in Henry S. Commager, ed., *Documents of American History*, New York: Appleton-Century-Crofts, 1963, Vol. II, pp. 128–32; Stuart I. Rochester, *American Liberal Disillusionment in the Wake of World War I*, University Park and London: Pennsylvania State University Press, 1977, pp. 58, 44.

26   Thomas Mann, *Betrachtungen eines Unpolitischen*, ed. H. Helbling, Franfkurt am Main: Fischer, 1988, pp. 49–50, 375.

27   Ibid., p. 24.

years excluded Soviet Russia). On the eve of the Second World War, it was
the international body based in Geneva that was branded as a tool used by
its hegemonic powers to proclaim a moral and religious crusade against their
enemies and transform a 'war between states' into 'an international civil
war'. As regards the new conflict looming on the horizon, once again it was
the 'western democracies' that were threatening to ideologize it and represent it as a 'war of doctrines'.[28] Underlying this denunciation was the
experience of the gigantic clash two decades earlier, which was transfigured
into a crusade for democracy and peace by the Entente and, with especial
eloquence, by Wilson.

Following US intervention in the Second World War, the main culprit for
Schmitt was America, which, while it regarded itself as 'the land of salvation
of the elect', viewed Europe as a kind of 'infected zone'.[29] From this attitude
there could result either an isolationism jealous of its own purity and wary
of any source of potential contamination, or a missionary, aggressive interventionism equally foreign to any respect for others: 'When self-isolation
from the rest of the world is converted into discrimination against this world,
war becomes a punitive, purgative action that discriminates against the
adversary as a criminal.' Elevating itself to the role of judge, 'the US government holds in its own hands discrimination against others' and it is then
clear that 'it also has the right to incite peoples against their own governments
and to transform war between states into civil war'. Thus, American-style
discriminatory world war is converted into a 'global civil war of a total,
global kind', with 'armed intervention not only in all the political spaces,
but also in all the social relations, of the earth'.[30]

Was the advent of 'international civil war' attributable exclusively to
Germany's enemies? It is true that between 1914 and 1918 the Wilhelmine
Reich developed an ideology of war fundamentally different from its opponents. Eschewing universalistic themes, it was an ideology that stressed
defence of Germany's peculiar culture and history, and sought to justify and
transfigure the enormous carnage as a kind of gigantic sacrificial rite or
spiritual exercise which, through the experience of pain and proximity to
death, made it possible to attain the dimension of authentic existence and
community.[31] However, tendencies to an appeal for international civil war

---

28   Carl Schmitt, *L'unità del mondo e altri saggi*, ed. A. Campi, Rome: Pellicani, 1994, pp.
187, 194.

29   Ibid., pp. 282–3.

30   Ibid., pp. 288, 295.

31   See Domenico Losurdo, *Heidegger and the Ideology of War: Community, Death and the West*,

are not absent from the German *Kriegsideologie*. Illuminating in this respect is a book by a social-democratic deputy, whose title presents the conflict as a *Weltrevolution*, with Germany, embarked on the road to socialism and engaged in a fight to the death against the capitalist or 'plutocratic' coalition, as its protagonist.[32] Hence even before October, like the appeal to 'global civil war', the appeal to 'world revolution' formed part of the ideological armoury of both sides in the First World War. The elements of international civil war are even clearer when it comes to the Eastern campaign. German propaganda did not fail to echo themes and attitudes typical of 'democratic interventionism'. Social-democracy even invoked Marx and Engels, in an attempt to transfigure the war against Czarist Russia into a major contribution to the cause of the 'victory of liberty' and the emancipation of oppressed peoples, such that Hindenburg became 'the executor of the will of Marx and Engels'. The author of this ironic observation was Rosa Luxemburg, who very effectively described the prevailing climate in Europe in 1916: 'every sovereign by the grace of God is called a fool, an ungrateful wretch, by his cousin on the other side'; and every government condemned its counterparts as 'worthy of the contempt of the world', as a 'catastrophe' for the people it claimed to represent, as an enemy against whom it became a 'holy' task to fight to the bitter end. International civil war and crusades were already a reality.[33]

Not just the ideology, but the reality of international civil war made its appearance with the outbreak of the First World War. It has justly been remarked that, as the Wilhelmine army advanced on Paris, the German government and high command developed and implemented 'a long-range programme of subversion', aiming in the first instance to incite populations in colonial or semi-colonial conditions in the British and Russian empires.[34] As regards Europe proper, while the Central Powers sought to incite Poles, Irish and Russian Jews to rebel, the Entente appealed to the Armenians and national minorities of the Hapsburg Empire, branded as a prison of nationalities. This is the context of the tragic Easter Uprising in Dublin in 1916. Less well-known, perhaps, are the successes scored by the Czarist Empire which, in the name of 'Slav solidarity', engaged in intense propaganda among

trans. Marella and Jon Morris, Amherst, NY: New York, 2001, Chapter 1 and *passim*.

32   See Paul Lensch, *Drei Jahre Weltrevolution*, Berlin: Fischer, 1917, p. 212 and *passim*.

33   Rosa Luxemburg, *Politische Schriften*, ed. O.K. Flechtheim, Frankfurt am Main: Europäische Verlagsanstalt, 1968, Vol. II, pp. 20, 33, 86–9.

34   See Fritz Fischer, *Griff nach der Weltmach. Die Kriegszielpolitk des kaiserlichen Deutschland 1914/18*, Düsseldorf: Droste Verlag, p. 138.

Czechs and Slovaks, to whom it held out hopes of national independence. In 1916, there were between 250,000 and 300,000 Czech and Slovak prisoners in Russian hands. Not a few of them let themselves be 'persuaded to join the armies of the Entente against the Central Powers'.[35] On the other side, a Finnish battalion fought alongside Germany, which also sought to spark rebellion by Jews living in the Czarist Empire, which responded by deporting them. The Turkish government, against which the Entente sought to stir up Arabs and Jews, thought it identified the hand of the Russians and British behind Armenian agitation and responded with a large-scale massacre – in fact, with genocide. The reality of the international civil war ended up impacting on, or brushing, territorially dispersed ethnic groups, who hardly represented a danger: 'various anti-German pogroms' occurred in Russia;[36] and a similar climate developed in the USA against 'Huns' and 'aliens' in general.

In calling for imperialist war to be transformed into revolutionary civil war, Lenin in some ways merely released from its hypocritically one-sided character the watchword that had already been issued by the two sides exclusively against one another, and generalized it. Thus we can understand the Bolshevik leader's polemic against Kautsky, who, 'rejecting freedom of separation for the oppressed nations of Hapsburg Austria', recognized it in the case of 'Russian Poland'. Chauvinists and social chauvinists in general were propagandizing for the war solely in the enemy camp, but 'do not uphold the freedom to secede for colonies and nations oppressed by "their own" nations'.[37]

Moreover, the internal structure of the states engaged in the world war also involved an internal division of certain nations on the battlefield. At the Zimmerwald conference, the Polish delegation condemned the conflict as 'doubly fratricidal' for Poles,[38] who were forced to shed their blood in a civil war between members not only of the same (proletarian) class, but also of the same nation (Poland), dismembered by the great powers now at grips in mortal combat. In this instance, at any rate, loyalty towards one's own state did not avert – in fact, it implied – civil war within a single nation. Sometimes, different types of civil war became entangled. In particular, this

---

35   François Fejtö, *Requiem pour un empire défunt. Histoire de la destruction de l'Autriche-Hongrie*, Paris: Le Lieu commun, 1988, pp. 188–9.

36   Mikhail Agursky, *The Third Rome: National Bolshevism in the USSR*, Boulder, CO: Westview Press, 1987, p. 146.

37   V.I. Lenin, *Collected Works*, London: Lawrence & Wishart, 1960–, Vol. 22, p. 156.

38   Ibid., p. 155.

occurred in Persia: the dominant class split into two opposed factions – one pro-British, the other pro-German – and faced a revolt by the Kurds, on the one hand, and peasants and popular masses, on the other.[39] To the extent that it succeeded, Lenin's appeal stimulated civil wars (within a particular state community), but tended to put an end to civil wars of another type (those triggered within a particular national community, and sometimes within the same state community, by the rivalry and clash of the imperialist great powers).

Not only did the Bolshevik October not signal the start of international civil war, but the Russian Revolution can be situated in a context of international civil war. According to some historians, an important role was played in February by the 'German lobby'.[40] Above all, however, it was the events of subsequent months that were denounced in Entente ranks as the result of a 'Judeo-German' conspiracy. Not only Mussolini,[41] but (as we shall see) Churchill himself, advanced such an interpretation. The reasoning is readily explicable: having sought to arouse the Jews against the Romanov dynasty, here was Germany removing Russia from the war through a revolution that involved the active participation of Jews. To the last, Kerensky continued to insist on the role of the Wilhelmine empire's high command in the October events. No doubt he was speaking out of the resentment and frustration of defeat, but there is something in what he said, even if, once again, it was pathologically inflated.[42]

While the impact of the Russian and Bolshevik model on it was clear, the November Revolution that broke out in Germany the following year cannot be detached from the propaganda and attitude of the Entente. The US administration answered the German request for an armistice at the start of October 1918 by demanding profound political changes in the defeated country. The people of the world, it stated, could have no confidence in the declarations of Germany's current rulers, and the US government would only deal with representatives of the German people in a position to offer greater constitutional guarantees.[43] The victorious powers subsequently

39   Accademia delle Scienze dell'URSS, *Storia universale*, Italian trans., Milan: Teti, 1975, Vol. VII, pp. 498–9.

40   Agursky, *The Third Rome*, p. 148.

41   Meir Michaelis, *Mussolini and the Jews: German-Italian Relations and the Jewish Question in Italy 1922–1945*, New York: Oxford University Press, 1978, p. 35.

42   See Alexander F. Kerensky, *The Kerensky Memoirs: Russia and History's Turning Point*, London: Cassell, 1966, Chapter 18.

43   See Ritter and Miller, eds, *Die deutsche Revolution 1918–1919*, p. 27.

sought the trial of Wilhelm II and the Prussian high command! The role of Britain and, above all, France in the overthrow of the Hapsburg dynasty appears to have been even more significant.[44]

The collapse of the home front in Germany (stimulated by the Entente) was matched by the collapse of the home front in Russia (stimulated by the Wilhelmine empire); and the theory of the 'stab in the back' articulated by German chauvinists is the pendant of the theory, fostered by the Entente, explaining the Bolshevik October by a German or Judeo-German conspiracy. In conclusion, the countries defeated in the First World War were the site of revolutions or civil wars, which were also the result of enemy propaganda and manoeuvring. The preventive civil war on a much larger scale unleashed by Hitler, in preparation for a new bid for world power by Germany, was also a response to the 'stab in the back' and the victorious conduct of the 'international civil war' by the Entente.

The regime born in October 1917 immediately became the target of the international civil war that was already underway. An episode directly signals the transition from one phase of the 'international civil war' to the next. Its protagonist was the Czech Legion, formed with the help of the Entente in the hope of creating an autonomous Czechoslovak state on the ruins of the Hapsburg Empire, which subsequently (once again at the instigation of Britain and France) helped trigger and exacerbate the Russian Civil War even before the end of the world war. Ideologically, the transition from one phase to the next is apparent in an author like Salvemini. Having already distinguished himself in interpreting the First World War as a 'global civil war' and anti-German democratic revolution, he hastened to interpret the intervention against Soviet Russia, invoked by him in July 1918, in identical terms. 'To save' the country 'from the Bolsheviks and German penetration', it was necessary to promote a

predominantly American-Czech intervention . . . The 60,000 Czechoslovaks who are concentrated in Vladivostok should not return to Europe, but turn to Russia, mingling with Americans, as interpreters with a good knowledge of the country, in which they have lived for three years . . . The Entente has an interest in the revolution not being lost to the cause of world democracy.[45]

---

44 See Fejtö, *Requiem pour un empire défunt.*
45 Salvemini, *Opere*, Vol. III, pt. 2, pp. 197–9.

Defeat of the Bolsheviks would also facilitate recruitment of a Russian volunteer army, led by 'old officers', which would make an effective contribution to the war against Prussian militarism and despotism.

'Splendid Little War', Total War and Civil War

Hence October cannot be separated from the international civil war which the two sides engaged in the First World War sought to trigger in competition and confrontation with one another. But the civil war from which the Bolshevik Revolution derived also possesses a complex dialectic of its own, which, while it united or tended to unite soldiers called upon to fight and kill one another, saw the opposing high commands united in a way by a shared concern to prevent or repress such phenomena. Curzio Malaparte's analysis is no less lucid for coming from a novelist:

At the start of 1917, events of exceptional gravity occurred in all the belligerent armies of Europe. Pronunciamentos, revolts, and acts of collective insubordination had become frequent. In France as in Germany and Austria, in Russia as in Italy, the community of the trenches showed signs of exhaustion and impatience. The threat of the gravest punishments was insufficient to curb the mania of desertions. Entire divisions refused to return to the front.

The rejection of war tended to find expression in acts of war. Men who were ready to mutilate themselves in order to escape death and the horror of the carnage could easily take up arms against those they deemed responsible for it all. On the Italian front, resort was had to decimation, while on the other side 'ever more ferocious' became the 'hunt for carabinieri', who formed the execution squads and who sometimes, arms in hand, drove reluctant soldiers into battle: 'The carabinieri killed in the trenches are not counted; countless are those hanged or stabbed behind the front line.'[46] In Russia, notwithstanding a lack of munitions, the high command did not hesitate to order the use of artillery against units displaying insufficient

---------•

46   See Curzio Malaparte, *Viva Caporetto! La rivolta dei santi maledetti*, Milan: Mondadori, 1981, pp. 94–108. On episodes of self-mutilation, see Enzo Forcella, 'Apologia della paura', preface to Forcella and A. Monticone, eds, *Plotone di esecuzione. I processi della prima guerra mondiale*, Bari: Laterza, 1972, pp. xvi, xlvii.

fighting zeal.[47] Even across the Atlantic, in Canada, machine gun fire was required to mow down a revolt by 'deserters' who, with pistols and rifles, protested against conscription.[48]

While they were rebelling and pursuing (or harbouring) vendettas against those they considered responsible for starting or continuing the massacre, soldiers from the two sides engaged in fraternization. In this phenomenon, which officers sought to block at all costs, Lenin saw the 'seed' of 'proletarian socialist revolution' – in fact, its commencement: 'Long live fraternisation! Long live the *rising* world-wide socialist revolution of the proletariat!'[49] Once again, it is evident that the transformation of the imperialist war into a civil war was a tendency that the Bolshevik leader did not create, but on which he was able to confer conscious, organized form.

And that is the paradox. Nolte, who presumes to compress the interpretation of such a complex, contradictory century into the category of civil war, ends up forgetting or repressing it when it is self-evidently called for. Thus, the Bolshevik October is represented as a mere coup d'état. Furet (not to mention others) concurs with this thesis. However, let us examine events in the wake of the reconstruction provided by exponents of historical revisionism themselves. Nineteen-seventeen was also a year of 'mutinies' in the French army: 'it was not the mutinies . . . that were so surprising but the fact that there had not been more of them sooner and on a massive scale', such was the burden of suffering and horror caused by the war.[50] Two years prior to the Bolshevik October, Alain, 'philosopher and moralist of democratic humanism', condemned the on-going slaughter: 'We shall pay for all this, believe me; everyone will find out who his true enemies were.'[51] The February Revolution already seemed to him like a settling of accounts: 'all I saw were men in a state of revulsion, constantly dreaming of ways of ending the massacre and, when finding no solution, plotting vengeance'. Citing this passage, the French historian comments: 'Here Alain points to the universal turn taken by events in Russia – the fall of czarism took second place to the revolt of soldiers and civilians alike against the war.'[52]

---

47   W. Bruce Lincoln, *Passage through Armageddon: The Russians in War and Revolution 1914– 1918*, New York and Oxford: Oxford University Press, 1994, p. 147.

48   Martin Gilbert, *The First World War: A Complete History*, New York: Henry Holt and Company, 1994, p. 413.

49   Lenin, *Collected Works*, Vol. 24, p. 318.

50   Furet, *The Passing of an Illusion*, p. 36.

51   Ibid., pp. 49, 53.

52   Ibid., p. 53.

Hence October was already implicit in February. The military mutiny and popular revolt that overthrew the Czar did not signal the end of the struggle. The crucial issue – war or peace – had not been resolved. Miliukov professed to regard the political mutinies of February as a vehicle for giving new impetus to the war, and bolstering the Russian people's 'enthusiasm' and 'spirit of sacrifice', so as to accomplish conquest of the coveted Straits.[53] In the soviets, meanwhile, albeit amid contradictions, the rising tide of rejection of the interminable massacre became ever more powerful. To put an end to this situation, the Right as a whole looked to a Cavaignac capable of meeting the exigencies of war – and a total war at that – at the front and in the rear. Having become premier in July, 'under the constant pressure of the ambassadors of the Allies, Kerensky seriously thought about establishing a kind of dictatorship in an emergency situation', and to that end called on the collaboration of the Cossack general and supreme commander, Kornilov,[54] who set about restoring iron discipline in the army. He re-introduced the death penalty at the front; and on 9 July issued his order to 'fire with machine guns and artillery on units that abandon their positions on their own initiative'.[55] These were warning signs of a civil war tending to envelop the whole country. At the beginning of August, Savinkov, deputy war minister and intermediary between Kerensky and Kornilov, wrote a four-point programme providing for 'the extension of the death penalty to troops in the rear, the militarization of railroad transport, the application of martial law to war industries, and the restoration to officers of disciplinary authority with a corresponding reduction in the power of army committees'.[56]

A new trial of strength was impending. Kornilov regarded himself as the man to fight the latent or actual civil war to a conclusion. The coup d'état attempted by him in September, which was foiled only with the decisive aid of the Bolshevik Party, led to increased antagonism between officers and soldiers. The latter set about ejecting, or physically liquidating, officers in contact with the general leading the coup or suspected of so being.[57] The opposing options (peace or war) increasingly became embodied in two political sides, but also in two opposing organs of power and principles of

53   Arno J. Mayer, *Origins of the New Diplomacy, 1917–1918*, New York: Vintage Books, 1959, pp. 70–1.

54   Nolte, *Der europäische Bürgerkrieg*, p. 54.

55   Gérald Walter, *La Rivoluzione russa*, trans. F. Della Pergola, Novara: De Agostini, 1990, p. 85.

56   Pipes, *The Russian Revolution*, p. 443.

57   Walter, *La Rivoluzione russa*, p. 89.

legitimation: the Provisional Government and the soviets. 'For the big bourgeoisie and the army leaders' of Russia, it was time 'the soviets [were] got rid of, the Bolsheviks arrested, [and] their leaders shot'.[58] The Mensheviks were no strangers to these preparations, convinced as they now were of the need to 'employ force against their rebel brothers'. Given the inexorability of the conflict, and in a situation marked by the collapse of state structures and the existence of dual power, the trial of strength was inevitable, 'and it is pointless asking who started it'.[59]

The latent or blazing civil war, fuelled by Kornilov, resulted in victory for the Bolsheviks – a victory that did not betoken the end of the civil war itself. According to Nolte himself, in securing victory and conquering power, the Bolsheviks were able to utilize the 'universal phenomenon' of 'reactions against those responsible for the war', identified with the 'ruling classes' and the 'bourgeoisie' as a whole.[60] In a sense, not only October, but even its socialist content, derived from the objective pattern of the struggle against the war as well as Bolshevik ideology:

> Mass popular pressure to enjoy what they had hitherto been deprived of – self-esteem, participation, culture – took the most disparate forms. Even if Lenin had wanted to, it would have been difficult for him to prevent the workers taking control of their factories and people referring ever more frequently to *socialism*, which was to be achieved by nationalizing industry and immediately extended triumphantly to the whole world.[61]

This identification of the dominant classes as the culprits for the war was not as ingenuous and primitive as Nolte seems to think. If the First World War resulted from the explosion of contradictions between the great powers, it was also the terminus of an aspiration that in a way united the dominant classes of the various countries. No war has ever been so ardently invoked as a 'prophylaxis', as 'an instrument of domestic politics', as a lifeline for an *ancien régime* that felt itself increasingly menaced by the rise of the labour and socialist movement.[62] Having remarked the agitation in London's

58   Ferro, *Nicholas II*, p. 221.
59   Marc Ferro, *La Révolution russe de 1917*, Paris: Aubier, 1967, p. 467.
60   Nolte, *La crisi dei regimi liberali e i movimenti fascisti*, pp. 45–6.
61   Nolte, *Die europäische Bürgerkrieg*, p. 58.
62   See Arno J. Mayer, *The Persistence of the Old Regime: Europe to the Great War*, London and New York: Verso, 2010, pp. 304–5.

working-class districts, Cecil Rhodes reached a clear conclusion in 1895: 'If you want to avoid civil war, you must become imperialists.' Or, in the words of a French contemporary (a certain Wahl), 'impatience, irritation and hatred are accumulating in all the countries of the old civilisation and are becoming a menace to public order; the energy which is being hurled out . . . must be given employment abroad in order to avert an explosion at home'.[63] In analogous terms, Admiral Tirpitz likewise motivated his policy of naval rearmament by the need to find an antidote to 'Marxism and the political radicalisation of the masses'.[64] The way out of the 'civil war' feared by Rhodes was ubiquitously identified as what the US ambassador in London celebrated as a 'splendid little war'[65] in the aftermath of Spain's defeat; as the 'victorious little war' desired by the Russian Interior Minister, Plehve;[66] as the war capable of repulsing socialism (to cite Vilfredo Pareto this time) 'for at least a half-century'.[67] The adventure of war was invoked not only to divert attention from domestic social conflicts, but also to create a new spiritual climate, capable of sweeping away the materialism in which the demands of the labour movement were rooted. The warrior's thirst for glory and conquest was summoned to replace or challenge the socialist agitator's petty calculations and philistinism. Such was the political context in which the celebration of war in an aesthetic and pedagogical key is to be located.

When war with Spain broke out, the *Washington Post* carried an editorial of the utmost significance:

> A new consciousness seems to have come upon us – the consciousness of strength, and with it a new appetite, a yearning to show our strength . . . ambition, interest, land-hunger, pride, the mere joy of fighting, whatever it may be, we are animated by a new sensation . . . the taste of blood in the jungle.

And let us now turn to Theodore Roosevelt, an implacable critic of 'sentimental humanitarians', regarded by him as worse than the 'professional criminal class':

---

63 Quoted in Lenin, *Collected Works*, Vol. 22, pp. 257, 262–3.
64 Quoted in Paul M. Kennedy, *The Rise of the Anglo-German Antagonism 1860–1914*, London and New York: Ashfield Press, 1987, p. 416.
65 Walter Millis, *The Martial Spirit*, Chicago: Elephant Paperbacks, 1989, p. 340.
66 Ferro, *Nicholas II*, p. 65.
67 Vilfredo Pareto, 'Perche?', in *Scritti politici*, ed. G. Busino, Vol. II, Turin: UTET, 1974, pp. 414–15.

Who has in him any real power of joy in battle knows that he feels it
when the wolf begins to rise in his heart; he does not then shrink from
blood or sweat or deem that they mar the fight; he revels in them, in the
toil, the pain, and the danger as but setting off the triumph.

Such themes and accents are likewise to be found in Germany in Ernst
Jünger.[68]

Long coveted, the splendid little war was transformed into the 'homicidal
civil war' Rhodes precisely wished to avert via an imperialist adventure of
limited proportions. And the rejection of war had its principal reference-point in the country where revolution had already triumphed. If only
from a military standpoint, the Entente had an interest in extinguishing it
in Russia. If only in order to survive, Russia's new rulers had an interest in
further encouraging it in other countries.

In Search of the Origins of the 'International Civil War'

We cannot ignore the reality of the 'international civil war', which was
underway prior to the October Revolution. Schmitt, and the literature
inspired by him, realizes this. The decline of the *jus publicum europaeum* and
traditional inter-state war, now replaced by the crusade and a new edition
of the wars of religion, is dated from the advent of Jacobinism, rather than
Bolshevism.[69] It has to be said that, well before this literature, Edmund
Burke had denounced the French Revolution as 'a revolution of doctrine
and theoretick dogma', which, with its 'spirit of proselytism', recalled the
Protestant Reformation,[70] even if it was a proselytism in the service of an
impious, atheistic doctrine. But the thesis of Schmitt, Schnur and Nolte is
actually refuted by the British author and statesman who, having inveighed

---

68   Quoted in Peter Karsten, 'Militarization and Rationalization in the United States,
1870–1914', in J.R. Gillis, ed., *The Militarization of the Western World*, New Brunswick and
London: Rutgers, 1989, p. 38; Richard Hofstadter, *The American Political Tradition and the Men
Who Made It*, New York: A. Knopf, 1967, pp. 206, 209; Losurdo, *Heidegger and the Ideology of
War*, Chapter 6, §7.

69   See Carl Schmitt, *The* Nomos *of the Earth in the International Law of the* Jus Publicum
Europaeum, trans. G.L. Ulmen, New York: Telos Press, 2006; Schmitt, *Theory of the Partisan*;
Hanno Kesting, *Geschichtsphilosophie und Weltbürgerkrieg*, Heidelberg: Winter, 1959; Roman
Schnur, *Revolution und Weltbürgerkrieg. Studien zur Ouvertüre nach 1789*, Berlin: Duncker &
Humblot, 1983; Nolte, 'Weltbürgerkrieg 1917–1989?'

70   Edmund Burke, *The Works: A New Edition*, London: Rivington, 1826, Vol. VII, pp. 13–14.

against the godless revolution in incendiary language, launched an appeal for a general war against France – a war that was represented as 'a religious war' in the literal sense of the term.[71] It was a war 'in many respects entirely different' from traditional conflicts between one nation and another; what was involved was 'a Civil War' of international dimensions.[72] 'Religious War' and international 'Civil War': the two central categories employed by Schmitt to prosecute the French Revolution found their initial explicit formulation in the first great opponent of such revolutions, who adopted them in a uniquely positive connotation as the banner of a struggle on behalf of a sacred cause!

The year is 1790. The Jacobins were not as yet in power, but already the Parisian royalist press called upon Europe's crowned heads to intervene in France with a veritable holy war on behalf of a descendant of St Louis, forced, like Jesus Christ, to carry the cross and suffer the outrages inflicted on him by revolutionaries and a whole 'sinful' nation.[73] And Burke too seemed intent on a veritable crusade, whose protagonists were to be regarded as 'the Avengers of the injuries and outrages which have been offered to the Human Race'.[74] At stake was 'the Cause of Humanity', the cause of the 'happiness of the whole Civilized World', the salvation of 'the civilized World from impiety and barbarism'.[75]

It is no coincidence if the British statesman was the recipient of a letter from the Pope, who blessed his noble engagement in defence of the '*causa humanitas*'.[76] And nor was it a coincidence if, in launching his appeal for a general war against France, Burke referred to the example of the alarm aroused throughout Europe by the Anabaptist unrest in its time.[77] In this sense, contrary to Schmitt's thesis, the wars of religion had not in fact ceased, not even in Europe. It is just that the heretics ever more clearly became revolutionaries and those subverting the social order. Obviously, the crusade theorized and proclaimed here was not a limited war. It was intended not only to confront the French armies, but also to extirpate Jacobinism 'in its place of origin', and eventually to proceed to

---

71   Ibid., p. 174ff.

72   Edmund Burke, *Correspondence*, ed. Th. W. Copeland and J.A. Woods, Cambridge: Cambridge University Press, 1958–, Vol. VII, pp. 387, 432.

73   Jean-Paul Bertaud, 'La presse royaliste parisienne, l'idée de guerre et la guerre, 1789–1792', in F. Lebrun and R. Dupuy, eds, *Les Résistances à la Révolution*, Paris: Imago, 1987, pp. 206–7.

74   Burke, *Correspondence*, Vol. VII, p. 472.

75   Ibid., pp. 354, 382.

76   See the letter from Pius VI, in ibid., p. 420.

77   Burke, *The Works*, Vol. V, p. 278.

'exemplary punishment of the principal Authors and Contrivers of [France's] ruin'.[78] Here it is the British Whig, esteemed by Schmitt and Nolte, who criminalizes the enemy, treating him like a common criminal.

Such criminalization was the result not of a fit of anger, but of a thought-out, developed theory. Transcribing Vattel, and naturally omitting all those passages where the Swiss jurist insists on every state's equal right to autonomy and sovereignty, Burke stressed the legitimate right of – in fact, the moral obligation on – the community of European states 'to repress, chastise . . . a nation of restless and mischievous disposition' and 'put it ever after out of its power to injure' other countries.[79] Some years later, Genz stressed that it was illegitimate to absolutize 'the principle that no state has the right to interfere in the internal affairs of another state'. A country that elevated the 'overthrow of all juridical relations' into a theory could not count on the international community's neutrality and inertia. The passivity of other states could certainly not be demanded in the face of legislation that proclaimed the legitimacy of 'assassination' and 'armed rapine'. This especially applied to Europe and the 'system of European states':

> Through their geographical location, their many links, the homogeneity of their customs, their laws, their needs, their way of life and their culture, all the states of this region of the world form a league (Bund) that has rightly been defined as the European republic. The various units making up this league of peoples (Völkerbund) form part of a community so close and indissoluble that no significant change in any one of them can be a matter of indifference to the others.[80]

Quite the reverse of representing an obstacle, it was precisely the sentiment of the community of European peoples, the pathos of the *jus publicum europaeum*, which prompted the criminalization of France, ruled at the time not by the Jacobins but by Napoleon.

The least that can be said is that the return of the war of religion cannot be attributed exclusively to the revolutionary party. Historical revisionism once again ends up aligning itself with the experience of the latter's

---

78   Burke, *Correspondence*, Vol. VII, pp. 387, 384.

79   Emer de Vattel, *Le Droit des gens ou principes de la loi naturelle*, ed. J. Brown Scott, Washington: Classics of International Law, 1916, Bk. II, Chapter 4, §53 (Vol. I, p. 296). Cf. Burke, *The Works*, Vol. VII, p. 201.

80   Friedrich von Gentz, *Ausgewählte Schriften*, ed. W. Weick, Stuttgart and Leipzig: Rieger, 1836–8, Vol. II, pp. 195–8.

opponents. In its comprehensive condemnation, it does not bother analysing the oppositions internal to the French Revolution. On many occasions, Robespierre strongly criticized any idea of exporting revolution. His diatribe against Cloots, 'inopportune preacher of the one and indivisible republic' identified with counter-revolutionaries, was harsh.[81] His irony against those who wanted heaven knows what, 'the republic or a universal conflagration', was caustic.[82] His admonition not to forget that 'no one loves armed missionaries' was lucid.[83] Paris was not 'the capital of the world' and starting-point for 'conquering the world'.[84] The 'yearning to make a nation happy and free despite itself' was senseless. On the contrary, 'all the kings would have been able to vegetate or die with impunity on their blood-stained thrones, had they known how to respect the independence of the French people'.[85] Europe, Robespierre repeated in his speech of 8 Thermidor, was not being subjugated through 'bellicose deeds', but was being influenced and attracted by the 'wisdom of our laws'.[86] Naturally, we can find lapses in Robespierre too. Yet his basic position unequivocally rejected the theory of exporting revolution.

While, on the one hand, it conflates Robespierre with Cloots and the Jacobins with the Girondins, on the other, historical revisionism once again proves inadequate in its inability to develop an adequate comparativism. What are the most important ideas of mission expressed in the history of the West? On the eve of the American Civil War, opponents of the abolitionist revolution denounced the North for an idea of mission that not only threatened the slaveholding states, but also tended to spread to an international level. It is true that representatives of the South branded this attitude as Jacobin or neo-Jacobin.[87] In reality, however, much more so than to the French Revolution, it went back to Puritanism and, via Puritanism, to the Old Testament and the idea of the 'chosen people'. Not by chance, in the course of its history, has the USA frequently cast itself as a new Israel invested with a Manifest Destiny.[88] This is the idea of mission that has proved

---

81   Maximilien Robespierre, *Oeuvres*, Paris: Presses Universitaires de France, 1912–, Vol. X, p. 275.

82   Ibid., p. 267.

83   Ibid., Vol. VIII, p. 81.

84   Ibid., Vol. X, p. 361.

85   Ibid., p. 230.

86   Ibid., p. 568.

87   See Eugene D. Genovese, *The Slaveholders' Dilemma: Freedom and Progress in Southern Conservative Thought, 1820–1860*, Columbia: University of South Carolina Press, 1995, p. 83.

88   See Domenico Losurdo, *Democrazia o bonapartismo*, Turin: Bollati Boringhieri, 1993,

most dynamic historically (as we shall see, even the Democrat Clinton spoke of an eternal 'mission' falling to his country). But if we exclude Schmitt, it is difficult to find a critic of the American political tradition among the other representatives of historical revisionism, all of whom engage exclusively in denunciation of the French and Bolshevik revolutions.

However, let us set aside the idea of mission and examine the aspect of international civil war that involves a challenge to state and national borders during crises and conflicts with an international dimension. What occurred during the American Civil War can be attributed to the revolutionary tradition: volunteers from various neutral countries rushed to fight the slaveholding South and, according to Lord Russell's reproach, the Union incited British subjects to disobey their government's declaration of neutrality.[89] But it is difficult to impute what happened during the war between the USA and Mexico in the mid-nineteenth century to Jacobinism. Frustrated and resentful at the discrimination they suffered in the North American republic, a not insignificant number of Irish and Catholics went over to the 'enemy' and fought bravely alongside an army and population that was likewise victim of the racial contempt of WASPs (White Anglo-Saxon Protestants).[90]

Finally, we can and must ask whether, working backwards in search of the origins of the 'international civil war', it is legitimate to stop at 1789. A climate of latent civil war developed in Britain itself during the revolt of the American colonies, which (it should not be forgotten) were allied with Britain's two traditional enemies – namely, France and Spain. However, this did not prevent Fox, leader of the opposition, from expressing himself as 'a passionate partisan of the insurgents'. A storm sank some British ships off the coast of America, causing the loss of all hands. The news, noted a loyalist political representative with scorn, was received by some with open 'parricide joy'. The US Congress invited a prominent representative of the British democratic movement to cross the Atlantic to take charge of managing the new state's finances. Although obliged to decline the invitation for safety reasons, the addressee was unstinting in his praise for the Assembly, which he characterized as 'the most respectable and important in the world'. Feeling himself a spiritual citizen of the new republic, the author of this encomium

---

Chapter 3, §§9–10.

89   Jefferson Davis, *The Rise and Fall of the Confederate Government*, ed. J.M. MacPherson, New York: Da Capo Paperback, Vol. II, pp. 224–5.

90   Richard Slotkin, *The Fatal Environment:The Myth of the Frontier in the Age of Industrialization 1800–1890*, New York: Harper Perennial, 1994, p. 187.

was Richard Price,[91] who some years later also enthused over the French Revolution and was met with harsh criticism by Burke, engaged in denouncing the illicit missionary spirit of the new rulers in Paris.

Working backwards in search of the genesis of 'international civil war' ultimately means researching the origins of democracy. As public opinion develops, it can reject the foreign policy of a country's government and come into contradiction with patriotic loyalties in wartime. The conflict becomes even more dramatic when the figure of the mercenary or professional soldier is replaced by the citizen-soldier, who, in the event of general mobilization, tends to express potential disagreement on the battlefield, where his very life is at stake. It scarcely needs saying that rejection of war played a very important role in the Italian Resistance and the formation of partisan groups.

Those who so wish may regret with Joseph de Maistre the disappearance of the good old days, when war took the form of a kind of sacred rite, from whose fascination man could in no wise escape:

Can you not hear the earth crying out and praying for blood? . . . Have you not noticed that on the field of death man never disobeys? He can kill Nerva or Henry IV. But the most abominable tyrant, the most insolent butcher of human flesh, will never hear it said: *We no longer wish to serve you.* A revolt on the battle-field, an agreement to embrace in disowning the tyrant, is something unheard of.[92]

Events in the First World War and the October Revolution supervened to refute Maistre and, despite everything, it is highly unlikely that his view of war will altogether come back into fashion.

---

91   William E.H. Lecky, *A History of England in the Eighteenth Century*, London: Longmans, Green & Co., 1883–8, Vol. IV, pp. 68–70.

92   Joseph de Maistre, *Oeuvres complètes*, Hildesheim, Zurich and New York: Olms, 1984, Vol. V, pp. 24–5.

Historical Epoch and the Concrete Analysis of Wars

According to Nolte, 'had Burke and Robespierre still been alive in 1815, they would have had to note that the main feature of the quarter-century following 1789 had been global civil war'.[93] In truth, while Burke would have had no difficulty recognizing himself in Wellington, it is hard to believe that the Jacobin leader would have been able to recognize himself in Napoleon. In the course of his controversy with the Girondins, he not only vigorously rejected the idea of exporting revolution, but also warned revolutionary armies against emulating the fatal course of Louis XIV's expansionism: 'If you are the first to violate their territory, you will vex the peoples of Germany . . . among whom the cruelties committed by generals in the Palatinate have left more profound impressions than can now be created by a few banned little books'; a French invasion could only 'reawaken the idea of the burning of the Palatinate'.[94] Judging from these passages at least, it might be said that Robespierre legitimized the *Befreiungskriege* – the anti-Napoleonic war – in advance. The twenty-five years of wars and armed conflict between 1789 and 1815 can indeed be interpreted as principally revolving around a confrontation between opponents and supporters of the *ancien régime* – hence as an extended period of latent or declared 'international civil war'. But this tells us little or nothing about the concrete nature of the particular phases and particular wars.

In this connection it is interesting to examine the thinking of the figure who, along with the French Jacobin leader, is branded by revisionist historiography as the monomaniacal prophet of international civil war. Lenin observed:

> the wars of the Great French Revolution began as national wars and indeed were such. They were revolutionary wars – the defence of the great revolution against a coalition of counter-revolutionary monarchies. But when Napoleon founded the French Empire and subjugated a number of big, viable and long-established national European states, these national wars of the French became imperialist wars and *in turn* led to wars of national liberation *against* Napoleonic imperialism.[95]

---

93   Nolte, 'Weltbürgerkrieg 1917–1989?', p. 35.
94   Robespierre, *Oeuvres*, Vol. VIII, pp. 61, 82.
95   Lenin, *Collected Works*, Vol. 22, p. 309.

The fact that the main content of the epoch that began in 1789 (or 1783 — i.e. with the American Revolution) was the destruction of feudalism on an international scale, the reality of the so-called international civil war, in no way excludes the occurrence of national wars — national wars which can contain a change of front, in the sense that the victims become aggressors, progress becomes reaction, 'left' becomes 'right' and vice versa. In other words, the new politico-social system can also emerge from a struggle against those who were the first to promote it. Lenin probably had in mind a page in Engels that dates the start of the bourgeois revolution in Germany from 1808–13[96] — in other words, not with Napoleon's victory, but with devclopment of resistance against the country guilty of having transformed the promise of 'perpetual peace' into 'a war of endless conquest',[97] with the realization of the anti-feudal reforms required by the national liberation struggle against post-revolutionary France. We can then understand the highly positive assessment of the *Befreiungskriege* and the uprising by Germans against those who even presumed to compel them 'to provide troops to assist the victor to conquer other nations'.[98]

Similar considerations apply to what for Marx and Lenin was the epoch of the transition from capitalism to socialism. Appeals for struggle against the capitalist bourgeoisie did not prevent them supporting national movements led by the bourgeoisie (one thinks of the Italian Risorgimento), or even hegemonized ideologically by the Catholic priesthood (one thinks of Poland and Ireland). The transition from capitalism to socialism constituted the main content of the epoch for whose onset Lenin called with the conversion of imperialist war into revolutionary civil war. But this only defined the general picture. In July 1916 — Wilhelm II's army was at the gates of Paris — although reiterating the imperialist character of the war, the Bolshevik leader observed that were it to end 'in victories like Napoleon's and in the subjugation of a number of viable national states . . . then a great national war in Europe would be possible'.[99] Accordingly, although what defined the epoch as a whole was the transition to socialism, the possibility of a national war could not be excluded even in the capitalist world. At all events, it was on the agenda in the colonial and semi-colonial world.

---

96 See Karl Marx and Friedrich Engels, *Werke*, Berlin: Dietz, 1955–, Vol. VII, p. 539.
97 Ibid., Vol. XX, p. 239.
98 Lenin, *Collected Works*, Vol. 27, pp. 105, 186.
99 Ibid., Vol. 22, p. 310.

Hence we can indeed interpret the period that began with the October Revolution and ended in 1945 or 1989 as principally characterized by a global struggle between Communism and capitalism, or between Bolshevism and Nazism and Fascism – a struggle which, more or less running through all the states engaged in the conflict, may be interpreted as an 'international civil war'. But this definition does not exempt us from a concrete analysis of the various contradictions and multiple conflicts marking this historical epoch. Along with the struggle between capitalism and socialism, there was the rivalry between the great powers (which exploded in 1914 after decades of incubation) and there were wars of national liberation in the colonial world (which had begun to show signs of unrest before October 1917) and, sometimes, in Europe. The struggle between capitalism and socialism could itself take very different forms: as war (hot or cold) between states, as a struggle between national liberation movements and colonial powers, as genuine civil war within a single national community. In all three instances, elements of civil war (at a national or international level) were present, which sometimes constituted the principal aspect, sometimes the secondary.

Lenin professed himself in full agreement with late Engels' thesis that 'the victorious proletariat can force no blessings of any kind upon any foreign nation without undermining its own victory by so doing'.[100] This was an 'absolutely internationalist principle' for the Bolshevik leader, who inferred from it that as long as the victorious proletariat continued to display chauvinistic or hegemonic tendencies, 'revolutions – against the socialist state – and wars are possible'.[101] If, objectively at any rate, Robespierre seems to justify in advance resistance movements against the expansionism of revolutionary or post-revolutionary France, Lenin explicitly theorized the legitimacy of movements of struggle and emancipation that developed in Yugoslavia, Hungary, Czechoslovakia and Afghanistan against the hegemonic pretensions of the socialist Big Brother. As we can see, Lenin's 'internationalism' had very little to do with the theory of international civil war imputed to him by historical revisionism, wherein all cows are black.

---

100   Marx and Engels, *Werke*, Vol. XXXV, p. 358.
101   Lenin, *Collected Works*, Vol. 22, pp. 352–3.

The October Revolution, Nazism and Fascism, and the Colonial Question

Thus we arrive at the main phenomenon repressed by revisionist historiography: the colonial and national question. Not only is its starting-point 1917 rather than 1914, but it forgets that, in addition to calling for the transformation of imperialist war into revolutionary civil war, the Bolsheviks also appealed to the slaves of the colonies to break their chains and wage wars of national liberation against the imperial domination of the great powers. Such repression makes it impossible adequately to understand Nazism and Fascism, which also presented themselves as a movement in reaction – extreme reaction – against this second appeal. It is no accident if the three countries that took the initiative in unleashing the Second World War were ones which, having arrived late at the colonial banquet, were frustrated in their ambitions and directly threatened by rising anti-colonialism. Thus, Japan sought its 'living space' in Asia; Italy in Ethiopia, Albania and elsewhere; and Germany in Eastern Europe and the Balkans. On the eve of the official commencement of the Second World War, before attacking Poland and the USSR, Hitler dismembered Czechoslovakia and explicitly declared that Bohemia-Moravia was a 'protectorate' of the Third Reich. The lexicon and institutions of the colonial tradition were explicitly invoked and their sphere of application extended to Eastern Europe. Hitler's model was Britain's colonial empire, of whose civilizing function and mission he held a very high opinion: 'there has never been in Europe, since the disintegration of the old German Empire, any State which . . . could compare with the British'. Hitler even expressed concern about 'the state of anarchy that will follow British withdrawal from India' in the wake of the Axis's triumph. The Ukraine was 'the new empire of the Indies' and its inhabitants, like those of Eastern Europe generally, were repeatedly characterized as 'natives'. The Italians were called on by the Führer to emulate the British colonial model in Egypt and Africa.[102]

The close link between Nazism and Fascism and attempts to block the historical process of liberation of colonial peoples that began with the October Revolution did not escape the most attentive observers at the time.

---

102   Adolf Hitler, *Hitler's Table Talk 1941–44*, London: Weidenfeld & Nicolson, 1973, p. 562 (conversation of 5 July 1942, evening); *Monologue im Führerhauptquartier 1941–1944. Die Aufzeichnungen Heinrich Heims*, ed. W. Jochmann, Hamburg: Albrecht Knaus, 1980, p. 196 (12–13 January 1942) and p. 110 (26 and 27 October 1941); *Hitler's Table Talk*, p. 574 (9 July 1942).

It was not only the Communist International that defined Fascism as the 'terrorist dictatorship of the most reactionary, the most chauvinist and most imperialist elements of finance capital'. In the same years, the future leader of independent India, Jawaharlal Nehru, observed that 'a victory of fascism in Europe or elsewhere will strengthen imperialism; its retreat will weaken imperialism. Equally, the triumph of a liberation movement in a colonial or subject country is a blast against imperialism and fascism.' Imperialism was certainly not coterminous with fascism. The then leader of an important national liberation movement ironized about Britain, 'the greatest of the imperialist powers, posing as the defender of world peace while it bombs and ruthlessly oppresses subject peoples'. Such irony indicates an awareness that being consistently anti-fascist entailed rejecting imperialism and colonialism. It was no accident, stressed Nehru, if one of the British colonial empire's most fervent admirers was precisely Hitler.[103]

There is something we should reflect on. The Second World War began as a colonial war (against colonies and the territories which the aggressors intended to convert into colonies). One thinks of the Italian conquest of Ethiopia, the Japanese conquest of China, and the German invasion (albeit legalized by the Munich treaty) of Czechoslovakia. Eurocentric prejudice prevents us appreciating a fact that did not escape a Third World leader like Mao Zedong. In May 1938, he observed: 'By now one-third of the world's population has entered the war. Look! Italy, then Japan; Abyssinia, then Spain, then China. The population of the countries now at war amounts to almost 600 million, or nearly a third of the total population of the world . . . What will come next? Undoubtedly Hitler will fight the great powers.'[104]

For that very reason, from its outset the second global conflict exhibited radically different characteristics from the first. The main difference consisted in the emergence of a new political subject. In a way, of course, the latter had already emerged between 1914 and 1918, with the enrolment of non-white troops in Entente ranks in a conflict of which they knew nothing. Twenty years later, the new wave of colonial expansion pursued by the Nazi and Fascist states was confronted (as Mao further observed) by 'revolutionary wars' and liberation movements that had now achieved political subjectivity, thanks also to the epochal break represented by the October Revolution.

---

103   Giuliano Procacci, *Dalla parte dell'Etiopia. L'aggressione italiana vista dai movimenti anticolonialisti d'Asia, d'Africa, d'America*, Milan: Feltrinelli, 1984, pp. 54–5.

104   Mao Tse-tung, 'On Protracted War', in *Selected Military Writings of Mao Tse-tung*, Beijing: Foreign Languages Press, 1967, p. 223.

If, at the end of the First World War, notwithstanding their promises to the peoples they had needed as cannon fodder, the victorious powers not only maintained their empires intact, but calmly appropriated the colonial booty abandoned by the losers (one thinks, in particular, of the Middle East), the picture changed radically with the Second World War. The Resistance was an international phenomenon investing a very wide arc of countries, European and non-European. Not a few of these, within and without Europe, had been reduced to colonial or semi-colonial conditions. We can therefore easily understand why such revolutions, having developed at a global level, should have continued beyond 1945 in a tempestuous dynamic of anti-colonial struggle encompassing all continents.

It should be added that the Third Reich's attempt to relaunch colonial expansionism at the expense of countries on its eastern borders, and the 'Napoleon-style victories' initially won by its army, exacerbated the national question in Europe itself, as Lenin had foreseen. We even have the instance of a country (Italy) which, having participated in unleashing world war with explicitly imperialist slogans (the conquest of a place in the sun and the return of Empire to the 'fateful hills of Rome'), was subsequently forced to fight to avoid itself becoming a province of the Greater German Reich. In this sense, despite the bitter elements of civil war it contained (something more or less characteristic of any independence struggle), the Italian Resistance is also to be regarded primarily as a war of national liberation.

Colonial War from Abyssinia to Eastern Europe

Given its utterly undifferentiated view of international civil war, it is not surprising that justification of colonialism, and repression of the colonial and national question, is a political and theoretical constant in Schmitt and historical revisionism. Fascist Italy's aggression against Ethiopia seems to perfectly embody the ideal type of the civilizing crusade and total, holy war on which the great political thinker's critical acumen is exercised. Mussolini professed his desire to help spread European civilization, liquidating the 'age-old slavery' that scandalously persisted in the African country (see below, Chapter 7, §2). The regime's propaganda declared that what was at stake was putting an end to the 'horrors of slavery'. In Milan, Cardinal Schuster blessed and consecrated the enterprise which, 'at a cost in blood opens the gates of Ethiopia to the Catholic faith and Roman civilization' and which, by abolishing 'slavery, will dispel the darkness of barbarism'.[105] The civilizing conquest proceeded with the massive recourse to mustard and poison gas, large-scale massacres of the civilian population, and use of concentration camps. But Schmitt intervened energetically in defence of the crusaders in 1936. The fact was that limited war presupposed 'homogeneity in terms of civilization'; and that could not be conceded to Abyssinia.[106] There was nothing objectionable about a discriminatory war of annihilation against barbarians. Fascist Italy was right to regard and treat 'the Negus not as a head of state but as a gang leader with extremely uncertain power over feudal tribes' – hence as a subject in no wise entitled to the rights of 'a member of the general community of international law'. In fact, 'the Negus' possession' – Abyssinia – 'did not exhibit either the ethical-legal or the organizational minimum in the absence of which one cannot speak of a state and hence of an effective member of the community of international law'.[107]

How are we to explain support for a war that was so expressly discriminatory? It might be said that the disappearance of rules is inevitable when dealing with countries that do not feel bound by the *jus publicum europaeum*. So let us see what occurred in Ethiopia. Italian troops systematically violated *jus in bello*. Without any declaration of war, they invaded. In defiance of the Geneva Convention, they resorted to 'systematic use of poison gas', hanged prisoners, and decimated the intellectuals.[108] Even so, the Negus issued an appeal (widely answered by the population) calling for full 'respect for the laws of war', not making the Italians pay for 'the atrocities they have visited on our people'.[109]

Shortly after Mussolini's aggression in Africa, Schmitt justified German intervention in Czechoslovakia, its dismemberment, and the establishment of the Protectorate of Bohemia and Moravia, with the argument that 'international law presupposes in any state a minimum of organization internally and of the power to resist externally':[110] 'a people incapable' of providing itself with a state – in fact, a state commensurate with modern war – could not be regarded as a 'subject of international law'. Schmitt explicitly

105   Luigi Salvatorelli and Giovanni Mira, *Storia dell'Italia nel periodo fascista*, Milan: Oscar Mondadori, 1972, Vol. II, pp. 254, 294.

106   See Losurdo, *Heidegger and the Ideology of War*, Chapter 3, §8.

107   Carl Schmitt, *Positionen und Begriffe im Kampf mit Weimar-Genf-Versaille 1932–1939*, Berlin: Duncker & Humblot, 1988, pp. 212–13.

108   Angelo del Boca, *Il Negus. Vita e morte dell'ultimo Re dei Re*, Rome and Bari: Laterza, 1995, pp. 140, 177, 181–2.

109   Ibid., p. 193.

110   Schmitt, *Positionen und Begriffe*, p. 285.

acknowledged that he was applying a category peculiar to the history of colonialism to Europe, when, in corroboration of the theory just formulated, he remarked: 'At the start of 1936, for example, it was revealed that Abyssinia was not a state.'[111]

Like Abyssinia, the USSR could not be recognized as possessing 'homogeneity at the level of civilization', or 'the national and *völkisch* affinity of the European peoples', declared Schmitt, explicitly invoking the 'Führer and Reichskanzler'.[112] It is now clear that the campaign of extermination in the East is incomprehensible if we ignore the colonial tradition behind it and refer exclusively to the category of international civil war.

In keeping with his defence of the colonial adventures of Fascist Italy (in Ethiopia) and of the Third Reich (in Eastern Europe), Schmitt likewise refused any legitimacy to anti-colonial liberation movements in the post-war period. Only now his main argument was not some lack of homogeneity with civilized peoples, but the fact that they were the expression of the international civil war launched from Moscow. In Schmitt's view, the revolutions in Algeria, Indochina or China were not autonomous. Yet the start of the revolution in the last-named preceded the Bolsheviks' assumption of power. In fact, the formation of Lenin's political thought cannot be separated from the maturing of the anti-colonialist wave from the second half of the nineteenth century: the Taiping, the Boxers and, subsequently, the advent of the republic in China; the Mahdi's revolt in Africa; the Cuban rebellion against Spanish domination, the guerrilla war against the USA in the Philippines, the Mexican revolution, and so forth. The Bolshevik leader's critique of capitalism was also a denunciation of its colonial policy.

All this is erased or repressed. For Schmitt, the twentieth-century partisan in action in the Third World was 'a key figure of world history'.[113] In fact, he was subject to 'international and supranational control, which helps and supports, but only in its own interests': 'the partisan . . . ceases to be essentially defensive. He becomes a manipulable tool of global revolutionary aggressivity', intent on world revolution and 'destruction of the existing social order'.[114] To be damned thus was the anti-colonialist movement in its entirety. Partisan struggle as a people's war? In reality, 'a few terrorists are able to threaten great masses'.[115] Their motives were anything

---

111   Ibid., p. 310.
112   Ibid., pp. 212–13.
113   Schmitt, *Theory of the Partisan*, p. 77.
114   Ibid., pp. 74–7.
115   Ibid., p. 73.

but noble: in Asia, an important role was played by 'racial enmity against the white, colonial exploiter'.[116] And who was responsible for mass terror? In Indochina, the partisans 'perpetrated all types of terrorist acts in order to cause the French to initiate acts of counter-terror against the indigenous population, which incited even more hatred against the French'.[117] In reality, the terrorist actions' planned by Salan 'against . . . the Algerian civilian population' drew on the 'methods of subversive warfare and psychological mass terror' experienced by French officers in Indochina.[118] It was clear that 'with a partisan, one fights like a partisan'.[119] Schmitt's sympathy for the OAS and supporters of French Algeria is evident: Salan 'soon became bitterly disappointed in his expectations that General de Gaulle would defend unconditionally France's territorial sovereignty over Algeria, which was guaranteed in the constitution'.[120] Along with the justification of reprisals by the French army there emerges, albeit indirectly and allusively, justification of reprisals by the Wehrmacht. And how could it be otherwise if, at bottom, these were different episodes in one and the same struggle – against the international civil war unleashed by the Bolsheviks and the USSR?

Historical Revisionism from Denunciation to Proclamation of the Crusade

Revealing in any conflict, however seemingly remote and specific, the manoeuvres and objectives of a single, omnipresent, planetary enemy, the 'international civil war' calmly represses the national and colonial question. Besides, the relevant category is remarkably vague, chronologically and conceptually. Generally, two periods are distinguished: 1789–1815 and from 1917–89/91. In-between comes 1848 (the 'first European civil war'),[121] and Marx.[122] According to Schmitt, a direct line leads from the *Communist Manifesto* of 1847 and the revolutionary wave of 1848 to the 'general global

---

116   Ibid., p. 59.
117   Ibid., p. 72.
118   Ibid., pp. 61–3.
119   Ibid., p. 81.
120   Ibid., p. 63.
121   Carl Schmitt, *Donoso Cortés in gesamteuropäischer Interpretation*, Köln: Greven, 1950, p. 7.
122   Schmitt, *L'unità del mondo e altri saggi*, p. 304.

civil war',[123] or the 'civil cold war',[124] whose conclusion Nolte dated and saluted in 1989.[125] Hence the category is sometimes used to define an acute struggle between revolution and counter-revolution at an international level (only in this sense can 1848 be referred to as a 'European civil war'). At other times, international civil war seems to presuppose the existence of a state calling for insurrection in countries with which it is at war, whether latent or declared. (In this instance, it is not clear why 'international civil war' should be regarded as having ended in 1989. During the Gulf War, Saddam Hussein called on the Arab masses to rise up against their 'traitorous' governments, allied with the West. Even today, the USA clearly continues to incite the Cuban or Iraqi people to revolt against 'tyranny'.) Finally, on occasion what is meant by 'international civil war' is simply calls for revolution in a series of countries made by a political party or movement. (But then it is not clear why the party of 'international civil war' is only Marx's and not also, for example, Mazzini's.)

The vagueness of the definition yields surprising results. According to Nolte, Hitler was the leader of the party of international civil war in Germany. More precisely, however, the Nazi Party was the party of international civil counter-war (the initiative in declaring war was taken by Lenin). At a certain point, the Führer became the interpreter not only of German national unity, but of a German national unity that was seamless. Notwithstanding the concentration camps, after the triumph of the *Blitzkrieg* on France, 'all Germans, without exception, were in agreement at a certain moment, at least in some of their convictions and emotions, with Hitler's resolute assertions and actions'.[126]

In his turn, Schmitt suddenly confronts us with the thesis that 1936–8 were 'the years in which Spain defended itself in a war of national liberation against the danger of falling into the hands of the international communist movement'.[127] Generally ubiquitous, the category of international civil war vanishes precisely as and when it would seem self-evident. It would be a mistake to read such a declaration as nothing more than a tribute to Franco's Spain, whose guest Schmitt was at the time he made it. There is a more profound reason

---

123   Schmitt, *Donoso Cortés*, pp. 85–6, 18–19.
124   Schmitt, *L'unità del mondo*, p. 299ff.
125   See Nolte, 'Weltbürgerkrieg 1917–1989?'
126   Ernst Nolte, 'Deutsche Identität nach Hitler', Italian trans. in *Dramma dialettico o tragedia? La guerra civile mondiale e altri saggi*, ed. F. Coppellotti, Perugia: Settimo Sigillo/ University of Perugia Press, 1994, p. 118.
127   Schmitt, *The Theory of the Partisan*, p. 56 (trans. modified).

for the sudden capsizal of the category of international civil war into that of war of national liberation. Let us revert to Burke, who condemned the French revolutionaries as fanatics in the grip of a missionary zeal, hence as protagonists of an international civil war, while branding them as 'savages' or 'Turks' alien to Europe and hence as external aggressors. Politico-moral distance tends to translate into geographical and territorial distance. And Communists seem all the more alien to the German political thinker because they refer to the Soviet Union, which is alien to the *jus publicum europaeum* and civilization. On the other hand, Nolte invokes Burke to compare the Bolsheviks, as well as the Jacobins, with Islam.[128] Thus they are once again reduced to the status of foreigners and external enemies of Europe and genuine civilization.

When underscoring the Western roots of Communist ideology (Marx, Hegelian philosophy of history, Jacobinism), and its menacing presence in the West, Schmitt (and historical revisionism) refers to international civil war; when stressing Moscow's leadership of the global subversive movement, he calls for resistance to the Oriental enemy by individual nations and the West as a whole. From this standpoint, even wars conducted by some European power or other to preserve their colonial possessions assume the form of national or Western wars of liberation or national resistance.

Once used to erase or repress the multiplicity and complexity of real contradictions, the category of international civil war ends up yielding a kind of tortuous justification even of the most infamous aspects of the Third Reich's policy: 'The civil war character of the Germano-Soviet conflict . . . meant the resumption of the Russian Civil War between "reds" and "whites" . . . With the "commissar order", Hitler simply reinstituted one of its most horrendous rules' (the Geneva Convention applies solely to inter-state conflicts). In this light, what otherwise 'seems like an incomprehensible, execrable fact – for example, the "commissar order" or even the "final solution of the Jewish question"' – becomes 'understandable'. Not only is the horror of the 'conquest' in the East disconnected from the colonial tradition that the Third Reich sought to revive and radicalize. It is explained on the basis of an international civil war in which, whatever the barbarism of the methods employed (under Asiatic and Bolshevik influence, moreover), Hitler ends up proving 'historically right'.[129]

---

128   Nolte, 'Weltbürgerkrieg 1789–1989?', p. 40.
129   Ernst Nolte, 'Der europäische Bürgerkrieg 1917–1945', Italian trans. in *Dopo il comunismo. Contributi all'interpretazione della storia del XX secolo*, trans. P. Sorge, Florence: Sansoni, 1992, pp. 41, 44–5.

Rather than being deprecated or analysed, the international civil war is proclaimed and declared, accompanied by condemnation of those who hesitate to register a terrible reality and fully commit themselves in the merciless struggle necessitated by it. We have seen Nolte deplore the USA's delay in participating in the struggle against the 'armed fanatics' of Moscow. The 1960s witnessed the development of anti-colonial movements and the emergence of the Third World, on the one hand, and the first steps towards 'peaceful coexistence', on the other, while the Sino-Soviet conflict split the 'socialist camp'. Yet Schmitt felt obliged to repeat his rigidly bipolar conception of the world: 'peace today is only a manifestation of real enmity. Enmity also does not cease in so-called cold war, which is not half war and half peace, but rather a situation of enmity with other than open violent means. Besides, only weaklings and illusionists are able to be deceived.'[130] Schmitt's repeated reference to Donoso Cortés is significant. During the 'European civil war of 1848', the latter, polemicizing against a chattering political class incapable of taking drastic decisions, bluntly called for a choice between 'Christ' and 'Barabbas'. Following in the footsteps of the Spanish author, Schmitt likewise excludes the Jacobins from the 'Christian West', summoning the latter to energetically confront Proudhon's 'satanism' and the 'abyss' represented by Marx.[131] Much more so than the Jacobins or Bolsheviks they denounce and sometimes analyse brilliantly, it is Schmitt and Nolte, like the authors admired by them, who express a crusading spirit and a Manichaean view of international conflicts.

Historical Revisionism, Neo-Liberalism and Anti-Colonial Revolution

Furet's judgement of the anti-colonial revolution is not very different from that of the two German authors. According to him, 'Mao, Ho Chi Minh, Castro, Guevara and, later, Ortega, the hero of "Sandinistan" Nicaragua', are not actors in major movements that have changed the face of the world, but bizarre cult objects of an 'exotic fanaticism'.[132] Here we have a further point of convergence between historical revisionism and neo-liberalism. An explicit

---

130   Schmitt, *Theory of the Partisan*, p. 60.
131   Carl Schmitt, *Dictatorship: From the Origin of the Modern Concept of Sovereignty to Proletarian Class Struggle*, trans. Michael Hoelzl and Graham Ward, Cambridge: Polity Press, 2014, p. xliv; Schmitt, *Donoso Cortés*, pp. 34–46, 81.
132   Furet, *The Passing of an Illusion*, p. 495.

rehabilitation of colonialism is ventured by the theoretician of the 'open society' himself. Popper seems to offer an unequivocally positive assessment of the centuries-long domination of the rest of humanity by the great European and Western powers: 'We freed these states too quickly and too simplistically.'[133] (The years when Arendt denounced the policy of genocide implemented by colonialism – in the Congo, for example – and identified colonial domination as the initial laboratory of totalitarian regimes seem far off.) To formulate his condemnation of anti-colonial revolutions, Paul Johnson employs the category applied by historical revisionism to other revolutions: abandonment of the royal road of gradualism, or, in this instance, a 'gradualist approach to self-rule'.[134] Once again, the rupture and the intro-duction of superfluous, disastrous violence are attributable to the revolutionary intellectual, 'the religious fanatic reincarnated as professional politician', who in this instance too proved himself 'the great destructive force of the twen-tieth century'.[135] In the revolution in Russia, as in the colonies or ex-colonies, we find the same intellectual and political strata in action:

> Lenin's Bolsheviks of 1917, Mao's CCP cadres of 1949 and the Congress-men of India came to power by different routes. But they had this in common. All three new ruling groups were men who had never engaged in any other occupation except politics and had devoted their lives to the exploitation of a flexible concept called 'democracy'.[136]

The contiguity of revolution and Nazism is even apparent in seemingly moderate anti-colonial movements: Gandhi 'was a year older than Lenin, with whom he shared a quasi-religious approach to politics, though in sheer crankiness he had much more in common with Hitler, his junior by twenty years'.[137]

Now, after the catastrophe, there is no alternative in 'a great many third-world countries' to the 'revival of colonialism' – indeed, an 'altruistic revival of colonialism': 'there is a moral issue here; the civilized world has a mission

---

133   Karl Popper, 'Kriege führen für den Frieden', interview in *Der Spiegel*, 23 March 1992, p. 208.

134   Paul Johnson, 'Colonialism's Back – and Not a Moment Too Soon', *New York Times Magazine*, 18 April 1993.

135   Paul Johnson, *Modern Times: The World from the Twenties to the Nineties*, New York: Harper Collins, 1991, p. 655.

136   Ibid., p. 470.

137   Ibid.

to go out to these desperate places and govern'. According to Johnson, intervention is required not only in countries that are incapable of self-government, but also in those self-governing countries which display a tendency to 'extremism'. Reagan was right to intervene in Grenada and overthrow its government.[138]

Even more important than the directly political positions adopted by it is the historical balance sheet that emerges from revisionist historiography. To a certain extent, colonial expansion was a 'reluctant and involuntary process', initiated with the voyages undertaken at the dawn of the modern age by Dutch, Portuguese and British merchants, who landed on the coasts of Africa in search of business.[139] Not so much as a vague reference to the slave trade. This enormous instance of repression is starkly apparent in the assertion that, with the Pale of Settlement imposed on Jews in Czarist Russia, we have 'the first modern exercise in social engineering, treating human beings (in this case the Jews) as earth or concrete, to be shovelled around'.[140] In reality, on the basis of the definition of social engineering offered here, it should be said that a key chapter in its history was the history of the domination of colonial populations. In fact, were account to be taken of the slave trade and the deportation of Native Americans, the USA would turn out to be the architect of the most colossal experiments in social engineering.

The rehabilitation of colonialism and the repression of its most tragic aspects also cast a shadow over the abolitionist revolution. In a familiar argument, revisionist historiography condemns it for interrupting a process of the gradual extinction of slavery, already in train, with Jacobin frenzy and superfluous violence; while liberal literature seems to ignore that revolution because it erases the ensuing tragedy from the historical record. This explains the habitual celebration of Calhoun as 'a strong individualist'.[141] But can such a definition be regarded as accurate in the case of an author who denied an individual character to blacks, who were condemned by him to perpetual slavery and degraded to the status of mere work tools? On other occasions, Calhoun is promoted to the rank of 'defen[der] of minority rights against the abuse of an overbearing majority';[142] to the status of theoretician of the

---

138 Johnson, 'Colonialism's Back', pp. 22, 43–4.
139 Ibid., pp. 43–4.
140 Paul Johnson, *A History of the Jews*, New York: Perennial Library, 1988, p. 358.
141 C. Gordon Post, Introduction to John C. Calhoun, *A Disquisition on Government*, New York: Liberal Arts Press, 1953, p. vii.
142 Ross M. Lence, Foreword to John C. Calhoun, *Union and Liberty*, ed. Lence, Indianapolis: Liberty Classics, 1992, p. xxiii.

moderation and self-limitation that should typify majorities.[143] What is forgotten is that his appeal to the majority for moderation was an appeal to central power not to interfere in the 'peculiar institution', which involved the white master's absolute, unbounded power over black slaves.

Repression of the colonial question makes it impossible to understand the Second Thirty Years' War adequately. We have noted Furet's thesis that the crimes 'perpetrated in the name of the proletarian revolution in the Soviet Union' far exceeded those of the Third Reich, 'until 1941'.[144] Let us linger for a moment over this comparison between two political movements, one of which gave impetus to the process of de-colonization, while the other was committed to containing and repulsing the 'inferior races' and to reviving the colonial tradition in Europe itself. Yet the contrast is made with the eve of Operation Barbarossa as its basis, as if the plans for colonial expansion into Eastern Europe already heralded by *Mein Kampf* could be expunged from Nazism! For the purposes of condemning the French Revolution, it is uncoupled from the abolition of slavery effected in the colonies and contrasted with an American Revolution wherein the fate of blacks and Native Americans has been repressed. To liquidate the 'proletarian revolution', the French historian first disconnects it from the anti-colonial movement which it promoted and then contrasts it with a Third Reich that he would like to purge of the colonial war of extermination. We have seen Hitler comparing the 'natives' of Eastern Europe to the 'redskins' of the Far West. Revisionist historiography impartially neglects both.

So deep-rooted and self-evident is the exclusion of the barbarians from the historical picture that Furet dates the start of the Second World War from 3 September 1939.[145] Not only are China, Ethiopia, and so forth not taken into account. Nor is Poland, invaded two days earlier. The Second World War began with Britain and France's declaration of war on Germany – that is, with the struggle between the Western great powers. Repression of the colonial question, and revisionist condemnation of the anti-colonial revolution, sets off a chain reaction. Why should we continue to regard Churchill as a hero of world history if, by dint of his anti-German intransigence, he ended up putting the colonial empire he sought to defend, and whose retention had been guaranteed by Hitler, into liquidation? Would it

---

143   See Giovanni Sartori, *Democrazia e definizioni*, Bologna: Il Mulino, 1976, p. 151, and *The Theory of Democracy Revisited*, New Jersey: Chatham, 1978, pp. 239, 252.

144   Furet, *The Passing of an Illusion*, pp. 357–8.

145   Ibid., Chapter 9.

not have been preferable to come to an arrangement with Germany, conceding it the colonial empire to which it too aspired? The fact is that, by erasing the colonial and national question, repressing the desperate resistance of the 'natives' of Eastern Europe and 'under-men' in general, and further repressing the struggle against any 'imperial race' that developed in the colonies in the wake of the 'master race's' defeat,[146] it becomes impossible to understand the great democratic, emancipatory significance of the Second World War.

The outbreak of the dreadful conflict could supposedly have been avoided by timely colonial concessions to Japan, Italy and Germany: thus argue prominent representatives of American revisionism. Because of its population growth, the land of the Rising Sun required its own area of expansion. Promoting the spread of capitalism and civilization in Asia, it played a positive role and, in any event, formed a bulwark against the Soviet threat.[147] Manchuria had never really been an integral part of China.[148] Japan merely aspired to an Asian Monroe Doctrine and to establish over a region crucial to its national security and economic space a control analogous to that exercised over Mexico by the USA. In both cases, the 'feelings' of the population or local politicians cannot be taken into account.[149] Ethiopia harboured an 'aggressive attitude' towards the African colonies of Italy, which needed to extend its territorial domains to find an outlet for a colossal flow of emigrants, whose access to the United States and other countries was denied or impeded by 'restrictive laws'.[150] As regards the Third Reich, even sectors of British diplomacy acknowledged the reasonableness of its request for the colonies lost at Versailles to be restored to it. Hitler even displayed a spirit of 'conciliation' over Eastern Europe, making proposals which on the very eve of war proved 'surprisingly moderate'.[151] It was Stalin who sowed discord and incited war between the capitalist countries.[152] Instead of encouraging a regional compromise, the USA proclaimed 'a crusade against aggressor nations' and unleashed 'economic warfare' first against Italy and then against

---

146   John Charmley, *Churchill: The End of Glory*, London: Hodder & Stoughton, 1993, p. 438.

147   Cf. Frank Paul Mintz, *Revisionism and the Origins of Pearl Harbor*, Boston and London: University Press of America, 1985, pp. 11–15, 59.

148   Charles C. Tansill, *Back Door to War: The Roosevelt Foreign Policy 1933–1941*, Chicago: Regnery, 1952, p. 137.

149   Ibid., p. 141.

150   Ibid., pp. 168–9.

151   Ibid., pp. 546, 548.

152   Harry E. Barnes, *Revisionism: A Key to Peace*, New York: Revisionist Press, 1973, pp. 19–20.

Japan.[153] It thereby played into the hands of the USSR, which encouraged China and Ethiopia in their intransigence and waved the banner of anti-colonialism in order to weaken capitalist enemies by turning them against one another.[154] It is no accident if the US historian Tansill, cited at some length here, ended his days engaged in the struggle against the second Reconstruction and defending racial segregation.[155]

The rehabilitation of colonialism, or repression of the colonial question, betokens the triumph of historical revisionism. On the other hand, interpreting the Second World War in accordance with the Entente's schema of democratic interventionism means legitimizing the idea of crusades and exporting revolution which historical revisionism denounces in Jacobinism and Bolshevism. And if the interpretation of the First World War as a crusade for democracy is rendered problematic or absurd by the presence in the anti-German alliance of Czarist Russia or Imperial Japan, interpretation of the Second World War in that key proves even less credible, given the alliance of the Western powers with a Soviet Union decidedly worse, according to historical revisionists, than the Third Reich itself.

---

153   Tansill, *Back Door to War*, p. 237.
154   Ibid., pp. 136, 197.
155   Warren I. Cohen, *The American Revisionists: The Lessons of Intervention in World War I*, Chicago and London: University of Chicago Press, 1967, p. 240.

CHAPTER FOUR

'White Civil War', 'International Civil War', the 'American Century' and the 'Second Thirty Years' War'

Historical Revisionism and the Two World Wars

Numerous historians refer to the two worlds wars as the Second Thirty Years' War. As early as 1905, as the contradictions between the great powers became ever more acute, Jaurès evoked the catastrophe of the seventeenth century, whose historical memory also disturbed Chancellor Bethmann-Hollweg on the immediate eve of the conflagration.[1] For an understanding of the twentieth century, the category of the Second Thirty Years' War proves much more satisfactory than that of international civil war. As in the twentieth century, so in the seventeenth, a struggle for hegemony and even, to a certain extent, the struggle of some countries for national independence was bound up with ideological (or religious) war.

Closely connected with the advance of revisionism, the success of the category of international civil war not only involves silence on the national and colonial question, but also obscures the conflict between the great powers, in a further simplification of the historical picture. In a remarkable contradiction, however, this was precisely the terrain on which the revisionist cultural and political current first proved itself. From the 1920s, a lively historiography developed in the USA which, under the watchword of 'revisionism', engaged in severe criticism of what one of its brilliant representatives, Charles A. Beard (who had earlier felt the appeal of Wilson's crusade), defined as the 'Sunday-school theory' of the war consecrated by the Versailles Treaty. 'Three pure and innocent boys' (Russia, France and Britain) were attacked by two brutes (Germany and Austria), who conspired to commit

---

1 Arno J. Mayer, *The Persistence of the Old Regime: Europe to the Great War*, London and New York: Verso, 2010, pp. 317–18.

'cruel deeds in the dark'.[2] But what role did Czarist Russia's push in the direction of the Straits, and France's chauvinism and its aspiration to recover Alsace and Lorraine at any cost, play in causing the conflagration? An ideological, Manichaean interpretation left no room for a reconstruction of the texture of geopolitical conflicts and rivalry for hegemony.

The Second World War became the occasion for a new, intense phase of revisionism. Was the attack on Pearl Harbor sufficient to explain US intervention? In reality, far from coming as a bolt from the blue, it was the wholly foreseeable – and possibly foreseen or even desired – result of a long tussle between the United States and Japan. In that tussle, Franklin Delano Roosevelt's initiative or provocation was considerable. Intent on playing an active role in the war, he was determined to force or provoke the Asian or European enemy to fire first, so that he could override the neutralist orientation of Congress and American public opinion. On closer examination, Pearl Harbor proves to be a kind of 'back door' taken by the US president to intervene against Germany (and Japan itself) and, ultimately, to participate in the great powers' competition for hegemony, acquitting the planetary mission with which he felt himself invested. Such is the main theme of a historical literature, published shortly after victory, which was felt on its appearance to be needlessly and provocatively debunking and anti-patriotic.[3]

In translation, some of these texts met with particular favour and interest in Germany, which subsequently became the protagonist of a second wave of historical revisionism. According to Hillgruber, after the outbreak of war in Europe, in which he had decided to intervene, Roosevelt sought to push Hitler into 'rash steps in an attempt to extricate himself from the dilemma of his difficulties with Congress'. As for the other front, given Japan's total dependence on imported oil, the embargo imposed by the US president confronted the Asian country 'in fact with the alternative of political capitulation to America or seizing raw materials in South-East Asia by force, unleashing an attack against the USA and its allies'. Such, allegedly, was the true origin of Pearl Harbor.[4]

---

2   Deborah E. Lipstadt, *Denying the Holocaust: The Growing Assault on Memory and Truth*, New York and Toronto: Free Press/Macmillan, 1993, p. 32.

3   George Morgenstern, *Pearl Harbor: The Story of the Secret War*, Newport: Institute for Historical Review, 1991; Charles C. Tansill, *Back Door to War: The Roosevelt Foreign Policy 1933–1941*, Chicago: Regnery, 1952.

4   Andreas Hillgruber, *Die Zerstörung Europas. Beiträge zur Weltkriegsepoche 1914 bis 1945*, Frankfurt am Main and Berlin: Ullstein/Propyläen, 1988, p. 284.

At stake here is the overall interpretation of the Second Thirty Years' War. While it finds expression in the title (*Crusade in Europe*) of the 1948 book by the supreme commander in Europe and future president, Eisenhower, the USA's official ideology was sharply challenged two years later by William Henry Chamberlin. He recalled how the 'first crusade' – proclaimed by Wilson – was not in fact the requisite response to bare-faced provocations by the Wilhelmine empire (the *Lusitania* was carrying munitions and the submarines that sank it were an understandable German counter to the British naval blockade). The fact is that 'Americans, more than any other people, have been inclined to interpret their involvement in the two great wars of the twentieth century in terms of crusades for righteousness.'[5]

In addition to constituting a mystification, such a view supposedly generates disastrous outcomes. *Perpetual War for Perpetual Peace* is the title of a collective volume edited in 1953 by Harry Elmer Barnes. It starts with the ideology developed by the Entente during the war that was supposed to end all wars and ensure peace, but which in reality, by criminalizing the alleged aggressors, ended up laying the bases of a new, more ruinous world war.[6] In this context, revisionism is represented as a prerequisite for establishing relations of mutual understanding and respect between the countries of the West, whose unity is dictated by the emergence of an Asiatic, brutal, menacing power whose image had been transformed by its decisive participation in the anti-fascist 'crusade'. These are theses to be found developed at the time in a suggestive historico-theoretical framework by Carl Schmitt, who began to move in this direction as early as the inter-war period. 'Revisionist' themes and ideas circulated on both sides of the Atlantic.

It is understandable that US historiography, along with its German counterpart, should be the main protagonist in the revisionist challenge. The USA is an absolutely privileged observation post. On the eve of the intervention in the First World War, it was the US ambassador in London, Walter Page, who telegraphed his government to note that 'it is not improbable that the only way of maintaining our preeminent trade position and averting a panic is by declaring war on Germany'. Immediately after the intervention, in a letter to Colonel House, Wilson wrote of his 'allies' as follows: 'When the war is over we can force them to our way of thinking, because by that time

---

5   William H. Chamberlin, *America's Second Crusade*, Chicago: Regnery, 1950, pp. 6, 3.

6   See Harry E. Barnes, ed., *Perpetual War for Perpetual Peace*, Idaho: Caldwell, 1953, and Barnes, *Revisionism: A Key to Peace*, New York: Revisionist Press, 1973.

they will, among other things, be financially in our hands.'[7] However, this did not prevent either the president, or his ambassador, from celebrating their country as the protagonist of 'a holy war – the holiest in all history', a veritable crusade suffused by divine light. Perhaps that is why Wilson seemed to Keynes in 1919 to be the 'greatest fraud on earth'.[8]

We cannot go on interpreting the two world wars identifying with the experience of the protagonists (or opponents) of the two crusades. Despite the persistence of myths created from 1914 onwards, certain results may now be regarded as established, courtesy, in the first instance, of American and Anglophone historiography in general, albeit that furthest removed from historical revisionism proper. Alluding to Wilson's thesis that in order to establish lasting or permanent peace, 'nations should with one accord adopt the doctrine of President Monroe as the doctrine of the world', Kissinger observes:

> Mexico was probably astonished to learn that the president of the country which had seized a third of its territory in the nineteenth century and had sent its troops into Mexico the preceding year was now presenting the Monroe Doctrine as a guarantee for the territorial integrity of sister nations and as a classic example of international cooperation.[9]

We find a similar impartiality in a book published in Britain in the mid-1950s, in which A.J.P. Taylor, mocking the ideology of democratic interventionism, comments as follows on the rebellion in Ireland during the First World War: it was 'the only national rebellion in any European country during the First World War – an ironical comment on the British claim to be fighting for freedom'.[10] Above all, in the very title of another work the British historian clarifies that what was involved was not a struggle between despotism and democracy, or militarism and the cause of peace, but a 'struggle for mastery': 'German power had increased vastly in the preceding generation, and her existing position in Europe no longer corresponded with her resources of

---

7   Quoted in Robert Skidelsky, *John Maynard Keynes – A Biography. Hopes Betrayed: 1883–1920*, London and Basingstoke: Macmillan, 1983, p. 336; Henry Kissinger, *Diplomacy*, New York: Simon & Schuster, 1994, p. 224.

8   Quoted in Skidelsky, *John Maynard Keynes*, p. 371.

9   Kissinger, *Diplomacy*, pp. 224, 235.

10   A.J.P. Taylor, *English History 1914–1945*, Oxford: Oxford University Press, 1965, p. 56.

power.'[11] Hence it is the change in the balance of power, economically, commercially and militarily, which explains the emergence and subsequent explosion of Anglo-German antagonism.

A fundamental work has been devoted to this subject by Paul Kennedy, whose concrete historical analysis once again ends up mocking the mythology of 'democratic interventionism'. What led to war was, primarily, an implacable objective dialectic: 'the Reich's booming overseas trade was more or less totally dependent upon British goodwill as its merchant ships steamed up and down the Suez Canal'.[12] Hence the Wilhelmine empire's intensive rearmament programme, which could not go unanswered:

> the impression left upon one after a study of the documents of both sides is the *absolute incompatibility* of British and German naval aims. What the Germans supporting Tirpitz desired, whether the vaguer 'world political freedom' or the more specific security for German commerce in the event of war, they could not have without affecting Britain's existing naval supremacy. What the latter in turn wished to preserve, command of those waters vital for her own safety as a maritime nation, would be impossible if Germany's goal was reached. What one power wanted, the other would never voluntarily concede; security for one meant danger to the other.[13]

Were the coalitions that clashed on the battlefields of the First World War significantly different in their political set-up at least? In reality, the alliance that cast itself as the protagonist of a crusade for democracy contained Czarist Russia and a Japan led by an emperor invested by a sacred aura and venerated as a god. Let us ignore these ideologically inconvenient allies. It is not clear why Germany in 1914, characterized as it was by a multi-party system and where the Reichstag at any rate was elected on the basis of male 'universal' suffrage, should be unequivocally regarded as less 'democratic' than Britain and the United States, where censitary or racial discrimination persisted. In particular, in the case of the North American republic we should note that blacks were widely excluded at the time from civil rights as well as political rights. They were subject to apartheid, semi-servile labour relations, and racist violence that not infrequently ended in lynching.

---

11   A.J.P. Taylor, *The Struggle for Mastery in Europe 1848–1918*, Oxford: Clarendon Press, 1954, p. 536.

12   Paul M. Kennedy, *The Rise of the Anglo-German Antagonism 1860–1914*, London and New York: Ashfield Press, 1987, p. 421.

13   Ibid., pp. 422–3.

If the situation in the New World was peculiar (in positive and negative senses), in the case of the old continent the two opposed alliances were largely homogeneous as regards internal structure and social relations. It is no coincidence if an eminent American historian has dated the real, definitive collapse of the aristocratic regime, which (notes a British historian) proved especially deep-rooted and dynamic in Britain, from the First World War.[14]

Even if we take the category of democracy in the sense of the limitation of power, we do not arrive at significantly different results. The thesis that Wilhelmine Germany was a semi-absolute monarchy does not withstand historical examination. It is contradicted by the vitality of the parliamentary and trade-union dialectic and the presence of a strong social-democratic party which, thanks to its ideological influence and ample diffusion and ramification (ensured by press organs, networks of cooperatives, etc.), became the reference-point for the European and international working-class movement. With the outbreak of war, it was the countries of the Entente, much more so than Germany, which effected an absolute centralization of political and economic power and seamless total mobilization. In the USA, in particular, pacifists and doubters were met with an iron fist much more relentlessly than in Germany; control of information and education of any kind was perfected. Post-war German culture and journalism were marked by amazement and chagrin at the superior capacity for total mobilization and iron regimentation of the population demonstrated by Germany's enemies, directed by leaders who were much more powerful than Wilhelm II or Nicholas II – in fact, vested with a panoply of historically unprecedented (or well-nigh unprecedented) powers. Nazism was also an attempt to remedy this unanticipated disadvantage; it was a kind of revitalization in anticipation and preparation for the second stage of the Second Thirty Years' War.[15]

The second stage displayed radically different characteristics. Very much present, rivalry between the great powers was nevertheless a secondary aspect of the gigantic conflict, which on the Third Reich's part was an attempt to cancel or repulse a secular historical process of emancipation. However, this is not a reason to stick with conventional images. Once again, American culture makes a significant contribution to their refutation. Let us read Kissinger. It was Roosevelt who imposed the 'test of strength' in Asia.[16]

---

14   Mayer, *The Persistence of the Old Regime*; David Cannadine, *The Decline and Fall of the British Aristocracy*, New Haven and London: Yale University Press, 1990, pp. 8–15.

15   See Domenico Losurdo, *Democrazia o bonapartismo*, Turin: Bollati Boringhieri, 1993, pp. 160–3.

16   Kissinger, *Diplomacy*, p. 377.

Imposing an embargo and demanding abandonment of previous conquests in return for its lifting, he 'must have known that there was no possibility that Japan would accept'. It would, and did, react emulating the model tried and tested during the war against Russia nearly forty years earlier. Something similar may be said of the other front: even before Pearl Harbor, 'to all practical purposes, America was at war on the sea with the Axis powers'. In engaging in a military conflict with the Third Reich, the US president, operating 'on the fringes of constitutionality', did not await a formal declaration of war by Hitler.[17]

Revisionist historiography compares Lincoln's policy of challenging and provoking the Confederacy with that adopted some decades later by Roosevelt towards Japan and Germany.[18] Albeit with the opposite value judgement, a similar thesis is found in Kissinger: 'like Lincoln, Roosevelt sensed that the survival of his country and its values was at stake, and that history itself would hold him responsible for the results of his solitary initiatives'.[19] The comparison between the two statesmen is commonplace today: it even constitutes the main theme of a collective volume to which the preface by David Eisenhower (nephew of the supreme commander in Europe and subsequent US president), and the dedication 'to the American soldiers of the Second World War', give something of an official flavour. Refusing to evacuate Fort Sumter, Lincoln sought to compel the Confederacy to fire the 'first shot', which 'would unite and galvanize the people of the North'. The oil embargo on Japan, and war measures in the Atlantic Ocean adopted by Roosevelt, 'hoping to goad Nazi submarines into attacking', corresponded to a similar design. The attacks on Fort Sumter and Pearl Harbor had the same effect: 'a rush of national adrenalin, a fusion of rage, energy, and principle into unparalleled unity'.[20] Hence the debt of gratitude which, in Kissinger's words, 'free peoples' have towards the two American presidents is similar.[21]

However, Truman and his administration constantly justified use of the atomic bomb by referring to the treacherous surprise attack on Pearl Harbor. In the light of reinterpretations of the outbreak of war in Asia, how is the

---

17   Ibid., pp. 392, 387.

18   Thus Tansill, quoted in Lipstadt, *Denying the Holocaust*, p. 40.

19   Kissinger, *Diplomacy*, p. 393.

20   Robert V. Bruce, 'Toward Sumter and Pearl: Comparing the Origins of the Civil War and World War II', in Gabor S. Boritt, ed., *War Comes Again: Comparative Vistas on the Civil War and World War II*, New York and Oxford: Oxford University Press, 1995, pp. 24–9.

21   Kissinger, *Diplomacy*, p. 393.

horror of Hiroshima and Nagasaki now to be justified? Especially given that, at least according to eminent American historians, the erasure of the two cities and their populations from the face of the earth would not appear to have answered to any real military exigency; utterly defeated, Japan was already set to surrender. We can now understand the emergence of a Japanese revisionism involving not just historians, but also, in the front rank, the cities of Hiroshima and Nagasaki, which have long vainly sought from successive American administrations, if not apologies, then at least an expression of regret for 'us[ing] a genocidal weapon on innocent non-combatants'.[22]

The Roosevelt who emerges from the most recent American historiography is a president who, operating on the fringes of constitutional legality and sometimes violating it, led the country to intervene not only to defeat Nazism, but also on the basis of clear 'imperial ambitions': his 'democratic and capitalist ideology had always been expansive in nature'.[23] In 1914, the year that signalled the start of the Second Thirty Years' War, the future president wrote: 'Our national defense must extend all over the western hemisphere, must go out a thousand miles into the sea, must embrace the Philippines and over the sea wherever our commerce may be.'[24] Not by chance, as a young man his 'admiration' for his cousin – the 'herald of modern American militarism and imperialism',[25] Theodore Roosevelt – 'knew no bounds';[26] and he attentively read Mahan, the major US theoretician of geopolitics and the strategic importance of a navy and naval bases.[27] 'Long before the famous destroyer-for-bases deal of 1940', Roosevelt 'expressed an interest' in acquiring British bases in Caribbean. He consistently and lucidly aimed at winning world leadership,[28] thus defeating Germany but also supplanting Great Britain. War preparations, massive rearmament in peacetime, and subsequent intervention in the war were constitutive elements of a strategy encapsulated in the slogan of the 'American century',

22   Gar Alperovitz, *The Decision to Use the Atomic Bomb and the Architecture of an American Myth*, New York: Knopf, 1995, p. 565.

23   Robert E. Herzstein, *Roosevelt and Hitler: Prelude to War*, New York: Paragon House, 1989, pp. 247, 293.

24   Robert Dallek, *Franklin D. Roosevelt and American Foreign Policy 1932–1945*, New York and Oxford: Oxford University Press, 1995, p. 9.

25   Richard Hofstadter, *The American Political Tradition and the Men Who Made It*, New York: A. Knopf, 1967, p. 207.

26   Ibid., p. 6.

27   Herzstein, *Roosevelt and Hitler*, pp. 351, 411; Dallek, *Franklin D. Roosevelt and American Foreign Policy*, p. 7.

28   Herzstein, *Roosevelt and Hitler*, pp. 288, 294.

which was desired and celebrated even before the attack on Pearl Harbor by Henry Luce, who controlled a news empire and who, though a Republican, was a fervent supporter of Roosevelt's interventionist foreign policy.[29]

The American century dawned with the eclipse of the British century. Thus, the emergence of revisionist tendencies in Britain as well becomes intelligible. The US president's opposite number was Churchill, who regarded 'the Americans as a branch of the "English-Speaking Peoples"'. In fact, however, 'they were . . . foreigners who disliked the British Empire even more than did Hitler', and who transformed Great Britain into a kind of US 'protectorate'.[30] Perhaps things would have gone differently if Britain had pursued a policy of compromise with Hitler, who was always a fervent admirer of the British Empire . . .

The Drama of German Culture: From Weber to Nolte and Hillgruber

When it comes to assessing the Second Thirty Years' War, German culture finds itself in a difficult position. On the one hand, a tradition combining lucid attention to the material and geopolitical dimension of what was at stake in the two world wars with a tendency to historiographical (if not specifically political) revanchism remains dynamic. While the guns were still firing, Weber mocked the self-styled democratic interventionism of the Entente. He highlighted how in America – the country now at the head of the anti-German coalition and crusade – blacks, excluded from political rights, were subject to a meticulous regime of racial segregation and targeted by laws strictly prohibiting mixed marriages.[31] But it was above all during the discussion of war 'guilt' either side of Versailles that Weber stressed the presence of a 'war ideology' in the USA as well – in particular, among the 'best layers of "young" America'. In fact, in 1904 an eminent US scholar had given credence to the 'theory' of 'the alleged need for a war for trade' that had spread to every country, but which was 'completely wrong'. Indeed, in Veblen's book one could 'read the gleeful conclusion that the time was coming when it would once again become a sound business view to wrest

29   Ibid., pp. 340, 358.

30   John Charmley, *Churchill: The End of Glory*, London: Hodder & Stoughton, 1993, pp. 429–30, 431, 440.

31   Max Weber, *Zur Politik im Weltkrieg. Schriften und redden 1914–1918*, ed. W.J. Mommsen with G. Hübinger, Tübingen: Mohr, 1988, p. 354.

world trade from one another through war, so that a warlike spirit would be revived and a sense of dignity substituted for squalid money-making'.[32] Not by chance, Weber was among the first to signal the advent of what would two decades later be called the 'American century': the irresistible rise of a power set on conquering 'economic supremacy' and 'world power' in the footsteps of ancient Rome.[33]

However, a capacity to demystify the Manichaean character of the interpretation ventured by the victors of the First World War was not matched by a self-critical evaluation of the history of German imperialism. This was despite the fact that Weber, as the similarly gratified late-nineteenth-century prophet of an imminent end to the 'intermezzo of seemingly peaceful competition' between the great powers, was certainly no stranger to that history.[34] Focusing on the conflict with Czarist Russia, the great sociologist continued to vindicate Germany. Had not German social-democracy itself acknowledged that 'a war against *this* system was a just war'?[35] Indeed, a war aimed at the '*destruction of Czarism*' was a 'good war'.[36] Criticized on the part of the Entente, democratic interventionism was wholly legitimate in the case of the Second Reich's Eastern campaign. Yet this ideology ends up being refuted by Weber himself, when he declares: 'We have destroyed Czarism, but the confrontation with the East will never end.'[37] Rather than to a political system, the eternal character of the struggle theorized here seems to refer to geopolitics or, worse, the antithesis of Slavs and Germans. At all events, the subject of Weber's self-critical reflection was not the war against France, traditionally interested in having 'a weak neighbour',[38] let alone that — inevitable and just — against Russia: 'our misfortune was and is that this war has also become a war against the West, against the Anglo-Saxon world'.[39]

It is true that in the heat of the controversy over war 'guilt' and 'atrocities', Weber did not hesitate to denounce the 'manifestly illegal' and

---

32   Max Weber, *Gesammelte politische Schriften*, ed. J. Winckelmann, Tübingen: Mohr (Siebeck), 1971, pp. 495, 585; Weber, *Zur Politik im Weltkrieg*, p. 44.

33   Wolfgang J. Mommsen, *Max Weber. Gesellschaft, Politik und Geschichte*, Frankfurt am Main: Suhrkamp, 1974, pp. 92–3.

34   On Weber and imperialism, cf. Losurdo, *Democrazia o bonapartismo*, pp. 176–80.

35   Weber, *Gesammelte politische Schriften*, p. 492.

36   Quoted in Wolfgang J. Mommsen, *Max Weber und die deutsche Politik, 1890–1920*, Tübingen: Mohr (Siebeck), 1974, p. 528.

37   Weber, *Zur Politik im Weltkrieg*, p. 356.

38   Weber, *Gesammelte politische Schriften*, p. 492.

39   Weber, *Zur Politik im Weltkrieg*, p. 356.

inhumane 'British naval blockade', which had claimed 'around 750,000' victims among the German civilian population.[40] Yet the basic historiographical and political project was to repair the deplorable divide between Germany and the Anglo-Saxon countries and restore the unity of the civilized world, putting Czarist and then Bolshevik Russia in the dock. The same tendency is evident in Schmitt. Immediately after the First World War, he condemned Britain's 'maritime war' and 'naval blockade' as a form of total war, which cancelled 'the continental distinction between combatants and non-combatants' and indiscriminately hit 'the entire population of the area under blockade'.[41] Denunciation of tendencies to 'a sheer war of destruction'[42] was resumed after the Second World War and extended to the conduct of the Anglo-American air force. Yet Schmitt principally pointed an accusing finger at the revolutionary tradition culminating in the Bolshevik October. It was to be regarded as responsible for the advent of total war and for the massacres and genocides that marked the twentieth century. Germany's Western enemies were above all culpable of undermining the *jus publicum europaeum* and the unity of the genuinely civilized world.

Naturally, critical references to Dresden are also to be found in Nolte, who in fact underscores an 'openly and explicitly genocidal' intention on the part of Churchill, who in April 1941 declared: 'There are less than seventy million malignant Huns – some of whom are curable and others killable – many of whom are already engaged in holding down Austrians, Czechs, Poles, French, and the many other ancient races they now bully and pillage.'[43] To substantiate his thesis, the German historian translates 'others' by 'die Anderen', as if all the others, with the exception of a few salvageable Germans, were to be killed. Yet despite this highly forced reading (even if it is clear from the context that Churchill had in mind a drastic thinning out of the 'Huns'), Nolte once again focuses his denunciation on Asiatic and Bolshevik barbarism. Compression of the multiple aspects of the Second Thirty Years' War into the category of international civil war also has the function of demonstrating that the sole real contradiction of these decades

---

40 Weber, *Gesammelte politische Schriften*, p. 494.

41 Carl Schmitt, *Positionen und Begriffe im Kampf mit Weimar-Genf-Versailles 1932–1939*, Berlin: Duncker & Humblot, 1988, p. 238; Schmitt, *Verfassungsrechtliche Aufsätze*, Berlin: Duncker & Humblot, 1985, p. 382ff.

42 Carl Schmitt, *The Nomos of the Earth in the International Law of the Jus Publicum Europaeum*, trans. G.L. Ulmen, New York: Telos Press, 2006, p. 317.

43 Winston Churchill, *Complete Speeches 1897–1963*, Vol. VI, New York and London: Chelsea House, 1974, p. 6384 (speech of 27 April 1941); Ernst Nolte, *Der europäische Bürgerkrieg 1917–1945*, Frankfurt am Main and Berlin: Ullstein, 1987, p. 503.

opposed the West as a whole (including Germany) to Communism. It then becomes difficult to explain the fact that until Operation Barbarossa the Second World War did not involve the Soviet Union. The German historian tends to get himself off the hook by pointing up the 'paradoxical' character of such developments.[44]

Hillgruber can be situated in the same context. True, he draws attention to the fact that it was the British government which pushed 'for a general transfer of the population of the eastern German territories and the Sudetenland'; it was the Under-Secretary of State Sargent who hypothesized 'the transfer of the Germans of eastern Prussia and Upper Silesia to Siberia'. We even encounter a glimpse of Stalin reluctantly acceding 'to Benes' pressure for the expulsion of the Sudeten Germans from a restored Czechoslovakia'.[45] However, such details prove irrelevant when it comes to an overall assessment: barbarism is once again located exclusively outside the West to which Germany hopes to be ultimately readmitted with full honours. Such is the main theme of German historical revisionism in general. On the other hand, praise and acknowledgement of Nolte do not prevent Furet, as historian of the twentieth century, identifying with the experience of the anti-German crusade. And as with conflicts between the great powers, so with possible conflicts between the various revisionisms, attempts are made to resolve them, restoring the unity of the West and denouncing the oriental Bolshevik October.

It is the history of the USSR that must be rewritten. In recent years, there has been no shortage of books committed to demonstrating that Operation Barbarossa slightly preceded a planned attack on Germany by Stalin.[46] But this thesis risks undermining a key count in the indictment of the Bolshevik Revolution, which according to Furet resulted in a regime that proved a loyal ally of Hitler to the end. Perhaps in order to avoid such contradictions, historical revisionism prefers to follow a different line of argument. It seeks to show that the USSR's war against Germany was similar to that launched by the Third Reich with Operation Barbarossa: the Soviet counter-offensive in Eastern Europe spared neither prisoners nor the civilian population. According to Hillgruber, rather than to some desire for revenge, all this seems to 'come down . . . to the Soviet way of conceiving war', with its inherently 'barbaric' character.[47]

---

44   See Luciano Canfora, *Marx vive a Calcutta*, Bari: Dedalo, 1992, p. 96.

45   Hillgruber, *Die Zerstörung Europas*, p. 365.

46   See Joachim Hoffmann, *Stalins Vernichtungskrieg 1941–1945*, Munich: Verlag für Wehrwissenschaften, 1995, pp. 18–64.

47   Andreas Hillgruber, *Zweierlei Untergang. Die Zerschlagung des Deutschen Reiches und das*

The aprioristic character of such assertions is immediately apparent from the fact that there is no hint of a comparative analysis either of the other fronts in the Second World War, or the behaviour of anti-Bolshevik, collaborationist Russian troops, who in Carnia for example sowed terror.[48] Above all, any comparison with the conduct of the Czarist army in eastern Prussia during the First World War is lacking. On 23 August 1914, a collaborator of Ludendorff noted in his diary: 'There has never been, and no doubt will never again be, a war like this – fought with such bestial fury. The Russians are burning down everything.'[49] Still less do we find in Hillgruber a self-critical reflection on pre-Hitlerite Germany's contribution to the interpretation of the life-and-death struggle in the East in a racial key. On the eve of the First World War, Wilhelm II foresaw a 'final battle between the Slavs and the Germans'; 'it is not a major political problem, but a racial issue . . . It involves the existence or non-existence of the Germanic race in Europe.'[50] Even the objectives to be pursued were out of the ordinary. The Second Reich aimed to 'provoke the break-up of Russia so as to drive our eastern neighbour back inside borders predating those established by Peter the Great'.[51] After the Brest-Litovsk peace treaty and the onset of the Civil War, influential circles in the Wilhelmine empire sought a further extension of territorial conquests and even the disintegration of Russia as a whole. For Wilhelm II, 'peace is not in fact possible between Slavs and Germans'.[52] Such was the programme subsequently inherited and radicalized by Hitler.

Moreover, Hillgruber's thesis is refuted by the very collection of documents to which he refers.[53] The reality of particular massacres certainly transpires from them. But we also find appeals to soldiers from the Soviet political and military authorities to respect prisoners and the civilian population, avoiding 'behaviour unworthy of the Red Army'. There are frequent warnings of the need to make distinctions on the enemy side, bearing in mind that 'our task is to get the soldier of the German army to side with

---

Ende des europäischen Judentums, Berlin: Wolf Jobst Siedler Verlag, 1986. Cf. also Hoffman, *Stalins Vernichtungskrieg 1941–1945*.

48   Mario Rigioni Stern, Introduction to Leonardo Zanier, *Carnia, Kosakenland, Kazackaja, Zemlja*, Udine: Mittelcultura, 1996.

49   Quoted in Martin Gilbert, *The First World War: A Complete History*, New York: Henry Holt and Company, 1994, p. 49.

50   Quoted in Fritz Fischer, *Griff nach der Weltmach. Die Kriegzielpolitik des kaiserlichen Deutschland 1914/18*, Düsseldorf: Droste Verlag, 1971, pp. 40–1.

51   Ibid., p. 144.

52   Quoted in ibid., p. 781.

53   Hillgruber, *Zweierlei Untergang*, p. 102 n. 9.

the Red Army'. As the editor of the collection remarks, there was indeed a marked discrepancy between instructions from above and actual behaviour on the battlefield and in the occupied territories.[54] But it remains the case that in early February 1945 the Soviet authorities 'made every effort to check the vengeful fury of their troops', who, crossing through 'the most lacerated provinces of Europe's Second Thirty Years' War',[55] were confronted with a spectacle which (as we shall see) caused Roosevelt to say that he felt 'more bloodthirsty than ever toward the Germans'. As regards the Soviet soldiers, there was an aspect of personal revenge on the part of recently recruited peasants, a high percentage of whom had had relatives killed, tortured or deported as slaves by the invaders. It was not a policy of extermination: 'Russian barbarities' were met by the high command with sometimes 'ferocious' repression, which consigned those responsible to 'penal battalions'.[56]

On the other hand, Hillgruber himself reveals that in the First World War – and before the October Revolution – the 'idea of an ethnic-racial re-composition of territory' emerged 'during the nationality struggles on the periphery of Europe'.[57] Why, then, refer to 'the Soviet way of conceiving war', unless for the ideological purposes of equating Nazi 'barbarism' and Soviet 'barbarism'? In truth, the clear difference between the two emerges from the picture drawn by the German historian. Hitler aimed at 'building a German empire in the East, on the ruins of the USSR, by exterminating the Bolshevik ruling class, decimating the Slav masses, and systematically eliminating the Jews'.[58] In contrast, the 'veritable battle for survival' imposed on the USSR pushed Stalin 'to seek security via an eastwards expansion of Soviet territory and a sort of inversion of the "cordon sanitaire" established by Western powers in 1919–20 out of hostility to the USSR'.[59] Although pursued with all manner of brutality, the objective of integrating Germany into Moscow's sphere of influence had nothing in common with the project of reducing the 'natives' of Eastern Europe to the status of 'redskins'.

---

54   Alfred M. de Zayas, ed., *Die Wehrmachtuntersuchungsstelle. Deutsche Ermittlungen über alliierte Völkerrechtsverletzungen im zweiten Weltkrieg*, Munich: Universitas, 1984, pp. 287–9.

55   Arno J. Mayer, *Why Did the Heavens Not Darken? The Final Solution in History*, London: Verso, 2012, p. 422.

56   Christopher Duffy, *Red Storm on the Reich: The Soviet March on Germany, 1945*, New York: Atheneum, 1991, pp. 273–5.

57   Hillgruber, *Zweierlei Untergang*, p. 67.

58   Ibid., p. 45.

59   Ibid., p. 56.

It makes no sense to accuse the regime produced by the October Revolution of appealing for international civil war and, at the same time, for a war of racial annihilation. These two types of conflict are radically different; underlying them are two types of de-specification that must not be confused. The boundary between politico-moral de-specification and naturalistic de-specification is labile and was clearly crossed in some appeals that dehumanized the German people as such. But what we have here is the influence of an old cultural and political tradition, rather than of the ideology of war generated by October. We shall see the systematic efforts made by the Soviet side to attract the maximum number of enemy soldiers, officers and even generals. Triggering civil war in Germany presupposed its trans-versal division, not its configuration as a single accursed mass. Even Nolte is obliged to acknowledge 'a merit of Soviet Communism':

> Only for a brief period was the war depicted in what is today called 'racist' form – Slavs against Germans. It fairly soon reverted to a depic-tion wherein the German people contained National Socialists or fascists, anti-fascists, non-National Socialists and anti-National Socialists. The subject to be dealt with was National Socialism or perhaps the monopoly capitalism behind it. This was a historical representation, whereas in the West, curiously and paradoxically, a kind of replica of the image fostered by National Socialism emerged, according to which the subjects were peoples. The Allies' war literature also proceeded thus: from Arminius to Hitler, from Luther to Hitler, etc.[60]

In her turn, a historian opposed to revisionism condemns Communists for having taught that 'it was the fascists (not Germans) who killed Communists (not Jews)', therewith abolishing the 'specifically Jewish' nature of the trag-edy that occurred under the Third Reich.[61] We shall soon see the problematic, even arbitrary, character of this claim. Albeit with a decidedly negative value judgement, however, it acknowledges that Marx's lesson in concrete analysis impeded or prevented identifying the Germans with the Nazis.

With his insistence on the objective characteristics of imperialism, Lenin had already refused to attribute the outbreak of the First World War exclu-sively to an imaginary German people, massively and consistently militaristic

---

60   Martin Schmidt and Dieter Stein, *Im Gespräch mit Ernst Nolte*, Potsdam: Junge Freiheit, 1993, p. 29.

61   Lipstadt, *Denying the Holocaust*, p. 7.

and bellicose throughout its history. One fact is especially significant. Although the Bolshevik leader regarded the Brest-Litovsk peace as rapacious, he compared Soviet Russia's struggle against German imperialism to the struggle against Napoleon's invasion and the occupation waged by Prussia, albeit that it was led by the Hohenzollerns, while Napoleon was in turn defined as 'another plunderer like the Hohenzollerns'.[62] The line of demarcation between progress and reaction, and between forces of peace and forces of war, is not definable once and for all; at all events, it never coincides with an ethnic boundary. What is required is concrete analysis of a concrete situation. If, amid the lightning victories of the Wilhelmine army, Lenin evoked the possibility of wars of national liberation against German imperialism in Europe itself, he subsequently denounced the national oppression suffered by the German people. With its economic clauses and exclusive attribution of war guilt to Germany, the Versailles Treaty seemed to the Bolshevik leader even more vindictive and ferocious than Brest-Litovsk. Hence it was an expression of the imperialist rapacity that the Entente powers regarded as an intrinsic characteristic of Germans or Huns. There is no place in Lenin's conceptual universe for the racialization of the Germans as Huns and Vandals which, as we shall see, was diffused among Germany's Western enemies.

On the other hand, the revolutionary break shattered the unity of Russian history: the first fascist squads – the white guards – were compared by Lenin with the Black Hundreds – that is, the armed reactionary groups in Czarist Russia. In the wake of this lesson in historical concreteness, after Hitler's arrival in power Kirov denounced 'German fascism, with its pogrom ideology, its anti-Semitism, its views on higher and lower races' as the inheritor of the Russian Black Hundreds.[63] Not even Hitler's invasion repaired the break in Russian history. Notwithstanding the untold losses and suffering caused by the aggression, and despite the fact that the latter seemed to go back directly to the Teutonic knights, who were explicitly invoked in *Mein Kampf*,[64] despite all this, Stalin was not in fact inclined to racialize Germans en bloc. In February 1942, he declared that 'it would be ludicrous to identify Hitler's clique with the German people, with the German state. The

---

62   V.I. Lenin, *Collected Works*, London: Lawrence & Wishart, 1960–, Vol. 27, pp. 187, 105–6.

63   Quoted in Robert C. Tucker, *Stalin in Power: The Revolution from Above, 1928–1941*, New York and London: Norton, 1990, p. 258.

64   See Adolph Hitler, *Mein Kampf*, trans. Ralph Mannheim, London: Pimlico, 1992, p. 128 and n. 1.

experience of history indicates that Hitlers come and go, but the German people and the German state remain.'[65] Stalin was so little inclined to equate the history of Germany with the Third Reich that, although he issued an impassioned appeal for national unity in the 'patriotic war' against the invaders, he denounced the Nazi regime as the continuator in certain crucial respects of the Czarism overthrown by the Russian Revolution:

> In point of fact the Hitler regime is a copy of that reactionary regime which existed in Russia under tsardom. It is well known that the Hitlerites suppress the rights of the workers, the rights of the intellectuals and the rights of nations as readily as the tsarist regime suppressed them, and that they organize medieval Jewish pogroms as readily as the tsarist regime organized them.
>
> The Hitlerite party is a party of enemies of democratic liberties, a party of medieval reaction and Black-Hundred pogroms.[66]

This was not an isolated point. The Nazis were repeatedly branded as the 'heroes of pogroms', who vainly sought to camouflage or embellish their 'reactionary pogromist character'.[67] Whatever our political and moral judgement of Stalin, it remains the case that, with Lenin's lesson in mind, he stressed that the genesis and modality of war 'cannot be explained by the

---

65   Marshal Stalin, *On the Great Patriotic War of the Soviet Union*, London, New York and Melbourne: Hutchinson, n.d. [1944], p. 27. Unsubstantiated is the thesis that, 'during World War Two', Stalin declared 'the entire German people an enemy of socialism and the Soviet peoples': Roman Rosdolsky, 'Friedrich Engels und das Problem der "geschichtslosen Völker"', *Archiv für Sozialgeschichte*, Vol. IV, 1964, p. 149 n. 11.

66   Stalin, *On the Great Patriotic War of the Soviet Union*, p. 16.

67   J.V. Stalin, *Über den Grossen Vaterländischen Krieg der Sowjetunion*, Frankfurt am Main: Dokumente der Kommunistichen Weltbewegung, 1972, p. 137. Without troubling to support his assertion in any way, Furet declares: 'after the advent of Nazism, Stalin had never shown the least compassion for the Jews' (*The Passing of an Illusion*, trans. Deborah Furet, Chicago and London: University of Chicago Press, 1999, p. 382). In fact, as regards the years under analysis here, the denunciation of anti-Semitism played an important and, in one instance, even a lethal role in the positions adopted by the Soviet leadership. At Katyn, as we shall see, Polish officers were massacred as 'anti-Semites'. Ardent anti-Communism possibly leads the representative of revisionism to confuse different historical periods in the relations between the Soviet Union and the world of Jewry. At the end of the war, the USSR enjoyed such great sympathy from 'Zionists the world over' that the latter went so far as 'to admire all things Russian'. The author of this observation is Arendt who, as late as May 1948, deplored the pro-Soviet orientation of the Zionist movement, which was inclined to condemn Britain and the United States as 'anti-Semitic' (Hannah Arendt, *Essays und Kommentare*, ed. E. Geisel and K. Bittermann, Berlin: Tiamat, 1989, Vol. II, pp. 36, 88–90).

personal characteristics of the Japanese and the Germans'.[68] When, towards the end of the war, the writer Ehrenburg, getting carried away, asserted that the Germans were 'all one gang', *Pravda* intervened firmly to condemn such stereotypes and recall the Soviet leader's declaration of August 1942.[69] This stance may well have answered to diplomatic calculations and propaganda exigencies, but it does not thereby lose its significance.

The Drama of German Culture: From Schumpeter to Habermas

Running alongside, and in contrast to, the historiographical and cultural tradition issuing in the revisionism of Nolte and Hillgruber, there is a different tradition. It is characterized by the illusion of promoting Germany's democratic, anti-bellicose regeneration by accepting the ideology of the victors in subaltern fashion. In the defeated Central Powers in the years immediately following 1918, liberal circles or those close to social-democracy, desirous in the latter case of drawing a veil over their approval of war credits and of countering Lenin's influence, seemed to rally to the cause of the 'democratic interventionism' of the Entente, and especially the USA and UK. The great Russian revolutionary had identified the causes of the First World War in the objective dialectic of capitalism and rivalry between the great imperialist powers. So here we have Kautsky and Hilferding underlining the radical differences between the Anglo-American world and Germany. While the former, with particular reference to Wilson, is transfigured in a 'pacifist' key, the latter is branded as the sole true locus of militarism, as well as a cult of the state and the 'impulse' harboured by it to 'assert and expand its power'.[70]

This view was given its most complete 'scientific' formulation by Joseph Schumpeter, Austrian Finance Minister in 1919–20. According to him, far from pertaining to the 'highest stage of capitalism' as Lenin had argued, imperialism was an expression of backwardness and pre-capitalist survivals. The United States supposedly demonstrated this unequivocally. It could easily have annexed Canada or Mexico and other vast areas of the Western hemisphere. Instead, it remained stubbornly loyal to its peaceful vocation. Thus an edifying

---

68   Stalin, *Über den Grossen Vaterländischen Krieg der Sowjetunion*, p. 192.

69   See Isaac Deutscher, *Stalin: A Political Biography*, New York: Oxford University Press, 1967, p. 539; Giuseppe Boffa, *Storia dell'Unione Sovietica*, Milan: Mondadori, 1979, Vol. II, pp. 273–4.

70   See Domenico Losurdo, *La catastrophe della Germania e l'immagine di Hegel*, Milan: Guerini, 1987, Chapter 2, §12.

picture emerges of the foreign policy of a great power which, in the time frame considered by Schumpeter, did not hesitate to theorize the necessity and beneficial character of a policy of the 'big stick'. Clearly, repeated US military interventions in Latin America are not to be included in the category of war; and the great economist has no inkling that Lenin identified and denounced such omission as typical of the arrogance of imperialism, which wages 'a number of wars, which were not regarded as wars because very often they amounted to sheer massacres, when European and American imperialist troops, armed with the most up-to-date weapons of destruction, slaughtered the unarmed and defenceless inhabitants of colonial countries'.[71]

It would be easy to set against Schumpeter's thesis the much more realistic assessment made by Anglo-American authors. Kissinger refers to US policy in Latin America with a quite distinct impartiality. On the other hand, we have seen Veblen, alluded to by Weber, examining the relationship between wars to conquer markets and capitalist economic calculation. Underlying such analysis was experience of the inter-meshing in the USA between industrial development and diffusion of the martial spirit. In 1895, having celebrated his country as the architect of 'a record of conquest, colonization and expansion unequalled by any people in the Nineteenth Century', the influential US Senator Henry Cabot Lodge demanded a further powerful forward thrust: 'From the Rio Grande to the Arctic Ocean there should be but one flag and one country . . . For the sake of our commercial supremacy in the Pacific we should control the Hawaiian Islands and maintain our influence in Samoa.'[72]

Thus was ushered in the 'American century', which was in the process of supplanting the century that had seen Great Britain as hegemon in terms of industrial development and colonial expansion alike. In the mid-nineteenth century, a British liberal, Richard Cobden, observed self-critically:

We have been the most combative and aggressive community that has existed since the days of the Roman dominion. Since the Revolution of 1688 we have expended more than fifteen hundred millions of money upon wars, not one of which has been upon our own shores, or in defence of our hearths and homes . . . this pugnacious propensity has been invariably recognized by those who have studied our national character.[73]

---

71   Lenin, *Collected Works*, Vol. 31, p. 216 and Vol. 24, p. 400.
72   Quoted in Walter Millis, *The Martial Spirit*, Chicago: Elephant Books, 1989, p. 27.
73   Quoted in Daniel Pick, *War Machine: The Rationalisation of Slaughter in the Modern Age*, New Haven: Yale University Press, 1993, p. 21.

In these authors there is no trace of the transfiguration of the Anglo-American world and developed industrial society that is so evident in Schumpeter. The latter presumes to demonstrate the inherently pacific nature of capitalism from its supposed refusal to establish 'professional armies'. The very country taken as a model by Schumpeter is today characterized by its formidable military potential, which can count on professional soldiers ready to intervene in any part of the world to bomb it back to the Stone Age. But the most astonishing thing is this. Obliged to acknowledge the presence of non-pacifist forces in the USA, Schumpeter disposes of them by attributing them to pre-capitalist survivals represented by immigrants from the most backward countries of Europe![74] Thus, at the heart of a 'scientific' explanation of imperialism are, in fact, national stereotypes. Furthermore, they immediately turn out to be incoherent. We need only recall that European immigrants swelled the ranks of the socialist and pacifist movement in the United States and that, in denouncing the expansionism of his country in the mid-nineteenth century, Cobden reproved the 'national character' of the English, who formed the original stock of the North American republic.

It might be said that the USA is analysed and appraised by Schumpeter on the basis not of objective political and social relations, but of the apologetic self-image with which it has traditionally transfigured its reality and activity on the international political scene. Similar considerations might be applied to such authors as Hayek, Mises and Popper (likewise intellectuals of Austrian origin who, having arrived in the coveted Anglo-Saxon world, celebrated it with the zeal of converts). To see that this is the case, we need only compare their judgements of the role of Britain and the USA in the two world wars with those we have read in authors like Taylor and Kissinger, not to mention Keynes, at times scornful of Wilson.

In a way, the internalization of the victors' ideology seems to make itself felt even in contemporary German historiography and culture. Although it has the merit of incontrovertibly refuting the pitiful legend of the Second Reich's involuntary, imperceptible slide into the tragedy of the First World War, Fritz Fischer's weighty monograph, published in the early 1960s, makes the mistake of always declining imperialism in the singular, as if the German variety alone were operative,[75] and as if Germany (including Hitlerite Germany) had not constantly looked to the model represented by the British

---

74 Joseph A. Schumpeter, *Imperialism and Social Classes*, trans. Heinz Norden, New York: A.M. Kelly, 1951, p. 72.

75 See Fischer, *Griff nach der Weltmacht*.

Empire with envy and admiration! Habermas must be located in the same context. His sharp polemic against historical revisionism proceeds under the sign of the celebration of 'Western life forms'.[76] Without intending to, the philosopher coincides here with Nolte, more zealously committed than anyone to demonstrating the Oriental, Asiatic character of Nazism. And in both we once again note repression of the influence of the Western colonial tradition – especially the Anglo-Saxon variant – on Hitler's imperial plans and war of extermination in the East.

The War in Asia: Whites and Non-White Populations

While Hillgruber denounces the 'barbarism' with which the 'Soviet' war was conducted, Nolte is obliged to acknowledge that elements of racialization of the German people were much more widespread among its Western enemies than in the USSR. In reality, this is a 'merit' entailed by the international civil war and revolutionary tradition branded by him as the root of all evil. Where this tradition was inactive, or weak, naturalistic de-specification of the enemy encountered few obstacles. This was demonstrated during the war between Japan and the USA. The war crimes committed by the Japanese are well known. In retaliation for the indiscriminate bombing of their cities, they sometimes showed no pity to prisoners, shooting them or, more commonly, reducing them to the status of slaves fated to die in large numbers from exhaustion while engaged in work on military projects.[77] It is now appropriate to take a look at a less well-known chapter of history. The ideology that inspired US soldiers has been described as follows: in the case of '99 [out] of 100 people in the army', the 'strongest motives are (a) nationalism . . . and (b) race prejudice' against enemies equated with 'blacks', often defined as 'jackals', 'monkey-men' or 'sub-humans', and systematically de-humanized.[78] Against these 'sub-humans', who (according to numerous American newspapers) represented a 'racial threat', a war of

---

76   Jürgen Habermas, 'Nachspiel', Italian trans. in G.E. Rusconi, ed., *Germania: un passato che non passa*, Turin: Einaudi, 1987, p. 167.

77   See Eric Markusen and David Kopf, *The Holocaust and Strategic Bombing: Genocide and Total War in the Twentieth Century*, Boulder, CO, San Francisco and Oxford: Westview Press, 1995, and Robert S. La Forte and Ronald E. Marcello, *Building the Death Railway: The Ordeal of American POWs in Burma, 1942–1945*, Wilmington: SR Books, 1993.

78   Paul Fussell, *Wartime: Understanding and Behavior in the Second World War*, New York: Oxford University Press, 1989, pp. 137, 117–18.

a particular kind and severity, a 'racial war', was to be waged. It was a war which, even before Pearl Harbor, was defined as 'merciless' by General (and subsequently Secretary of State) George C. Marshall.[79]

And here is what happened at the front, according to two American authors far removed from historical revisionism:

> the marines loved to use the few Japs who came forward to surrender as amusing rifle targets, just as they felt intense satisfaction watching them twist and writhe when set on fire by the napalm of the flame-thrower. Japanese skulls were not the only desirable trophies: treasured also were Japanese gold teeth, knocked out, sometimes from the mouths of the still-living, by a USMC Ka-bar knife-hilt.[80]

Thus one historian. Let us now attend to a war correspondent:

> We shot prisoners in cold blood, wiped out hospitals, strafed lifeboats, killed or mistreated enemy civilians, finished off the enemy wounded, tossed the dying into a hole with the dead, and in the Pacific boiled the flesh off enemy skulls to make table ornaments for sweethearts, or carved their bones into letter openers.[81]

Convinced that 'the Japanese skull was some 2,000 years less developed than ours', an eminent anthropologist thought it appropriate to inform the president accordingly.[82] This discovery facilitated relaxation of the usual inhibitions: 'Dealing that way with the skull of a German or Italian, that is, "a white man," would be clearly inappropriate, perhaps sacrilegious.' The commander-in-chief of the Pacific Fleet was forced to intervene to stop or impede such behaviour towards the 'yellow men'.[83]

Given the naturalistic de-specification of the enemy, we can understand the emergence of plans that tended towards genocide. The most moderate was perhaps Roosevelt, who for a time harboured the idea of forced sterilization ('people pass through a narrow passage and the . . . brrrrr of an electrical apparatus'), or 'enforced cross-breeding with South Sea islanders

---

79   Markusen and Kopf, *The Holocaust and Strategic Bombing*, pp. 191, 165.
80   Fussell, *Wartime*, p. 120.
81   Quoted in David E. Stannard, *American Holocaust: The Conquest of the New World*, Oxford: Oxford University Press, 1992, p. 252.
82   Ibid., p. 252.
83   Fussell, *Wartime*, pp. 117–18.

to eradicate the barbarism of the Japanese'. Further than the US president went his son Elliott, who was in favour of bombing of the enemy country 'until we have destroyed half the civilian population'.[84] Even more radical suggestions and promptings were not wanting. According to an opinion poll of November 1944, 13 per cent of Americans were inclined to the annihilation of the whole Japanese people. Questioned about what to do with the now destroyed, prostrate Asian country, a group of officers trained to be members of the future military government replied: 'Let the yellow bastards starve.'[85] Finally, Paul V. McNutt, president of the War Manpower Commission, declared for a kind of final solution, demanding 'the extermination of the Japanese in toto'.[86]

A question inevitably arises: is there a link between processes of racialization and the indiscriminate bombing campaign that culminated in Hiroshima and Nagasaki? Hatred of 'yellow men' was widespread in the period prior to the outbreak of hostilities. Even before Pearl Harbor, the 'merciless' war foreseen and planned by General George C. Marshall explicitly targeted 'civilians' and envisaged incendiary attacks to set the wooden and cardboard structures of densely populated cities ablaze. Plans of this kind date back to the early 1930s. During the war, along with incendiary bombs, time bombs were dropped that hampered rescue operations.[87] When deciding to use atomic weapons, Truman silenced critics and his moral scruples with this significant argument: 'When you are dealing with a beast you have to treat him as a beast'; 'in their conduct of the war [the Japanese] had been vicious and cruel savages'.[88]

Skin colour certainly played a role in processes of racialization. But it would be wrong to isolate or absolutize this factor. Japan sometimes seemed to appeal to a struggle against the 'white empires',[89] but its worst crimes were committed in China and Korea against other 'yellow men', who had the misfortune to belong to the colonial population to be subjugated, subject to forced labour, or used as guinea pigs in experiments in biological

---

84   See Hugh Thomas, Armed Truce: The Beginnings of the Cold War 1945–46, London: Sceptre, 1988, pp. 891, 585.

85   Quoted in George Friedman and Meredith Lebard, The Coming War with Japan, New York: St. Martin's Press, 1991, p. 95.

86   Quoted in Markusen and Kopf, The Holocaust and Strategic Bombing, p. 190.

87   Ibid., pp. 165, 173, 178.

88   Quoted in Alperovitz, The Decision to Use the Atomic Bomb, pp. 563–4.

89   See George Morgenstern, Pearl Harbor: The Story of the Secret War, Newport: Institute for Historical Review, 1991, p. 101.

warfare.[90] And the ideology and conduct of the Americans also harks back to the colonial tradition. The yellow enemy was assimilated to blacks or redskins, formed part of the non-white populations. The practice of 'carving' the skulls or bones of the dead went back to the war against the Native Americans, when President Jackson himself had distributed souvenirs of the kind 'to the ladies of Tennessee'.[91] A US historian cited by us several times – Paul Fussell – compares the American war ideology in Asia with that of the Third Reich in Eastern Europe. But as we have seen it was Hitler himself who compared the Polish or Russian 'natives' with 'redskins'.

Moral Pathos and Racialization of the Enemy

Let us now examine the war in the West. From 1914 onwards, Germany became the target of a campaign of politico-moral de-specification. It was branded as an expression of despotism, militarism and the *ancien régime*. However, another motif became inter-meshed with this one, which ultimately goes back to the revolutionary tradition (we shall set aside the debate that developed in the wake of 1789 and 1917 about the legitimacy or feasibility of exporting revolution). It singled out the barbarian horde of 'Goths', or the 'descendants of the Huns and Vandals'.[92] Similar considerations apply to the USA's war ideology: the democratic crusade sometimes ceded to depiction of the Germans as 'barbarians' challenging 'civilization', as 'Huns', or as savages who were situated even lower than 'the red Indians of America and the black tribes of Africa'.[93]

The alternation and inter-meshing of politico-moral de-specification and the naturalistic variety, and the tendency to switch from one to the other, were accentuated during the Second World War. Unforgiving denunciation of the Huns came from Churchill and Eisenhower,[94] who wrote to his wife:

---

90   Sheldon H. Harris, *Factories of Death: Japanese Biological Warfare and the American Cover Up*, London and New York: Routledge, 1994.

91   Fussell, *Wartime*, pp. 137–8, and Stannard, *American Holocaust*, p. 252.

92   See Domenico Losurdo, *Hegel and the Freedom of the Moderns*, trans. Marella and Jon Morris, Durham, NC: Duke University Press, 2004, Chapter 12, §1.

93   Ralph H. Gabriel, *The Course of American Democratic Thought*, New York, Westport and London: Greenwood Press, 1986, pp. 394–9.

94   Fraser J. Harbutt, *The Iron Curtain: Churchill, America and the Origins of the Cold War*, New York and Oxford: Oxford University Press, 1986, p. 28; Stephen E. Ambrose, 'Eisenhower and the Germans', in Günter Bischof and Ambrose, eds, *Eisenhower and the German POWs: Facts against Falsehood*, Baton Rouge and London: Louisiana State University Press, 1992, p. 31.

'God, I hate the Germans.'[95] It was an 'undying hatred' that permitted of no escape: 'the German people must not be allowed to escape a sense of guilt, of complicity in the tragedy that has engulfed the world'.[96] And that meant − the clarification is not irrelevant − a 'personal sense of guilt', which implicated every individual member of the German people.[97] Moral sentiment generates an ever more uncontainable indignation and hatred: 'the German is a beast'. There seems to be no space for distinctions within this accursed community: 'I intend to really punish [them] when I can turn my attention in that direction'; they had to be treated 'rough'.[98] The US high command as a whole worked on the assumption that 'all Germans were guilty, [but] some were more guilty than others'. This explains a policy that seemed to treat 'all Germans as lepers',[99] and which initially forbade occupying troops to fraternize with the population of the defeated country.[100]

Moral fanaticism seems to have played a role in the Morgenthau Plan (named after the US Treasury Minister), which proposed radical dismantlement of Germany's industrial apparatus and its consequent 'pastoralization'. On the one hand, such a plan answered to concrete economic and political objectives: the USSR envisaged seizing a sizeable amount of Germany's machinery (in compensation for the losses and dismantlement suffered during the war); and Britain intended to seize a welcome opportunity to rid itself of a dangerous rival in world markets. On the other hand, there were representatives of the US administration who consciously aimed to keep the German population at mere 'subsistence level', so as to make them 'suffer for their sins' and impose on them 'the tortures they have inflicted on others'.[101]

Ignoring the ruthless persecution to which the Third Reich had subjected its domestic opponents, moral indignation now invested a whole people

---

95   Günter Bischof and Stephen E. Ambrose, Introduction to *Eisenhower and the German POWs*, p. 25.

96   Dwight D. Eisenhower, *Crusade in Europe*, New York: Doubleday, 1948, pp. 470, 287.

97   Ambrose, 'Eisenhower and the Germans', p. 33; my emphasis.

98   Eisenhower, quoted in James Bacque, *Other Losses: An Investigation into the Mass Deaths of German Prisoners at the Hands of the French and Americans at the End of World War II*, Toronto: Stoddart, 1989, pp. 35–6, 21.

99   Ambrose, 'Eisenhower and the Germans', p. 33; Bischof and Ambrose, Introduction to *Eisenhower and the German POWs*, p. 12.

100   Ambrose, 'Eisenhower and the Germans', pp. 33–4.

101   The US War Secretary Stimson noted this polemically. Cf. Henry L. Stimson and McGeorge Bundy, *On Active Service in Peace and War*, New York: Octagon Books, 1971, pp. 571–9.

indiscriminately. But this outcome was only made possible by the now indis-
soluble admixture of moral de-specification with naturalistic de-specification.
In as much as the enemy can be regarded as guilty and sinful en bloc, it
comes to be represented as a race or stock, whose conduct is attributable
less to history than to nature. We have seen Churchill brand the Germans
as 'malignant Huns'. Having declared at Yalta that he felt 'more bloodthirsty
than ever toward the Germans',[102] on account of the atrocities committed
by them, Roosevelt unwittingly ended up adopting a plan advanced during
the First World War by a pious pastor who commanded a wide audience.[103]
The US president formulated it thus: 'We have got to be tough with Germany
and I mean the German people, not just the Nazis. We either have to castrate
the German people, or you have got to treat them in such a manner that
they can't just go on reproducing people who want to continue the way
they have in the past.'[104] The idea of 'castration' is the culmination of the
process of racialization of the enemy. We can understand Benedetto Croce's
indignant reaction during the First World War. He noted that interpretation
of it as a struggle between 'Germanism' and 'Latinity' lost nothing of its
odious character once it was adopted by the Italian (or French or British)
side with the opposite value judgement. The thesis that condemned the
German people en bloc as a 'reprobate people' was no 'less foolish' than
celebration of it as the 'chosen people'.[105] During the Second World War,
while reiterating the 'historical character' of the 'evil' represented by the
Hitlerite regime and ideology, Croce stressed that references to 'sterilization'
actually mimicked the 'example furnished by the Nazis themselves'.[106]
Indeed, during the Third Reich the 'final solution' was preceded by recurrent
programmes or suggestions of 'mass sterilization' of Jews.[107]

Endowing the enemy with permanent, if not immutable, characteristics,
and allowing of no distinctions within it, naturalistic de-specification paves
the way for forms of violence that tend towards genocide. In this case too,
there is probably a relationship between the processes of racialization analysed

---

102   Quoted in Bacque, *Other Losses*, p. 27.

103   See Susan Canedy, *America's Nazis: A Democratic Dilemma*, Menlo Park: Markgraf, 1990,
pp. 10–11.

104   Quoted in Bacque, *Other Losses*, p. 21.

105   Benedetto Croce, *L'Italia dal 1914 al 1918. Pagine sulla guerra*, Bari: Laterza, 1950,
pp. 75, 64.

106   Benedetto Croce, *Scritti e discorsi politici (1943–1947)*, ed. A. Carella, Vol. I, Naples:
Bibliopolis, 1993, pp. 157–8.

107   Richard D. Breitman, *The Architect of Genocide: Hitler and the Final Solution*, New York:
Knopf, 1991, pp. 141, 153.

and the decision of the British government and high command to conduct aerial bombing aimed at causing the maximum number of casualties among the German civilian population, with the systematic destruction primarily of working-class districts (where population density was highest).[108] Among the architects of this plan was the supporter of the crusade against the 'malignant Huns'. Churchill did not allow himself to blot from the record the fact that at the end of the First World War he had fought for German pilots, responsible for bombing that was doubtless limited, to be tried as war criminals.[109] A similar consideration applies to Roosevelt: in 1939, he had invited the belligerents to abstain from the 'inhuman barbarism' of bombing civilians.[110] During the subsequent development of the total war against enemies who were increasingly assimilated to barbarians and savages, the US president promoted much more massive, indiscriminate destruction than that which he had deplored.

The racialization of the enemy continued to have damaging consequences after the end of the war. Recently, the Canadian historian James Bacque has accused Eisenhower of having consciously caused the death, through exhaustion and hunger, of hundreds of thousands of German prisoners of war; and for this reason has called for removal of the statue erected in honour of the American general and statesman. Although committed to defending the memory of his hero and denying the most serious charges, the director of the Eisenhower Center at the University of New Orleans concedes that

There was widespread mistreatment of German prisoners in the spring and summer of 1945. Men were beaten, denied water, forced to live in open camps without shelter, given inadequate food rations and inadequate medical care. Their mail was withheld. In some cases prisoners made a 'soup' of water and grass in order to deal with their hunger.[111]

Concentration camp guards who claim to have 'witnessed the atrocities' paint an even more tragic picture:

---

108   Frederick J.P. Veale, *Advance towards Barbarism: The Development of Total Warfare*, Newport: Institute for Historical Review, 1979, pp. 18–19; David Irving, *The Destruction of Dresden*, London: W. Kimber, 1963, Chapter 2.

109   See Alex P. Schimd, *Churchills privater Krieg. Intervention und Konterrevolution im russischen Bürgerkrieg, November 1918–März 1920*, Zurich: Atlantis, 1974, p. 322.

110   Paul Johnson, *Modern Times: The World from the Twenties to the Nineties*, New York: Harper Collins, 1991, p. 424.

111   Ambrose, 'Ike and the Disappearing Atrocities', *New York Times Book Review*, 24 February 1991, p. 31.

There was certainly no water shortage; we were right on the Rhine, yet we denied the prisoners sufficient water. Maddened with thirst, some of them crawled under the wires and ran toward the river in open fields in broad daylight while American guards machine-gunned them. A friend in the camp kitchen showed me our abundant supplies and admitted we could feed the prisoners more. When I threw some of my surplus rations over the wires to them, I was threatened with imprisonment. I protested to my officers, and they said the starvation diet was ordered by 'higher-ups' and was general policy.

Another testimony concludes: 'We sometimes stepped over the boundary of civilized behavior and resembled to some extent what we were fighting against.'[112]

While what lay behind the theme of the democratic crusade was, in a sense, the revolutionary tradition, the representation of the enemy as barbarian stock goes back to a very different tradition that has often targeted revolutionaries, equated by their opponents with 'Turks', 'savages' and barbarians erupting from without to destroy or threaten civilization. As we have seen, according to Tocqueville, after the Parisian June of 1848 the rebellious workers seemed like 'Vandals' and 'Goths' to much of public

---

112   Letters, *New York Times Book Review*, 14 April 1991, pp. 26–7; cf. also Michael C.C. Adams, 'Retelling the Tale: Wars in Common Memory', in Gabor S. Boritt, ed., *War Comes Again: Comparative Vistas on the Civil War and World War II*, New York and Oxford: Oxford University Press, 1995, p. 217. The lack of self-critical reflection on processes of racialization of the enemy explains the persistence of historical appraisals in which tendencies to attribute guilt to an entire people continue to play a role. A successful American historian characterizes anti-Semitism and even 'exterminationist antisemitism' as a 'common property of the German people'. Once the concentration camps, the emigration, and the ruthless preventive civil war unleashed by Nazism to prevent a repetition of the November Revolution have been excluded from the record, what is intended to be a pitiless requisitory risks turning into its opposite: Hitler becomes the protagonist of 'a peaceful revolution willingly acquiesced to by the German people' (paradoxically, a recurrent theme of the Third Reich's propaganda is adopted). Goldhagen tirelessly underscores the mass consensus in Germany over the anti-Jewish persecution culminating in the 'final solution'. But, it might be asked, what consensus was there in the USA over, for example, the confinement of citizens of Japanese origin in concentration camps, the atomic bombs on Hiroshima and Nagasaki, and suggestions for a massive thinning out or annihilation of the 'yellow' enemy? Certainly, the temptation of genocide cannot be equated with actual genocide. In the absence of any comparative analysis, however, Goldhagen's insistence is not only worthless historically, but also unacceptable as testimony of moral indignation (cf. Daniel J. Goldhagen, *Hitler's Willing Executioners: Ordinary Germans and the Holocaust*, London: Little, Brown & Company, 1996, pp. 454–6, 49ff., and passim).

opinion. During the Second Thirty Years' War, the Germans became 'Vandals', 'Goths' and 'Huns'. This kind of de-specification, which establishes a geographical, anthropological and ethnic distance between oneself and the enemy, culminated in attitudes towards populations located within zones of colonial expansion. With the explosion of especially bitter conflicts, however, not even 'civilized' populations are spared processes of racialization. Long habituated to campaigns against blacks and 'redskins', Americans had no difficulty stigmatizing the Japanese as 'yellow men'. More complex and more interesting is the dialectic that developed in Europe. In the early months of the Second World War, having assimilated Hitler to Attila, Churchill invited the Italians, in despite of Mussolini, to refuse to make common cause with Germany in these terms: 'In the last war against the barbarous Huns we were your comrades . . . It is one man who . . . has arrayed the trustees and inheritors of ancient Rome upon the side of the ferocious pagan barbarians.'[113] Whereas, prior to the Second Thirty Years' War, barbarism for Churchill was situated exclusively outside Europe, in the colonial territories, it was now identified with the Huns, who had already threatened civilization at the time of ancient Rome. Thus we understand the sign that towards the end of the Second World War warned soldiers entering a now defeated Germany from Holland: 'Here Ends the Civilized World'.[114] Given that the boundaries between civilization and barbarism are self-proclaimed, the peoples or countries with which one is engaged in a bitter war are liable at any moment to be reduced to barbarians. The ideology developed to legitimize and celebrate ventures against the barbarians also ends up materializing in the capitalist metropolis.

This process was facilitated by the fact that the area of civilization may be differently and alternatively defined in peacetime. Schmitt draws attention to this fact. Dropping his habitual indictment of the revolutionary tradition, he feels compelled to refer to the Monroe Doctrine and the world-view underlying it. America demarcates the boundaries between civilization and barbarism differently from European statesmen and politicians, and in contradiction with them. Civilization remains synonymous with the West, but now it crosses the Atlantic: 'Strangely enough, the term "Western Hemisphere" was opposed precisely to Europe, the old West, the Old Occident. It was not opposed to old Asia or to old Africa, but rather to the old West. The

---

113   See Winston Churchill, *Great Destiny*, ed. F. W. Heath, New York: Putnam & Sons, 1965, pp. pp. 687–8 (radio message of 23 December 1940).

114   Bischof and Ambrose, Introduction to *Eisenhower and the German POWs*, p. 17.

new West claimed to be the true West, the true Occident, the true Europe.' Thus, 'old Europe' ends up suffering the same fate as Asia and Africa, invariably excluded from civilization.[115]

In fact, in his farewell message Washington called upon his fellow citizens to steer well clear of 'the toils of European Ambition, Rivalship, Interest, Humour or Caprice'. Europe's conduct recalled that of the Native Americans: 'while in Europe, wars or commotions seem to agitate almost every nation, peace and tranquillity prevail among us, except on some parts of our western frontiers, where the Indians have been troublesome, to reclaim or chastise whom proper measures are now pursuing'.[116] The tendency to expel Europe from civilization re-emerged in the 1812 war against Britain. Already denounced in the Declaration of Independence for having resorted to the aid of 'savages' in its struggle with the colonists, Britain was now accused by Madison of behaving like redskin 'savages', as demonstrated by its naval bombardments, which indiscriminately struck the civilian population, not sparing women or children.[117]

This tendency became more intense during the Second Thirty Years' War. In the weeks and months immediately succeeding the outbreak of the First World War, condemnation fell equally on both parties, which (observed an editorial in *The Times* of 2 August 1914) 'have reverted to the condition of savage tribes'.[118] In his speech of 26 October 1916, Wilson reprehended 'the whole European system'. With 'its combination of alliances and agreements, a developed web of intrigue and espionage, which . . . drew the whole family of nations into its web', it had dragged them into a disastrous war.[119] Subsequently, with US intervention alongside the Entente, denunciation was focused exclusively on the Germans, branded (as we know) as 'Huns' and 'barbarians' who were lower even than 'the redskins of America and the black tribes of Africa'. A similar dialectic developed during the Second World War. In April 1939, Roosevelt accused European countries in general of having found no better means for composing their differences than those employed 'by the Huns and Vandals fifteen hundred years ago'. Fortunately, thanks to a 'typically American institution' – the union embracing all the countries of

---

115   Schmitt, *The Nomos of the Earth*, p. 290.

116   George Washington, *A Collection*, ed. W.B. Allen, Indianapolis: Liberty Classics, 1988, pp. 525, 555.

117   Henry S. Commager, ed., *Documents of American History*, New York: Appleton-Century-Crofts, 1963, Vol. I, pp. 208–9.

118   Quoted in Gabriel, *The Course of American Democratic Thought*, p. 388.

119   Quoted in Schmitt, *The Nomos of the Earth*, p. 268.

the 'American family' – 'the republics of the Western world', or the American
continent, had managed 'to promote their common civilization under a system
of peace' and to protect the 'Western world' from the tragedy that had struck
the 'Old World'.[120] Following intervention in the war, the US president
directed his fire exclusively at Germany, without unduly concerning himself
about internal distinctions, as is evident, in particular, from the idea (already
noted) of forced sterilization of the German people.

White War of Independence in the West
and Colonial War in the East

In the years and decades preceding the outbreak of the Second Thirty Years'
War, the countries of the West all prided themselves on belonging to an
exclusive family – in fact, a race (or family of races) destined to subjugate
'inferior races'. It was a 'great race', an 'expansionist race' (to use Theodore
Roosevelt's terms),[121] or an 'imperial race' (in Macaulay's),[122] a race variously
defined as Nordic, Aryan or Teutonic. It was 'almost universally admitted',
wrote a respected British ethnologist in 1842, that the 'collective body of
the European nations' descended from 'the Aryan or the Indo-European
race'. Some decades later, a eulogist of British imperialism celebrated the
British and Germans as the 'two main currents of the Teutonic race'.[123] In
1899, the British Colonial Secretary himself, Joseph Chamberlain, called
upon the United States and Germany to enter into a 'Teutonic' alliance with
his country.[124] Only with the First World War were such categories converted
from a vehicle of unanimous self-celebration of Europe and the West (especially their leading countries) into tools of 'fratricidal' struggle. With the
USA's intervention in the war against Germany, the term 'Teuton' lost the
positive, celebratory connotation it had hitherto had in wide cultural and
political circles, becoming an insult directed at the new enemies.[125]

120   Commager, *Documents of American History*, Vol. II, p. 414.
121   Theodore Roosevelt, *The Letters*, ed. E.E. Morison, J.M. Blum and J.J. Buckley,
Cambridge, MA: Harvard University Press, 1955–, Vol. II, pp. 377, 620; Roosevelt, *The
Strenuous Life: Essays and Addresses*, New York: The Century, 1901, pp. 251, 275.
122   Quoted in Charmley, *Churchill: The End of Glory*, p. 424.
123   Quoted in Hugh A. MacDougall, *Racial Myth in English History: Trojans, Teutons, and Anglo-
Saxons*, Montreal and London: Harvest/University Press of New England, 1982, pp. 120, 98.
124   Kissinger, *Diplomacy*, p. 186.
125   Thomas F. Gosset, *Race: The History of an Idea in America*, New York: Schocken Books,
p. 341.

This division of Europe, the West and the Aryan race created bitter controversies and heartfelt regrets. The war raged, but there were German authors who regretted the spectacle of a bloody conflict between two 'sister nations of Germanic stock', on the one hand, and 'the fraternization of Indo-Germanic Great Britain with Mongol Japan', on the other.[126] Especially painful was the presence in the Entente's ranks, and, worse still, among the troops occupying defeated Germany, of black soldiers, who were accused of a propensity for rape. Did the victors' vendetta extend to 'mak[ing] mulattos' of the defeated? Protests against this unprecedented violation of white solidarity and racial (and social) hierarchy appealed to the whole civilized world and the Holy See:

> With horror and disgust, Germany sees itself menaced in the purity of its blood . . . They are ruining the blood, ruining the purity of our blood which for years will have to mix with the blood of more primitive races, and we shall become a population of mulattos. We do not want to suffer such an affront! And given that the other European peoples have no sense of European solidarity in this matter, they do not see the danger threatening the whole of Europe should Germany be inhabited by a proletarianized, ungodly, half-caste population.

The 'Cry for pity by German women' called for an immediate end to this kind of racial civil war: 'With ours heads veiled, we present ourselves to you, men and women of the white race; we open our broken hearts . . . so that . . . you too will raise a voice of protest which will be testimony to universal indignation at the race of brutes which, in debasing us, debases the world's entire white race.'[127]

These were themes that also circulated widely on the other side of the Atlantic. Lothrop Stoddard (who rapidly achieved international notoriety and was lauded by two US presidents, Harding and Hoover) deplored the 'white civil war', or the 'new Peloponnesian war' of 'white civilization'.[128]

---

126   Thus Ernst Haeckel, quoted in Rudolf Buchner and Winfried Baumgart, eds, *Quellen zum politischen Denken der Deutschen im 19. und 20. Jahrundert. Freiherr vom Stein–Gedächtnisausgabe*, Darmstadt: Wissenschaftliche Buchgesellschaft, 1976, Vol. VII, p. 417.

127   Quoted in Emma Fattorini, 'Il colpo di grazia sessuale. La violenza delle truppe nere in Renania negli anni venti', in A. Bravo, ed., *Donne e uomini nelle guerre mondiali*, Rome and Bari: Laterza, 1991, pp. 47–50.

128   See Lothrop Stoddard, *The Rising Tide of Color against White World-Supremacy*, Westport, CT: Negro University Press, 1971, pp. vi, 172. President Harding's laudatory judgement is reported on the opening page of the French translation (cf. Stoddard, *Le Flot*

It involved a fratricidal conflict which, destroying 'white solidarity' and dismembering Europe in the first instance – the 'white homeland, the heart of the white world' – amounted to 'white race-suicide'. Just as the American Civil War brought the enrolment of blacks in the Union's ranks, so the First World War had involved massive recourse to coloured troops by the Entente. This division of the white, civilized world, with its abolition of the boundary between civilization and barbarism, was consummated by Bolshevism. Engaged in constructing a global alliance with colonial peoples against the West and the whites, and inciting 'the rising tide of the peoples of color', it was to be regarded as 'the renegade, the traitor within the gates, who would betray the citadel' – an 'arch-enemy of civilization and the race'.[129]

Spengler reached the same conclusion, denouncing the 'burning hatred of Europe' and 'white peoples' nurtured by the Bolsheviks, who were allies and, indeed, an integral part of 'the earth's coloured population'. The German writer offered a historical reconstruction of this disastrous parabola. It began with Britain's recourse to the aid of the Native Americans in its struggle against the rebel colonists (this resumed a theme consecrated in the American Declaration of Independence); continued with the French Jacobins' alliance with the blacks of Haiti in the name of the 'rights of man'; developed with the Entente's employment of coloured troops;[130] and finally culminated in the Bolshevik Revolution.

Such themes and suggestions are active in Hitler, who in *Mein Kampf* set out a programme of colonial expansion in the European East in an attempt to avoid a fratricidal conflict with Britain. Immediately after coming to power, he declared to a British reporter that the First World War had been a tragedy for the 'two great Germanic nations'. A year later, speaking to another British journalist, the Führer expressed the idea that 'Germanic nations such as ours ought to be friends by sheer force of natural instinct.' On 4 September 1937, the *Daily Mail* reported a letter by Hitler in which, having celebrated 'the historically unique colonial aptitude and the naval power of Britain', he desired an agreement between it and Germany, to be

montant des peuples de couleur contre la suprematie mondiale des Blancs, trans. A. Doysié, Paris: Payot, 1925). For the praise bestowed on Stoddard by Hoover, cf. Stefan Kühl, *The Nazi Connection: Eugenics, American Racism and German National Socialism*, New York and Oxford: Oxford University Press, 1994, p. 61.

129   Stoddard, *The Rising Tide of Color against White World-Supremacy*, pp. vi, 179, 196, 219–21.

130   Oswald Spengler, *The Hour of Decision*, trans. Charles Francis Atkinson, London: George Allen & Unwin, 1934, p. 209.

subsequently extended to the 'adhesion of the American nation', so as to hold high the banner and 'the interest of the white people'. Some years earlier, the Nazi leader had defined a potential war between Germany and Great Britain, and between the 'Germanic nations' in general, as 'a racial crime'.[131] In similar fashion, Rosenberg sang the praises of the 'creative values' and 'entire culture of the west', or 'Teutonic European values', threatened by 'racial chaos'.[132]

Once he had failed to avert war in the West, the Führer largely respected the *jus publicum europaeum* during the conflict with France – repression of the partisan resistance, for the particular problems of international law it raises, would merit a separate discussion. From the outset, however, he theorized and practised the war of extermination against the 'natives' of the colonial empire he proposed to build. While he criticized the British (used, unlike the Germans, to going to war with 'foreigners' and barbarians) for bombing cities and failing to respect the 'customs of chivalrous war', Hitler professed to 'attach no importance to a formal, juridical end to the war on the Eastern Front'.[133] It was an explicitly colonial war against barbarians. After the conquest and colonization of the new territories, 'we must meet [a flood from Asia] with a living wall'.[134] The sentiment of the unity of the Germanic nations that continued to inspire the Third Reich is the obverse of a racial contradistinction from the Orient. Equally, notwithstanding total war, the radical naturalistic de-specification of the 'Asiatic' enemy inhibited a naturalistic de-specification of Western enemies, who were still situated within the ambit of civilization.

At the war's close, Himmler surrendered to a 'racially akin enemy' – the 'Anglo-Saxons' who had always formed 'part of the Nordic family of races'. The Nazi ringleader was possibly under the illusion that he would meet with understanding.[135] After all, it was in the East, on the 'natives', that the Third Reich had waged pitiless war. This attitude had a long history behind it. Reference has sometimes been made to 'a double standard in the American

---

131   See Louis C. Kilzer, *Churchill's Deception: The Dark Secret that Destroyed Nazi Germany*, New York: Simon & Schuster, 1994, pp. 122–3.

132   Alfred Rosenberg, *The Myth of the Twentieth Century: An Evaluation of the Intellectual-Spiritual Confrontations of Our Age*, Newport Beach, CA: Noontide Press, 1993, pp. 40–1.

133   Adolf Hitler, *Hitler's Table Talk 1941–44*, London: Weidenfeld & Nicolson, 1973, p. 92 (conversation of 26–27 October 1941); *Monologe im Führerhauptquartier 1941–1944. Die Aufzeichnungen Heinrich Heims*, ed. W. Jochmann, Hamburg: Albrecht Knaus, 1980, pp. 110, 393–4 (conversations of 26 and 27 October 1941 and 6 September 1942).

134   *Hitler's Table Talk*, p. 40 (25 September 1941, midday).

135   Breitman, *The Architect of Genocide*, p. 7.

way of waging war', depending on whether the enemy were whites or Native Americans. This even manifested itself during the conflict between North and South. The violence that marked it is in no wise comparable to the contemporaneous extermination of rebellious native populations, even though they posed no real threat to the Union. The orders were unequivocal: no prisoners were to be taken. In 'the infamous Sand Creek Massacre' of 1864, women and children were also killed.[136] In reality, the 'double standard' was a feature of the Western history as a whole. In America, it is immediately apparent only because the colonial populations were located within the metropolitan territory itself. The 'double standard' celebrated its triumph with the Third Reich: the more or less 'chivalrous' duel desired in the West, in the context of a persistent, deplorable white civil war, was inseparable from the colonial campaign of extermination against barbarians posted outside civilization.

Total War and 'Barbarians'

This undermines the thesis dear to Schmitt (and historical revisionism) that blame for the advent of total war is to be pinned exclusively on the revolutionary political tradition and the international civil war declared by it. This is an unsustainable schema, and not only because theoreticians of conservatism and reaction proclaim their own crusade during acute crises. Rather than ideological fanaticism and politico-moral de-specification, it is the irruption of the barbarians that radically undermines the *jus publicum europaeum* and *jus in bello*. What occurred during the American Civil War is revealing. As it went on, becoming more bitter, southern and northern blacks enrolled in the Union army en masse. Jefferson Davis and the Confederacy not only called on white world public opinion to revolt at the scandal of barbarians, members of an 'inferior race', being enrolled in Union ranks. They also refused to treat blacks and white officers leading military units of colour as normal prisoners of war; the latter deserved to die in as much as they were guilty of instigating 'slave insurrection'.[137]

---

136   Mark Grimsley, *The Hard Hand of War: Union Military Policy toward Southern Civilians 1861–1865*, Cambridge: Cambridge University Press, 1995, p. 18.

137   William E.B. Du Bois, *Black Reconstruction in America 1860–1880*, ed. D.L. Lewis, New York: Atheneum, 1992, pp. 113–14.

We are reminded of the white civil war, deprecated above all in Germany and the USA for the intervention of coloured troops in a conflict between civilized peoples. If, despite everything, it survived during the first phase of the Second Thirty Years' War, the *jus publicum europaeum* fell radically into crisis in the second. Like the Confederacy in the case of blacks, the Third Reich placed the 'natives' of Eastern Europe outside international law. Meanwhile, the treatment reserved for white commanders of black units recalls the treatment meted out by Hitler to the Red Army's political commissars and state and party cadres, as well as Jews, who were regarded as the backbone of Bolshevism and for that reason assimilated to the preceding categories. That is why the severest crisis of the *jus publicum europaeum* occurred in the East and why its architect was the country leading the crusade for white and Aryan revival.

The American Civil War is also significant in another aspect. To compel the South to submit, the Union systematically destroyed crops and sometimes burnt down towns. But it is important to note that 'Sherman's march had its roots in colonial- and revolutionary-era campaigns', which also furnished 'the personnel and the military doctrine that Americans carried into their imperial adventures in Latin America and the Philippines'.[138] In other words, during serious conflicts between members of the civilized community, forms of war traditionally employed against barbarians tend to emerge within it as well. It seems that Sherman inspired Hitler,[139] who explicitly invoked the war against the Native Americans during his war of extermination against the 'natives' of Eastern Europe.

At this point, Schmitt's charge against the revolutionary political tradition of having destroyed the *jus publicum europaeum* – the limitations that governed war between civilized peoples – appears in a different light. This theme has a long tradition behind it, dating back to Plato. He distinguished between *polemos* – war proper, which was unlimited and saw the Greeks confronting barbarians (who in the event of defeat were killed or enslaved) – and *stasis* – the civil war pitting Hellenes against one another, which, if it could not be averted, must occur within precise limits (the killing or enslavement of the vanquished was impermissible). Armed conflict with a 'blood relation' (*suggenes*) could not proceed in the same way as the total war of one *genos* against an utterly alien, barbaric *genos*.[140] In his turn, Cicero made a clear

---

138   Richard Slotkin, *The Fatal Environment: The Myth of the Frontier in the Age of Industrialization 1800–1890*, New York: Harper Perennial, 1994, pp. 304, 322.

139   See Kilzer, *Churchill's Deception*, pp. 53, 185.

140   See Plato, *Republic*, 469c–471b.

distinction between a war where what was at stake between the contending parties (who in some sense respected and recognized one another) was hegemony, and war where the issue was survival. The latter involved confrontation not between one *competitor* – rival – and another, but between one *inimicus* – total enemy – and another. This was true, for example, of the war between the Cimbri and the Teutones, where at stake was 'who was to survive, not who was to exercise dominion' (*uter esset, non uter imperaret*). In this light, whereas the destruction of the foundations of Carthage and Numantia posed no problem, the similar fate that befell Corinth, a civilized city and people, inspired reservations (as early as ancient Troy, Greece had been engaged against the 'barbarians').[141]

Plato's pan-Hellenic community became the *res publica christiana* in Erasmus, who translated *polemos* by *bellum* and *stasis* by *seditio*, it being understood that *seditio* must be limited and contained as much as possible.[142] Sometimes this extended to yearnings for the end of any conflict within the Christian community. This was the case with Saint-Pierre, who added that the European states could thereby seize 'the opportunities to cultivate military genius and talents' in the struggle against the 'Turks', the 'corsairs of Africa' and the 'Tartars'.[143] A few decades later, Fichte condemned Napoleon for having shattered the unity of the 'community of Europe', the 'sole true fatherland' of 'European Christians'. The French warlord's expansionist dynamism would have been better deployed outside the 'realm of civilization', where there were still 'sufficient barbarians' to subjugate through wars wherein 'European youth' might be tempered.[144] The pan-Hellenic community, the *res publica christiana*, and the 'community of Europe' are finally configured in Schmitt as the Western community united not by perpetual peace, but by the *jus publicum europaeum*. The *polemos* and *bellum* referred to by Plato and Erasmus now become discriminatory wars and wars of annihilation, which can and absolutely must be averted within – and only within – the civilized world. *Stasis* or *seditio* is the war-duel that must never become 'civil' to the point of lacerating the European or Western community and the states belonging to it, with appeals for crusades and a no-holds-barred conflict. With its exalted universalism, which forgets or abolishes the

---

141 Cicero, *De Officiis*, I, 35–8 and III, 99.

142 See Erasmus, *The Complaint of Peace*, New York: Da Capo Press, 1973.

143 Thus, at least, according to Rousseau's summary: see *Oeuvres complètes*, ed. B. Gagnebin and P. Raymond, Paris: Gallimard, 1959–, Vol. III, pp. 585–6.

144 See J.G. Fichte, *Werke*, ed. I.H. Fichte, Berlin: de Gruyter, 1971, Vol. VII, pp. 204–5 and Vol. XI, p. 426.

historical and geographical concreteness of the *nomos*, the revolutionary political tradition is guilty (according to Schmitt) of abolishing or volatilizing the distinction between the civilized and the barbarian, thereby undermining the distinction between *stasis* and *polemos*, *seditio* and *bellum*, war as duel and discriminatory, exterminatory war.

Schmitt refers to a 'great and courageous thinker of the *ancien régime*', Joseph de Maistre. Before accusing the French Revolution of having rendered chivalrous 'European war', where 'soldier only fought soldier, while nations were never at war', barbaric and pitiless, Maistre celebrated the 'enthusiasm of the carnage' and even seemed to justify the extermination of the Native Americans – those 'degraded men' whom 'the Europeans' rightly refused to recognize as 'their fellows'. The disappearance of chivalrous war was deplored only as regards that part of the globe which 'the divine spirit' suffused in a very special way. Elsewhere, it was clear that, amid the 'constant carnage' forming part of the economy of the 'great totality', there were 'certain nations' which the 'exterminating angel' persisted in drenching in blood.[145] It is a matter of fact that in the lengthy assessment of the emergence of discriminatory wars and wars of annihilation in *The Nomos of the Earth*, there is no room for critical analysis of wars of colonial extermination, including that unleashed by Hitler against the 'natives' of Eastern Europe.

Exclusion from Europe is also exclusion from Christianity (it is precisely an excommunication). Given that, as Schmitt explains, 'the distinction between civilized peoples and uncivilized or semi-civilized peoples' in fact 'secularizes' the 'distinction between Christian peoples and non-Christian peoples',[146] here we have war against barbarians still tending in the mid-twentieth century to be configured as a war of religion in the sometimes literal sense of the term. Boutroux condemned Germany for not yet being 'fully converted to the Christian doctrine of the God of love and goodness'.[147] Churchill, as we have seen, called for a struggle against those 'savage pagan barbarians', the Germans or Huns.

Condemnation of the revolutionary tradition for having abolished the distinction or dichotomy between civilization and barbarism is sealed in Schmitt with condemnation of the anti-colonial revolution. The figure of the

---

145   Joseph de Maistre, *Oeuvres complètes*, Hildesheim, Zurich and New York: Olms, 1984, Vol. IV, p. 83 and Vol. V, pp. 18–28; Carl Schmitt, *Theory of the Partisan: Intermediate Commentary on the Concept of the Political*, trans. G.L. Ulmen, New York: Telos Press, 2007, p. 53.

146   Schmitt, *Positionen und Begriffe*, p. 163.

147   Émile Boutroux, *Études d'histoire de la philosophie allemande*, Paris: Vrin, 1926, p. 234.

partisan inspired by Marxism, and active in the anti-colonial liberation movements, 'caused nothing less than the destruction of the whole Eurocentric world that Napoleon had hoped to rescue and that the Congress of Vienna had hoped to restore'.[148] With it goes the eclipse of 'a Eurocentric international law: the *jus publicum Europaeum*'.[149]

---

148   Schmitt, *The Theory of the Partisan*, p. 53.
149   Schmitt, *The Nomos of the Earth*, p. 49.

CHAPTER FIVE

The Colonial Tradition, Total War and Genocide

Total War and Total Manipulation

The particular interest German conservative circles have in shaking off the burden of Auschwitz is understandable. In Franz Joseph Strauss's words, Germany must once again become 'a normal nation' and 'walk with its head held high'.[1] The easiest way to achieve this objective is to negate the reality of the genocide. We should not immediately cry scandal; among the most illustrious casualties of the Second Thirty Years' War is truth. Wars have always been accompanied by attempts to defame the enemy and skilful construction of propaganda interwoven with lies. In particular, this is a weapon used against ethnic groups deemed foreign to civilization. 'Barbarians' are branded such by reference to their 'atrocious' practices. In the USA, the more ruthlessly the erasure of Native Americans from the face of the earth proceeded, the more repugnantly they were depicted. Discriminatory wars and wars of annihilation against colonial populations, whether external or internal to the metropolis, were justified by dehumanizing them; and this was achieved by sheer invention of 'atrocities' or by an inflation and one-sided reading of atrocities actually committed. The legend of ritual murder attributed to Jews for centuries, as evidence of their incorrigible foreignness to civilization as such, can be located in this context.

In as much as intensification in the conflicts between 'civilized' peoples involves expulsion of the enemy from the civilized community, a weapon traditionally reserved for the struggle against 'barbarians' is deployed against it. That is how the belligerents in the American Civil War, especially the North, proceeded. But in our century we note a qualitative leap. Along with

---

1 Quoted in Jürgen Habermas, 'Nachspiel', Italian trans. in G.E. Rusconi, ed., *Germania: un passato che non passa*, Turin: Einaudi, 1987, p. 163.

the industrial, mass production of death emerges the industrial, mass production of lies and half-truths intended to criminalize the enemy and destroy his image. The Spanish-American War, which closed the nineteenth century and inaugurated the twentieth, was prepared for ideologically by the USA through the diffusion of 'news', completely invented, identifying the Spanish as responsible for having killed defenceless prisoners and massacred 300 Cuban women.[2] We witness a further escalation during the First World War. Although undertaken by both sides, the campaign of defamation soon registered the clear prevalence of the Entente:

> Western allegations of German atrocities began with the violation of Belgian neutrality by the Germans in August 1914. The Germans, it was said, had ravished women and even young children, impaled and crucified men, cut off tongues and breasts, gouged eyes and burned down whole villages. These reports were not only carried in sensationalist newspapers but also endorsed by leading writers from John Buchan and Arthur Conan Doyle to Arnold Toynbee, to mention but a few. This propaganda continued throughout 1914 and 1915, decreased somewhat in intensity in 1916, but reached a new peak in April 1916 when the British press began to publish news and comments about the use of the corpses of fallen soldiers by the Germans for the production of lubricants such as glycerine and soap. As an afterthought, probably for the benefit of China and the Muslim countries, it was added that pig food was also made of the corpses.
>
> There were indeed such installations in Germany (*Kadaververwertungsanstalten*) but they were processing animals' cadavers, not human corpses. However, such news items were not the exception; even highly reputable newspapers such as the *Financial Times* carried stories according to which the Kaiser himself had ordered the torturing of three-year-old children and had personally specified what tortures should be applied. The *Daily Telegraph* reported in March 1916 that the Austrians and the Bulgarians had killed 700,000 Serbs using asphyxiating gas.[3]

In the mid-1920s, speaking in the House of Commons, the British Foreign Minister Austen Chamberlain admitted that 'the story of the corpse factory

---

2   See Walter Millis, *The Martial Spirit*, Chicago: Elephant Paperbacks, 1989, p. 60.

3   Walter Laqueur, *The Terrible Secret: Suppression of the Truth about Hitler's 'Final Solution'*, New York: Penguin, 1980, pp. 8–9.

had been without foundation'.[4] Today, we know that the testimony, statements, images and stills documenting the atrocities of Wilhelmine Germany
were the result of skilful manipulation, to which the nascent US cinema
industry, shooting scenes in New Jersey of the savage, barbarous behaviour
of German troops in Belgium, made a splendid contribution![5] Two details
in the 'atrocities' attributed to the Germans give particular pause for thought.
The story of women being raped and having their breasts sliced off returns
us to the image with which official ideology in America sought to create
'sexual and racial anxieties' about Native Americans.[6] Then there are the
'crucified' men: it is as if the practice of ritual homicide is now being attributed to the Germans. In addition, as early as the First World War, an even
more serious suspicion began to hang over them. According to Bergson, as
the 'chosen race', the 'Germanic race' reserved 'an absolute right to life'
exclusively for itself. At most 'tolerated' in peacetime, 'the other races' were
destined to suffer 'annihilation' in wartime. Germany 'will not only come
to blows with combatants: it will massacre women, children, the elderly; it
will sack and burn. The ideal would be to destroy cities, villages, the whole
population'.[7] As we can see, the accusation of genocide is deduced here *a
priori* from the ideology attributed to Wilhelmine – eternal – Germany.

   We can now understand the arguments of historical revisionism or of
so-called 'negationism'. Why should the systematic extermination of Jewry
attributed to the Third Reich not itself be a myth? Are we dealing with a
new, more acute formulation of the charge of ritual murder laid against the
Germans, consummated in the Holocaust of a people blessed by the Bible?
Let us see who Germany's main accusers were. As a representative of the
Wilson administration, Franklin Delano Roosevelt had taken an active part
in the campaign against the 'German atrocities' during the First World War.[8]
As for Stalin, he even tried at Nuremburg to offload the Soviet execution
of Polish officers at Katyn onto the Nazis.

   Finally, it should be noted that as regards the theme of massacres and
genocides the line of demarcation between historical revisionists and

---

   4   Ibid., p. 9.
   5   Martin Gilbert, *The First World War: A Complete History*, New York: Henry Holt and
Company, 1994, p. 432.
   6   See Colin G. Calloway, *The American Revolution in Indian Country: Crisis and Diversity in
Native American Communities*, Cambridge: Cambridge University Press, 1995.
   7   Henri Bergson, *Mélanges*, ed. A. Robinet, Paris: Presses Universitaires de France, 1972,
p. 1113.
   8   Robert E. Herzstein, *Roosevelt and Hitler: Prelude to War*, New York: Paragon House,
1989, p. 65.

negationists, on the one hand, and historians respectful of the tragedy of the victims, also at the level of historical memory, on the other, is fairly labile and cannot be fixed definitively. We have seen Laqueur include in the list of invented atrocities the liquidation of hundreds of thousands of Serbs by poison gas. This would not appear to be the opinion of Hillgruber, even though he is generally counted among the 'revisionists'. While he exculpates the Austrians and pins the blame exclusively on the (eastern) Bulgarians, as evidence of the genocidal character that war was already tending to assume in the First World War Hillgruber records the testimony of a journalist from the *Frankfurter Zeitung*, released on 20 November 1917 by the Secretary of State von Kühlman: 'the Serbs are being "wiped out" (*erledigt*) administratively: they are taken for purposes of cleansing to disinfection centres and eliminated by gas'.[9]

Even more interesting is the present-day controversy over the Armenian tragedy. In this case, it is descendants of the victims of the Turkish massacres who accuse eminent representatives of international Jewish culture, engaged in demonstrating the uniqueness and incommensurability of the Holocaust, of being negationists or revisionists. Why should it be legitimate to deny or downgrade the Serbian or Armenian genocide and not the Jewish one? All the more so in that, while Germany has an interest in shaking off the infamy of Auschwitz, rival or potentially rival powers might have an interest in assigning it eternal responsibility for a crime 'unique' in history. To seek to establish an official truth by law, as is the practice in some countries, is contrary to any ethic of scholarly research and, furthermore, can only create suspicions that the victors wish to conceal the truth more stubbornly than they did on the morrow of the First World War.

We shall see that historical investigation has no need of external support to document the tragic particularity of the fate reserved for Jewry by Nazism. Perhaps that is why revisionism seems to downgrade the horror of the Third Reich by pursuing a secondary, different strategy. In its initial phase, at any rate, the imprisonment of Jews in German concentration camps was supposedly comparable to that of German citizens in French and British concentration camps, or of American citizens of Japanese origin in American concentration camps. In both cases, this was a measure typical of total war, which does not hesitate to target en bloc ethnic groups suspected of a lack of patriotic

---

9 Bernhard Guttmann, *Schattenriss einer Generation 1888–1919*, Stuttgart: Koehler, 1959, p. 146. On this cf. Andreas Hillgruber, *Die Zerstörung Europas. Beiträge zur Weltkriegsepoche 1914 bis 1945*, Frankfurt am Main and Berlin: Ullstein and Propyläen, 1988, p. 110.

loyalty. And that Hitler's suspicions were no less legitimate than those harboured by Roosevelt is allegedly demonstrated by the 'declaration of war' on Germany made by Chaim Weizmann in the name of Zionist organizations.[10]

Against this thesis it is pointless proclaiming the innocence of the Jews. This is an argument which obviously applies to American citizens of Japanese origin (particularly since women and children were also confined in the US camps), as it does to the German exiles, most of them anti-fascist, confined in French concentration camps immediately after the outbreak of the war with Germany. As a total institution, the concentration camp involves cancellation of the principle of individual responsibility. And, be it said in their honour, the Jews were not victims who passively waited for the sacrifice to be performed. They often sought to counter the plans of their oppressors and butchers on an international scale. They collaborated with the Resistance and were active in the partisan struggle. These are the years when Arendt hoped that Jewish fighters, at 'war' with Nazism since the advent of Hitler and engaged 'on all the fronts of the world', would finally unite in an autonomous 'Jewish army' waging the struggle with its own identity alongside the other armies of the anti-fascist coalition.[11] On the other side, we should not trivialize the fate of Americans of Japanese origin. Bearing in mind the elements of negation and differentiation in comparativism, we can offer a comparison between the two ethnic groups referred to here. Hanging over Americans of Japanese origin was likewise an old racial prejudice, which for decades had warned the 'white race' against the 'yellow peril', or thundered against the 'progeny of Asiatic slaves'. Accused of never having sought to 'assimilate' to the people receiving them, and remaining obstinately attached to 'racial solidarity',[12] Americans of Japanese origin, like German Jews, suffered a kind of expropriation (they were forced to sell their goods). There then began a journey into the unknown, which occurred in uncomfortable conditions, sometimes on 'decrepit, sluggish trains', and lasted up to ten days. 'Black shades covered the windows day and night', while controlling the 'passengers' were 'armed guards, who aimed guns at the Japanese Americans'. The unfortunates were

10   See Ernst Nolte, *Der europäische Bürgerkrieg 1917–1945. Nationalsozialismus und Bolschewismus*, Frankfurt am Main and Berlin: Ullstein, 1987, pp. 317–18, 509–10.

11   See Hannah Arendt, *Essays und Kommentare*, ed. E. Geisel and K. Bittermann, Berlin: Tiamat, 1989, Vol. I, p. 154 and Vol. II, pp. 167–71.

12   Peter Irons, *Justice at War: The Story of the Japanese American Internment Cases*, New York and Oxford: Oxford University Press, 1983, pp. 9–10, 225, 237.

eventually housed 'in deserts and swamps, the most desolate, hostile areas of the country', in a further 'shock to the refugees, most of whom had spent their lives in temperate California'. The accommodation, of extremely modest proportions, was not less than twenty miles from the closest small town.[13] The temptation of even more drastic measures arose: we have seen Roosevelt entertain the sterilization of the Japanese proper (the analogy with projects targeting the Jews in Germany once again leaps out at us). The *Los Angeles Times* thundered menacingly: 'A viper is always a viper wherever the egg is hatched – so a Japanese American, born of Japanese parents, grows up to be a Japanese not an American.' It involved (repeated a general) a 'race' that was much more dangerous than Italian Americans or German Americans: hence, one could not rest in peace until it had been 'wiped out'.[14] What would have happened in the event of an invasion of US territory or a genuine threat of invasion? After the Battle of Midway, problems of military security can no longer be invoked. Yet Americans of Japanese origin continued to be deprived of their liberty. The last of them were only able to leave their concentration camps in mid-1946, almost a year after the end of the Second World War. Even slower was the return home of Latin American citizens of Japanese origin from the USA, deported by thirteen Latin American countries. Only in 1948 were the last able to leave the 'internment' or concentration camp of Crystal City in Texas.[15]

The effects of the coincidence of total war (which indiscriminately struck ethnic and social groups suspected of insufficient loyalty) with naturalistic de-specification, which tended to block any escape route for members of that group, were potentially terrible. Yet we shall see that the comparison suggested by historical revisionism is not convincing – and not only because the temptation to genocide can be more or less strong, more or less deep-seated. However, one cannot simply respond to such comparisons with an indignation that does not deign to enter into the merits of the problem raised. Such is Furet's reaction. On the one hand, he credits Nolte with having 'quickly gone beyond the prohibition against putting Communism and Nazism in the same bag', thereby breaking a 'taboo' long widespread in European anti-fascist circles. On the other, he deems 'both shocking and

---

13   Eric Markusen and David Kopf, *The Holocaust and Strategic Bombing: Genocide and Total War in the Twentieth Century*, Boulder, CO, San Francisco and Oxford: Westview Press, 1995, p. 190; Deborah Gesensway and Mindy Roseman, *Beyond Words: Images from America's Concentration Camps*, Ithaca and London: Cornell University Press, 1987, pp. 43–4.

14   Markusen and Kopf, *The Holocaust and Strategic Bombing*, pp. 189–91.

15   Irons, *Justice at War*, p. 7; *International Herald Tribune*, 30 August 1996, p. 6.

false' the argument in question, which 'can no doubt be attributed to a basic fund of humiliated German nationalism for which Nolte's adversaries have reproached him for twenty years and which in large part motivates his books'.[16] It is undeniable that a desire to lessen German culpability plays an important role in the German historian's work. But it is not clear why such motivation should be invoked to liquidate *a priori* some of his theses, rather than others. Besides, exposure of the psychological, or politico-social, genesis of a particular proposition does not constitute its refutation. Instead, it might be said that for Furet the hermeneutic of political suspicion renders superfluous a scholarly response to an argument perceived by him as irritating or disturbing. The fact is that, albeit involuntarily and to a limited extent, Nolte has broken a taboo that is much more deeply rooted, and much more formidable, than the one referred to by the French historian. The latter seems to accept a comparativist approach on condition that it is restricted to comparing the Third Reich and the USSR, without involving the other actors, or the true victors, of the Second Thirty Years' War.

As regards the latter, Nolte himself makes do with a few allusions or the odd rapid sally. This is not attributable to a lack of courage, or even diplomatic caution in conducting an operation intended to result in relativizing or minimizing the horror of the Third Reich, but to the goal of the readmission of Germany, thus rehabilitated and rescued from its brief 'Asiatic' parenthesis, into the sacred heart of the West. There is a further reason. Once the history of the twentieth century is depicted as an international civil war lasting until 1989, which saw the various Western countries ranged against the USSR at different times and in different ways, it is clear that the polemic must be focused on the Bolsheviks. And, in fact, according to Nolte, the century's horrors began with the deplorable October 1917. In sum, this is also the view of Furet, who, although stressing the epochal character of the turning-point of 1914, does so only to point up the constant bellicose frenzy of the likes of Lenin, Mussolini and Hitler. What is lacking is any examination of the political order which, starting with 'total mobilization', began to emerge in all the countries engaged in the war.

---

16   François Furet, *The Passing of an Illusion*, trans. Deborah Furet, Chicago and London: University of Chicago Press, pp. 518–19 n. 13.

Total Mobilization, Totalism and Totalitarianism

By way of example, let us turn to a liberal country like Italy. It has rightly been observed that the situation following intervention in the war seemed 'to anticipate the *"univers concentrationnaire"* experienced by the world in subsequent decades':[17] compulsory conscription, military tribunals, execution squads; emergency legislation or state of siege constricting not only the army, but the civilian population itself, in an iron grip. At the front, in order not to die, so as not to be forced to die, soldiers not infrequently committed self-mutilation, sometimes with horrific consequences. But military justice was blind; its spies were everywhere; and not a few of those who had mutilated themselves were condemned to death. So as not to waste time, one general – Andrea Graziani – always carried out trench inspections with execution squads in tow.[18] There were instances of decimation, which (reported the high command) commanders had an 'absolute, inescapable duty' to resort to, where necessary.[19] Even when seriously wounded, soldiers enjoyed no respite. Gaetano Salvemini pointed out to the government that it was inadvisable to let them spend their convalescence with their family, because their talk about the tragic reality of the war would have 'extremely dangerous psychological effects'.[20] As far as possible, soldiers' relatives must be kept in the dark about the horrors of the front, but were nevertheless jointly responsible for the behaviour of their kin: 'for psychological purposes the high command requested punitive measures against the kin of deserters, even if they were uninvolved in the crime of their relative'.[21]

With practices of decimation and transversal punishments or vendettas, we are far beyond terror of the Jacobin variety, which precisely did not abrogate individual responsibility, even if it 'ascertained it' on the basis of mere inklings or suspicions. Here, by contrast, the totalitarian universe clearly emerges: decimation was used to end numerous human lives at random, on the basis not even of vague suspicion, but solely for the pedagogical purposes of restoring rigid discipline among slave-soldiers destined for sacrifice and death. Added to this was a paranoid hunt for foreign agents, requiring the dismissal from their jobs of citizens of Austro-German origin

---

17　Enzo Forcella, 'Apologia della paura', preface to Forcella and A. Monticone, eds, *Plotone di esecuzione. I processi della prima guerra mondiale*, Bari: Laterza, 1972, p. xxi.

18　Ibid., pp. xvi, xlvii.

19　See Mario Isnenghi, *Il mito della grande guerra*, Bari: Laterza, 1970, pp. 293–4.

20　Quoted in Forcella, 'Apologia della paura', pp. lvi–lvii.

21　Ibid., pp. lvi–lvii.

or with Austro-German parents, as well as a ubiquitous, rigid network of control. Encompassing the whole population, it even stipulated the character and length of obituaries,[22] and spied on private life, correspondence and conversations so as to prevent and punish any diffusion of rumours or news 'whereby public peace might be disturbed in any way or the public interest damaged'.[23] Jurisdiction was devolved onto military tribunals, which were manipulated by the high command in every aspect and phase of their activity. They seemed to demand not only obedience 'but also enthusiasm'; in fact, what they wanted was that certain 'expressions should not even be thought'.[24]

The state, Weber observed in 1917, 'is accorded "legitimate" power over life, death, and liberty'.[25] This also applies to countries with the oldest liberal traditions. In the USA, a Committee on Public Information was created that would appear to afford the first example of effective total mobilization of the means of information. Emergency legislation allowed for maximum prison terms of twenty years for anyone using 'disloyal, profane, scurrilous, or abusive language about the form of the government of the United States, or the Constitution of the United States, or the military or naval forces of the United States, or the flag . . . or the uniform of the Army or Navy of the United States'.[26] The logic of such developments was made clear by the US Justice Department which, in demanding the rapid enactment of laws against sedition (they were approved by the House of Representatives in under four hours), observed: 'Our soldiers temporarily surrender their liberties of thought and speech and action in order that they may save them for the future. The whole Nation must subject itself to discipline until after the war. Otherwise in defending liberties in detail, we may lose liberty altogether.'[27]

Military discipline tended to be extended from the front to the rear, in accordance with the inexorable logic of 'total mobilization', 'total war' and 'total politics'. This is where we must start to explain the genesis of the term and reality of 'totalismo' (as it was initially called), or 'totalitarianism'

---

22 Ibid., pp. lii, liv.
23 Quoted in ibid., p. xiv.
24 Ibid., p. lviii.
25 Max Weber, 'The Meaning of "Ethical Neutrality" in Sociology and Economics', in Weber, *Methodology of the Social Sciences*, ed. and trans. Edward A. Shils and Henry A. Finch, New Brunswick, NJ: Transaction Publishers, 2011, p. 46.
26 Henry S. Commager, ed., *Documents of American History*, New York: Appleton-Century-Crofts, 1963, Vol. II, p. 146.
27 Quoted in Christopher N. May, *In the Name of War: Judicial Review and War Powers since 1918*, Cambridge, MA, and London: Harvard University Press, 1989, p. 140.

proper.[28] And an integral part of this totalism or totalitarianism was the combination of terror from above with terror from below. In the USA, anti-sedition laws were also justified by the need to prevent resort to lynching by exasperated 'patriots' ready to take the law into their own hands. In reality, vigilante squads were openly encouraged by the authorities, with the result that a '"hang-them-all-at-sunrise" attitude' spread towards those suspected of treason or lack of patriotic zeal.[29]

For a rounded picture, we must take a rapid look at what occurred in the colonies. In Egypt, peasants caught in the bazaars were 'arrested and sent to the nearest mobilization centres'. Those who fled did not get far; for the most part, they were 'captured in outlying villages and sent to barracks under escort'.[30] In the words of a British historian, 'some 50 million Africans and 250 million Indians were involved [by Britain], without consultation, in a war of which they understood nothing'.[31] The more or less forced labour extracted by the metropolis in the colonies needs to be added to the cannon fodder.

In different ways, and to varying degrees of intensity, the totalitarian logic of total war manifested itself in all the countries involved in the conflict. In the USA, Theodore Roosevelt proclaimed that there was no room for divided loyalties: anyone claiming to have them 'is necessarily a traitor to at least one country'. People therefore had to be on their guard: 'the Hun within our gates masquerades in many disguises; he is our dangerous enemy; and he should be hunted down without mercy'. Given that the death sentence intimated here was bound up with a concrete form of behaviour, there was still a way out, which tended to narrow or disappear completely as and when the enemy was subject to a process of racialization. Suspected of forming a fifth column, German 'aliens', required by Wilson to register

---

28   These are watchwords that were subsequently consecrated in two works published in Germany in the inter-war period: Ernst Jünger's 'Total Mobilization' (in Richard Wolin, ed., *The Heidegger Controversy: A Critical Reader*, Cambridge, MA, and London: MIT Press, 1983) and Erich Ludendorff's *Der totale Krieg* (Munich: Ludendorff, 1935). While the former celebrated 'total mobilization', the second identified 'total politics' as the presupposition of 'total war' and its victorious conduct. The term *Totalismus* made its appearance immediately after the war. See Alfons Paquet, *Im Kommunistischen Russland. Briefe aus Moskau*, Jena: Diederichs, 1919, p. 111 and Nolte, *Der europäische Bürgerkrieg*, p. 563.

29   See May, *In the Name of War*, pp. 136–8.

30   Academy of Sciences of the USSR, *Storia universale*, Italian trans., Milan: Teti, 1975, Vol. VII, p. 496.

31   A.J.P. Taylor, *English History 1914–1945*, Oxford: Oxford University Press, 1965, p. 1.

officially, became the target of a campaign of terror. Their property and businesses were seized at the behest of the Justice Secretary. Sometimes, along with other potential traitors, they were marked out with a yellow symbol. As we know, there were also those who invoked the sterilization of a genetically tainted race.[32] Measures of expropriation against a national minority (suspected of insufficient patriotic loyalty, and whom it was therefore a good idea to neutralize and punish economically); the yellow symbol; and the emergence, finally, of the idea of the forced sterilization (and 'mercy killing') of entire ethnic groups – these put us in mind of the Third Reich.

Historical revisionism ignores such glaring facts, claiming to deduce *a priori* the *univers concentrationnaire* from the revolutionary project. Yet it was precisely that political tradition which denounced the totalitarian effects of war in advance, seeking in vain at two crucial points in contemporary history to avert them. War, observed Robespierre between the end of 1791 and the beginning of 1792, concentrated 'all the forces of the state in the hands of executive power', whose 'popularity' and 'dominance' grew.[33] Executive power was – or felt itself – entitled 'to take decisions on its own',[34] sweeping aside any resistance by diffusing a 'spirit of blind, absolute obedience' or, if needs be, by resorting to martial law and placing 'under military command our border cities'.[35] In conclusion:

> War is always the primary aspiration of a powerful government that wants to become even more powerful . . . It is during war that executive power deploys the most formidable energy and exercises a kind of dictatorship, which cannot but threaten nascent liberty. It is during war that the people forget deliberations of fundamental importance to their civil and political rights and concern themselves exclusively with external events.[36]

War was therefore 'the greatest scourge threatening liberty in the circumstances in which we find ourselves', and risked placing the 'fate of the state' in the hands of 'an army, a general'.[37] In effect, having led to the institution

---

32 Susan Canedy, *America's Nazis: A Democratic Dilemma*, Menlo Park: Markgraf, 1990, pp. 10–12. For Theodore Roosevelt's position and the yellow symbol, cf. H.C. Peterson and Gilbert C. Fite, *Opponents of War 1917–1918*, Madison: University of Wisconsin Press, 1957, pp. 81, 197.

33 Maximilien Robespierre, *Oeuvres*, Paris: Presses Universitaires de France, 1912–, Vol. VIII, pp. 37, 87.

34 Ibid., p. 100.

35 Ibid., pp. 87, 48.

36 Ibid., pp. 47–8.

37 Ibid., pp. 40, 61.

of the Terror, the interminable conflict with the anti-French coalition resulted in 1799 in a coup d'état by a warlord who exploited the glory he had won on the battlefield to establish a new kind of despotism. Paradoxically, Robespierre analysed and denounced in advance not only Bonapartism, but the very Jacobin dictatorship of which he became a protagonist.

Something similar occurred in the relationship between the Marxist and Bolshevik movement, on the one hand, and twentieth-century totalitarianism, on the other. Towards the end of the nineteenth century, Engels warned against the inevitably disastrous effects of the impending European conflagration. Already, increasing militarization and 'rivalry in conquest have tuned up the public power to such a pitch that it threatens to swallow the whole of society and even the state'.[38] Once war had broken out, Lenin referred to this analysis,[39] but it was developed by Bukharin in particular. The latter saw looming on the horizon a 'new Leviathan compared with which Thomas Hobbes' fantasy seems like child's play'. It was not limited to controlling production and manpower, reduced to more or less servile conditions. The qualitative leap involved went far beyond the political and economic spheres: 'Philosophy, medicine, religion and ethics, chemistry and bacteriology – everything has been "mobilized" and "militarized", just like industry and finance.' This is unquestionably an early analysis of totalitarianism, even if the word had yet to feature. In addition, Bukharin lucidly grasped the phenomenon subsequently termed the 'nationalization of the masses', meticulously listing the countless associations diffused in society (e.g. in France) that organized and regimented it in unanimous support of colonial expansion and military policy.[40] It can be said that this super-Leviathan also ended up materializing in the state of which Bukharin was a leader and, subsequently, a victim. At all events, it remains the case that the first critical analysis of the totalitarian phenomenon was developed on the basis of an ideology from which historical revisionism claims to deduce it.

That is not all. In the late eighteenth century, the Jacobin press drew attention to the dynamic whereby war created the 'horrors of fanaticism' and familiarized soldiers and citizens 'with blood, butchery, and the daily

---

38   Karl Marx and Friedrich Engels, *Werke*, Berlin: Dietz Verlag, 1955– , Vol. XXI, p. 166.

39   V.I. Lenin, *Collected Works*, London: Lawrence & Wishart, 1960– , Vol. 25, pp. 390–1.

40   N.I. Bukharin, *Lo Stato Leviatano. Scritti sullo Stato e la guerra 1915–1917*, ed. A. Giasanti, Milan: Unicopoli, 1984, pp. 130–43. On the 'nationalization of the masses', cf. George L. Mosse, *The Nationalization of the Masses: Political Symbolism and Mass Movements in Germany from the Napoleonic Wars through the Third Reich*, New York: Howard Fertig, 1974.

spectacle of combat', thus creating contempt for 'the tranquil, pacific liberty which is our happiness'.[41] This is a diagnosis readily applicable to the delight in bellicose adventures and blood that found expression in the twentieth century, in authors like Theodore Roosevelt and Ernst Jünger. Likewise during the First World War, it was the Marxist tradition that first highlighted its genocidal tendencies. While Bukharin referred to a 'nightmarish corpse factory',[42] Luxemburg went even further. On the battlefields 'mass murder' and 'genocide' (*Völkermord*) were becoming such 'daily, tediously monotonous realities' that 'a climate of ritual murder' was prevalent in the rear.[43] This denunciation was contemporaneous with the tragedy of the Armenians. On account of the First World War – a gigantic, interminable sacrificial rite – ritual homicide tended to be transformed from myth into reality.

In the two key moments of contemporary history referred to above, it was the political and social classes targeted by the revolutionary movement that celebrated the marvellous impact of war in regenerating and reconstructing national unity. We have already mentioned the myth of the 'splendid little war', which was widespread on the eve of the First World War. It should be remembered that the creation of political and social 'harmony', and the containment and roll-back of the revolutionary movement, were objectives likewise pursued by supporters of bellicose adventures in France.[44] Invoked as an antidote to revolution, the international conflict gave them powerful impetus. And this ended up burdening the revolutionary movement itself with the disastrous effects it had denounced in the war. A similar dialectic is manifest in 1792 and 1917.

Terror from the War to the Post-War Period

Let it be said firmly and clearly: our intention is not in fact to deny the influence of ideology in the Jacobin Terror or the Bolshevik Gulag. There is no doubt that, in addition to the 'circumstances' for which Furet has utter contempt, the Terror also derived from the discrepancy between political

---

41   Quoted in Marc Belissa, *Le Cosmopolitisme du droit des gens (1713–1795). Fraternité universelle et intérêt national au siècle des lumières et pendant la Révolution française*, doctoral thesis, Paris: Panthéon-Sorbonne, Paris I, 1996, pp. 621, 624.

42   Bukharin, *Lo Stato Leviatano*, p. 45.

43   Rosa Luxemburg, *Politische Schriften*, ed. O.K. Flechtheim, Frankfurt am Main: Europäische Verlagsanstalt, 1968, Vol. II, pp. 19–20, 31, 33.

44   See Belissa, *Le Cosmopolitisme du droit des gens*, pp. 618, 621.

project and historical situation. Pursuing the fantastic utopia of a reconstruction of the ancient polis, Robespierre embarked on a quixotic endeavour. This believed it possible to eliminate anything that did not correspond to its project or utopia by means of violence, but inevitably resulted in the re-emergence of modern economic and social relations, very different from those features of the ancient polis to which the Jacobin leaders passionately aspired. In this sense, the Terror contained a surplus of violence vis-à-vis the objective situation. This was pointed out by Marx himself. He repeatedly underlined the weaknesses, illusions and mirages of Jacobin ideology, which was not simply the product of individual madness, but itself referred to a broader historical context. There is no reason not to apply the same methodology when analyzing the revolution that drew its inspiration from Marx. A manifestly negative role was played by basic theoretical weaknesses in the Bolshevik leaders' political project: the idea of a rapid transition to a society without a state, market, religion, borders and national identity generated a surplus of violence against civil society. Expectations of the imminent realization of a society without conflicts of any kind distracted attention from the need to legally regulate continuing conflicts through general norms and forms. The utopianism derived from Marx made it impossible to confront the state of emergency adequately, therewith prolonging it unnecessarily. All this is true. But it does not mean that we can ignore the state of emergency and deduce everything from ideology. Yet this is what historical revisionism does. The arbitrary abstractions already identified in the liquidation of Jacobinism are, with a few variations, once again evident in the case of Bolshevism: silence about total war and a lack of any serious comparative analysis of the totalitarian tendencies that emerged in its wake in very different countries.

Let us see how Lenin described the situation in the post-war period: 'Either the whiteguard, bourgeois terrorism of the American, British (Ireland), Italian (the fascists), German, Hungarian and other types, or Red, proletarian terrorism. There is no middle course, no "third course", nor can there be any.'[45] In the USA, notwithstanding the armistice of 11 November 1918, the state of war was formally ended only three years later, with the signature of the peace treaties. Without in practice being impeded by judicial power, the federal government exploited it to employ 'the full panoply of its war powers', which allowed it, *inter alia*, to control post, to exercise a censorship whose 'magnitude . . . cannot be overstated', to

---

45   Lenin, *Collected Works*, Vol. 32, p. 356.

'tak[e] civil and criminal action against strikers, to prosecut[e] radicals', to launch 'a frontal attack on dissidents' – in fact, to declare and wage a 'war on radicalism'. That phrase comes from the *New York Times*, which highlighted why the iron fist already wielded against potential supporters of Germany was also being deployed against Bolsheviks and subversives. In fact, 'bad as was the German spy, he was not worse nor more dangerous than is the would-be destroyer of all civilized government'.[46] Of especial significance was the persistence of a combination of violence from above and violence from below, with the participation of vigilante groups and, in particular, the Ku Klux Klan, which revived from 1915 onwards. The xenophobia fuelled by the massive conflict survived its conclusion and was directed at Catholics, Jews, Communists and, above all, blacks, all of them regarded as alien to genuine 'Americanism'. In 1921, having been subject to violence by white gangs (tolerated or protected by the police), the black districts of Tulsa (in Oklahoma) were attacked by land and bombed with dynamite by one or more planes. For an inhabitant caught up in this full-blown, warlike offensive (intended to prevent a feared black reaction to earlier gang aggression), one seemed to be witnessing the German invasion of France or Belgium: 'The firing of guns was renewed in quick succession. People were seen to flee from their burning homes, some with babes in their arms and leading crying and excited children by the hand; others, old and feeble, all fleeing to safety.' The survivors were subsequently expelled en masse by the police and imprisoned in 'internment camps'.[47]

Let us turn to Ireland. The nationalists believed they were in position to take advantage of the war to achieve their dream of independence. At Easter 1916, on 22 April, they rose up in Dublin. Although their hatred of Britain was age-old, as was their experience of harsh repression, they had not fully understood the reality of total war: 'The insurgents' training had been based on the assumption that they would have to face nothing more than small-arms fire; they thought it would be impossible that the British would use artillery in the centre of an historic city.' The dispelling of their illusions was tragic. A few days later, the city centre was in ruins. Forced to surrender, even seriously wounded rebels were shot after summary, secret 'trials', conducted on the basis of martial law. Suspected sympathizers were interned without trial in concentration camps in their thousands. But the worst was still to come. With

---

46   See May, *In the Name of War*, pp. 1, 133–4, 144.
47   See Scott Ellsworth, *Death in a Promised Land: The Tulsa Race Riot of 1921*, Baton Rouge and London: Louisiana State University Press, 1992, pp. 59–72.

the end of the war came a resumption of pressure for independence, which increasingly took the form of armed struggle. The spiral of terror and counter-terror became infernal. The authorities resorted to reprisals: paramilitary groups indiscriminately opened fire on a crowd of soccer fans; whole districts were destroyed. A manifesto warned: 'If in the vicinity a policeman is shot, five Sinn Feiners will be shot . . . Stop the shooting of the police, or we will lay low every house that smells of Sinn Fein.' This was a practice that did not scandalize Lloyd George: 'You cannot in the existing state of Ireland punish a policeman who shoots a man whom he has every reason to suspect is concerned with political murders. This kind of thing can only be met with reprisals.' Or, in the words of another government representative, 'terror must be met by greater terror'.[48] Such was precisely Lenin's view.

Still in the years immediately following the First World War, the so-called Free Corps (*Freikorps*) went into action in Germany. They did not limit themselves to restoring 'order' in their own country, but also intervened in the Baltic countries in defence both of persistent German colonial ambitions and of civilization against 'Asiatic' and Bolshevik 'barbarism'. In Riga, 'liberated' by them (with the at least initial agreement of the social-democratic government and the Entente itself), the Free Corps proceeded to massive summary executions without trial on 22 May 1919. Sometimes they resorted to the façade of martial law, which provided for the death penalty for crimes like 'failure to report to a drum-head court martial, sympathy for Bolshevism, being found in the streets of Riga after 6.00 pm, and using a private telephone'.[49] As regards Germany itself, rather than the action without legal and humanitarian scruples of the Free Corps (which broadly merged into Nazism and formed the initial backbone of the SS),[50] it is well to remember that (as acknowledged by Nolte himself, albeit the Nolte not yet identified with historical revisionism), 'the ruthless repressive measures of Noske' and the social-democratic government went far beyond the 'ventures of the Spartacists', just as in Hungary Horthy's 'white terror' proved much more radical than the preceding 'red terror'.[51] The atmosphere of these years is

48   See Paul Johnson, *Ireland: A Concise History from the Twelfth Century to the Present Day*, Chicago: Academy, 1992, pp. 178–94.

49   Robert G.L. Waite, *Vanguard of Nazism: The Free Corps Movement in Postwar Germany 1918–1923*, Cambridge, MA: Harvard University Press, 1970, pp. 118–19.

50   See Arno J. Mayer, *Why Did the Heavens Not Darken? The 'Final Solution' in History*, London: Verso, 2012, p. 138.

51   Ernst Nolte, *La crisi dei regimi liberali e i movimenti fascisti*, trans. E. Gamaleri and A. Caiani, Bologna: Il Mulino, p. 43.

perhaps best characterized by the position adopted by Justice Minister Schiffer, according to whom, faced with an acute state of emergency, the federal president could 'use poisoned gas against cities if, in a given case, this is the necessary measure for the restoration of security and order'.[52]

Corresponding to British paramilitary groups and the German Free Corps were Italian fascist squads and the American Ku Klux Klan. Of particular significance on the early post-war Western scene is not so much the terror practised by the state apparatus proper, as recourse to armed bodies of a seemingly 'private' or 'semi-private' character. The right to engage in reprisals, even indiscriminate reprisals, could not be officially declared by the British government, which in fact tolerated or encouraged them via a kind of reserve state apparatus not constrained by ordinary law.

Lenin referred to such developments in the 'bourgeois' camp to explain and justify Bolshevik terror. At the same point in time, Churchill stated that he wanted to confront the state of emergency in Ireland drawing inspiration from the measures of the 'Russian government' and 'making life intolerable' in the areas where the rebels operated.[53] Who really initiated the terror? The Bolsheviks or their opponents? And was it the October Revolution or the total war against which it revolted? Rather than shifting the blame back and forth, students today should attempt to analyse the objective dialectic of the phenomenon and the influence on its development of different situations, as well as different ideologies and different ruling groups. Contrary to Furet's programmatic declarations, however, here too historical revisionism prefers to identify with the experience of one of the antagonists engaged in a massive conflict.

Even more horrible was the face of war in Russia. While it did not scant on artillery to maintain internal discipline, the retreating Czarist army resorted to scorched earth tactics. But let us see in what conditions: 'People were torn away from their homes with but a few hours in which to settle their affairs. Their stores of food and at times even their houses were burned before their very eyes.' A forced mass migration resulted: a stream of thousands, hundreds of thousands, up to one million exiles, without shelter, without means of transport, without a destination, without food; women carried new-born babies at their breasts who died of hunger.[54] Patriotic

---

52   We quote from the paraphrase in Carl Schmitt, *Dictatorship: From the Origin of the Modern Concept of Sovereignty to Proletarian Class Struggle*, trans. Michael Hoelzl and Graham Ward, Cambridge: Polity Press, 2014, p. 176.

53   Johnson, *Ireland*, p. 190.

54   W. Bruce Lincoln, *Passage Through Armageddon: The Russians in War and Revolution 1914–1918*, New York and Oxford: Oxford University Press, 1994, pp. 156–7.

hysteria and the demands of total war set off an anti-German manhunt: a 'vicious anti-German pogrom' occurred in May 1915 in Moscow and, more generally, 'anyone overheard speaking German risked lynching'.[55]

But the main victims were obviously the Jews. The Russian high command warned against their espionage activities. Some were taken hostage and threatened with death in the event of the 'Jewish community' displaying insufficient loyalty to the Czarist army. Alleged 'spies' were shot.[56] Above all, the deportation of Jews overrun by the advance of the Wilhelmine armies was decided. A Duma deputy described the modalities of the operation. At Radom, at 23.00 hrs,

> the people were informed that they had to leave, with a threat that anyone found at daybreak would be hanged . . . Old men, invalids, and paralytics had to be carried in people's arms because there were no vehicles. The police and gendarmes treated the Jewish refugees precisely like criminals. In one case . . . a train was completely sealed and when finally opened, most of the inmates were found half dead.

Of the half-million Jews subject to deportation measures, 100,000 did not survive.[57] Following the two revolutions, there was a marked intensification in anti-Semitic agitation, which, gunning for Jews branded as Bolsheviks, now intersected with the civil and international war against the new Soviet power. While the latter countered the bloody agitation with draconian laws, in summer 1918 British forces carried out a massive air-drop of anti-Semitic leaflets.[58] A few months later, pogroms of shocking proportions occurred in which around 60,000 Jews lost their lives and which, it would seem, enjoyed the secret support of 'the Allies, then engaged in their invasion of Russia'.[59] This is a chapter of history that seems to be a direct prelude to the Nazi genocide.[60]

---

55   Richard Pipes, *The Russian Revolution*, New York: Vintage Books, 1990, p. 220.

56   Lincoln, *Passage Through Armageddon*, p. 141.

57   Nora Levin, *The Jews in the Soviet Union since 1917*, London and New York: I.B. Tauris, 1990, Vol. I, pp. 28–9.

58   Léon Poliakov, *The History of Anti-Semitism*, trans. Richard Howard et al., Philadelphia: University of Pennsylvania Press, 2003, Vol. 4, p. 203.

59   George L. Mosse, *Fallen Soldiers: Reshaping the Memory of the World Wars*, New York: Oxford University Press, 1994, p. 160.

60   Norman Cohn, *Warrant for Genocide: The Myth of the Jewish World-Conspiracy and the Protocols of the Elders of Zion*, New York: Harper & Row, 1967, p. 125. Mayer writes in similar terms in *Why Did the Heavens Not Darken?*, p. 5.

Nolte's Development

In Nolte's view, however, the horror of the Third Reich took the form of a replica of, and prophylactic measure against, the horrors hailing from Soviet Russia. But the revisionist ideologue who claims to have identified October 1917 as the primordial source of the catastrophe of the twentieth century is contradicted by the historian obliged to recognize that the deportation of the Armenians marked 'the first great act of genocide in the twentieth century'.[61] This was a deportation that occurred prior to the fateful date – in fact, during the war against which the Bolsheviks rebelled. But this is not the only oscillation or inconsistency in Nolte, on whose development it is worth dwelling.

In his early phase, the German historian sought the origins of Nazism and the genocide elsewhere. He underscored the Social Darwinist motifs in Hitler and his links with 'the great stream of counterrevolutionary thought'.[62] He highlighted the decisive role played by appeals to struggle against the Judeo-Bolshevik conspiracy, by the denunciation of the Jew as a pathogenic agency in society, as a bacillus of dissolution and subversion to be destroyed: 'The explosive political effect of this identification of Jewry with bolshevism is obvious . . . Not, of course, that it was Hitler's invention; it was the common property of a whole literature from Henry Ford to Otto Hauser – one might even be tempted to say that Hitler was *its* invention.'[63]

Particularly interesting here is the reference to Ford, whom we shall see supporting the thesis of the racial (Jewish), as opposed to political, origin of the Bolshevik October. In this phase, Nolte explained Hitler not with reference to the USSR and Lenin and Stalin, but to the USA and a magnate of the American automobile industry. The Third Reich was viewed as inspired not by the 'Asiatic' model represented by Bolshevism, but by the ideology that branded Bolshevism and Judaism alike as Asiatic phenomena alien to the West. If analogies with Nazism could be discovered among Germany's enemies, they were to be found in the nationalist movements. In his chauvinist frenzy, an author like Charles Maurras indissolubly equated Nazism

---

61   Ernst Nolte, 'The Past That Will Not Pass: A Speech That Could Be Written but Not Delivered', in *Forever in the Shadow of Hitler? Original Documents of the Historikerstreit, The Controversy Concerning the Singularity of the Holocaust*, trans. James Knowlton and Truett Cates, New Jersey: Humanities Press, 1993, p. 21.

62   Ernst Nolte, *Three Faces of Fascism: Action Française, Italian Fascism, National Socialism*, trans. Leila Vennewitz, New York: Mentor, 1969, p. 418.

63   Ibid., p. 419.

and the German people, so that the only possible 'de-Nazification' would be 'de-Germanization'. Such a view, commented the non-revisionist historian, 'is the outright expression of the inclination (if not personal, at least factual) toward genocide, which links [Maurras] with Hitler'.[64] Early Nolte was well aware of the naturalistic and racial character of the Third Reich's de-specification of the enemy. Precedents and analogies were to be sought other than in the revolutionary tradition.

At this stage of Nolte's development, far from representing a mere riposte to Bolshevism, Fascism and Nazism had a pre-history pre-dating October 1917 and which, moreover, did not refer exclusively to the struggle against the democratic and socialist movement. A prominent role was played by growing international tensions, the increasingly evident antagonism between the various capitalist countries. Even before the outbreak of the First World War, movements existed in France at whose core was 'hero worship and the spell of bloodshed'. They declared 'holy war' on the republic, prayed for Jaurès' death, stated their intention of drowning Parliament in the Seine, smelt the presence of Jewish espionage and treason, and unleashed squads against socialists and anti-militarists. Along with Action française, the Camelots du Rois, whose name was 'synonymous with terror' − a terror manifestly attuned to preparing for the impending gigantic conflict -- especially distinguished themselves. Having cleared the streets of any resistance to the introduction of the three-year military draft, they boasted of having acted as '*Gendarmes supplémentaires*'. Early Nolte aptly comments: 'Flouters of the law as auxiliary police: a strange union with more than a hint of things to come!'[65] It is clear that the constitutive elements of Fascism were already present and, according to the non-revisionist historian, the original experience of Mussolini's terror derived not from Lenin but precisely from the Camelots, even if the news of their evil deeds initially filled his 'Marxist heart . . . with angry contempt'.[66]

Turning from France to Germany, we see 'right-wing totalitarianism' emerging prior to October in 'a classical formulation'. Nolte is referring to a book published anonymously in 1912 by the president of the Pan-German League.[67] We are once again referred to the climate preceding and heralding

---

64   Ibid., p. 122.
65   Ibid., pp. 127–31.
66   Ibid., p. 130.
67   Heinrich Class (Daniel Frymann), *Wenn ich der Kaiser wär'. Politische Wahrheiten und Notwendigkeiten*, Leipzig: Dieterich'scheVerlagsbuchhandlung, 1912. See Nolte, *La crisi dei regimi liberali e i movimenti fascisti*, p. 49.

the outbreak of the Great War, which was prayed for by Heinrich Class (the author in question) as a remedy for the 'current malady' and 'a moment of revival in the people of all its good, healthy and energetic forces' – the forces it required to decisively repulse the democratic movement, if necessary by a coup d'état. No doubt the war with the other powers would prove hard and difficult; and it might end in defeat and increased chaos. But people should not be unduly concerned about this: the 'powerful will of a dictator' would ensure the restoration of 'order' and prepare for revenge, after having swept away 'Jewish-socialist propaganda' for 'a revolution intended to destroy the German people for ever'.[68] Only a 'catastrophe' serving to liquidate the Jewish 'ferment of decomposition', and socialist and 'Jewish dissolution', could pave the way for a real renaissance of 'national policy'.[69]

Such talk, which seems to prophesy Nazism, and offer a clear statement of the justification for Hitler's regime, is clairvoyant and sinister. At stake was averting the threat of annihilation that Jews and socialists posed to Germany. This ideological theme of 'counter-annihilation', not taken seriously by early Nolte, is at the heart of his subsequent reading of the twentieth century. Throughout his development, the German historian has rightly paid particular attention to Nietzsche and, above all, to the appeal, which emerged in the last years of the philosopher's conscious existence, to the 'annihilation', the destruction 'without pity', of anything degenerate. Thus, stressed early Nolte, the working-class movement inspired by Marxism was 'confronted with the desperate comradeship in arms of the martial society and the culture proceeding from it with its battle cry of "salvation" and "annihilation"'. This pitiless conflict would end in the triumph of 'the future lords of the earth'. A new type of man would emerge, capable (in Nietzsche's words as reported by Nolte) of 'cruelty merely at the *sight* of much suffering, perishing, and destruction'. He would be 'cruel in hand and deed (and not merely with the eyes of the spirit)', and prove capable of 'experiencing pleasure' in suffering. Thus, 'many decades in advance, Nietzsche provided the political, radical anti-Marxism of fascism with its original spiritual image, an image of which even Hitler never quite showed himself the equal'.[70] In this phase, Nazism was the inheritor of a reactionary radicalism that contained a terrible charge of violence and developed decades before the Bolshevik October.

---

68   Rudolf Buchner and Winfried Baumgart, eds, *Quellen zum politischen Denken der Deutschen im 19. und 20. Jahrhundert. Freiherr vom Stein – Gedächtnisausgabe*, Darmstadt: Wissenschaftliche Buchgesellschaft, 1976–, Vol. VII, pp. 313–15.

69   Class, *Wenn ich der Kaiser wär'*, pp. 36–9.

70   Nolte, *Three Faces of Fascism*, pp. 556–7.

True, Nietzsche might be considered a riposte to Marx. However, for the non-revisionist historian it made no sense to seek to put the two philosophers on a par:

> It is true that the bourgeoisie saw itself threatened politically with destruction by the socialist program. But it is equally true that it was a legacy of Marxism if scarcely anywhere did the socialist parties attempt to bring about such destruction (even in Russia they did so only hesitantly and in the struggle for their own survival). For Marxists regard 'the expropriation of the expropriators' rather as the radical removal of an already tottering obstacle than an actual battle, and certainly not as physical extermination. It is precisely Nietzsche's thought which proves that the fascist idea of destruction must not be regarded primarily as a homogeneous reaction [to the challenge represented by Marx].[71]

Whereas Nolte links Nazism with the anti-democratic reaction of the nineteenth century, the idea of physical extermination proves foreign not only to Marx, but also to the Bolsheviks. Some years later, although correctly underscoring the 'horror' of the Gulag, when reporting the assertion of a Bolshevik newspaper that 'our war is not directed against individuals, but we seek to destroy the bourgeoisie as a class', the German historian regarded it as 'incontrovertible' that 'the "destruction of the bourgeoisie" as a class does not mean killing every single bourgeois'.[72] Shortly before his revisionist turn, Nolte defined the Bolsheviks as 'the greatest force of planned destruction', but entered two important caveats: 'the white terror was at least equal in cruelty to the red terror' and, in any event, the Bolsheviks' planned destruction was to be regarded as 'anti-Marxist'. It was alien to Marx for reasons bound up with his scientific methodology. In fact, observed Nolte, Marx's definition of classes was never purely sociological (it might be said that in Marx 'actual sociological analysis' was 'comparatively irrelevant'): 'party struggle' was not immediately identified with 'class struggle'. Depending on circumstances or 'conduct', the same social group, or individuals from the same social group, could be included in the category of proletariat, lumpenproletariat, or plebs. The same was true of the bourgeoisie. Elements from its ranks could become part of the working-class movement, even leaders of

---

71 Ibid., p. 666 n. 42 (trans. modified).
72 Nolte, *La crisi dei regime liberali e i movimenti fascisti*, p. 38.

it.[73] The category of class genocide, which subsequently became the war horse of historical revisionism, is exposed here as a nonsense: what defines genocide is precisely the irrelevance of the conduct of the individual, naturalistically included in a group whose fate she or he simply cannot escape.

In today's historical revisionism, there is no reference to Maurras and Ford: it is a question of exclusively indicting the revolutionary tradition from 1789 to 1917. In tracing the history of conspiracy theory, Furet establishes a dizzying line of continuity between the French Revolution and Nazism: the 'aristocrats' and class enemies sniffed out first by the Jacobins, and then by the Bolsheviks, become the Jews who were the object of Hitler's paranoia.[74] Not a word is spent by the French historian on his esteemed Burke, who was among the first (as we shall see) to detect a Jewish hand in the unprecedented events across the Channel. Little or no attention is paid to the extraordinary vitality of the myth of the Jewish conspiracy supposedly underlying revolutionary upheavals. In the course of the struggle against the October Revolution, this myth celebrated its triumph not only in Germany, but throughout the West. The initial head of the crusade against the Judeo-Bolshevik conspiracy was Henry Ford, the American automobile magnate. To foil it, he founded a paper with a large print run, the *Dearborn Independent*. The articles published in it were collected in 1920 in a volume entitled *The International Jew*, which immediately became a reference point for international anti-Semitism, to the extent that it 'probably did more than any other work to make the *Protocols* world-famous'.[75] Much later, front-rank Nazi leaders like von Schirach and even Himmler claimed to have been inspired by Ford or to have started out from him. In particular, the second recalls having understood 'the Jewish danger' only after reading Ford's book: for Nazis it came as a 'revelation'. Reading of the *Protocols of the Elders of Zion* followed: 'These two books indicated the road to follow to liberate humanity from the affliction of the greatest enemy of all time, the Jewish international.'[76] According to Himmler, along with the *Protocols*, Ford's book played a

---

73   Ernst Nolte, *Marxismus und industrielle Revolution*, Stuttgart: Klett-Cotta, 1983, pp. 402–3, 525–6.

74   Furet, *The Passing of an Illusion*, p. 45.

75   Cohn, *Warrant for Genocide*, p. 159. Cf. also Poliakov, *History of Anti-Semitism*, Vol. 4, pp. 251–2.

76   As regards von Schirach, see William L. Shirer, *The Rise and Fall of the Third Reich: A History of Nazi Germany*, London: Pan, 1964, p. 188; for Himmler, cf. Poliakov, *History of Anti-Semitism*, Vol. 4, pp. 254, 387 n. 138, which makes perfunctory mention of the testimony of Felix Kersten, Himmler's Finnish masseur, conserved in the *Centre de documentation Juive et contemporaine* (*Das Buch von Henry Ford*, 22 December 1940, No. CCX-31).

'decisive' (*ausschlaggebend*) role in the Führer's formation, as well as his own.[77] What is certain is that *The International Jew* continued to be published with great fanfare in the Third Reich, with prefaces underlining the decisive historical merit of the American industrialist (for having shed light on the 'Jewish question') and disclosing a kind of direct line from Henry Ford to Adolf Hitler![78]

Blithely ignored by Furet, all this is allowed to lapse by the later Nolte, committed as he is to the goal of Germany's readmission into the authentic West. Attention must now be concentrated exclusively on the East. Everything is clear: the Nazi genocide is to be imputed to 'Asiatic' barbarism, imitated by Hitler with his focus on the October Revolution. Was the idea of annihilation already present in late nineteenth-century culture? In reality, it was tantamount to an idea of 'counter-annihilation', in reaction to the programmes of physical liquidation of the bourgeoisie and exploiting classes already inscribed in black and white in the socialist movement.[79] 'With the Bolshevik Revolution, for the first time in European history a negation of the right to existence not only in theoretical terms, but in historical reality, came to fruition. All this was precisely postulated by Marxism.'[80] First Nietzsche, then Hitler, reacted to the threat of annihilation: *The Anti-Christ* responded to the *Manifesto of the Communist Party*, just as *Mein Kampf* took up the challenge of *The State and Revolution*!

The Savage, the Work Tool and the Bacillus

A pity that this ingenious reconstruction does not withstand textual analysis! Late Nietzsche's relentless polemic against socialists must not lead us to forget the motif of the 'destruction of the decadent races'.[81] The philosopher expressed the hope that the '"barbarism" of the methods' used by the conquistadors 'in the Congo and wherever', and an awareness of the need

---

77   See n. 76 for the evidence of Felix Karsten.

78   See, for example, the *Vorwort* by the German publisher to the 29th and 30th editions, dated 'June and August 1933': Henry Ford, *Der internationale Jude*, trans. P. Lehmann, Leipzig: Hemmer, 1933, pp. 3–5.

79   Ernst Nolte, *Nietzsche und Nietzscheanismus*, Frankfurt am Main and Berlin: Propyläen, 1990, p. 193.

80   Ernst Nolte, *Intervista sulla questione tedesca*, ed. A. Krali, Rome and Bari: Laterza, 1993, p. 54.

81   Friedrich Nietzsche, *Sämtliche Werke, Kritische Studienausgabe*, ed. G. Colli and M. Montinari, Munich: DTV, 1980, Vol. XI, p. 69.

to maintain 'mastery of barbarians', would end up putting paid to the habitual, hateful 'European sentimentality'.[82] This takes us back to revisionism's other colossal repression. While the first ignores total war, the second abolishes the history of colonialism. According to Nolte, in developing his programme and methods of struggle, Hitler constantly had in mind the treatment meted out to prisoners of the 'Chinese Cheka': 'They place a cage containing a half-starved rat in front of his head. The interrogator threatens to open the door.'[83] This was the kind of horror to which Nazism felt compelled to respond. The revisionist historian's argument is the one with which colonialism has traditionally justified its brutality. Let us read a contemporary American historian:

> The Filipinos were fighting the kind of war that is based on terror; the Americans fought back just as cruelly. They developed a 'water torture' that made even the Spanish cringe. If a captured Filipino refused to divulge military information, four or five gallons of water were forced down his throat until his body became 'an object frightful to contemplate'. Then the water was forced out by kneeling on his stomach. The treatment was repeated until the prisoner talked or died.[84]

Torture is not an invention alien to the West, which Nazism could only have imitated by looking to Asiatic, Bolshevik barbarism. But Nolte sticks with his schema: like the barbarism of the means of struggle generally, so the genocides of the twentieth century descend from the October Revolution. With the latter, a 'qualitatively new thing was entering into world history' – 'the collectivist appraisal of guilt and the acts of annihilation that resulted from it'.[85] Once again, both total war (and the practice of decimation), and the history of colonialism, disappear from the revisionist historian's view. Yet it was precisely to this history that an anti-Semitic deputy made explicit reference in the Reichstag in the late nineteenth century, when demanding the mass expulsion of the Jews uninhibited by compassion for particular individuals. In India, he stated, the British 'exterminated this whole sect [the

82   Ibid., Vol. XII, p. 471.

83   Ernst Nolte, 'The Past That Will Not Pass', p. 21. On Nolte's inaccuracies in this connection, cf. Hans-Ulrich Wehler, Le mani sulla storia, trans. A. Missiroli, Florence: Ponte alle Grazie, 1989, pp. 115–21.

84   Robert Leckie, The Wars of America, New York: Harper Collins, 1992, p. 570.

85   Nolte, 'Standing Things on Their Heads: Against Negative Nationalism in Interpreting History', in Forever in the Shadow of Hitler, p. 151.

Thuggee], without regard to the question whether any particular member of the sect already had committed a murder or not'.[86]

But let us return to the rebellion in the Philippines, basing ourselves on the reconstruction of another American historian. The guerrillas were faced not only with the systematic destruction of crops and livestock, but also by mass imprisonment of the population in concentration camps, where it was scythed down by starvation and disease. A general (Jacob H. Smith) issued explicit orders to transform a village into a 'howling wilderness', resorting, *inter alia*, to the killing of all males over the age of ten. This was not an isolated gesture: it was necessary (as the War Secretary himself made clear) to employ 'methods which have proved successful in our Indian campaigns in the West'.[87]

Hitler constantly referred to white and European expansion in the Far West, as well as to the British conquest of India. Underlying genocide is an act of naturalistic de-specification and this goes back in the first instance to the history of colonialism. Naturalistic de-specification can in fact take very different forms. We may start with the observations of a historian of slavery, who summarizes a few centuries of Western history as follows: 'Negroes . . . were stolen in Africa to work the lands stolen from Indians in America.'[88] Or, in the words of Hobson (the British left-wing liberal closely read by Lenin), colonial expansion proceeded *pari passu* with extermination of 'inferior races', who were 'incapable of profitable exploitation by the superior white settlers'.[89]

On the one hand, then, we have work tools, applicable to whom are the categories developed by Aristotle and antiquity to define the institution of slavery, which southern ideologues in the USA continued until the Civil War to celebrate as the foundation of civilization. There was no question about the utility of blacks. Ownership of slaves was an index of wealth and the development of production: the 'breeding' of blacks became a flourishing economic activity in some southern states.[90] Naturally, a presupposition of

86 Quoted in Raul Hilberg, *The Destruction of European Jews*, New York and London: Holms & Meier, 1985, Vol. I, p. 18.

87 Quoted in Brian McAllister Linn, *The U.S. Army and Counterinsurgency in the Philippine War, 1899–1902*, Chapel Hill and London: University of North Carolina Press, 1989, pp. 27, 23.

88 Eric Williams, *Capitalism and Slavery*, London: Deutsch, 1990, p. 9.

89 J.A. Hobson, *Imperialism: A Study*, Ann Arbor: University of Michigan Press, 1983, p. 253.

90 John H. Franklin, *From Slavery to Freedom: A History of Negro Americans*, New York: Knopf, 2000, p. 132.

the profitability of such investments was that the work tools, or 'beasts of burden' as they were sometimes dubbed, remained such. That was why, as Tocqueville reports, severe penalties, including death, attached to teaching slaves to read and write.[91]

Barely touched by civilization, blacks continued to be regarded as 'barbarians'. Although adopting mildly abolitionist positions, on the assumption that 'the real distinctions which Nature has made' could not be surmounted or challenged, Jefferson came down in favour of deporting emancipated slaves to Africa, so as to avoid a conflict that would end in 'the extermination of the one or the other race' (the laws of the *jus publicum europaeum* were inapplicable in this instance).[92] In the late nineteenth century, Theodore Roosevelt repeated that, should one of the 'inferior races' attack the 'superior' race, the latter would be bound to respond with a 'war of extermination': like 'crusaders', white soldiers would be called upon 'to put to death man, woman and child'.[93] These were years when strong-arm groups committed to reasserting white supremacy, despite the defeat of the slaveholding South, were unleashed. In some circles, the temptation arose of 'wip[ing]' the blacks 'from the face of the earth', thereby definitively averting 'the hideous, ominous, national menace' that loomed over American civilization.[94] With a view to 'unloosing the Gordian knot of American politics', dynamite could be used so that blacks were 'gradually exterminated from the face of the whole earth', as had occurred or was occurring in the case of the Native Americans.[95]

So the fate of the Native Americans was to serve as a warning to the slaves or ex-slaves. According to an ideologue on the eve of the Civil War, 'they are threatened with violent extermination. The fate of the Indians shows that they will be exterminated if they continue so useless and so troublesome.'[96] But to the extent that normality obtained, or could be

---

91   Alexis de Tocqueville, *Oeuvres complètes*, ed. Jacob-Peter Mayer, Paris: Gallimard, 1951– , Vol. I, pt. 1, p. 377 and Vol. III, p. 117.

92   Thomas Jefferson, *Writings*, ed. Merrill D. Peterson, New York: Library of America, 1984, p. 139.

93   Theodore Roosevelt, *The Letters*, ed. E.E. Morison, J.M. Blum and J.J. Buckley, Cambridge, MA: Harvard University Press, 1951–, Vol. I, p. 377.

94   See C. Vann Woodward, *Origins of the New South 1877–1913*, Baton Rouge: Louisiana State University Press, 1951, pp. 352–3.

95   Quoted in Thomas F. Gosset, *Race: The History of an Idea in America*, New York: Schocken Books, 1965, pp. 262–3.

96   Thus Fitzhugh, quoted in Richard Slotkin, *The Fatal Environment: The Myth of the Frontier in the Age of Industrialization 1800–1890*, New York: Harper Perennial, 1994, p. 233.

restored, it would be foolish to abandon useful work tools or cheap forced labour.

While it only emerged with states of emergency in the case of blacks, the temptation to destroy the Native Americans was constant. They were of little or no economic value: 'The Spaniards discovered that one Negro was worth four Indians.'[97] The difference in the fate meted out by whites to the two races clearly emerges from reading Tocqueville: 'the Europeans have not been able to change the character of the Indians; and though they have had the power to destroy, they have never been able to subdue and civilize them'. In other words, the Native Americans were more resistant than blacks to being reduced to work tools. In any event, while the Europeans wanted to exploit the blacks' labour-power, they sought to grab the Native Americans' land. This is something the liberal author expresses in an ideological, subtly apologetic register, almost as if the blacks and Native Americans were responsible for their fate at white hands: 'The servility of the one dooms him to slavery, the pride of the other to death.' The fact was that 'civilization has little hold over' the 'redskin'; 'far from desiring to conform his habits to ours, he loves his savage life as the distinguishing mark of his race and repels every advance to civilization'. That was why 'not only have these wild tribes receded, but they are destroyed'.[98]

The radical difference in the fate that befell the two unfortunate races becomes clear. The blacks were deported from Africa and their presence was highly welcome, because it did not challenge the social and natural hierarchy – an outcome easy enough to achieve, given that nature itself rendered the slaves or work tools instantly recognizable by their skin colour. By contrast, the Native Americans had to be removed from those fertile lands which Providence had in fact reserved for the Europeans. Successive deportations, ever further West towards an increasingly remote horizon, were at once a terrible reality and a metaphor for a journey into the void. Whites merely confined themselves to collaborating more or less directly with God's design, depending on the strength of their moral scruples. In addition to the Native Americans' removal, such collaboration could take other forms. In 1790, Franklin wrote: 'if it be the design of Providence to extirpate these savages in order to make room for the cultivators of the earth, it seems not improbable that rum may be the appointed means. It

---

97   Williams, *Capitalism and Slavery*, p. 9.
98   Alexis de Tocqueville, *Democracy in America*, London: Everyman, 1994, Vol. I, pp. 334–7.

has already annihilated all the tribes that formerly inhabited the seacoast.'[99] Rum was a kind of euthanasia for a race that was already condemned and already dying. There was no inviolable boundary separating recourse to alcohol from the tailor-made spread of contagious diseases, the devastation of land, the razing of villages, and the use of firearms against the civilian population. And such a boundary was all the more easily crossed in that the victims' resistance seemed stubborn and irrational. Between the end of the nineteenth century and the beginning of the twentieth, Theodore Roosevelt called for 'putt[ing] down savagery and barbarism': 'I don't go so far as to think that the only good Indians are the dead Indians, but I believe nine out of every ten are, and I shouldn't like to inquire too closely into the case of the tenth.'[100]

A fate similar was suffered in southern Africa by 'the jungle men and Hottentots', who (Gumplowicz observed) were regarded and treated by the 'Christian Boers' 'as "beings" (Geschöpfe) whom it is permissible to exterminate like wild game'.[101]

The fate of the Jews was different. The diaspora, and the legislation enacted against them, severed them from land ownership at a stroke. Hence they could not be assimilated to those 'savages' the wealth of whose land had to be exploited lest it be doomed to sterility. Furthermore, given the culture and professional skills that profoundly integrated them into bourgeois modern society, Jews could certainly not be assimilated to the kind of dross represented by the Native Americans and kindred races, of which the engine of civilization somehow needed to be rid so as to be able to proceed more rapidly. They could not even be compared with blacks. It was difficult to include the people of the Book in the category of work tools; for a series of historical reasons, moreover, they had been deeply involved in the liberal arts. By virtue of their culture, by dint of their skin colour, Jews did not represent alterity instantly recognizable as such. But the less visible it was, the more insurmountable such alterity proved. Hence it had to be exhibited (by means of ghettos or marks of recognition), in order to contain and control this alien, perfidious element nestling in the very heart of civilization and threatening to undermine its integrity and health. That is why Luther

99   Quoted in Slotkin, The Fatal Environment, p. 79.

100   Theodore Roosevelt, The Strenuous Life: Essays and Addresses, New York: The Century, 1901, p. 294; quoted in Richard Hofstadter, The American Political Tradition and the Men Who Made It, New York: A. Knopf, 1967, p. 209.

101   Ludwig Gumplowicz, Der Rassenkampf. Soziologische Untersuchungen, Innsbruck: Wagner'sche Universitätsbuchhandlung, 1883, p. 249.

referred to 'a plague, a pestilence'.[102] Hence the metaphor of the *foetor judaicus*. As an eighteenth-century British pastor, Thomas Woolston, observed, 'if their Bodies neither do or ever did stink living', it remained the case that 'the World according to the Proverb, and common belief of Mankind, may be said to stink with them'.[103] The category of *foetor judaicus* was merely an initial formulation, as yet insufficiently 'scientific', of the charge levelled against Jews of constituting a vehicle of infection, a bacillus which, by its very presence, imperilled the health of the social organism.

The Third Reich and the Natives

With the unleashing of the war in the East, Hitler set about constructing the 'German Indies', as they were sometimes called, or conquering a *Lebensraum* similar to the Far West. The First World War and the British naval blockade had demonstrated the geopolitical vulnerability of Germany's previous colonial expansion. Assessing this negative experience, *Mein Kampf* stressed that 'the New Reich must again set itself on the march along the road of the Teutonic Knights of old', in order to build a robust continental empire.[104] This involved exploiting the disintegration of Czarist Russia, avoiding a 'fratricidal' conflict with the Anglo-Saxon powers, and preserving Germanic or Aryan solidarity intact. In this optic, the war with the 'natives' of Eastern Europe was equated with the 'war against the Indians', with 'the struggle in North America against the Red Indians'. In both cases, 'victory will go to the strong',[105] and be secured by the methods appropriate to colonial war: 'in the history of the expansion of the power of great peoples, the most radical methods have always been applied with success'.[106]

It might be said that Hitler sought his Far West in the East and identified the *Untermenschen* of Eastern Europe and the Soviet Union as 'Indians' to be chased ever further beyond the Urals in the name of the march of civilization. This was not a fleeting suggestion, but a long-premeditated programme spelt out in detail. Furet aptly draws attention to the fact that Hitler compared

---

102   Quoted in Hilberg, *The Destruction of the European Jews*, p. 17.
103   Quoted in Poliakov, *History of Anti-Semitism*, Vol. 3, pp. 66–7.
104   Adolf Hitler, *Mein Kampf*, trans. Ralph Mannheim, London: Pimlico, 1992, p. 154.
105   Adolf Hitler, *Hitler's Table Talk 1941–44*, London: Weidenfeld & Nicolson, 1973, p. 621 (conversation of 8 August 1942).
106   Quoted in Hans-Adolf Jacobsen, 'Kommissarbefehl und Massenexekutionen sowjetischer Kriegsgefangener', in *Anatomie des SS-Staates*, Munich: DTV, 1989, Vol. II, p. 216.

the great spaces he readied himself to conquer to a 'desert'.[107] But he does not breathe a word about the history behind this metaphor, which pertained to the history of colonialism and, above all, the expansion of the continental empires. In the mid-nineteenth century, Mexico seemed like a set of 'desert wastes . . . untrodden save by the savage and the beast' to chauvinistic circles in the USA, who aspired to conquer it, at least in part.[108] Going further back, here is how Tocqueville described the immense territories of North America on the eve of the Europeans' arrival:

> Although the vast country that I have been describing was inhabited by many indigenous tribes, it may justly be said, at the time of its discovery by Europeans, to have formed one great desert. The Indians occupied it without possessing it. It is by agricultural labour that man appropriates the soil, and the early inhabitants of North America lived by the produce of the chase. Their implacable prejudices, their uncontrolled passions, their vices, and still more perhaps, their savage virtues consigned them to inevitable destruction. The ruin of these tribes began from the day when Europeans landed on their shores; it has proceeded ever since, and we are now witnessing its completion.

In a way, the genocide that was in the process of being completed formed part of a divine plan – what, around a decade later, would be called the Manifest Destiny with which the white colonizers were invested:

> They [the indigenous tribes] seem to have been placed by Providence amid the riches of the New World only to enjoy them for a season; they were there merely to wait till others came. Those coasts, so admirably adapted for commerce and industry; those wide and deep rivers; that inexhaustible valley of the Mississippi; the whole continent, in short, seemed prepared to be the abode of a great nation yet unborn.[109]

The advance of the American white, engaged in his lone 'struggle against the obstacles that nature opposes to him', against 'the wilderness and savage life', was unstoppable and beneficial.[110] Indeed, the native 'has nothing to

---

107   Furet, *The Passing of an Illusion*, p. 337; *Hitler's Table Talk*, p. 68 (conversation of 17 October 1941, evening).

108   See Slotkin, *The Fatal Environment*, p. 184.

109   Tocqueville, *Democracy in America*, Vol. 1, p. 25.

110   Ibid., p. 434.

oppose to our perfection in the arts but the resources of the wilderness'.[111] There is an especially significant expression: 'the Indians were the sole inhabitants of the wilds whence they have since been expelled'.[112] The desert becomes genuinely inhabited only with the entry of the Europeans and the flight or deportation of the natives.

This was the colonial tradition that lies behind Hitler, who was likewise concerned to populate the 'desert' of Eastern Europe: 'In a hundred years' time there will be millions of German peasants living here.' The settlement of civilians went together with measures to contain and deport the barbarians:

> Given the proliferation of the natives, we must regard it as a blessing that women and girls practise abortion on a vast scale . . . we must take all the measures necessary to ensure that the non-German population does not increase at an excessive rate. In these circumstances, it would be sheer folly to place at their disposal a health service such as we know it in Germany; and so – no inoculations and other preventative measures for the natives! We must even try to stifle any desire for such things, by persuading them that vaccination and the like are really most dangerous!

Even traffic accidents or similar kinds of incident could prove useful: 'Jodl is quite right when he says that notices in the Ukrainian language "Beware of the Trains" are superfluous; what on earth does it matter if one or two more locals get run over by the trains?' For the processes of racial de-specification to proceed unhindered, 'to avoid all danger of our own people becoming too soft-hearted and too humane towards them, we must keep the German colonies strictly separated from the local inhabitants'.[113]

As the conquest proceeded, it was necessary to push the *Untermenschen* or 'Indians' of Eastern Europe back ever further, possibly beyond the Urals, so as to create space for Germanic elements and civilization. On the other hand, the objective situation dictated rapid colonization of the conquered territories and their endowment with a new ethnic identity. This entailed massive 'tasks of population policy' (*volkspolitische Aufhaben*). The process that had taken centuries in the Far West or other colonies had to be completed

---

111   Ibid., p. 335.
112   Ibid., p. 337.
113   *Hitler's Table Talk*, pp. 624, 588–9 (conversations of 9 August, evening and 22 July 1942, after dinner) (trans. modified).

or configured in its essentials in the space of a few years and in conditions of total war. The 'mass catastrophe' (*Volkskatastrophe*) of the subjugated peoples and the death of 'tens of millions of men' was inevitable.[114] The decimation of the indigenous populations could not be entrusted to the long-term effects of rum, or infectious diseases, or the destruction of bison. Where starvation and the brutality of deportation proved insufficient, bombers could be called upon to raze Leningrad and Moscow to the ground (according to Hitler's plan in July 1941), as could execution squads charged with thinning out populations 'of primarily Asiatic composition' and 'Asiatics of poor quality'.[115]

The natives had hitherto been assimilated to the Native Americans, who could be unceremoniously depleted. In another respect, they ended up being represented as work tools, 'slaves in the service of our civilization',[116] and hence as blacks. The new continental empire had to seize land from the 'Indians' (therewith condemned to deportation and decimation), and procure work tools – the slaves who could not be imported from Africa, and who were all the more imperative because of the war's economic and military requirements.

From the outset, the Third Reich's colonial policy suffered from this contradiction or tension: in the new territories, it was necessary both to conquer the Far West and Africa, deporting and decimating savages, and to utilize sufficient servile or semi-servile manpower. Resolving this problem – reducing the residual 'native' population to a simple pool of slaves for the master race – was not easy. As with the slaves in the southern USA referred to by Tocqueville, they were certainly to be deprived of education in the interim. Hitler explained: 'I am in favour of teaching a little German in the schools simply because this will facilitate our administration. Otherwise every time some German instruction is disobeyed, the local inhabitant will come along with the excuse that he "didn't understand".'[117] But Eastern Europe was not the America conquered by whites; nor was it the Africa of the golden age of the slave trade. Here the 'Indian savage' and black slave did not exist in a natural state: they had to be created by erasing centuries of history and artifice (from the standpoint of Nazi Social Darwinism),

---

114   See Helmut Krausnick, *Hitlers Einsatzgruppen. Die Truppen des Weltanschauungskrieges 1938–1942*, Hamburg: Fischer, 1985, pp. 96, 114.

115   Ibid., pp. 137–8.

116   Thus the Reichsführer of the SS, quoted in Jacobsen, 'Kommissarbefehl und Massenexekutionen', p. 141.

117   *Hitler's Table Talk*, p. 589 (conversation of 22 July 1942, after dinner).

restoring the laws and aristocracy of nature. The attempt to revive the colonial tradition in twentieth-century Eastern Europe entailed a gigantic programme of dis-emancipation and a horrendous train of atrocities and barbarism. The death penalty with which, according to Tocqueville, the South threatened those who offered education to slaves, now had to target an entire social stratum. The Führer clearly explained the inexorable logic governing the construction of the new empire: 'For the Pole there must be *a single master*, and that is the German; . . . therefore all the representatives of the Polish intelligentsia must be killed. This sounds cruel, but it is the law of life.' Hitler's order, formulated as early as the start of the campaign in Poland, was obsessively repeated by the Nazi ruling group. It was necessary 'to prevent the Polish intelligentsia structuring itself as a leading group'; it was necessary to systematically liquidate the clergy,[118] the nobility, and social strata capable of preserving the national consciousness and historical continuity of the nation, so that the new colonies could supply the requisite slaves. As the blacks were destroyed by the slave (or semi-slave) labour they were forced to perform, they were transformed into 'redskins', dross that must somehow or other be disposed of, in accordance with the schemas of the colonial tradition, which now assumed its most sanguinary and repugnant aspect. The pressure of time and war dispelled any residual scruples.

'Natives', Jews and Bolsheviks

Jews were a significant presence in the new colonial territories. Themselves 'natives', they thus shared the condition of blacks (they were an integral part of the world of forced labour) and Native Americans (they were marked down for decimation or liquidation). In so far as they were included among the intelligentsia of the new territorial colonies, Jews were destined to suffer an even worse fate than the mass of 'natives'. They had to be liquidated so that the natives resigned themselves to the condition of Native Americans or blacks.

The fate of Bolsheviks in Russia was similar to that of Jewry. They were a constitutive element of the intelligentsia to be destroyed because, by its very existence, it hampered the construction of the coveted colonial empire or rendered it impossible. Hitler clearly defined his objective. Once the 'Judeo-Bolshevik intelligentsia' had been eliminated by 'employing the most

---

118   See Krausnick, *Hitlers Einsatzgruppen*, pp. 27, 70, 35, 51.

brutal violence', he would finish by 'crushing the Russian people'.[119] The liquidation of Jewish and Bolshevik intellectuals (the two categories tended to be identified) was the precondition for depriving the huge Asiatic state of any ruling, unifying element and configuring it as a shapeless amalgam of internecine struggles between tribes resigned to their yoke.

Up to this point, we have been dealing with the operations required to build the German colonial empire. With the attack on the USSR, however, a new element enters the picture: that of the holy war in defence of civilization. Denunciation of October as a Judeo-Bolshevik conspiracy now reached its most tragic conclusion. General Blum communicated the orders received: 'Eastern Jewry constitutes the intellectual reserve of Bolshevism and hence, in the Führer's opinion, must be destroyed.'[120] As well as building the new colonial empire, the crusade in the East now aimed to detect and destroy the bacillus of dissolution wherever it was to be found. The 'poison of dissolution' that acted via Bolshevik cadres was to be neutralized once and for all,[121] but without forgetting that 'the chief "carriers of the Bolshevik infection"' were the Jews.[122] In Goebbels' words, 'Jewish terror' was the core of 'eastern Bolshevism', that mortal enemy of civilization.[123] The Jews were doubly Oriental and doubly barbarous. They were an 'Asiatic people' alien to Europe and the West, as had been stressed by Houston Chamberlain and the anti-Semitic tradition that fed into Nazism;[124] they therefore formed part of the 'native' populations. Furthermore, they were the inspirers of 'eastern Bolshevism' – were, in fact, the ethnic basis of the virus eroding civilization that was to be eliminated for good.

From Revolutionary Virus to Jewish Bacillus

But what is the history behind this fateful identification of Jewry with subversion? Let us return to traditional representations of the Jew as a source of contagion. It was essential to neutralize this pathogenic agent, constituted

---

119   Quoted in ibid., p. 101.
120   Quoted in ibid., p. 138.
121   See ibid., p. 101.
122   Mayer, *Why Did the Heavens Not Darken?*, p. 309.
123   Joseph Goebbels, *Reden 1932–1945*, ed. H. Heiber, Bindlach: Gondrom, 1991, Vol. II, p. 175.
124   Houston Chamberlain, *Foundations of the Nineteenth Century*, Howard Fertig: New York, 2006, p. 330.

by an alterity (cultural, religious or racial) destructive of a society which was homogeneous or aspired to homogeneity. The task became all the more imperative in crisis situations that imperilled, or seemed to imperil, the community's very identity.

Events during the First Crusade are significant here. Before setting out for the Holy Land to do battle with the Arabs, Christian warriors invaded German cities with the highest Jewish presence. The logic of this detour is clear. Prior to dealing with the external enemy, it was necessary to confront the enemy within, especially because the latter might be in league with the former and, in any event, by its presence impeded the unanimous mobilization and unqualified enthusiasm demanded by Christianity. These events are paradigmatic of the subsequent fate of the Jews. The more total the conflict in which a particular community found itself embroiled, the more heavily a cloud of suspicion hung over them. The tragic crescendo in the fate of Jewry from the First to the Second World War, from Tsarist Russia to the Third Reich, marks the 'total' and 'totalitarian' crescendo of the Second Thirty Years' War.

Even more essential was the isolation and neutralization of the breeding ground in the event of revolution. To the extent that a ruling class sought to externalize the conflict, attributing it to the influence or aggression of external pathogenic agents attacking a fundamentally healthy social body, reference to the Jewish bacillus became self-evident and inevitable. Writing after the peasants' war, when the peasants presumed to interpret the liberty peculiar to Christians and realize it on earth, Calvin, reiterating that 'spiritual liberty is perfectly compatible with civic servitude', declared: 'it is a Jewish vanity to seek and include the kingdom of Christ under the elements of this world'.[125] As the theory that explained revolution by a conspiracy hatched by a group of intellectuals emerged and spread, Jews were increasingly compared to *philosophes* and freemasons, and targeted along with them. This is what we find in Barruel and Maistre. The latter, in particular, drew attention 'to the very important role played by Jews in the current revolution and their alliance with the illuministi'. In their turn, Jewish intellectuals could count on support from the financial power of the 'accursed sect'. Whence 'a monster composed of all the monsters, and if we do not kill it, it will kill us'.[126]

---

125   Calvin, *The Institutes of the Christian Religion*, trans. Henry Beveridge, Edinburgh: Calvin Translation Society, 1846, Book IV, Chapter 20, 'Of Civil Government', p. 899.

126   Maistre, quoted in Johannes Rogalla von Bieberstein, *Die These von Verschwörung 1776–1945*, Bern and Frankfurt am Main: Lang, 1976, p. 163

In his analysis of the French Revolution, Burke stressed the disastrous impact of general theories and abstract principles. Thus, condemnation of the French Revolution was at the same time a denunciation of the philosophy and the intellectuals that had ideologically paved the way for it. Once again, the Jews were brought into play. Denouncing as early as 1790 'a regular plan for the destruction of the Christian religion' orchestrated by the authors of the *Encyclopédie* and the *philosophes*, the British Whig also mentioned the obscure doings of Jewish finance. He subsequently received Abbé Barruel in London with full honours and was warmly appreciative of his work: 'The whole of the wonderful narrative is supported by documents and proofs with almost juridical regularity and exactness.'[127]

Burke's German translator was Gentz. Engaged as he was in siphoning money from Jews, he referred to them favourably and prudently in public, going so far as to revise certain lurid passages in *Reflections on the Revolution in France*. In private, however, it was a very different story:

Intelligence – that is the mortal sin of the Jews. All of them are more or less intelligent. But only let one be born in which a spark of heart, a spark of true feeling can be found. The curse pronounced on them, and it pursues them to the ten thousandth-generation, is that they can never leave the sphere of intelligence, in the narrower meaning of the word, to their own detriment and that of the world, but must make endless circles in it until their black souls descend into hell. That is why the monsters are at home everywhere where intelligence, stupid and criminal intelligence, arrogates the right to govern alone: born representatives of atheism, Jacobinism, Enlightenment and so on.

The revolution was attributed by Gentz to the work of 'professional revolutionaries' (*Revolutionisten von Profession*).[128] This phrase brings to mind an extremely famous formula of Lenin's. But we must beware of hasty, superficial comparisons. Metternich's advisor certainly did not have in mind a vanguard employed full-time in establishing a relationship with the masses for revolutionary purposes. The phrase 'revolutionaries by profession' is modelled on that of 'intellectuals by profession' (*Gelehrte von Profession*),[129]

127   Burke, quoted in ibid., pp. 163, 111 n. 3; Burke, *The Works*, Vol. V, p. 207.
128   Friedrich von Gentz, *Ausgewählte Schriften*, ed. W. Weick, Stuttgart and Leipzig: Rieger, 1836–38, Vol. II, p. 45 n.; quoted in Poliakov, *The History of Anti-Semitism*, Vol. 3, p. 297.
129   For Burke as translated by Gentz, see Edmund Burke, *Betrachtungen über die französische*

introduced by Gentz in a free translation of Burke's indictment of politicized intellectuals, prone to support any 'innovation' and pursue 'a regular plan for the destruction of the Christian religion'. Gentz's thinking is perhaps conveyed more accurately by a subsequent phrase – 'professional stokers of revolution' (*Revolutionsstifter von Profession*).[130] The external pathogenic element is identified as intellectuals (especially members of the people of the Book *par excellence*).

At roughly the same time, Bonald compared 'the Jews' *Sanhedrin* to the philosophers' *Convention*'.[131] The 'superstition' which, in Engels' words, reduces 'revolution to the iniquity of a handful of agitators'[132] refers back to an intellectual and Jewish conspiracy. Once revolution is derived from abstract and abstractly universalistic theories, elaborated by rootless intellectuals without links to the concrete historical tradition of a historically determinate country, it is clear that the Jews, those abstract intellectuals *par excellence*, are to be identified and denounced as the secret subject of revolutionary upheavals. In Germany, Heinrich Leo wrote that:

> The Jewish nation stands out conspicuously among all other nations of this world in that it possesses a truly corroding and decomposing mind. In the same way as there exists some fountains that would transmute every object thrown into them into stone, thus the Jews, from the very beginning until this very day, have transmuted everything that fell into the orbit of their spiritual activity into an abstract generality.[133]

The liberal and conservative critique of the revolution insists that, underlying the incessant upheavals in France, are visionary intellectuals with messianic tendencies, full of resentment and rancour against the ruling classes, out of touch with reality and practical experience. And once again, increasingly explicitly, it is the Jews, 'the people of *ressentiment* par excellence', who are accused.[134] Nietzsche supported this thesis. For him the dialectic (that plebeian 'form of vendetta') was likewise typically Jewish,[135] just as the social

---

Revolution, ed. Lore Iser, Frankfurt am Main: Suhrkamp, 1967, p. 180. For the original text, see Burke, *The Works*, Vol. V, p. 207.

130   Gentz, *Ausgewählte Schriften*, Vol. II, p. 53.
131   Poliakov, *History of Anti-Semitism*, Vol. 3, p. 229.
132   Karl Marx and Friedrich Engels, *Werke*, Berlin: Dietz Verlag, 1955–, Vol. VIII, p. 5.
133   Quoted in Zygmunt Bauman, *Modernity and Holocaust*, Cambridge: Polity Press, 1991, p. 53.
134   Nietzsche, *Sämtliche Werke*, Vol. V, p. 286.
135   Ibid., Vol. VI, p. 70.

palingenesis dreamt of by revolutionaries was directly continuous with 'the shameful Jewish phrase *heaven* on earth'.[136]

These were themes subsequently developed by Sombart. Jews were motivated by *ressentiment*.[137] 'Lacking roots' and 'outside the world', they were only capable of moving 'in the abstract', be it 'trade' or 'literature'. The Jew embodied what would today be called the *homo ideologicus*:

> The Jewish spirit is rational and abstract. It lacks plasticity and tangible concreteness. Hence the Jew is a born doctrinaire and fabricator, a man of principles who willingly thinks in accordance with systems and, when it comes to their practical implementation, believes it possible and desirable to structure reality in accordance with these logical systems. What the Jew lacks is a feeling for what has grown, become, the 'organic', for historical society and its bases, for a concretely individual people with its absolutely specific history. The Jew knows only abstract individuals and an abstract humanity . . . The abstractness of his thought is matched by a highly developed capacity for criticism which, in particular conditions, is readily conducive to a basically revolutionary attitude.

Jews were impelled in the same direction by 'an accentuated *ethical attitude* towards the world' and a *'fanaticism for justice'*, as well as '*messianism*' and 'hopes for the millenarian kingdom, for the redemption of evil in *this* world'.[138] Basing himself on the critique of the French Revolution by Burke, whom he esteemed and admired, Sombart denounced the Jew not only as the abstract individual, but also as the social experimenter or (as would be said today) the constructivist and social engineer *par excellence*. These themes are also to be found in Spengler, likewise an admirer of the British Whig who was the author of the first great requisitory against the revolutionary mentality. Finally, polemics against 'Jewish intellectualism',[139] or against the 'Jewish dialectic' to which Carl Schmitt alludes with explicit reference to *Mein Kampf*, became commonplace in Nazi literature.[140]

---

136   Ibid., Vol. VII, p. 121.

137   Werner Sombart, *Der proletarische Sozialismus*, Jena: Fischer, 1924, Vol. II, pp. 517, 153 and Vol. I, p. 57.

138   Ibid., Vol. II, pp. 154–6.

139   Karl Löwith, *Mein Leben in Deutschland vor und nach 1933. Ein Bericht*, Stuttgart: Metzler, 1986, p. 75.

140   Carl Schmitt, 'Die deutsche Rechtswissenschaft im Kamp gegen den jüdischen Geist', in *Deutsche Juristen-Zeitung*, No. 20, 15 October 1936, p. 1198.

Nor should it be thought that such developments were confined to Germany. After the 1905 revolution, 'anti-Jewish pogroms . . . accompanied by attacks on students and intellectuals' erupted throughout the Russian empire. This manhunt intensified in 1917.[141] Even before the Bolshevik October, Jews in Russia likewise tended to be identified with the subversive intellectuals plotting revolutions or conspiracies in the shadows.

In Tocqueville, denunciation of the abstract intellectual takes the form of diagnosis of 'a virus of a new and unknown kind', which explains the incessant, senseless revolutionary upheavals. This kind of explanation was widespread in Western culture following the outbreak of the October Revolution. On 5 November 1919, Churchill declared in the House of Commons that, by aiding Lenin to reach Russia, the Germans had as it were sent 'a phial containing a typhus or cholera culture to the water reservoirs of a big city'. The source of the contagion was embodied in a figure whom the British statesman branded as the 'high priest and head' of 'a formidable sect, the most formidable sect in the world', which was committed to 'destroy[ing] all the religious faiths' and replacing them by the idolatry of 'the international Soviet of Russian and Polish Jews'. It was no coincidence if the new regime spared 'Jewish interests and Jewish places of worship'.[142] The virus of subversion was manifestly Jewish; and that is why, in Henry Ford's view, 'the Russian upheaval is racial, not political nor economic'.[143]

The abstract, visionary intellectual, full of *ressentiment*, increasingly tended to acquire an ethnic and racial physiognomy. So much so that on the eve of the Romanovs' overthrow, Lenin himself noted that, as the main victims of Czarism's 'hatred', 'the Jews furnished a particularly high percentage (compared with the total Jewish population) of leaders of the revolutionary movement'. Above all, 'it should be noted to the credit of the Jews, they furnish a relative high percentage of internationalists'.[144] The process of identifying the subversive virus with Jewry culminated in Nazism. The two metaphors or categories with which the reactionary tradition has consistently viewed revolutionaries, branding them as madmen and foreign barbarians, had now completely merged. It was finally possible to identify the ethnic and racial basis of the revolutionary disease or frenzy. *Homo ideologicus* was

141   Pipes, *The Russian Revolution*, pp. 46, 41 and n.
142   Churchill quoted in Poliakov, *History of Anti-Semitism*, Vol. 4, pp. 206–07. Cf also Nolte, *Der europäische Bürgerkrieg*, p. 111.
143   Henry Ford, *The International Jew: The World's Foremost Problem*, Dearborn, MI: Dearborn Publishing Company, 1920, p. 219.
144   Lenin, *Collected Works*, Vol. 23, p. 250.

himself a barbarian alien to Europe and authentic civilization: he was the Jew. For Hitler there was no doubt: the external pathogenic agent attacking and dissolving society was the 'Talmudistic pettifogger', prone to 'verbal juggleries' and possessed only of 'a talent for bringing confusion into the simplest matters, for getting everything muddled up'.[145] 'Science' could now be invoked in support of this thesis:

> The discovery of the Jewish virus is one of the greatest revolutions that have taken place in the world. The battle in which we are engaged today is of the same sort as the battle waged, during the last century, by Pasteur and Koch. How many diseases have their origin in the Jewish virus! . . . We shall regain our health only by eliminating the Jew. Everything has a cause, nothing comes by chance.[146]

On the basis of this discovery, it was possible and necessary to proceed to a 'complete revision' in the politico-social sphere comparable to that which had occurred in biology: 'As long as students of biology believed in spontaneous generation, it was impossible to explain the presence of microbes.'[147] Now things were clear: 'Any and every nation which fails to exterminate the Jews in its midst will sooner or later finish by being itself devoured by them', whereas a 'people that is rid of its Jews returns spontaneously to the natural order'.[148] But this was not an exclusively national problem: 'It is Jewry that always destroys this order. It constantly provokes the revolt of the weak against the strong, of bestiality against intelligence, of quantity against quality . . . The Jew plays in nature the role of a catalysing element.'[149]

We are dealing with a people that, as early as Paul of Tarsus, had incited 'slaves of all kinds against the elite, the masters and those in dominant authority'; with a people that had been the agent of every subversion in the history of the West, including the massive subversion and conspiracy represented by two world wars, which had targeted both Germany and the hierarchical order of races and classes sanctioned by nature. Taking note, accurately and religiously, of the Führer's thoughts was Bormann, who in turn observed: 'Everywhere they have stirred up the plebs against the ruling

---

145 *Hitler's Table Talk*, pp. 117–18 (conversation of 5 November 1941, evening).

146 Ibid., p. 332 (conversation of 22 February 1942, evening).

147 Ibid., p. 88 (conversation of 25 October 1941, evening).

148 Ibid., pp. 678, 314 (conversations of 31 August, evening, and 17 February 1942, midday).

149 Ibid., p. 314 (conversation of 17 February 1942, midday).

classes. Everywhere they have fostered discontent against the established power . . . Everywhere they fan the flames of hatred between peoples of the same blood. It is they who invented class-warfare.'[150] It was therefore not enough to eliminate the breeding-ground of the subversive contagion in Germany. It was 'interesting to note the way in which this little Catholic priest who calls himself Tiso sends the Jews into our hands', Hitler enthused. In placing itself at the head of the anti-Jewish crusade, Germany was saving not only itself, but also civilization as such: the natural order founded on racial and class inequality and hierarchy. The profundity of the subversive danger, and the radicalism of Nazism's counter-revolutionary project, dictated a final solution. Given that *homo ideologicus* was embodied in a people – in fact, in a clearly defined 'race' (whose nature was absolutely immutable) – the problem of the struggle waged by abstract intellectuals was now configured as the Jewish question. And, in the light of new 'scientific' developments, this question was nothing but a chapter of parasitology. Ghettos and traditional anti-Jewish measures would no longer suffice. In one way or another, the bacillus had to be totally removed: 'until Jewry . . . is exterminated, we shall not have accomplished our task'.[151]

The unsustainability of the comparison between the concentration camps in which the Germans imprisoned Jews and those in which the Americans isolated citizens of Japanese origin – a comparison suggested by Nolte and other exponents of historical revisionism – is patent. The latter were not blacks – slaves forced to work for the master race (the USA had no need of forced labour). If, in the heat of battle, the Japanese enemy were sometimes compared with Indians, they were not 'natives' whose land had to be appropriated in order to build a colonial empire of a continental kind. Still less did they represent the race-virus, the race of the *homo ideologicus*, whose very existence posed a mortal threat to civilization. The concentration camps compared by historical revisionism shared but one thing in common: they answered to the exigency of total war that iron control should be exercised over ethnic or social groups who were regarded as enemies or suspected of disloyalty. In as much as these groups were subject to a naturalistic de-specification, the escape route for individuals belonging to them narrowed. But it is precisely a question of examining the modality and intensity of the process, or convergent processes, of naturalistic de-specification. Although far removed from historical revisionism proper, the most impartial US

---

150   Ibid., p. 722 (conversation of night of 29–30 November 1944).
151   Ibid., p. 676 (conversation of 30 August 1942, evening).

historiography has not hesitated to establish a comparison between the destruction of a whole city from the air and the Judeocide.[152] However, as with concentration camps for Americans of Japanese origin, so too in the case of Dresden, Hamburg and Nagasaki the principal aspect is total war. Although legitimizing recourse to forms of violence that struck at the enemy en bloc, without distinguishing between combatants and civilians, naturalistic de-specification was not yet autonomous. And even though it had now acquired greater weight, it was not really autonomous even in the US concentration camps where defeated Germans were subjected to cruel treatment. Not by chance, the outbreak of the Cold War rapidly made it possible to displace the friend/enemy dichotomy and include Germans and Japanese among the friends. The process of racialization and naturalistic de-specification culminated in Eastern Europe and, quite especially, in the campaign against Jewry.

The historical context in which the Judeocide was implemented is now clear. (I take the term Judeocide from an American historian of Jewish origin, Arno J. Mayer, who correctly prefers it to the Holocaust, which is too charged with theological resonance and hence more apt to stimulate religious meditation than concrete scholarly investigation.) Similarly clear are two further facts. First, it was a process that developed in stages (dis-emancipation of the Jews with the Nuremburg Laws; plans for mass deportation to an island-ghetto outside Europe so as to prevent any contact between the race-virus and civilization; forced sterilization of women and the people generating the virus; formation of special corps to accelerate the Germanization of the empire by decisively confronting the 'native' question, Bolshevik and Jewish; measures to screen Jews and identify and liquidate the virus). Secondly, it was a process that developed amid contradictions, changes of mind and conflicts internal to the Third Reich. In this light, the issue of the gas chambers seems of secondary importance. 'Negationists' are committed to destroying this 'legend' or 'lie'. But in any event the effort is misplaced. Subsequent historical research may clarify the number of victims and the methods of extermination: execution squads; condemnation of Jewish slaves to die of work, exhaustion and maltreatment; the employment, probably in the final stage, of poison gas, which had already been used in one way or another to liquidate the mentally ill and other categories of human beings, equated with 'redskins' as burdensome dead wood to be cleared away to make room for Germans and Aryans, who flowed into the Greater Reich

---

152   Markusen and Kopf, *The Holocaust and Strategic Bombing*.

and its colonial empire from all sides.[153] However that may be, what incontestably emerges from the explicit pronouncements of Nazi leaders themselves is the reality of the dual naturalistic de-specification to which Jews were subject: they were natives alien to civilization whose drastic depletion was the presupposition for building and Germanizing the new colonial empire; and a race fatally doomed to generate the bacillus of social decomposition and subversion in its various forms and, in particular, its most extreme form – namely, 'eastern', barbaric Bolshevism. In conditions of total war, this dual de-specification left very little room for escape.

The Bolsheviks and the 'Liquidation of the Kulaks as a Class'

However, the royal road taken by historical revisionism to relativize the horror of the Judeocide is its equation with the 'political genocide' or 'class genocide' of which the Jacobin-Bolshevik tradition is accused. This category proves immediately instrumental if not examined in a comparative historical optic and when applied unilaterally. During the French Revolution, the Girondin Isnard threatened the Jacobins with the destruction of Paris ('soon one would seek in vain on the banks of the Seine whether Paris ever existed').[154] When reference is made to instances of political genocide, the massacre of hundreds of thousands of Communists in Indonesia in 1965 is rarely mentioned. Over and above the logic of total war, which tends to undermine the principle of individual responsibility (one thinks of the practice of decimation during the First World War), what enormously increased the number of casualties in this case was the collective guilt whereby whole family groups were regarded as jointly responsible and therefore killed.[155] Precisely this detail is of the utmost interest: the massacre approximates to genocide through the influence exercised by social relations and a tribal ideology that certainly do not pertain to the revolutionary tradition (in the case of Indonesia, they were even pre-modern). Naturally, in determinate circumstances a revolutionary movement can indeed intersect with pre-modern social relations and ideological survivals (it is likely that something of

---

153   See Mayer, *Why Did the Heavens Not Darken?* and Götz Aly, *'Endlösung'.Völkerverschiebung und der Mord an den europäischen Juden*, Frankfurt am Main: Fischer, 1995.

154   Quoted in François Furet and Denis Richet, *La Révolution française*, Paris: Hachette, 1999, p. 198.

155   See Paul Johnson, *Modern Times: The World from the Twenties to the Nineties*, New York: Harper Collins, 1991, p. 480.

the kind occurred in Pol Pot's Cambodia). But there remains a basic contradiction between the two elements.

According to Nolte, Bolshevism and Nazism are both characterized by 'collectivist thinking' that creates 'stigmas' from which 'individuals can free themselves . . . only with great difficulty' – 'criticism of "the" Jews, "the" Russians, "the" Germans, or "the" petite-bourgeoisie'.[156] In fact, we have seen the German historian, when not yet a revisionist, underscoring the weight that history, ideology and the concrete conduct of individuals and groups have in Marx's analysis of classes and political parties. It is not only the *Communist Manifesto* that highlights the revolutionary role of transfugues from the dominant class. The thesis is prominent in *What Is to Be Done?*, which insists even more forcefully on the decisive contribution of intellectuals from the bourgeoisie, or other 'exploiting' classes, to the development of revolutionary theory. In its turn, the tribune of the people has the task of diffusing this theory not only within the proletariat, but also among all the popular classes. Moreover, class membership does not always possess the same significance. There is a national bourgeoisie which plays a progressive role not only in colonial countries, but also (according to Lenin) in situations where imperialist oppression has put the national question on the agenda. And it is Furet himself who, as proof of Stalin's unscrupulous realpolitik, notes that 'republican Spain under the Soviet influence . . . [left] the bourgeoisie in place so long as it was pro-Soviet'.[157] On the other hand, we have seen the revisionist Nolte stressing that the 'collectivist' view of the Germans as a single reprobate mass played a much more prominent role among Germany's Western enemies than in the USSR.

The collectivization of agriculture imposed by Stalin is generally adduced as an example of class genocide, with particular reference to the Ukraine. In reality, what we have here is a civil war ruthlessly waged on both sides – a civil war which, far from developing on tribal lines, sometimes divided family units internally.[158] To refute Nolte's thesis, we shall largely draw on testimony that cannot be suspected of sympathy for the Soviet regime: reports from fascist Italy's diplomats. Let us glance at the picture that emerges. The countryside responded to what historians have defined as the 'revolution from above', or 'war on the peasantry', unleashed by Stalin, with

---

156 Nolte, 'The Past That Will Not Pass', pp. 22–3.
157 Furet, *The Passing of an Illusion*, p. 254.
158 See Sheila Fitzpatrick, *Stalin's Peasants: Resistance and Survival in the Russian Village after Collectivization*, New York and Oxford: Oxford University Press, 1994, p. 248.

an 'insurrectionary movement' and partisan struggle: witness a 'bomb set off not far from Vladikavkaz as a train full of GPU agents went past'.[159] The rebellion invested centres of power (here and there 'representatives of the Soviet government' at local level were 'forced to evacuate the city'),[160] and also threatened members of the 'Ukrainian government and, first and foremost, the President of the Republic'. Thus the civil war that succeeded the October Revolution was rekindled, all the more so in that the rebellious peasants seemed to be inspired by 'those former Socialist Revolutionaries who had only transferred to Communism at a second stage'.[161]

The clashes in the countryside were reflected at the highest levels of government. The Ukrainian Communist leaders, allied with Stalin in his battle against Bukharin and for the collectivization of agriculture, changed their minds in the light of the evidence of the extremely high social and human costs of the political turn. Ryutin 'circulated a document in the party' that was not only highly critical, but even went as far as to 'openly [desire] the removal and, it would seem, the elimination of Stalin'. In vain, the latter demanded the arrest of his opponent and enemy. The Central Committee would only agree to his expulsion from the party.[162] (The dictatorship of the party had not yet been replaced by a personal dictatorship.)[163]

The peasant uprising took the form of a 'nationalist' and 'separatist movement' intersecting with 'banditry with a political substratum'.[164] This explains the atrocious methods sometimes adopted by the guerrilla: 'a little boy was taken . . . from a party big wig and found dead one morning in front of the house, with his eyes gouged out and a board on his chest: this in return for what you make us suffer'. The son of another government representative was 'kidnapped, chopped into pieces, and the pieces were cast before the father's door'.[165] A ruthless reaction was not slow to materialize: 'fifteen villages [that] had rebelled and responded to the GPU's intervention with weapons . . . were bombed by aeroplanes so that no stone was left standing'.[166] The brutality of the repression created deep divisions among the 'red

---

159 Andrea Graziosi, ed., *Lettere da Kharkov. La carestia in Ucraina e nel Caucaso del Nord nei rapport dei diplomatici italiana, 1932–33*, Turin: Einaudi, 1991, pp. 70, 69.

160 Ibid., p. 108.

161 Ibid., pp. 229–30.

162 Andrea Graziosi, Introduction to *Lettere da Kharkov*, p. 20.

163 Robert C. Tucker, *Stalin in Power: The Revolution from Above, 1928–1941*, New York and London: Norton, 1990, p. 120.

164 Graziosi, ed., *Lettere da Kharkov*, pp. 73–4.

165 Ibid., pp. 138, 148.

166 Ibid., p. 71.

troops' themselves, who in some cases 'firmly sided with the peasants – that is, the relatives of the majority of soldiers'. Disagreement even manifested itself in high places and sometimes in tragic form, with cases of suicide and insanity among prominent leaders of the party and military apparatus.[167]

All this has nothing to do with the bureaucratically administered genocide of a clearly defined group, whose members had no way out regardless of their actual conduct. Rather, what comes to mind in some ways is colonial warfare. Given that the revolution from above invested a countryside inhabited by national minorities, the moral de-specification characteristic of revolutionary ideology could sometimes intersect with forms of naturalistic de-specification. Immediately after the October Revolution, Gorky, who was critical of Bolshevism at the time, spoke with contempt of the peasants of his immense country as 'non-Russian nomads'. And it has even been written that the great writer 'hated the Russian peasants, who for him embodied the Asiatic-Mongol biological heritage that, he felt, had ruined [and retarded] Russia'.[168] More than a decade later, when repression of the rebellious, 'counter-revolutionary' countryside reached a tragic peak, the aforementioned diplomatic correspondent had 'a Jew, a big wig of the local GPU', say that in the Ukraine 'the "ethnographic material" is being changed'.[169]

While the remark about the great Russian writer is possibly exaggerated, and testimony about the war in the countryside is not wanting in anti-Jewish prejudice, it is true that the culture of the time – European rather than Russian – already contained all the presuppositions for the relationship between town and countryside in Russia being configured as a relationship between Europe and Asia and between civilization and barbarism (traditionally coinciding with the capitalist city, civilization was identified post-October with the socialist city). Prior to its implementation, forced collectivization was compared to the capitalist process of original accumulation by an economist close to the Trotskyist opposition, Preobrazhensky. He even seemed to indicate, as a precondition of the development of socialist industry, the 'exploitation' of a kind of internal 'colony', composed of agriculture and sectors where 'pre-socialist economic forms' were dominant. In warning against the temptation or danger of a 'St Bartholomew's Night of rich peasants', Bukharin correctly pointed out that the vague category of 'colony'

---

167   Ibid., pp. 78, 173.
168   Mikhail Agursky, *The Third Rome: National Bolshevism in the USSR*, Boulder, CO: Westview Press, 1987, p. 162.
169   Graziosi, ed., *Lettere da Kharkov*, p. 168.

objectively encompassed, 'with the exception of Great Russia, an enormous number of peasants' and (one might add) the totality of national minorities. Indeed, the agrarian question was closely bound up with the national and religious questions, given that the non-Russian national minorities were precisely concentrated in the countryside, and attachment to religion, which in turn often represented a way of expressing and defending national identity, was strongest there.

The ruthless repression brought with it the spread of the constitutive features of the *univers concentrationnaire* (the Gulag, deportation, forced labour), which, having emerged in Europe itself during the process of the original accumulation of capitalism (one thinks of the 'work houses' to which 'vagabonds' and even members of their family, often held in conditions of mutual isolation, were sent), constantly marked Western expansion into colonies thereafter. It might be said that, to a certain extent, the picture painted by Preobrazhensky in 1924 of the methods of original capitalist accumulation (including 'dispossession in the form of taxes on natives, the appropriation of their belongings, livestock, land and stockpiles of precious metals, the reduction of the population to slavery, and the infinitely various systems of violent extortion')[170] also ended up applying to the methods employed by the original socialist accumulation he had theorized.

Nevertheless, we cannot speak of genocide. Even in the years when repression of the 'counter-revolution' was pitiless, it was combined with initiatives that tended in different, contrasting directions: 'In various centres, the soldiers have been sent to the countryside to collaborate on rural work; the agricultural machinery factories are taken care of by workers who rush around the countryside doing makeshift repairs on machines that only work intermittently.'[171] We are also far removed from ethnocide:

> Alongside this action to destroy any Ukrainian separatist ambitions, the policy of promoting Ukrainian national characteristics has been intensified . . . That is, they want to replace a separatist kind of Ukrainian nationalism which looks towards Poland with one of centripetal stamp, attracting Poland's Ukrainians into a possible or desirable union with those of the USSR.

---

170   N.I. Bukharin and E.A. Preobrazhensky, *L'accumulazione socialista*, ed. Lisa Foa, Rome: Riuniti, 1969, esp. pp. 14–15, 50–1, 82–3 and 169 n.

171   Graziosi, ed., *Lettere da Kharkov*, p. 117.

This objective was pursued by encouraging free expression of the Ukrainian
language, culture and customs:

> At the military and civil review on 1 May, twenty children filed past in
> splendid Ukrainian national costumes. The previous evening, at the thea-
> tre of the Opera, following celebration of the red feast with a short speech,
> Ukrainian songs were sung and traditional Ukrainian and Cossack dances
> were performed on stage. In the various gatherings at the opening of 1
> and 2 May not only modern dances, but also and especially . . . Ukrainian
> ones, were performed.

And again:

> To supply the schools with Ukrainian teachers it has been decided to
> take 10,000 peasants from the Ukrainian kolkhozy and have them follow
> accelerated courses to turn them into Ukrainian primary school teach-
> ers. So they are in the process of establishing an orthodox Ukrainian
> nationalism, obedient to Moscow, a tool for attracting the Ukrainians
> of Poland.[172]

It is enough to compare this testimony with Hitler's explicit pronouncements
on the need to rear a caste of slaves in the colonies, reducing their education
to a minimum, to appreciate the absurdity of historical revisionism's thesis.
Only ideological *parti pris* can compare this with the Third Reich's policy
towards 'natives'.

Furthermore, the relationship between central government and the
Ukrainians was not uniformly tempestuous, but experienced highs and
lows. Between the end of the Civil War in Russia and the unleashing of
the war on the peasantry, 'the Ukraine experienced what was perhaps its
happiest modern period, and numerous nationalist leaders – largely militants in socialist parties who were opponents of the Bolsheviks in the Civil
War – returned home'. A new turn occurred at the end of the Second
World War, which was the consequence of premises already established in
the period of the most ferocious repression: 'Paradoxically, victory in war,
and the consequent territorial expansion, guaranteed the regime and Stalin
renewed credit not only among Russians, but *also* among the other Soviet
nationalities, and even among the Ukrainians.' People were grateful to

172   Ibid., pp. 229–32.

Stalin 'for having finally made possible the unification of all the Ukrainian territories'.[173]

We can therefore draw a conclusion. The politico-moral criminalization of a whole social class led to pitiless repression. The fact that it objectively struck 'backward' and 'barbaric' populations in the first instance facilitated transition from moral de-specification to the naturalistic variety on occasion. Even then, however, the fallacy of the deductive logic that presumes to deduce *a priori* the *univers concentrationnaire* from revolutionary ideology is evident. In reality, as well as from the exigencies of total war and ideological fanaticism, the ferocity of the repression also derived from the pre-revolutionary colonial tradition. Only thus can we understand the 'suicide of the GPU general Brodsky', disconcerted during an inspection in the course of which he cried out 'repeatedly this is not communism, but "horror"'.[174]

A permanent stance of naturalistic de-specification on the part of Soviet power and the Bolshevik Party proved impossible for ideological reasons. The year of the onset of forced collectivization of the countryside saw Stalin draw attention to the tragedy of the Armenian people. Condemnation of 'the Turkish assimilators – the most brutal of all assimilators' implicated not only 'the German-Prussian Germanisers' (of Polish territories), but also 'the tsarist-Russian Russifiers'. This position was the more significant in that it was bound up with a theoretical consideration of a more general kind. Contra Kautsky, Stalin stressed that, far from betokening the disappearance of national languages and peculiarities, socialism involved their further development and expression. Any 'policy of assimilation' was therefore to be condemned as an 'enemy of the people' and 'counter-revolutionary'. It was all the more disastrous because of 'the colossal power of stability of nations'. To 'declar[e] . . . war on national culture' was tantamount to being 'an advocate of colonisation'.[175] However crying their discrepancy with actual policy, declarations of principle are never null and void – especially in a political regime where the ideological formation and mobilization of party cadres and militants, and mass indoctrination, played such a significant role.

The Ukrainian was not a 'redskin' to be removed from the land at any cost, nor a bacillus to be eliminated, nor a work tool to be deprived of education and stripped of his or her cultural identity. At most, he can be

---

173   Graziosi, Introduction to *Lettere da Kharkov*, pp. 17, 47.
174   Graziosi, ed., *Lettere da Kharkov*, p. 173.
175   J.V. Stalin, *Works*, Moscow: Foreign Languages Publishing House, 1952–, Vol. 11, pp. 358–63 and Vol. 10, pp. 72–3.

compared to the black, by virtue of the fact that, as a 'counter-revolutionary', he was subjected to the forced labour required to industrialize the USSR. However, the 'mobility' contained in the non-naturalistic character of de-specification of the enemy was also manifest in the fate of members of a social class whom it was intended to liquidate as a class. Identification of them was beset by all kinds of contradictions and, as early as spring 1930, it was queried and retracted in a notable number of cases. Moreover, not all those branded as kulaks suffered deportation (actual political conduct played a role).[176] In 1934, the citizenship rights of which kulaks had been stripped were restored to them. At the end of 1935, referring to Stalin's statement that 'the son is not answerable for the father', *Pravda* announced an end to the discrimination which prevented the offspring of privileged classes attending university.[177] Obviously, the horror of the Gulag stands. Yet we should not erase or repress the differences that could emerge within the *univers concentrationnaire*. In 1931, sending Molotov suggestions for a speech he was about to deliver at the Congress of Soviets, Stalin called on him to explain 'with thorough documentation that the only ones among the deported kulaks who work are those who want to work and [that they do so] with all the rights of voluntary labor'.[178] It goes without saying that this presents a distorted image of reality. But such an image is an integral part of reality in that it expresses an ideology which, far from planning the biological destruction of a whole social class, proposed to liquidate it socially also by 're-educating' individuals. The outbreak of the war opened up an escape route from the Gulag for 'counter-revolutionaries' and even offered them the possibility of social mobility and promotion: 'many deportees asked to enrol voluntarily . . . some, especially officers and technical cadres who had survived, were liberated and re-joined the ranks'.[179] The basic difference between the various kinds of de-specification – a difference repressed or ignored by historical revisionism – emerges once more.

---

176   See Stefan Merl, '"Ausrottung" der Bourgeoisie und der Kulaken in Sowjetrussland?', *Geschichte und Gesellschaft*, Vol. 13, No. 3, 1987, pp. 368–81.

177   See Tucker, *Stalin in Power*, pp. 283, 329–30.

178   J.V. Stalin, *Letters to Molotov*, ed. L.T. Lih, O.V. Naumov and O.V. Khlevniuk, New Haven and London: Yale University Press, 1995, p. 228.

179   Thus Pasternak, quoted in Graziosi, ed., *Lettere da Kharkov*, pp. 47–8.

Ukraine, Bengal and Ireland

Reference has been made in connection with the Ukraine to a 'famine holocaust', death by starvation deliberately inflicted on a rebellious people by Stalin. But even were this to be true, the comparison with the Judeocide would be completely misleading. More satisfactory as a term of comparison would be the events that unfolded in Ireland in 1846–8. In the aftermath of a disease that destroyed the potato crop, Ireland lost 2.5 million people out of a total population of 9 million. Half of them emigrated to Canada and the USA, while the other half died of starvation. Sir Charles Edward Trevelyan, who was charged by London with monitoring the developing situation and dealing with it, detected in this terrible famine the hand of an 'all-wise Providence', seeking to solve 'the problem of Ireland's imbalance between population and food'. For this, the British politician has sometimes been branded as a 'proto-Eichmann', protagonist of a tragedy that should be regarded as the prototype of twentieth-century genocides.[180] Instead, we should first of all bear in mind the policy traditionally followed in the unfortunate island by its conquerors, whom we have seen banking on the rebels dying of starvation. We are also reminded of the policy towards the Native Americans pursued in the USA, not coincidentally frequently compared with British policy in Ireland. And Trevelyan's statements display some similarity to the previously cited view of Franklin, according to whom extermination of the Indians formed part of the design of Providence. It is true that British policy now proposed not to erase an ethnic group, but to reduce it drastically, without resorting to additional tools to those employed by God. But it remains the case that the mass starvation of a people long assimilated by the dominant British classes to other colonial populations was regarded as 'providential'.

But even this second term of comparison is inadequate. On the one hand, Ireland was not the theatre of a pitiless civil war in 1846–8; on the other, the Ukrainians were not subject to permanent racialization. A comparison might instead be made with India's experience between 1943 and 1944. Following the Japanese invasion of Burma, Bengal, already deprived of the ability to feed itself, found itself in the front line. Implementing their 'denial policy', the British military authorities sought to put the region's food supplies out of the reach of any potential future enemy advance – with catastrophic consequences, in the event, for the

---

180   Markusen and Kopf, *The Holocaust and Strategic Bombing*, p. 44.

civilian population. The reports filed by US journalists were controlled by the censors, who erased all reference to 'death by starvation', 'hunger', or 'bodies' slumped in the street. In February 1944, however, the US Congress authorized the UNRRA (United Nations Relief and Rehabilitation Administration) to send food to India. But Churchill denied that people in the British colony were suffering hunger:

> A deadly game was being played. Everyone knew that people were starving in Bengal, but the government of India (representing Churchill and British interests) refused to request UNRRA assistance. At the same time, the British in India paid UNRRA a contribution of $24 million, which made one of the poorest countries on earth the sixth-largest contributor . . . The human cost of the Bengal famine between 1943 and 1944 was 3 million lives.

Should we relate the position adopted by the British government to its struggle against the independence movement, and denounce a case of 'famine holocaust' in this instance as well? In reality, the interpretative key to the events is furnished by a declaration by US Vice President Henry Wallace. He explained the lack of food aid for a population mown down by starvation thus: 'The more food we can put into Russian stomachs, the more American blood will be saved.'[181] In the context of a titanic world war, the Bengal famine became a negligible quantity: lack of respect for a colonial population, and irritation at its unrest, would not appear to have played a significant role. An analogous conclusion can be reached in the case of the Ukrainian tragedy. It unfolded during a pitiless civil war at the height of the Second Thirty Years' War; rightly or wrongly, the USSR regarded collectivization of agriculture as the only option in the face of a conflict and 'aggression' it believed to be imminent. Famine struck with equal cruelty in certain regions of Russia. Yet the state grain reserves created for war were not drawn on. The aid measures decided in February 1933 aimed primarily to ensure sowing in the regions hit by hunger – and this in expectation of a new international conflict.[182]

---

181   Ibid., pp. 109–11.
182   See Merl, '"Ausrottung" der Bourgeoisie und der Kulaken in Sowjetrussland?', pp. 379–81.

International Civil War and the Katyn Massacre

Proof of the unsustainability of the Nazism/Bolshevism equation would not be complete without an analysis of one of the most terrible crimes committed by the Soviet Union: the Katyn Massacre. Let us return to the latent or open civil war which, between 1914 and 1918, developed in the trenches and pitted soldiers and officers against one another. This is something that did not end with the conclusion of the First World War. Hatred and a spirit of revenge were too deep-rooted. Many countries were far from having returned to normality, and it was not difficult to discern new massacres on the horizon, whose culprit already seemed to be known. It was the officer 'caste', tirelessly repeated Kurt Tucholsky in Germany,[183] saluting 'soldiers' enormous anger' against it. Prophetically anticipating the approach of a new war within twenty years, a poem of 1919 expressed uncontrollable anger against 'those who towered above, decorated from top to bottom with medals and who always and only ordered: Kill! Kill!'[184] Hatred of officers was all the more justified in that, having made a decisive contribution to spreading the chauvinist poison which resulted in war, they were in the front rank in Kapp's attempted putsch and the conspiracy to overthrow the republic and install a regime presaging new wars. Some years later, Tucholsky wrote: 'And just as gnats naturally dance, so crime, the commission of crime and the celebration of crime are equally natural for the murderers and their sons . . . May gas find its way into the bedrooms of your children.'[185]

This is a passage to which attention has aptly been drawn by Nolte, who uses it to equate quite different realities.[186] Tucholsky's truculent declaration demonstrates that the civil war begun in the trenches had not been extinguished. In Eastern Europe, where national and state borders were quite the reverse of fixed, persistent civil war seems to link the two world wars without any break. This is the context in which the Katyn Massacre must be situated. Both products of the break-up of the Czarist Empire, Soviet Russia and Poland clashed on the battlefield in 1920 and, albeit latently, the conflict continued thereafter. Polish intelligence, at the time regarded as among the best in Europe, managed to penetrate the Polish Communist Party so deeply that 'the Soviet leaders decided to

---

183   Kurt Tucholsky, *Gesammelte Werke*, ed. M. Gerold Tucholsky and F.J. Raddatz, Hamburg: Rowohlt, 1985, Vol. II, pp. 29, 135.

184   Ibid., Vol. II, pp. 11, 112–13.

185   Ibid., Vol. II, p. 336 and Vol. V, p. 266.

186   See Nolte, 'Standing Things on Their Heads', p. 152.

dissolve the Communist Party in Poland as the only means of saving the remnants of its membership from complete registration by the Polish security agencies'.[187] For a while, Poland seemed interested in Germany's scheming to attract it into the orbit of the Anti-Comintern Pact. In any event, 'Polish ambitions in the Ukraine' were explicit, to be realized, if needs be, with the aid of the Third Reich and under the benevolent gaze of the West, which was quite the reverse of hostile to the collapse of the country and regime created by the October Revolution.[188]

A Soviet book of 1935 explained that in the event of war the ordinary soldier taken prisoner could, 'according to the principle of proletarian solidarity, . . . expect a "brotherly" welcome'. By contrast, officers, who for the most part 'do not belong to the proletariat', would have to be 'converted to communism by . . . theoretical instruction'. These were rules that dated back to 1920 and the veritable Civil War of the time. In 1939, when entering Poland, the Soviets dropped leaflets from the air inviting soldiers to rebel and 'destroy' their officers and generals.[189]

Immediately after capturing them, the USSR envisaged ridding itself of the heavy burden of Polish officers by seeking to exchange them for Ukrainian prisoners in the hands of the Wehrmacht. But Germany refused an exchange. Unwanted on one side, because it was difficult to convert them to the cause of 'proletarian revolution', the Polish officers were no more welcome on the other, which was interested in procuring forced labour, not unproductive mouths to feed. (The Geneva Convention prohibited employment of officers as forced labour and, at the start of the war in the East, the Wehrmacht displayed residual scruples about international law.)[190] The Soviets initiated a programme of 'mass indoctrination' which, while achieving modest results among ordinary soldiers, got nowhere with officers. An exiguous group of Communists was formed, but for the rest attempts at ideological conversion proved a failure. Anti-Communists (the overwhelming majority) countered it with their 'esprit de corps' and 'the concept of an "Officer Honor" rooted in the faraway times of medieval knighthood'.[191] They reached the threshold of active resistance, boycotting film shows, disrupting lectures,[192] and

---

187   J.K. Zawodny, *Death in the Forest: The Story of the Katyn Forest Massacre*, London and Basingstoke: Macmillan, 1971, p. 132.

188   A.J.P. Taylor, *The Origins of the Second World War*, London: Penguin, 1991, pp. 241–3.

189   Zawodny, *Death in the Forest*, pp. 129–30.

190   Ibid., p. 128.

191   Ibid., pp. 133, 103, 142.

192   Ibid., pp.140–1.

engaging in 'punch-ups' with the tiny minority of 'reds'. This attitude sealed their fate: condemnation to death. In its very horror, the crime of Katyn turns out to be essentially different from practices of a genocidal kind, where individual conduct is irrelevant. Instead, even before their internment, the Polish officers were examined one by one, and a biography and a file was constructed for each of them. They were even accused of 'anti-Semitism'. We are so far from the idea of genocide that, in reality, the motive for the homicide sprang from the insurmountable obstacles erected by the officers' refusal to recruit and organize a Polish national army, certainly subaltern to Moscow, but Polish nevertheless.[193]

Moreover, the anti-Communist author whom we have followed in recon-structing the crime of Katyn draws attention to the subsequent regret and chagrin of Beria himself, who repeatedly declared: 'We have committed a great blunder'; 'We have made a great mistake.' The hypothesis of a misun-derstanding on Beria's part of an order from Stalin (which would add a grotesque note to a tragic event) cannot be excluded.[194] At all events, Zawodny draws a conclusion to which we can possibly subscribe: the massa-cre of the Polish officers was simultaneously an atrocious episode of civil war and a failed attempt to indoctrinate and recruit army cadres for inter-national civil war. For the Soviet secret police, 'dealing with the Poles provided . . . a valuable initial experience in conditioning and manipulating the attitudes of [German and Japanese] prisoners-of-war'. As early as a few months after the start of Operation Barbarossa, on 8 October 1941, the first conference of German prisoners-of-war (158 soldiers and junior officers) took place; in July 1943, the 'Free Germany Committee' was formed and, two months later, the 'German Officers Corps', to which officers of any rank could belong.[195]

All this did not prevent Stalin proposing a toast to the summary execu-tion of 50,000 German officers (hence a Katyn on a larger scale) at the Teheran Conference the same year. This was met with disdain by Churchill, whom we have seen formulating a much more 'radical' programme two years earlier (perhaps the British statesman was now already acting with an eye to the Cold War).[196] By contrast, Stalin encountered no objections from either Roosevelt (who seems to have revived the idea at Yalta), or,

193   Ibid., pp. 120, 134–6, 148.
194   Ibid., pp. 150, 127.
195   Ibid., pp. 160–1.
196   See James Bacque, *Other Losses: An Investigation into the Mass Deaths of German Prisoners at the Hands of the French and Americans at the End of World War II*, Toronto: Stoddart, 1989, p. 1.

still less, his son Elliott, who in fact went one further with a toast to the death of 'not only those fifty thousand . . . but many hundreds of thousands more Nazis as well', adding: 'and I am sure the United States Army will support it'.[197] In fact, Eisenhower expressed the idea that not only the 3,500 officers of the German General Staff, but also all members of the Gestapo, as well as the heads of the Nazi Party, from mayors upwards, should be killed: 'This', comments the Canadian historian we have already cited, 'would total about 100,000 people'.[198] What is revealed here is the horrible face of international civil war. The configuration of the friend/ enemy dichotomy in political, rather than national, terms and the identification of the enemy as Nazis rather than Germans seems to undermine the *jus in bello* traditionally governing war between states belonging to the 'civilized' world.

International Civil War, Racial War and Genocide

There is another side to the coin. International civil war can generate especially bitter conflicts and massacres, but it nevertheless halts at the threshold of genocide in the strict sense. Let us take a glance at some crucial moments in the history of international civil war. Proclaiming his crusade against revolutionary France, the Duke of Brunswick announced that Frenchmen caught with weapons would be regarded as rebels against the legitimate king and shot. The same fate would be suffered by 'all members of the Assembly, the department, the district, the municipality, the justices of the peace, the national guard', and so forth. In the event of disrespectful behaviour towards the king, France as a whole must expect 'an unprecedented revenge to be remembered for all eternity' and Paris, in particular, 'military execution and complete ruin'. Thus began, in Michelet's words, 'a strange new war, completely contrary to the law of civilized nations'.[199] Burke expressed the hope that it did not amount to a 'flourish Speech'.[200] Yet the Brunswick Manifesto's genocidal tendencies were objectively off-set by appeals for

---

197   Cf. Frederick J.P.Veale, *Advance to Barbarism:The Development of Total Warfare*, Newport: Institute for Historical Review, 1979, pp. 216–20; Bacque, *Other Losses*, p. 1.

198   Bacque, *Other Losses*, p. 19.

199   Jules Michelet, *Histoire de la Révolution française*, Paris: Gallimard, 1961, Vol. I, p. 945.

200   Edmund Burke, *Correspondence*, ed. Th. W. Copeland and J.A. Woods, Cambridge: Cambridge University Press, 1958–, Vol. VII, p. 169.

international civil war that divided the French people transversally and prevented their criminalization en bloc (its 'healthy part' was called upon to collaborate in restoring order).

Robespierre referred to the Brunswick Manifesto and the logic behind it when reproaching the British government, which 'has dared to state and proclaim that there is no need to respect any faith, any role of honour in this war with the French, given that they are a people of rebels who have infringed the most sacred rules'.[201] As the war raged more intensely, in the wake of indignation at attacks on Jacobin leaders attributed to a British conspiracy, the Convention issued the decree of 7 Prairial: 'no British or Hanoverian will be taken prisoner'.[202] This was probably not an order to shoot prisoners: episodes of the kind have not been confirmed (on the other hand, there was only a brief gap between Prairial and Thermidor). Rather, it seems to be an order for the war to be waged to the bitter end, looking for battles to destroy the enemy and having done with 'this Anglomania masked as philanthropy'. To express himself thus was Robespierre, who subsequently went further: 'I do not like the British', 'I hate the British people', 'that despicable nation' which, were it to continue to support its government, 'would have to slip back into the ocean'.[203]

What are forgotten or rejected here are the frequent appeals during the French Revolution, to 'denationalize the war'[204] and trigger international civil war, wherein the friend/enemy opposition is defined not by national borders but by political ideology. Now, by contrast, it might be said that the British are subject to a criminalization that does not seem to permit of any escape. On the one hand, this is the result of moral fanaticism and the international civil war. According to Robespierre, 'Those who make war on a people to block the progress of liberties and destroy the rights of man must be pursued not as ordinary enemies, but as assassins and rebel outlaws.'[205] On the other hand – and this is by far the more important aspect – what influenced the decree of 7 Prairial was a different logic, which clearly emerges from Barère's report to the Committee of Public Safety:

201   Robespierre, *Oeuvres*, Vol. X, p. 349.
202   Ibid., Vol. X, p. 473.
203   Ibid., Vol. X, pp. 348–9.
204   Quoted in Marc Belissa, *Le Cosmopolitisme du droit des gens (1713–1795). Fraternité universelle et intérêt national au siècle des lumières et pendant la Révolution française*, doctoral thesis, Paris: Panthéon-Sorbonne, Paris I, 1996, p. 824.
205   Robespierre, *Oeuvres*, Vol. IX, p. 463.

National hatred must be vented. For commercial and political communications, there must be an immense ocean between Dover and Calais; young republicans must imbibe hatred of the name of Britain with their mothers' milk. O my country! At the very name 'British', my blood boils and my soul is vexed. The fact is that, having been born in that part of Guyenne where the British wreaked devastation at the time of Charles VII and ruled with a rod of iron, my ears have since infancy heard a tradition of hatred that must become national, in order to save liberty in Europe and maintain the Republic in France.[206]

In other words, the need to mobilize all France's energies led to the re-nationalization of the war and its reinterpretation not as an international civil war, but as a clash between two eternal enemies. In this sense, the re-nationalization of the war was its re-naturalization, with *de facto* reversion to a pre-revolutionary ideology. This ideology had been given effective expression two years earlier by a right-wing speaker (he ended up first as an exile in Coblenz and then in London, where he entered Burke's circle) – namely, Cazalès, who polemicized against those who presumed to apply 'the vague principles of humanity' in international relations and war as follows: 'The *patrie* must be the exclusive object of our love . . . As for me, and I say it openly, it is not the Russians, the Germans, or the British whom I love; it is the French whom I hold dear: the blood of a single one of my fellow citizens is more precious to me than that of all the peoples of the world.'[207]

Among the revolutionaries, the re-nationalization and re-naturalization of war was neither definitive nor stable. Robespierre continued to hope for the 'explosion which liberty is bound to produce' in the country leading the counter-revolutionary coalition. Even when he declared his hatred for that 'despicable nation', the Jacobin leader added: 'As long as they remain shamefully enslaved to despots, I shall detest the British people with all my heart. Once they have become free, they will perhaps again have a right to my admiration.'[208] The revolutionary logic of de-naturalizing the war ends up prevailing.

Let us turn to the nineteenth century. If there is one moment when Marx and Engels (the second much more so than the first) came close to justifying indiscriminate massacre and thus, tendentially, genocide, it was around 1848,

---

206   Quoted in Belissa, *Le Cosmopolitisme du droit des gens*, pp. 828–9.
207   Quoted in ibid., p. 416.
208   Robespierre, *Oeuvres*, Vol. X, pp. 345, 349.

when they advanced the theory of the 'non-historic peoples'. Here the friend/enemy dichotomy seems to lose any historical, mobile character, dangerously constricting the escape route for an enemy who risks being represented in naturalistic terms. But the theory of the 'non-historic peoples', condemned en bloc and hence not traversed by class struggles, may be regarded as a pre-Marxian survival – one superseded, or contested at any rate, by Marx's polemic of 1859 against viewing Germany as the 'heart of human civilization'.[209]

    And now let us come on to the October Revolution. The Civil War and British intervention posed a deadly threat to Bolshevik power. But here is what Trotsky had to say:

> Soldiers of the Red Army! On all fronts you are encountering the hostile cunning of the British. The counter-revolutionary forces are firing on you with British weapons . . . the women and children of Archangelsk and Astrakhan are being killed and disabled by British pilots with British explosives. British ships are firing on our coasts . . . But even now, as you struggle bitterly against the British puppet Yudenich, I appeal to you: never forget that there is not only one Britain. As well as the Britain of profits, violence, corruption and bloodthirstiness, there is the Britain of labour, of strength of spirit, of great ideals, of international solidarity. Against us is the Britain of the stock market, an infamous Britain without honour. Working Britain and its people are with us.[210]

This is a text that might be compared with those by Robespierre cited above. In both instances, the threat to the revolution comes from Britain. However, although nurtured on historical culture, the Bolshevik leader avoids naturalizing the conflict and depicts it in terms that divide the enemy internally. Here too it might be said that the USSR came closest to indiscriminate massacre when it put a damper on the international civil war and reinterpreted the war with Germany in accordance with traditional, pre-revolutionary views as a mortal clash between Slavs and Germans.

    Despite proclaiming the anti-Bolshevik crusade, the Third Reich never really managed to distance itself from that representation of the war. The campaign in the East was cast, in Hitler's words, as a 'bitter racial war that

---

209   Marx and Engels, *Werke*, Vol. XIII, pp. 282–3.
210   Quoted in Alex P. Schmid, *Churchills privater Krieg. Intervention und Konterrevolution im russischen Bürgerkrieg, November 1918–März 1920*, Zurich: Atlantis, 1974, p. 265.

does not permit of legal limits of any kind'.[211] There was no reference to international civil war, which by definition divides different peoples and races transversally. Let us read an order from the German army's high command on the eve of Operation Barbarossa:

> The war against Russia is an inevitable consequence of the struggle imposed on us for the existence and, in particular, the economic autonomy of Greater Germany and the European space dominated by it. It is the ancient struggle of Germans against Slavs, the defence of European civilization against the Asiatic-Muscovite flood, the ejection of Jewish Bolshevism. The objective of this struggle is to reduce Russia to ruins and hence it must be waged with unprecedented severity.[212]

As we can see, the ideological crusade against Bolshevism does not cancel the element of racial war. The war with Russia continues to be interpreted with categories that had emerged prior to the October Revolution, such as the life-and-death struggle between Germans and Slavs. In fact, the ideological crusade ultimately ends up being subordinated to the racial war, because in line with the schemas of the reactionary intellectual tradition Bolshevism is branded as an ideology alien to Germany, Europe and civilization as such – as an inherently Asiatic, barbaric ideology: the struggle against Communism is an aspect of the racial struggle against barbarians. Thus, at least as regards the campaign in the East, Nazism did not – could not – contain a genuine appeal for international civil war. Obviously, the Third Reich was prepared to avail itself of the aid of collaborationist troops or groups and had an interest in disrupting the Soviet army and domestic front. But the arguments it deployed are significant. The fliers dropped from German aircraft called on Russians to refuse to shed their blood for 'Jewish commissars', and to put a stop to the 'criminal machinations of the Jewish clique', emulating Germany which, with the overthrow of the republic created by the November revolution, had rid itself of Jewish 'parasites'.[213] On the basis of this ideological platform, the Third Reich's troops incited bloody anti-Jewish pogroms in the various territories occupied by them. In other words, the motif of racial war was deployed even in the context of attempts to disaggregate the enemy. By disobeying 'Jewish

---

211   Quoted in Krausnick, *Hitlers Einsatzgruppen*, p. 70.
212   Quoted in ibid., p. 189.
213   Mayer, *Why Did the Heavens Not Darken?*, p. 211.

commissars', Russians would refuse to let themselves become embroiled in a civil war within the white and European race. In any event, civil war was a negative value. In fact, it could not even really be conceived among a people that had genuinely achieved civilization. The Hitlerite terror in Germany, which in the view of the contemporary historian appears as a preventive civil war in preparation for the bid for world power, was represented in Nazi ideology as a war of racial liberation.

Without abandoning attempts to disaggregate the enemy through an ideological crusade, Hitler was always very careful that the Bolshevik/ anti-Bolshevik dichotomy did not undermine or blur the dichotomy he regarded as primary and crucial – namely, that between barbarism and civilization, Slavs and Germans, the race of savages and slaves, on the one hand, and the master race, on the other. The thesis formulated here – the fundamental foreignness to Nazism of the category of international civil war – might be taken as a complimentary concession by the most fervent exponents of historical revisionism. In reality, however, such foreignness was only the flip side of an inability to go beyond naturalistic de-specification in its gravest form: racial de-specification. Precisely this largely precluded any escape for the 'natives' and, even more so, the Jews.

Holocaust and Holocausts

Promptings to reinterpret the Judeocide also hail from cultural and political circles that should not in any way be confused with historical revisionism. Some time ago, a debate developed in France that pitted Armenian intellectuals and Jewish intellectuals against one another. The former attacked Bernard Lewis as a revisionist and negationist. Concerned to reassert the incomparability of the Holocaust, he had rejected any attempt to equate, or even compare, it with the Armenian tragedy. The latter was to be interpreted as a 'simple' deportation which, in conditions of total war, objectively resulted in a large-scale massacre: 'no serious proof exists of a decision and plan by the Ottoman government to destroy the Armenian nation' as such. The angry reaction of descendants of the victims of this tragic episode in modern history is fully understandable, especially since for some time now they have been stressing that it was precisely to the genocide of their ancestors that Hitler referred when planning the war of extermination in the East: who, Hitler asked, now remembers the Armenians? And who, some decades hence, will bother about the drastic reduction in numbers of the natives that the Wehrmacht intends to carry out in the impending German colonial empire? In the history of the twentieth century, then, the Armenian genocide is not only the first chronologically, but the model inspiring the culprits of subsequent genocides.[214] The Jewish Holocaust is not a unique phenomenon, and not even the original genocide. This thesis provoked cries of scandal over the 'ultimate expedient of a more subtle revisionism' and a new riposte from the Armenian side: does drawing attention to 'genocides other than the Jewish one', and rescuing those suffered by the Armenians and Romany from oblivion, 'attest to a more subtle revisionism'?[215]

Romany likewise lament the lack of attention paid to the tragedy of their people:

> Romany are confined to oral culture and must speak the unspeakable to distracted ears in simple terms. They do not possess organic intellectuals who can express the collective anguish of exterminated families or scholars capable of analysing the specific character of Nazi legislation, describing the process of deportation, and quantifying the impact of the extermination.[216]

Identified as responsible for the first twentieth-century genocide, Turks not only reject the charge, but sometimes observe that behind their measures against the Armenians lay the experience of the concentration camps employed by the British against the Boers some years earlier.[217] This is a historical experience that refers us back to the history of colonialism and which, according to Arendt in *The Origins of Totalitarianism*, represents a key stage in the construction of the *univers concentrationnaire*.[218] Significantly, it was precisely then that a term and category destined to play a crucial role in today's debates began to make its appearance: the British pacifist press denounced the 'holocaust of child-life' which occurred during the

---

214   See Edward Alexander, *A Crime of Vengeance: An Armenian Struggle for Justice*, New York and Toronto: Free Press/Macmillan, 1991, pp. 1, 198.

215   On all this, see Marc Nichanian, 'Le droit et le fait: la campagne de 1994', *Lignes*, No. 26, October 1995, pp. 74–9.

216   Henriette Asseo, 'La spécificité de l'extermination des Tziganes', in Y. Thanassekos and H. Wismann, eds, *Révision de l'histoire. Totalitarismes, crimes et génocides Nazis*, Paris: Éditions du Cerf, 1990, p. 130.

217   See Alexander, *A Crime of Vengeance*, p. 135.

218   See Hannah Arendt, *The Origins of Totalitarianism*, New York: Harcourt, Brace & World, 1951, pp. 440–1.

suppression of the Boer rebels.[219] The latter in fact embodied the worst of the colonial tradition in their policy towards the natives, who met with the fate traditionally reserved for Indians and peoples regarded as dross. From Europe and Africa we thus pass to America. During the inauguration of the mausoleum dedicated to the Holocaust, survivors of the Native American population asked why a similar monument had not been erected in memory of the genocide committed in the Western hemisphere. Like the Romany, Native Americans cannot count on many organic intellectuals. Perhaps they have found an exception in the author of a book, at once committed and rigorous, devoted to the 'American Holocaust'. As early as the end of the sixteenth century, the 'discovery' of the New World had led to 60–80 million deaths, but 'the carnage was not over'.[220]

Intellectuals of Jewish origin do not challenge the fact that 'sheerly as a matter of quantity the Indian catastrophe is unparalleled' and, 'both absolutely and proportionally, surpasses the destruction of European Jewry'. In this instance, however, we are not dealing with the planned total destruction of an ethnic group.[221] To which the scholar on the Native American side of the question replies:

A traditional Eurocentric bias that lumps undifferentiated masses of 'Africans' into one single category and undifferentiated masses of 'Indians' into another, while making fine distinctions among the populations of Europe, permits the ignoring of cases in which genocide against Africans and American Indians has resulted in the *total* extermination – purposefully carried out – of entire cultural, social, religious, and ethnic groups.[222]

This thesis is fully confirmed by the picture drawn by a loyalist historian of the American Revolution. Ryerson observed of the policy of 'the destruction of the Six Indian Nations' adopted by the rebel colonists: 'Congress, by an order which, we believe, has no parallel in the annals of any civilized nation, commands the complete destruction of these people as a nation . . . including

---

219   See Stephen Koss, *The Pro-Boers: The Anatomy of an Antiwar Movement*, Chicago and London: University of Chicago Press, 1973, p. 229.

220   David E. Stannard, *American Holocaust*, Oxford: Oxford University Press, 1992, p. 95.

221   Steven T. Katz, *The Holocaust in Historical Context. Volume I: The Holocaust and Mass Death before the Modern Age*, New York and Oxford: Oxford University Press, 1994, p. 91.

222   Stannard, *American Holocaust*, pp. 95, 146, 151.

women and children.'[223] The oblivion or neglect suffered by this chapter in history is all the more serious because the experience of the Native Americans possesses a paradigmatic value. The USA tended to compare the enemies with which it clashed over the years to them. Moreover, the tragedy is on-going: while 'death squads' strike at the indigenous peoples in countries like Guatemala, in the Native American reservations of the USA the poverty rate is four times the national average. For all these reasons, the holocaust of which the Native Americans were the victims over the centuries is 'the worst human holocaust the world had ever witnessed'.[224] The contemporary historian quoted here does not refer to Hitler's comparison between the Native Americans and the natives of Eastern Europe, who in their turn demand that the 'forgotten Holocaust' of which the Poles (and not only they) were victims be rescued from oblivion.[225]

The fate of the Native Americans evokes that of the blacks, who were called on to replace or flank them in the forced labour required in the continent conquered by the Europeans. Descendants of the slaves deported from Africa in their turn underscore the centrality of the 'Black Holocaust', if only on account of its secular duration and the number of countries involved, including the most civilized – among them, the leader of the Western world today. A religious curse has long followed blacks. In Genesis (9, 21–7), we read that, after the great flood and following a copious libation, Noah slept naked and was discovered thus by his amused, disrespectful youngest son, Ham. When the patriarch awoke and realized what had occurred, he condemned Ham's descendants to be slaves of the descendants of Shem and Japheth (Noah's other sons). Blacks were subsequently identified and branded as descendants of Ham and their slavery was thus theologically sanctioned. Slave-owners and (after the American Civil War) theoreticians of white supremacy have referred to this motif for centuries. If anti-Jewish persecution was long justified by recourse to Christian theology and the theme of deicide, the persecution of Native Americans and blacks was justified by recourse to themes derived from the scriptures sacred to Jews and Christians alike. The Native Americans, and peoples assimilated to them,

223   Egerton Ryerson, *The Loyalists of America and Their Times: From 1620 to 1816*, New York: Haskell, 1970, Vol. II, p. 100.

224   Stannard, *American Holocaust*, pp. 258, 256, 146. Tzvetan Todorov, in *The Conquest of America: The Question of the Other* (trans. Richard Howard, London: Harper Perennial, 1992, p. 5), likewise speaks of the conquest of America as 'the greatest genocide in human history'.

225   See Richard C. Lukas, *Forgotten Holocaust: The Poles under German Occupation 1939–1944*, New York: Hippocrene Books, 1990.

were identified with the inhabitants of Canaan and blacks with the descendants of Ham.

Over the centuries, anti-Hamitism has raged alongside anti-Semitism; and Christians and Jews have participated in it. More than on any other people, the horror of world history has been focused on blacks. Unlike all others subject to persecution, noted Malcolm X, they cannot hide their skin colour and identity.[226] Consequently, we can understand the success of Islam among black American activists, who, to prove the uniqueness of the 'Black Holocaust', sometimes stress Jewish participation in the slave-trading from Africa. While the thesis of the exemplary character of the Armenian genocide sparks accusations of revisionism, the latter argument prompts the charge of anti-Semitism. But it is meaningless to brand as such an assertion corresponding to historical reality. The tendency to inflate the role of Jews in the black slave trade is certainly dangerous and inadmissible. Yet it would be absurd and unjust to claim that Jews alone were strangers to a historical experience and infamy whose protagonist was colonialism in its entirety, and to which Islam – often referred to by black militants in their polemic against the West (and the Judeo-Christian religious tradition) – was certainly no stranger.[227] Overall, however, rather than with an expression of anti-Semitism, we are dealing with claims for the negative primacy of anti-Hamitism in world history.

Even historical tragedies are a moment for constructing identities. Consequently, we can understand why the theme of genocide affords grounds for confrontation not only between the great powers, but between the victims themselves. Today, we witness attempts by Armenians, Romany, Native Americans, blacks and other ethnic and social groups (such as homosexuals) to rescue their tragedy from historical oblivion and force it to the centre of cultural and political attention. In so doing, they are objectively led to query the uniqueness of the Jewish Holocaust. However, notwithstanding appearances and superficial points of contact, all this has nothing to with historical revisionism in the strict sense.

In polemical mutual opposition, Jews, Native Americans and blacks seem to demand for themselves the characteristic attributed by Marx to the proletariat – namely, being the bearer of the sufferings of all humanity and, for

---

226   Malcolm X, *Malcolm X Speaks: Selected Speeches and Statements*, ed. George Breitman, New York: Merit Publishers, 1965, p. 169.

227   See David B. Davis, 'The Slave Trade and the Jews', *New York Review of Books*, 22 December 1994.

that reason, the symbol of its possible redemption. During the French Revolution, a utopian novel by Louis-Sébastien Mercier imagined the erection in 2440 of a 'single monument' in expiation of the slaughter of the Native Americans and enslavement of the blacks.[228] Perhaps, following the construction of a mausoleum in memory of the Jewish Holocaust, expectations on the part of Native Americans and blacks for this 'single monument' have become more impatient. But their aspiration seems to have no deep resonance in the dominant culture. In his inaugural address, Clinton celebrated his country as 'the world's oldest democracy'. In this historical depiction, blacks and Native Americans continue to be a *quantité négligeable*. The repression or trivialization of one or both of the tragedies that marked the fate of whole peoples serves the construction of genealogical myths, which are called upon to define a country's identity in the most positive terms possible and thereby justify its privileged role. The US president continued thus: America 'must continue to lead the world'; 'our mission is timeless'. The logic that motivates German historical revisionism is similar. Let us turn to Franz Joseph Strauss. It is necessary to desist from constant re-evocations of the horror of the Third Reich so that Germany, becoming 'a normal nation' once more, can 'again walk with its head held high' and 'accomplish its task in this world'. The 'economic giant' (to quote Ernst Nolte now) must be allowed to exercise 'due political power'.[229] Silence on the 'Black Holocaust' and the 'American Holocaust' is matched by trivialization of the Jewish Holocaust. Although, in justifying two different ideas of global 'mission' or 'task', the genealogical myths thus constructed can come into contradiction with one another, they fully converge in reinforcing a third genealogical myth. With the repression of the Native American and black tragedies, and the trivialization of the Judeocide – or, at any rate, its severance from the colonial tradition and assignment to Asiatic barbarism (the fact that the fate of the Jews was sealed by their dual stigmatization as Eastern 'natives' and bearers of eastern Bolshevism is ignored) – the West undergoes a dazzling transfiguration that affords no space for balanced historical assessments and relations of equality with the rest of the world.

While he characterizes the genocide of the Native Americans as the worst ever perpetrated, the author of *American Holocaust* suggests regarding each of the great genocides in the history of humanity as 'unique, for one reason

228   See Louis-Sébastien Mercier, *L'An deux mille cent quarante. Rêve s'il en fut jamais*, ed. R. Trousson, Paris: Ducros, 1971, pp. 201–6.

229   Habermas, 'Nachspiel', p. 163; Nolte, *Intervista sulla questione tedesca*, p. 79.

or another'.[230] At work here is a concern to put an end to the quarrels dividing the victims and their descendants. It is clear that historians must continue to examine the peculiarity of each of the great historical tragedies. Yet the horror of the dual naturalistic de-specification of which the Jews were victims in the twentieth century cannot be adequately appreciated if their experience is severed from the colonial tradition, which the Third Reich sought to resume and radicalize (at the same time proclaiming an exterminatory crusade against the 'barbarians' who challenged that tradition).

As is well known, following the fall of the Nazi regime, the most advanced German culture posed the problem of 'coming to terms with the past' (*Aufarbeitung der Vergangenheit*). We can discuss whether self-critical reflection went far enough. But it remains the case that nothing of the sort occurred in the case of the West as a whole. Such, in the final analysis, is the soil in which historical revision put down its roots.

---

230   Stannard, *American Holocaust*, p. 251.

CHAPTER SIX

Nostalgia for Empire: Historical Revisionism in Britain

From the Three Germanic Empires to the Two English-Speaking Empires

Not only has the West not achieved a genuine *Aufarbeitung der Vergangenheit*, but gestures and moves in this direction meet with fierce resistance and even explicit rehabilitation of the colonial tradition, with calls to resume it and recognize its contemporary relevance. We have seen Popper deprecating the 'haste' with which the process of de-colonization was carried out and Paul Johnson de-legitimizing the anti-colonial revolutions and mocking their leaders – not only those identified with Marxism and Leninism, but even Gandhi. However, if the anti-colonial revolutions are to be condemned, would it not have been better for Britain to arrive at a compromise with the Third Reich and thereby hold on to its empire, starting with India? As we know, this is the argument advanced by another British historian, John Charmley, who severely criticizes Churchill. The latter wanted to save the empire, but ended up losing it out of anti-German intransigence and his alliance with the Soviet Union – the country that had incited colonial populations to rebellion from its birth. Perhaps the prospect held out by Hitler (vigorously expressed in a letter to the *Daily Mail* on 4 September 1937) of an accord between the three empires of the 'white race' and 'Germanic' origin – the British, the American and the one he proposed to build in Eastern Europe in the tracks of the Teutonic knights – was not unfounded and unreasonable.[1]

---

1   Cf. above Chapter 3, §9 (for Popper and Johnson), Chapter 4, §6 (for Hitler's letter) and *passim* (for Charmley).

From here it is not difficult to discern the road leading to rehabilitation of the Third Reich itself. Such is the road unfortunately followed by another British author – namely, David Irving (who nevertheless has serious works of historical research to his credit). How are we to explain this startling political and intellectual involution? Hitler was the first to engage in rehabilitation of colonialism, which had been widely discredited by the carnage of the First World War (in which the scramble for empire had resulted), and became the target of the October Revolution's appeal to colonial slaves to cast off their shackles.

In face of the deadly threat looming over Western civilization, the Nazi leader had appealed for the unity of Germany, Britain and the USA, underscoring the three countries' common Germanic origins. Indeed, after having arrived in the British Isles, the Germans had also crossed the Atlantic. Hence (*Mein Kampf* stressed) the population of North America 'consists in by far the largest part of Germanic elements'.[2] In fact, repeated the so-called *Zweites Buch*, it was a population proud of its racial ascendancy: 'the American Union regards itself as a Nordic-Germanic state, not as an international mush of peoples'.[3] All the requisite conditions obtained for the unity of the three Germanic empires.

In adopting this position, Hitler revived a tradition that went far beyond his country. In the second half of the nineteenth century, numerous British authors had stressed the blood ties that bound England and Germany, these 'two great streams of the Teutonic race'.[4] Lord Robert Cecil (future Marquis of Salisbury and Prime Minister) contrasted 'the people of a southern climate' with those of 'Teutonic parentage'.[5] In 1899, Joseph Chamberlain (the Colonial Secretary) officially called on the United States and Germany to form a 'Teutonic' alliance with his country.[6] This is a vision not dissimilar from Hitler's. But such an ideological climate could not survive the antagonism that divided the three great Germanic or Teutonic powers during two world wars and the revelation of the horrors of which the Third Reich was guilty.

---

2   Adolf Hitler, *Mein Kampf*, trans. Ralph Mannheim, London: Pimlico, 1992, p. 260.

3   Adolf Hitler, *Hitlers Zweites Buch. Ein Dokument aus dem Jahre 1928*, ed. Gerhard L. Weinberg, Stuttgart: Deutsche Verlags-Anstalt, 1961, pp. 131–2.

4   Hugh A. MacDougall, *Racial Myth in English History: Trojans, Teutons, and Anglo-Saxons*, Montreal and London: Harvest/University Press of New England, 1982, pp. 120, 98.

5   Quoted in David Cannadine, 'The Context, Performance and Meaning of Ritual: The British Monarch and the "Invention of Tradition", c. 1820–1977', in Eric Hobsbawm and Terence Ranger, eds, *The Invention of Tradition*, Cambridge: Cambridge University Press, 1983, p. 101.

6   Cf. Henry Kissinger, *Diplomacy*, New York: Simon & Schuster, 1994, p. 186.

If we wish to understand contemporary ideological developments, we must begin with the turn that was already foreshadowed with the Second World War and then consolidated with the outbreak of the Cold War. When calling for a struggle against the danger to the West posed by Soviet and Eastern Communism, Churchill, in a letter to US President Eisenhower, invoked the 'unity of the English-speaking world' and stressed the key role within it of Great Britain, 'with her eighty million white English-speaking people'.[7] Appeals for the unity of the three Germanic or Teutonic countries ceded to appeals for the unity of the two principal Anglophone countries. Although he had never stopped thinking about it, Churchill did not refer to the British Empire or the American Empire while the global anti-colonial revolution was underway.

Thus we arrive at the present. David Irving is subject to general condemnation: his historical revisionism cannot prosper at a time when the rehabilitation and return of colonialism take the form of its transfiguration into a champion of the cause of democracy and human rights. On the other hand, Niall Ferguson has enjoyed extraordinary success. Rather than rehabilitating the three Germanic empires, he pays explicit, ringing tribute to the two English-speaking empires, overcoming the linguistic inhibitions apparent in Churchill at a time when the Communist movement exercised extremely strong influence among colonial peoples. So 'the question is not whether the British imperialism was without blemish. It was not. The question is whether there could have been a less bloody path to modernity. Perhaps in theory there could have been. But in practice?'[8] During the twentieth century, Empire had crossed the Atlantic, but without in any way losing its beneficial, progressive character: 'I have no objection in principle to an American empire. Indeed, a part of my argument is that many parts of the world would benefit from a period of American rule.'[9]

The overall picture is now clear. Before proceeding, it is worth reflecting on why this key episode in historical revisionism has occurred primarily in the United Kingdom. Its centre could not be a country like Germany or Italy, where the historical memory of the link between Nazism or Fascism

---

7   Peter G. Boyle, ed., *The Churchill-Eisenhower Correspondence 1953–1955*, Chapel Hill and London: University of North Carolina Press, 1990, p. 34 (letter to Eisenhower of 5 April 1953).

8   Niall Ferguson, *Empire: How Britain Made the Modern World*, London: Penguin, 2004, p. xxviii.

9   Niall Ferguson, *Colossus: The Rise and Fall of the American Empire*, London: Penguin, 2005, p. 2.

and the demand for 'living space' and celebration of colonial expansionism is still living. Nor could it be France, whose revolution inspired the first great anti-colonial revolution, mounted by the black slaves of San Domingo-Haiti and led by a 'black Jacobin' (Toussaint L'Ouverture). Finally, the centre could not be the United States – a country born out of a rebellion against the British Empire and which, during its ascendancy, frequently adopted anti-colonialist postures. Originating in the United Kingdom, the summons to the West to come to the rescue under the leadership of the American Empire, continuator and inheritor of the British Empire, meets with a wide echo in the USA, obviously, and in the West as a whole.

A Blood-Spattered 'Path' to a Problematic 'Modernity'

Over and above the two English-speaking empires, Ferguson rehabilitates the idea of (Western) Empire as such. It is called upon to exercise sovereignty, direct or 'informal', not only over countries that were de-colonized with excessive 'haste', or so-called 'failed states', or states infected with 'extremism' (as in Popper and Johnson), but ultimately on a planetary scale. This is all the more necessary because of the extremely perilous situation that has been created internationally. In the very title of a highly successful book (*Civilization: The West and the Rest*), Ferguson seems to adopt the commonplace of the West as an island of civilization surrounded, if not by barbarians, then by peoples of dubious value and reliability. The language used is militant. Unfortunately, the centre of global economic gravity is shifting to the East: 'what we are living through now is the end of 500 years of Western predominance'. Yet the gravest threat is 'our own loss of faith in the civilization we inherited from our ancestors'.[10] Recovering this 'faith' entails rediscovering the grandeur of the British Empire (and the 'path to modernity' indicated by it) and of the American 'empire of liberty' theorized by Jefferson.[11]

What immediately leaps to the eye is the historical fragility of this ideological construct. The 'empire of liberty' (more precisely, 'for liberty'), which was urged to annex not only Cuba but also Canada (to be seized from London's control by force) as rapidly as possible, and to become the

---

10   Niall Ferguson, *Civilization: The West and the Rest*, London: Penguin, 2011, pp. 322, 325.

11   Ferguson, *Colossus*, p. 2.

greatest and most glorious 'since the creation',[12] was conceived by the US statesman in bitter opposition to the British Empire, accused by him of the worst crimes. At least in his private correspondence, Jefferson had no problem acknowledging the horror of the war against the Native Americans. But in his view the culprit was the London government, which had incited these savage, sanguinary 'tribes'. This was a situation that 'will oblige us to pursue them to extermination, or drive them to new seats beyond our reach'. 'The confirmed brutalization if not extermination of this race in our America' was attributable to Britain, as was the analogous fate of the 'same colored man in Asia' and of the Irish (who, sharing their skin 'color', should have been the 'brethren' of the British). British policy, engaged in sowing death and destruction 'wherever else Anglo-mercantile cupidity can find a two-penny interest in deluging the earth with human blood', was at fault.[13] Jefferson's requisitory did not end there. According to him, the British Empire was even worse than the one built by Napoleon. While the latter would take his 'tyrannies' to the grave with him, in the case of the British Empire the protagonist seeking to impose absolute dominion over the seas was a whole 'nation', which was an 'insult to the human understanding'.[14] With its despotic, bellicose behaviour, which forced the young North American republic to embark on industrial development and rearmament, it was inspired by 'Satan'.[15] In any event, the relationship between the two countries could only be one of 'eternal war', destined to end with the 'extermination of the one or the other party'.[16] Of course, at the time Jefferson was writing the 1812–15 war between Britain and the USA was underway. But the ideological fury of these declarations makes a mockery of Ferguson's presumption in elevating the British and US empires to the pantheon of humanity's benefactors alongside one another – in fact, in fond embrace.

But let us dwell on the British Empire. It should be clear that, in order to form a balanced judgement, we must also attend to the voices of the colonized peoples. During the Second World War, Gandhi did not hesitate

---

12   Quoted in James Morton Smith, ed., *The Republic of Letters: The Correspondence between Thomas Jefferson and James Madison 1776–1826*, New York and London: Norton, 1995, Vol. III, p. 1586 (letter to Madison of 27 April 1809).

13   Thomas Jefferson, *Writings*, ed. Merrill D. Peterson, New York: Library of America, 1984, pp. 1312–13 (letter to A. von Humboldt of 6 December 1813).

14   Ibid., pp. 1272–3 (letter to Madame de Staël of 24 May 1813).

15   Ibid., p. 1357 (letter to W. Short of 28 November 1814).

16   Ibid., p. 1366 (letter to M.J. de La Fayette of 14 February 1815).

to compare the British Empire with Nazi Germany: 'In India we have Hitlerian rule however disguised it may be in softer terms.'[17] What in part prompted this judgement (whose appropriate severity is marred by its underestimation of the qualitative leap undergone by colonialist autocracy and violence with the Third Reich) was unquestionably resentment at the London government's stubborn refusal to concede independence. Let us now give the floor to Indian historians writing more than half a century since the end of British rule. This is how (on the second page of the cover of volume two of his book) one of them summarizes the repression that rained down on the sepoys' mutiny, or the first 'war of independence', which was waged with religious slogans (as often happens in cases of this kind): 'More than 10 million Indians – 7 per cent of the country's population – lost their lives, most of them massacred in cold blood by marauding British troops.'[18] Another Indian historian refers to a 'secret war' against the Indian people, not shrinking from genocide, in connection with the famine that struck Bengal during the Second World War. This is a serious, probably excessive accusation, but the ideology articulated by Churchill in these years seems to corroborate it: 'I hate Indians. They are a beastly people with a beastly religion.' Fortunately, an unprecedented number of 'white soldiers' were available to maintain order and defend civilization.[19] Britain was dealing with a race 'protected by their mere pullulation from the doom that is their due'. It would be good for Air Marshall Arthur Harris, the architect of the carpet bombing of Germany, to 'send some of his surplus bombers to destroy them'.[20]

According to Marx, India was 'the Ireland of the East'.[21] Let us turn then to what, by analogy, we might call the India of the West. The Irish were regarded and treated like the 'Amalekites' – the stock condemned by the Old Testament to be wiped off the face of the earth – by their British conquerors and colonists.[22] Marx's assertion will hardly impress an intellectual who also enjoys great success in the West because he disdains the

---

17   Mohandas K. Gandhi, *The Collected Works of Mahatma Gandhi*, New Delhi: Government of India, 1969–2001, Vol. LXXX, p. 200 ('Answer to Questions', 25 April 1941).

18   Amaresh Misra, *War of Civilisations: India AD 1857*, New Delhi: Rupa, 2008.

19   Quoted in Madhusree Mukerjee, *Churchill's Secret War: The British Empire and the Ravaging of India during World War II*, New York: Basic Books, 2010, p. 78.

20   Quoted in ibid., p. 246.

21   Karl Marx and Friedrich Engels, *Gesamtausgabe*, Berlin: Dietz, 1975– and Amsterdam: IMES, 1990–, Part I, Vol. 12, p. 166.

22   Karl Marx and Friedrich Engels, *Werke*, Berlin: Dietz, 1955– , Vol. XVI, p. 447.

'few die-hard devotees of Karl Marx'.[23] So we may cite the judgement expressed by Gustave de Beaumont, the French liberal who was a friend of Tocqueville. What obtained in Ireland was 'unimaginable religious oppression'. Taken together, the oppression, humiliations and suffering inflicted on this 'slave people' by the British 'tyrant' demonstrated that 'a degree of egotism and madness is present in human institutions whose limits cannot be defined'.[24] The domination of the unhappy island by the British Empire is referred to as if it were the extreme limit of evil, absolute evil. This is a representation reserved in our day for the Third Reich.

To complete the picture, let us finally take a look at Africa. Between 1952 and 1959, the Mau Mau rebellion occurred in Kenya. Drawing on the most recent historiography on the subject, a prestigious American liberal periodical has described the methods used by the British authorities to restore order in the colony. In the Kamiti concentration camp, women were 'interrogated, whipped, starved, and subjected to hard labor, which included filling mass graves with truckloads of corpses from other camps. Many gave birth at Kamiti, but the infant death rate was overwhelming. The women buried their babies in bundles of six at a time.'[25]

What of the American Empire? Celebration of it as an 'empire for liberty' did not prevent Jefferson from theorizing the need to exterminate the Native Americans, albeit blaming it on the rival British Empire. Nor did it prevent him from being a slave-owner and so de-humanizing his slaves as to sell, if necessary, individual members of the black families he owned as separate items or commodities. And all this – it is precisely Ferguson who highlights the fact – 'at a time when the movement for the abolition of slavery was already well under way on both sides of the Atlantic'.[26] It is no coincidence if the champion of the 'empire for liberty' was at the same time utterly committed to the political isolation and economic strangulation of the republic of Haiti, governed by former slaves who were the protagonists of a major revolution and struggle for liberty.

Over a century later – in the meantime, the Native Americans had largely been wiped from the face of the earth – the situation in the USA, in the

---

23   Ferguson, *Civilization*, p. 7.
24   Gustave de Beaumont, *L'Irlande sociale, politique et religieuse*, ed. Godeleine Charpentier, Lille: CERIUL/Université Charles de Gaulle-Lille III, 1989, Vol. I, p. 331 and Vol. II, pp. 306, 201.
25   Neal Ascherson, 'The Breaking of the Mau Mau', *New York Review of Books*, 7 April 2005, p. 29.
26   Ferguson, *Civilization*, p. 129.

summary of an authoritative American historian, was as follows: 'The effort to guarantee "race purity" in the American South anticipated aspects of the official Nazi persecution of the Jews in the 1930s.'[27] Yet again, we encounter the Third Reich! We must at once make it clear that it would be misleading to equate the latter with the two empires we are now more directly concerned with. But it would be even more misleading to transfigure two very different empires that somehow conjure up such a disturbing association into champions of the cause of freedom. At all events, the 'path to modernity', which in Ferguson's view the British and American empires had the merit of promoting, was much more 'bloody' than he believes.

Especially problematic is the very category of 'path to modernity' and the view that the peoples invested by Anglo-American (and Western) expansionism and rule embarked, thanks to it, and albeit at considerable human and social cost, on the road leading to 'modernity' – economic and political development, the 'rule of law', the affirmation and freedom of the individual. This discourse is manifestly unjustified in the case of the Native Americans, the aborigines of Australia and New Zealand, and all the peoples wiped off the face of the earth. But the evolutionistic schema suggested here is not even valid for other peoples.

Encouraged and promoted by colonial expansion, in the American colonies and then in the USA (which from the outset tended to be configured as a new, more powerful empire), a form of slavery obtained that involved an unprecedented de-humanization and commodification of slaves. Traditional religious restrictions having lapsed, the logic of the market radically asserted itself. The male slave's family (wife or partner and children) was broken up into its individual components, each of which was a commodity that could be put on the market separately. At the same time, the racial barrier between whites and blacks rendered emancipation virtually impossible and continued to pursue ex-slaves, who by dint of their skin colour were forever excluded from the race or community of freemen. The operative system was racial chattel slavery or, in the words of the English abolitionist John Wesley, 'the vilest that ever saw the sun'.[28] Anyone who so wishes may include it in the ambit of the 'path to modernity', but it is hard to equate the latter with some 'path to liberty'.

---

27   George M. Frederickson, *Racism: A Short History*, Princeton: Princeton University Press, 2002, pp. 2, 124.

28   Quoted in Robert Isaac and Samuel Wilberforce, *Life of William Wilberforce by his Sons*, London: Murray, 1838, Vol. I, p. 297 (letter to W. Wilberforce of 24 February 1791).

The vagueness of the category on which Ferguson bases his apologia for Empire is evident. Who represented 'modernity' during the war waged by Britain to force China to open its ports to opium imports? Which is more modern – free trade in opium or its prohibition? The laws in force today in virtually every country in the world would seem to attest to the 'modernity' not of the colonialist aggressor, but of its victim! And who represented 'modernity' when, in the mid-nineteenth century, China was torn apart and drenched with blood by a massive civil war? Was it the Taiping, headed by a leader reared on Christian literature and, albeit confusedly, inspired by the ambition to introduce radical reforms? Or the Manchu dynasty, guarantor of the *ancien régime*, clinging on to power and the Confucian tradition, and ultimately supported by Great Britain? Although an ardent chauvinist, who was even inclined to justify the genocidal practices deemed necessary to conquer Algeria,[29] Tocqueville had the required intellectual honesty to acknowledge a key point: 'We have rendered Muslim society much more wretched, disordered, ignorant and barbaric than it was before it knew us.'[30]

The category on which Ferguson relies to rehabilitate and celebrate the British and American empires proves even more debatable if we analyse it in the light of the phenomenon of fundamentalism – something at the heart of current political and ideological debates, but which is far from recent. Two historical episodes in two different continents are instructive. At the start of the nineteenth century, the United States witnessed the development of one of the first attempts to mount organized resistance to the invasion and devastation of the white colonists. This was the anti-colonialist movement led by Tecumesh and his brother. They blamed the tragedy consuming their people on the abandonment of old traditions. Among other things, their people must divest themselves of European clothing, which had been adopted, and return to leather apparel. This vision was less ingenuous than it might seem at first blush. White expansionism was all the more devastating in that it ran like a steamroller over the customs and identity of the subjugated populations, which were compelled or impelled to renounce Native American dances and feasts and adopt 'civilized' American clothing. Returning to one's origins was a desperate attempt to recover the negated, repressed identity, in order to mount a minimum of resistance. We are

---

29 See Domenico Losurdo, *Liberalism: A Counter-History*, trans. Gregory Elliott, London and New York: Verso, 2011, Chapter 7, §6.

30 Alexis de Tocqueville, *Oeuvres complètes*, ed. Jacob-Paul Mayer, Paris: Gallimard, 1951–, Vol. III, pt. 1, p. 323.

dealing with a total rejection of modernity, of a fundamentalist kind. But this was a reaction to colonial expansion, which thus, far from opening up the 'path to modernity', ended up obstructing it, rendering it hateful in the eyes of its victims.

Now let us turn back to the chapter of history that unfolded in China. Some decades after the repression whereby the Manchu dynasty, with British help, broke the Taiping rebellion, which had evinced profound hostility to the dominant power and the Confucian tradition, and looked with interest and sympathy to Christianity and the West, a movement developed with quite different, even contrary, characteristics. The year was 1900. Along with the invaders and their 'accomplices', the Boxers also targeted Western ideas and even technical inventions, while they fanatically defended indigenous religious and political traditions. The telegraph, railways and Christianity were not spared their frenzy. The penetration of these things into China had coincided with the deployment of the West's technological and ideological power and the country's consequent national humiliation. Anything regarded as alien to the authentic Chinese tradition and the good old days, or times rendered good by their transfiguration – China prior to the clash with the great colonial powers – was unequivocally condemned. Once again, we are dealing with a rebellion of a fundamentalist kind: it was the expression not of an endogenous evolution of the indigenous culture, but of a desperate attempt to resist colonialist aggression, which once more created an aversion to such oppressive 'modernity' in the subjugated peoples.[31]

Albeit in a different way, the effects of colonialism could also be devastating for the conquerors. We have evidence of this from India. Following the mutiny of the sepoys, Indians to all intents and purposes became 'negroes' as far as the British colonizers were concerned – members of an inferior race with whom it was necessary to avoid any form of contamination, including, in the first instance, sexual contamination: 'In the aftermath of the 1857 Mutiny attitudes towards interracial sex hardened as part of a general process of segregation . . . By 1901 racial segregation was the norm in most of the British empire.'[32] Is the advent of racism, or its exacerbation (in a process that had its bloody culmination in the Third Reich), to be included in the 'path to modernity'?

---

31   See Domenico Losurdo, *Il linguaggio dell'Impero. Lessico dell'ideologia Americana*, Rome and Bari: Laterza, 2007, Chapter 2, §6.

32   Niall Ferguson, *The War of the World: History's Age of Hatred*, London: Penguin, 2007, pp. 20–1.

Even if we focus exclusively on the economic dimension of the issue, 'there is no doubt that the influx of British-manufactured goods from 1913 led to very large de-industrialization in India'. Colonial rule entailed the collapse of handicrafts and the textile industry, and the reduction of the Asian country to a supplier of raw materials for the British textile industry.[33] Once again, the question dictates itself: was this the 'path to modernity'?

Between Repression and Transfiguration of US Colonialism

Over and above the British and American empires, what is celebrated in Ferguson is 'Western civilization' and its irresistible expansion from 1500 (i.e. from the discovery-conquest of America): 'No previous civilization had ever achieved such dominance as the West has achieved over the Rest . . . By 1913, eleven Western empires controlled nearly three-fifths of all territory and population and more than three-quarters (a staggering 79 per cent) of global economic output.' The 'eleven Western empires' referred to are listed as 'Austria, Belgium, France, Germany, Italy, Netherlands, Portugal, Spain, Russia, the United Kingdom and the United States'.[34]

Paradoxically, it is the leading country of the West that contests the spatial delimitation of Western colonialism celebrated by the British historian. On 27 February 2003, the then US Defense Secretary Donald Rumsfeld declared: 'We're not a colonial power. We've never been a colonial power.'[35] This was a declaration made on the eve of the second Gulf War and not long after the establishment of an infamous concentration camp at Guantánamo, on territory seized from Cuba. But such circumstances, which derive from the history of colonialism, do not trouble the good conscience of the US politician.

Oblivious of the fact, Rumsfeld could boast illustrious precedents in support of his thesis. Let us see how in 1919 Joseph Schumpeter refuted the thesis formulated by Lenin while the carnage of the First World War was still underway. Imperialism (and the war bound up with it) as the highest stage of capitalism? Nothing could be further from the truth, objected the great economist. To appreciate this, it was necessary to examine the United

---

33   See Paul Bairoch, *Economics and World History: Myths and Paradoxes*, Chicago: University of Chicago Press, 1995, pp. 88–9.

34   Ferguson, *Civilization*, pp. 5, 7.

35   Quoted in Ferguson, *Colossus*, p. 1.

States. It was precisely there, where capitalism was particularly developed, that the ideal of peace ruled unchallenged in political culture and practice. Traditionally absent were the aspirations to colonial expansion and domination and the bellicose sentiments widespread in Europe, where the influence of the pre-capitalist *ancien régime* was still strongly felt.[36] Forty years later, Hannah Arendt revived and radicalized the interpretation of the USA as a country without a colonial past: 'the colonialism and imperialism of European nations' was 'the one great crime in which America was never involved'.[37] In this depiction, in what was an incredible 'oversight' for two major intellectuals, there was no room for the war against Mexico and its dismemberment, for the colonization and annexation of Hawaii, for the conquest of the Philippines and the ruthless repression of its independence movement, sometimes explicitly drawing on the genocidal practices employed during the campaigns against the Native Americans.

We thus encounter a sensational instance of repression – namely, of the expropriation, deportation and decimation of the natives, for the purposes of acquiring land that was often cultivated by the forced labour of black slaves, who were deported from Africa on voyages marked by high mortality rates. Not by chance, as we have seen, this chapter of history inspired Hitler, who identified the 'natives' of Eastern Europe as Indians to be expropriated and decimated so as to enable the Germanization of the conquered territories, while the survivors were destined to work like black slaves in the service of the master race. Yet according to Arendt, this chapter of history, which encompasses the time span of the West's colonial expansionism and encapsulates all its horror, has nothing to do with the history of colonialism, at least as regards its initial American phase! And the philosopher formulated this thesis precisely when forced to come to terms with the struggle of African Americans, who, also under the impetus of the global wave of anti-colonialist revolution, aimed to put an end to the regime of white supremacy in the southern USA!

In reality, far from being absent from the history of the North American republic, the 'great crime' of colonialism was a decisive factor at the moment of its foundation in the wake of the War of Independence. What was the underlying reason for the conflict? We may give the floor to Theodore Roosevelt, US president from 1901 to 1909:

---

36   Joseph Schumpeter, *Imperialism and Social Classes*, trans. Heinz Norden, New York: A.M. Kelly, 1951, pp. 72–4.

37   Hannah Arendt, 'Reflections on Little Rock', *Dissent*, Winter 1959, p. 46.

The chief factor in producing the Revolution, and later in producing the War of 1812, was the inability of the motherland country to understand that the freemen who went forth to conquer a continent should be encouraged in that work . . . The spread of the hardy, venturesome backwoodsmen was to most of the statesmen of London a matter of anxiety rather than of pride, and the famous Quebec Act of 1774 was in part designed with the purpose of keeping the English-speaking settlements permanently east of the Alleghanies, and preserving the might and beautiful valley of the Ohio as a hunting-ground for savages . . .[38]

The colonialist and expansionist impulse behind the rebellion of the British colonists in America is lucidly and proudly stated here; and Arendt and Schumpeter are resoundingly contradicted. According to the latter, aspirations to peace characterize a purely capitalist country (the USA) without an *ancien régime* behind it. In reality, Roosevelt celebrated the foundation of the North American republic in the name of the white race's right to unlimited colonial expansion, imposed by force of arms. We are dealing with a statesman who is prominent in the republic's pantheon, but who hymned war as such, mocked those who 'shrink from blood', theorized a 'war of extermination' against the 'inferior races', and referred almost with amusement to the genocide of the natives (see Chapter 3, §3 and Chapter 5, §5). Not only in practice, but also in theory, colonialism and imperialism have played an essential, nefarious role in the history of the USA.

A professional historian cannot be unaware of all this, and Ferguson indeed observes: 'There were no more self-confident imperialists than the Founding Fathers themselves.' To take but one example, it was George Washington who referred to the country born out of the War of Independence as a 'nascent empire' or 'infant empire'.[39] We are dealing not only with imperialists, but with imperialists who were unscrupulous. Their priority was to rid themselves of the restrictions imposed by the British Crown on their westwards expansion at the expense of the Native Americans. This was an absolutely intolerable limitation for those ruled by an 'expansionist vision of the future – a vision of manifest larceny that was especially dear to property speculators like George Washington'.[40] The 'manifest destiny' that

38 Theodore Roosevelt, *The Strenuous Life: Essays and Addresses*, New York: The Century, 1901, pp. 246–7.
39 Ferguson, *Colossus*, pp. 33–4.
40 Ferguson, *Civilization*, pp. 114–15.

presided over the USA's irresistible expansion in the nineteenth century stands revealed for what, from the outset, it really was: 'manifest larceny'. Can one imagine a more radical demystification of US imperialism, its founding fathers and founding myths? However, for the British historian such remarks are quite the opposite of elements of condemnation or criticism. Whether his focus is on the past, the present or the future, Ferguson continues to refer reverently to the 'Empire for liberty'.

Possibly unawares, Ferguson joins up with the most enthusiastic champions of US imperialism. In the early twentieth century, Albert J. Beveridge paid tribute both to the 'gospel of liberty', which was embodied in the North American republic, and US imperialism.[41] He dated from Jefferson, 'the first imperialist of the Republic', the irresistible march of the 'people sprung from the most masterful blood of history', who were aided by God and were in fact to be regarded as 'His chosen people'. Thus were explained successive conquests: 'Hawaii is ours; Porto Rico is to be ours; at the prayer of her people Cuba finally is to be ours . . .; the flag of a liberal government is to float over the Philippines.'[42] Where the US Senator summoned the 'English people's league of God' to realize 'the permanent peace of this war-torn world',[43] around a century later an analogous function is attributed by the British historian to the providential handover whereby the American Empire replaced its British counterpart.

Ferguson feels wholly at ease in the political and cultural climate of the USA in the early twenty-first century. Not a few voices warmly greet the empire in the process of being constructed; there are even those who refer to the establishment of a Colonial Office with the task of administering the immense colonial and imperial space which, in one way or another, is subordinate to Washington. The British historian expresses his pleasure at the fact that US strategists, or at least the most open-minded among them, have finally recognized the reality and necessity of Empire, uninhibited by linguistic censorship.[44] Rumsfeld is therefore wrong to adopt an anti-colonial posture. In so doing, he is at odds with the Founding Fathers. It is necessary to face the facts: 'The United States has acquired an empire, but Americans themselves lack the imperial cast of mind. They would rather consume than conquer. They would rather build shopping malls than nations.' To summarize,

---

41   William J. Beveridge, *The Meanings of the Times and Other Speeches*, Freeport, NY: Books for Libraries Press, 1968, p. 50.

42   Ibid., pp. 47–50.

43   Ibid., p. 44.

44   Ferguson, *Colossus*, pp. 4–8.

what characterizes the people and leaders of the USA is, alas, 'the absence of the will to power'; and this risks ruining such a beneficent empire.[45]

This is an episode in the history of ideology that recalls one which occurred in the USA more than a century and a half ago. In the mid-nineteenth century, as the conflict that would issue in the Civil War intensified, John Calhoun, calling a halt to hesitant, shamefaced justifications of black slavery, declared that it was a 'positive good'. The South had nothing to be ashamed about; it could only be proud. In the years immediately following the dissolution of the USSR and, above all, NATO's triumphant war against Yugoslavia, empire and imperialism likewise seemed a 'positive good', which the West and the USA should not renounce and of which they could be proud. This was a short-lived ideological season, in part because the unexpectedly rapid rise of China led to the emergence of serious doubts about the durability of Western supremacy. These are doubts that Ferguson vainly seeks to flee.

Here, then, we have a remarkable combination of seeming demystification and actual apologia. The seeming demystification targets the linguistic interdictions that aim to camouflage imperialist practice and risk impeding it. The apologia concerns that practice, which is called upon to be deployed uninhibitedly, more decisively and energetically. This combination is a formula for success. Reviewers can celebrate Ferguson's books as 'brilliant and provocative'. Imperial governments and chancelleries receive encouragement and can pursue – even radicalize – their traditional policy safe from any real criticism.

Apologia for the West and Its *Enfant Terrible*

The combination in various forms of traditional apologia with an apparently debunking language marks Ferguson's discourse as a whole. Let us see how he treats the Opium Wars – the encounter-clash between the United Kingdom and the oldest civilization in the world. Like the other European powers, 'Britain too knew how to make war pay in the nineteenth century: something in the region of 40 per cent of the total defence budget for 1842 was covered by the £5.8 million indemnity exacted from China under the Treaty of Nanking; Palmerston even boasted to the House of Commons that the war had shown a profit.'[46] As we see, there is no room here for an

---

45   Ibid., p. 29.
46   Niall Ferguson, *The Cash Nexus: Money and Power in the Modern World*, London: Penguin, 2001, p. 394.

edifying vision à la John Stuart Mill, who celebrated the Opium Wars as a crusade for free trade and liberty as such: 'the prohibition of the importation of opium into China' violated 'the liberty . . . of the buyer' even more than that of 'the producer or seller'.[47] We find nothing of the sort in Ferguson. He reports Palmerston's statement in a paragraph whose title is eloquent in itself ('Giving War a Chance'), and which explains how 'expenditure on war can generate a visible return in the form of booty, indemnities from vanquished states or territories'.[48] Thus the debunking, or seemingly debunking, aspect of the discourse: the Opium Wars are recognized to have been wars of extortion, self-financing and even showing a profit.

But what were the consequences of such extortion for the people subject to it? The crisis exposed by the country's inability to defend itself against external aggression played a prominent role in causing the Taiping Rebellion (1851–64), which not coincidentally put the fight against opium on the agenda. This was a prolonged, extremely bloody civil war. The food situation deteriorated and hunger became the daily lot of a huge mass of people. Furthermore, the West set a fashion in Asia. The Japanese 'ended up copying everything, from Western clothes and hairstyles to the European practice of colonizing foreign countries'.[49] New wars of extortion occurred: 'The indemnity wrested from China by Japan in 1895 . . . amounted to more than three times total Japanese military spending in that year and around double the cost of the war.'[50] Five years later, 'eleven Western empires', including 'the United Kingdom and the United States',[51] launched a punitive expedition against the Boxers and the first anti-colonialist movements, which ended with the extraction of a new 'heavy indemnity',[52] even more exorbitant than the previous ones.

Is there, then, a link between such extortion and the drastic decline in the standard of living of the Chinese people? It is at this point – a crucial moment – that the debunking Ferguson is fond of disappears, in fact turning into its opposite. In his view, what has been described as 'China crucified'[53] was the result exclusively of an endogenous process of stagnation. In reality,

---

47   John Stuart Mill, 'On Liberty', in *Utilitarianism, Liberty, Representative Government*, ed. Harry B. Acton, London: Dent, 1972, p. 151.

48   Ferguson, *The Cash Nexus*, p. 394.

49   Ferguson, *Civilization*, p. 306.

50   Ferguson, *The Cash Nexus*, p. 394.

51   Ferguson, *Civilization*, p. 5.

52   Ferguson, *The War of the World*, p. 45.

53   Jacques Gernet, *A History of Chinese Civilization*, trans. J.R. Forster, Cambridge and New York: Cambridge University Press, 1996, p. 601ff.

as late as 1820 (prior to the Opium Wars), the great Asian country boasted a GDP that amounted to 32.4 per cent of global GDP, while 'Chinese life expectancy (and hence nutrition) was at roughly English levels (and so above Continental ones) even in the late 1700s'.[54] When it was founded in 1949, the People's Republic of China was the poorest country, or among the poorest, in the world. Although confirmed by other distinguished historians, this picture is challenged by Ferguson.

What leaps to the eye once more is the poverty and inadequacy of the conceptual apparatus of the British historian, who sticks to a heavily econ-omistic approach. The impact of the Opium Wars cannot be assessed exclusively in terms of the material devastation visited by them and the exorbitant indemnity in which they ended. It is not even enough to introduce into the calculation the territorial amputations and the large-scale destruction and theft of priceless artworks. It is evident that the forced introduction of opium had a devastating impact on Chinese society, which was felt for a long time. Even so, let us confine our attention to the economy in the strict sense and the data reported by Ferguson: 'By 1820 US per capita GDP was twice that of China; by 1870 it was nearly five times greater; by 1913 the ratio was nearly ten to one.'[55] It is legitimate to ask what contribution the wars of aggression and rapine made to the gap between China and the USA and the West as a whole. But it would seem difficult to deny any connection between the phenomena. Yet this is precisely what Ferguson argues. By a kind of miracle, wars which (as he concedes) significantly benefited the aggressor did no real harm to the aggressed!

This modus operandi also emerges in connection with the encounter-clash between the British Empire and India. Let us read Ferguson again. The kind of 'world war' that was the Seven Years' War 'decided one thing irrevocably. India would be British, not French. And that gave Britain what for nearly two hundred years would be both a huge market for British trade and an inexhaustible reservoir of military manpower. India was much more than the "jewel in the crown". Literally and metaphorically, it was a whole diamond mine.'[56] Thus is reconstructed and underscored the enormous advantage that Britain secured with the conquest of India. But how were things for the subjugated people? In 1835, the Governor General reported to London on

---

54   Kenneth Pomeranz, quoted in Mike Davis, *Late Victorian Holocausts: El Niño Famines and the Making of the Third World*, London and New York: Verso, 2001, p. 293.

55   Ferguson, *Civilization*, p. 304.

56   Ferguson, *Empire*, pp. 32, 35.

the consequences of the destruction of local textile handicrafts, swept aside by the major British industry: 'the bones of the cotton-weavers are bleaching the plains of India'.[57] The tragedy did not end there. Two years later, a famine broke out in some regions which was so terrible that – candidly stated another British source, wholly committed to celebrating the glory of the empire – 'British residents . . . could not take their evening drive, on account of the smell of corpses too numerous for burial.' Nor did there seem to be any improvement in the prospects for evening excursions: 'cholera and smallpox followed, sweeping away a multitude who had survived the dearth'.[58] Clearly, the British Empire did not benefit India and the Indian people: 'In the 100 years before independence in 1947, development averaged 0.2 per cent per year – at a time when Britain itself experienced growth almost ten times that rate. Life expectancy probably showed no improvement either, unlike Britain.'[59] Moreover, Ferguson himself writes that in 1913 'average life expectancy in England was nearly twice what it was in India'.[60] Once again the key question arises: is there a link between the 'diamond mine' of which the British Empire disposed, thanks to the subjugation of India, and the far from exalted condition of the Indian people? As a result of ignoring the connection, here too a seemingly critical discourse turns into its opposite – into an a-critical celebration, which registers the human costs involved in building empire with imperturbable cynicism.

On closer inspection, the *enfant terrible* of historiography proves to be an apologist or, to be more precise, the *enfant terrible* of the traditional apologetics engaged in transfiguring colonialism and imperialism.

Ferguson and the Mutilation of the Whole

In drawing up his balance sheet of Western colonialism, Ferguson rejects the habitual spatial amputation whereby, unlike Europe, the USA has nothing to do with this extended chapter of history – and rejects it to pave the way for an explicit apologia for the American Empire, from the Founding Fathers

---

57 Quoted in Karl Marx, *Capital: Volume One*, trans. Ben Fowkes, Harmondsworth: Penguin, 1976, p. 558.

58 Harriet Martineau, *British Rule in India: A Historical Sketch*, London: Smith, 1857, p. 297.

59 Michael Mann, *The Sources of Social Power. Volume Three: Global Empires and Revolution, 1890–1945*, Cambridge: Cambridge University Press, 2012, p. 43.

60 Ferguson, *Civilization*, p. 5.

to the present. On the other hand, in order to avoid dark clouds spoiling his apologia, he proceeds to a tacit temporal amputation of the history of Western colonialism, *de facto* excluding the Third Reich from it. Ferguson certainly stresses on several occasions that Germany cannot but be regarded as an integral part of the West. But when he celebrates the political and moral superiority of the 'West' over the 'Rest', he seems to forget that Hitler's Germany was an integral part of the 'West', not the 'Rest'.

There can be no doubt about this affiliation – and not only, and not so much, for geographical reasons. The Third Reich admired the British and American empires, taking them as its model. Hitler repeatedly stated that it was a question of building the 'German Indies' in Eastern Europe. Even more frequent, especially after the invasion of the Soviet Union, were comparisons with the expansion of the American colonists in the West and Far West, with the 'war against the Indians', the war 'waged on the Indians of North America'. In both cases, 'the strongest race will be the one to triumph': the 'natives' of Eastern Europe could not escape the fate of a radical reduction in their numbers and enslavement that awaited them (see Chapter 5, §6). The American model also exercised its fascination on Mussolini, who in November 1933, when preparations for the invasion and colonization of Ethiopia had already begun to be made, likewise paid homage to the 'harsh and alluring' 'great conquest' of the Far West (see Chapter 7, §2). Hence, together with the Third Reich, the Fascist Empire must likewise be included in a serious historical appraisal of Western colonialism.

While the expansion of England 'was a conscious act of imitation' of the Spanish Empire, which was 'the envy of the world',[61] the empires in whose construction Nazi Germany and Fascist Italy engaged, committing particularly odious crimes in the process, were a more or less conscious imitation of the British and American empires. Taken as a whole, the temporal cycle of Western colonialism commenced with the genocide of the Native Americans (summoned to replace them were the black slaves deported from Africa), and culminated in the twentieth century with the attempt to enslave the Slavs and exterminate the Jews, who were regarded along with the Bolsheviks as responsible for the insane revolt of 'inferior races' against white, Aryan and Western supremacy.

Furthermore, the Empire of the Rising Sun should not be excluded from any historical appraisal of Western colonialism that aims to be complete and

---

61   Ferguson, *Empire*, p. 2.

which, in formulating a moral judgement, takes account of the ethic of responsibility in the first instance. Certainly, at least prior to the mid-nineteenth century, Japan cannot be regarded as part of the West. But another truth, brought out by numerous historians, including Ferguson, is equally clear: Japanese colonialism and imperialism simply cannot be understood without bearing in mind the model they were inspired by – namely, the European and Western model.

Apologetics for the colonial tradition, and claims for the moral and political primacy of the West, are based on mutilation of the whole. In fact, the mutilation we have just noted is not the only one. Others occur, of varying kinds. Ferguson refers favourably to 'a young man, fresh from his first colonial war, Winston Churchill', who assigned the British Empire the glorious task of 'giv[ing] peace to warring tribes'.[62] However, when the First World War broke out, in the USA the most prestigious newspapers and public opinion as a whole denounced the European powers as 'savage tribes' incapable of understanding the cause of peace (Chapter 4, §5). Indeed, the characterization is apt, when we remember that what occurred on both sides on the Western front was 'the growth of a culture of "take no prisoners"', who were sometimes even 'executed with . . . [rifle] butts' – and all this not only in an explosion of anger from below, but often via orders from above.[63] The characterization as 'savage tribes' may well be apt. But in 1917 the United States, which decided to intervene in the war, joined them. And it was these 'savage tribes', European and Western, who forcibly dragged into the carnage the colonial peoples whom (according to Churchill as subscribed to by Ferguson) they had task of pacifying.

As regards the British 'savage tribe', or British Empire, it could call upon the 'inexhaustible reservoir of military manpower' which, according to the definition by Ferguson cited above, India represented. Indeed, 'in the autumn of 1914, around a third of British forces in France were from India; by the end of the war more than a million Indians had served overseas'.[64] Many were volunteers who, in return for their sacrifice, hoped (in vain) for independence or, at any rate, self-government for their people. With them fought countless Africans, who did not nurture hopes of any kind, but who were simply forced by the colonial power to fight and to die thousands of miles from home. Or to die in their own land, but in the service of a cause that

---

62   Ibid., p. xxvii.
63   Ferguson, *The War of the World*, pp. 125–8.
64   Ferguson, *Empire*, p. 255.

was not theirs: 'Total British losses in East Africa were over 100,000, the vast majority black troops and porters.'[65]

But all this was not enough for the British Empire, which also sought to obtain 'military manpower' from the semi-colonies. The first president of the Chinese Republic that emerged from the overthrow of the Manchu dynasty recounted the answer given by him to the British consul, who was pressing for China's intervention alongside the Entente during the First World War:

> Two thousand years ago we discarded imperialism and advocated a policy of peace . . . I consider your characteristic appeal to force as extremely barbarous . . . Because we have advanced two thousand years beyond you and have gotten rid of the old, savage, pugnacious sentiments and have attained . . . a true ideal of peace, and because we hope that China will forever cherish her moral code of peace . . . we are not willing to enter this great conflict.[66]

The least one can say is that the British Empire (and Western colonialism in general) can be credited with 'giving peace to warring tribes' only by completely ignoring a major historical episode in which, along with the natural resources of the subjugated peoples, human resources were plundered and converted into cannon fodder. During the Second World War, the picture did not change: 'The colonial commitment to the Empire proved every bit as strong as in the First World War.' Two-and-a-half million Indians fought in an army intended by Churchill to guarantee the permanence of the Empire and white or Western supremacy.[67]

By way of conclusive proof of the mutilation of the whole picture performed by apologetics for colonialism, which today finds its champion in Ferguson, we should pose a question: can the genesis of Fascism and Nazism be understood ignoring the First World War and, more generally, the scramble of the great capitalist powers for empire? As we know, 'total politics' – a substantive synonymous with ubiquitous totalitarian regimentation – was theorized in Germany in preparation for the *revanche* that would enable the country defeated in the First World War to recover the colonies

---

65 Ferguson, *The War of the World*, p. 115.
66 Sun Yat-Sen, *The Three Principles of the People*, trans. Frank W. Price, Vancouver: Soul Care Publishing, 2011, pp. 61–2.
67 Ferguson, *The War of the World*, p. 517.

annexed by the victors and to build the colonial empire for which it felt the need, and claimed the right, on a much larger scale (Chapter 5, §2).

In the course of this attempted *revanche*, something occurred that is worth reflecting on. Although expressing staunch support for the remorseless energy with which the conquest of Algeria was carried out, Tocqueville had expressed a concern: 'God save us from ever seeing France ruled by an officer of the army of Africa.'[68] In fact, Cavaignac, the general who had no hesitation in resorting to genocidal practices to eradicate Arab resistance, was some years later the architect of the bloody, ruthless repression that mowed down the barbarians of the metropolis – the Parisian workers who had risen up demanding the right to work and to life. Notwithstanding his earlier warning, Tocqueville extended constant, unwavering support to Cavaignac. But his warning was prophetic. Over a century later, the great theoretician of the Algerian Revolution, Frantz Fanon, characterized Nazism as an attempt to transform Europe (more precisely, Central-Eastern Europe) into 'a genuine colony' (Chapter 7, §1).

We may venture a more general observation. On closer inspection, the history of the West as a whole can be read in the light of a principle dear to Marx: any people that oppresses another is not free. The twentieth century was the century when the totalitarian domination and genocidal practices profoundly rooted in the colonial tradition irrupted into the very continent from which that tradition derived, in the wake of Hitler's endeavour to build a continental empire in Central-Eastern Europe, subjugating, decimating and enslaving the 'natives' who inhabited it and exterminating those (Jews and Bolsheviks) deemed responsible for the revolt of 'inferior races'.

The fact that the central categories and keywords of Nazi ideology go back to the colonial tradition – in particular, the US variant (Chapter 7, §2) – should give pause for thought. Colonial peoples and peoples of colonial origin have long expressed awareness of the close link between colonial racism and the Aryan mythology dear, in particular, to Nazism. This is true, above all, of African American activists, often compelled (as Martin Luther King stressed) to confront groups of white supremacists waving swastikas. An episode that occurred in New York in these years is emblematic. Without fully appreciating its significance, Hannah Arendt reported it in a letter to Karl Jaspers on 3 January 1960: 'A topic has been assigned to all the final classes of New York's high schools. Imagine a way of punishing Hitler. And this is what a black girl has suggested: he should be put in a black skin and

---

68 Tocqueville, *Oeuvres complètes*, Vol. III, pt. 1, p. 236.

forced to live in the United States.' In a spontaneous, ingenuous way, the black girl frankly imagined a sort of *lex talionis*, whereby those responsible for the Third Reich's racist violence were forced like blacks to suffer the humiliations and vexations of the regime of white supremacy tirelessly propagated, and remorselessly implemented, by them, but which in the southern USA would now rebound against them.[69]

Even anti-Semitic racism cannot be adequately understood if it is completely disconnected from the racism affecting colonial peoples, in which the British and American empires played a vanguard role. In his way, Ferguson ends up recognizing this when he writes: 'Since so few Germans emigrated to tropical countries, they were more likely to apply imported theories of Social Darwinism and "racial hygiene" to Jews – the nearest identifiable "alien race" – than to Africans or Asians.'[70]

The Third Reich's connection with the colonial tradition is strong and patent. After the Führer, perhaps the regime's major figure was Hermann Goering, who may be regarded as 'the initiator of the concentration camp system'. Yet his father, Heinrich, was the first imperial commissioner for German South-West Africa,[71] and it was there that Germany began to experiment with the system. Survivors of the campaign of extermination launched against the Herero by General von Trotha were imprisoned in concentration camps, where 'men, women and children were herded to be eliminated through work'.[72] As well as being utilized as rapidly consumed work tools, the natives were employed as guinea pigs for eugenicist experiments, conducted under the direction of Theodor Mollisson and Eugen Fischer, Joseph Mengele's teachers. With these teachers behind him, the future ideologue and organizer of the Third Reich's machinery of extermination joined the SA in 1933. It would appear that the original brown shirts worn by Hitler's squads were remnants of the uniforms worn by colonial troops in East Africa.[73]

However, when it began to construct its concentration camp system in Africa, Wilhelm II's Germany had precedents and models to draw on. Let

69   See Domenico Losurdo, *La non-violenza. Una storia fuori dal mito*, Rome and Bari: Laterza, 2010, Chapter 7, §1 and Chapter 6, §8.

70   Ferguson, *The War of the World*, p. 6.

71   Joel Kotek and Pierre Rigoulot, *Le Siècle des camps. Détention, concentration, extermination. Cent ans de mal radical*, Paris: Lattès, 2000, p. 94.

72   Ibid., p. 92.

73   See Klaus Hildebrand, *Vom Reich zum Weltreich. Hitler, NSDAP und koloniale Frage 1919–1945*, Munich: Fink, 1969, p. 40.

us see what happened in the British Empire, availing ourselves of Ferguson's reconstruction: 'To deprive the Boers of supplies from their farms, their wives and children had been driven from their homes and herded in concentration camps, where conditions were atrocious; at this stage, roughly one in three inmates was dying because of poor sanitation and disease.'[74] Rather than the Herero, the Boers call to mind the American colonists who, in their struggle against the central government, presumed to dispose at will of the natives, like human livestock owned by them. But it remains the case that we cannot come to grips with the Third Reich without coming to grips with the history of colonialism as a whole, with its terrible charge of violence, which sometimes even ended up striking sections of the self-styled master race.

From the Opium Wars to the 'Rape of Nanking'

However, Ferguson's main concern is to differentiate beneficent colonialism and imperialism from the maleficent variety. He effectively describes the 'murderous orgy' that visited China and, in particular, Nanking in the 1930s. The aggressors engaged in a 'killing competition'. In Nanking, 'between 260,000 and 300,000 non-combatants were killed'. The Japanese troops amused themselves assaulting women and practised sadism on men: some were 'buried alive' or covered in petrol and set alight; 'a few were hung by their tongues on metal hooks'.[75] Here is the British historian's conclusion:

> This was imperialism at its very worst. But it was Japanese imperialism, not British. The rape of Nanking reveals precisely what the leading alternative to British rule in Asia stood for . . . But it was also the collision between an Empire that had some conception of human rights and one that regarded alien races as no better than swine. In the words of Lieutenant-Colonel Ryukichi Tanaka, Director of the Japanese Secret Service in Shanghai: 'We can do anything to such creatures.' By the 1930s many people in Britain had got into the habit of rubbishing the Empire. But the

---

74   Ferguson, *The War of the World*, p. 6.
75   Niall Ferguson, *Empire: The Rise and Demise of the British World Order and the Lessons for Global Power*, New York: Basic Books, 2004, pp. 283–4; Ferguson, *The War of the World*, pp. 476–9.

rise of the Japanese empire in Asia during that decade showed that the alternatives to British rule were not necessarily more benign. There were degrees of imperialism, and in its brutality toward conquered peoples Japan's empire went beyond anything the British had ever done.[76]

This passage starts with an observation that is obvious, even banal: it is always useful and appropriate to apply the art of distinction. Compared with their competitors, both the Third Reich and the Empire of the Rising Sun appeared on the historical scene late. Because partition of the world had already been largely accomplished, they were led to target peoples of established or old and antique civilization, who could be reduced to the condition of savage tribes only through a massive dose of supplementary violence and brutality. They embarked on the work of colonial subjugation at a time when the anti-colonial revolution was already underway. In such circumstances, the barbarism of imperialism obviously underwent further escalation. However, even accepting the distinction between the British Empire and the Empire of the Rising Sun, it is not clear why an Asian country like China, of continental dimensions and antique civilization, had to choose between them.

We know that the Japanese Empire sought to learn, and did indeed learn, from its British counterpart. If we wish to reconstruct the process of ideological preparation of the 'Rape of Nanking', more than a few pages should be devoted to Great Britain and the West as a whole. At the start of the second Opium War, which ended with the sacking and burning of the splendid Summer Palace, John Stuart Mill called for the invading army to teach the Chinese barbarians a harsh lesson. It was not appropriate to quibble about formalities: 'appeals to humanity and Christianity in favour of ruffians, & to international law in favour of peoples who recognize *no* laws of war at all', were 'ridiculous'.[77]

Some decades later, in 1900, a new, more massive punitive expedition was launched against China. Haranguing German troops preparing to depart for Asia, Wilhelm II left them in no doubts about the modalities that should govern the repression of the Boxer Rebellion and the lesson to be taught the Chinese people as a whole: 'Give the world an example of virility and

---

76 Ferguson, *Empire: The Rise and Demise of the British World Order*, p. 284.

77 John Stuart Mill, *Collected Works*, ed. F.E.L. Priestley, John M. Robinson et al., London and Toronto: Routledge & Kegan Paul/University of Toronto Press, 1963–, Vol. XV, p. 528 (letter to E. Chadwick of 13 March 1857).

discipline! . . . No pardon will be given, and no prisoners will be taken. Anyone who falls into your hands falls to your sword! . . . Make the name German remembered in China for a thousand years so that no Chinaman will ever again dare to squint at a German.'[78] And indeed, let us take a glance at the sequel to the defeat of the 'barbarians':

> There then began systematic carnage and sacking, which went far beyond the excesses of the Boxers. In Beijing, thousands of men were massacred in a savage orgy of violence; women and whole families committed suicide so as not to suffer being dishonoured; the whole city was sacked; the imperial palace was occupied and robbed of the bulk of its treasures. A similar situation obtained in Tientsin and Baoding. 'Punitive' expeditions were undertaken in the rural areas of Zhili where missionaries had been attacked. Foreign soldiers razed entire villages to the ground and spared nothing. In Manchuria, where the Russians were responsible for the 'pacification', the atrocities were on the same scale. In reprisal for the shots fired on the city of Blagoveshchensk, thousands of Chinese – men, women and children – had their throats cut and their bodies were thrown into the Heilongjiang.[79]

The Rape of Nanking involved horror on a larger scale and even more unbridled barbarism. But it was thirty-seven years earlier that imperialist Japan had proved its mettle in China, participating in the punitive expedition of 1900 alongside Britain, the USA, France, Germany, Russia, Italy and Austria-Hungary.

Its horror did not elicit a wave of indignation in the West. In fact, the French general H.N. Frey credited it with having 'for the first time translated into reality the dream of idealist politicians – a United States of the civilised world'.[80] It was Lenin, the great critic of imperialism, who reported and ridiculed this assessment. He denounced the colonialist violence inflicted on 'the unarmed Chinese populace, who were drowned or killed, with no holding back from the slaughter of women and children, not to speak of the looting of palaces, homes, and shops'. Russian soldiers, and the invaders generally, had attacked 'like savage beasts, burning down whole villages,

---

78   Quoted in Ferguson, *The War of the World*, p. 44.
79   Jean Chesneaux, ed., *La Cina*, trans. David Mamo, Vol. II, Turin: Einaudi, 1974, p. 118.
80   Quoted in V.I. Lenin, *Collected Works*, London: Lawrence & Wishart, 1960–, Vol. 39, p. 684.

shooting, bayoneting, and drowning in the Amur River unarmed inhabitants, their wives, and their children'. Yet such infamy had been celebrated as a 'civilising mission' by the dominant classes, the 'press that kowtows to [them]' and, ultimately, by much (or even most) of public opinion, not only Russian, but Western in general.[81]

In any event, for having participated 'on an equal footing with the European [or Western] powers' in the punitive expedition against the Boxers, and made themselves jointly responsible for the horror, Japan was co-opted into the exclusive club of great powers (whose right to colonize and civilize barbarians was recognized).[82] This change was subsequently formally sealed: 'By the Anglo-Japanese Treaty Japan had become a Great Power, and so, in the statistics of the Dutch East Indies, had to figure among the European and not among the Asian states.'[83]

The First World War then intervened. The Empire of the Rising Sun fought on the side of the Entente, which recognized its right to inherit defeated Germany's colonial possessions in China. While imperialist and militarist Japan could now boast equal dignity with the great capitalist powers of the West, in Western eyes China remained Asiatic and barbarous and thus part of the colonial or colonizable world, even though it had rid itself of the Manchu dynasty and constituted itself as a democratic republic in the meantime. This is the starting-point for understanding the Japanese Empire's subsequent attempt to subject the most populous country on earth to its rule. The Rape of Nanking, and the other infamies bound up with it, cannot be separated from the history of imperialism as a whole – a history in which the great Western powers enjoyed a position of absolute pre-eminence. Basically, as Ferguson himself acknowledges, 'the Japanese merely inserted themselves into the privileged position hitherto occupied by the British'.[84] But it was the West that had much earlier defined the pyramid of peoples and 'races' – the hierarchy on the basis of which peoples and 'races' on a higher rung were granted the right to subjugate and, if needs be, drastically decimate people and 'races' of inferior rank.

The only thing we need add is that the processes of co-option were inherently fragile. While the Japanese treated the Chinese, degraded to the

---

81   Ibid., Vol. 4, pp. 372–4.

82   Carl Schmitt, *Donoso Cortés in gesamteuropäischer Interpretation*, Köln: Greven, 1950, pp. 204, 163.

83   Jan Romein, *The Asian Century: A History of Modern Nationalism in Asia*, trans. R.T. Clark, Berkeley: University of California Press, 1962, p. 71.

84   Ferguson, *Empire: The Rise and Demise of the British World Order*, p. 285.

status of an inferior race, with particular ferocity, they in turn suffered a process of racialization by the USA during the Second World War, which occasionally went as far as envisaging a kind of final solution of the Japanese question (Chapter 4, §4).

Oblivion of History and Geopolitics and Manichaean Essentialism

Ferguson does not tire of counter-posing 'the West' to 'the Rest' – a kind of worthless appendix of the genuinely civilized world. The contrast is primarily developed on the basis of a reading of the history of the American continent: 'independence from Spain left South America with an enduring legacy of conflict, poverty and inequality. Why did capitalism and democracy fail to thrive in Latin America? Why, when I once asked a colleague at Harvard if he thought Latin America belonged to the West, was he unsure? Why, in short, was Bolivar not the Latin Washington?'[85] The questions are peremptory: are they correctly formulated? We have seen Hamilton and Tocqueville stressing that what facilitated the USA's peaceful development and liberal order was a favourable geopolitical context. On the American continent, it did not have great powers on its borders or in its vicinity, while the Atlantic protected it from potential attempts at revenge by the defeated enemy (Chapter 2, §10). The same conclusion is reached by Hegel in his *Lectures on the Philosophy of History*: 'there is no neighbouring state in America with which the United States could have the kind of relationship which prevails among the European nations, a state which they would have to view with distrust and against which they would have to maintain a standing army'.[86] Contrasting North America and Latin America in the context of a comparison that totally ignores history and geopolitics, Ferguson neglects the convergent lesson of the three authors cited. The genesis and development of the United States profoundly altered the geopolitical framework and created that situation (the vicinity of a powerful and fearsome, if not threatening, state).

Hegel's *Lectures on the Philosophy of History* make a further observation. Over and above the favourable geopolitical situation, an important role was played in the USA by 'the outlet of colonisation': 'By this means, the principal

---

85   Ferguson, *Civilization*, p. 119.
86   G.W.F. Hegel, *Lectures on the Philosophy of World History: Introduction*, trans. H.B. Nisbet, Cambridge: Cambridge University Press, 1975, p. 169.

source of discontent has been removed, and the continued existence of the present state of civil society is guaranteed'. A safety valve of this kind was wanting in Europe, with profound consequences: 'if the ancient forests of Germany still existed, the French Revolution would never have occurred'. Or it would have occurred in a less radical, less tormented fashion. Generally speaking, it would have been easier to defuse social tension and political unrest. Given the radical difference of geopolitical contexts, 'a comparison between the free states of North America and the countries of Europe is therefore impossible'.[87] This represents a refutation *avant la lettre* of Ferguson's abstract comparativism.

The full implications of Hegel's second remark should be noted. 'Colonization' – the expropriation, deportation and decimation of the natives – made it possible for poor whites to access property, so that the reigning political power in the USA, already sheltered from attacks from without, did not have to fear the threat harboured by a bitter internal social conflict. In other words, the liberal state (for the white community) was only one side of the coin. The flip side took the form of terror against the natives, who were constantly exposed to the threat of expropriation, deportation and decimation. Hegel's analysis can be extended: the institution of slavery enabled iron control over the 'dangerous classes' at the point of production. And once again, social stability and the rule of law (for the white community) was the flip side of a complete lack of rights for slaves (and blacks in general).

However, in negatively contrasting the South with the North of the American continent, Ferguson focuses exclusively on one side of the coin – the liberty enjoyed by the white community in the British colonies and then in the USA – while the reverse side is persistently ignored and repressed. The remarkable thing is that the latter ends up emerging from the British historian's own descriptions. Let us first deal with the lot of the natives. George Washington 'was appalled when the Indians were effectively confirmed in their lands by the royal proclamation of 1763'. He thought this was an expedient to keep them on board during the Seven Years' War.[88] The leader of the rebellion against the London government had no doubt that expropriation and repression were the inevitable fate awaiting the natives. In short, 'in South America the Indians worked the land. In North America they lost it.'[89] To be precise, it was not only the land:

---

87   Ibid., pp. 168–70.
88   Ferguson, *Civilization*, p. 116.
89   Ibid., pp. 118–19.

In 1650 the American Indians had accounted for around 80 per cent of the population in both North America and South America, including also Brazil. By 1825, however, the proportions were radically different. In Spanish America indigenous peoples still accounted for 59 per cent of the population. In Brazil, however, the figure was down to 21 per cent, while in North America it was below 4 per cent.[90]

As regards the USA and Canada, what, in addition to immigration, yielded this result was the tenacious, consistent pursuit of a policy aimed at getting rid of the dross represented by the Native Americans.

Let us now contrast the fate of blacks in the South and North of the American continent, still availing ourselves of Ferguson's reconstruction:

> The lot of slaves in pre-revolutionary Latin America was not wholly wretched. Royal and religious authority could and did intervene to mitigate the condition of the slaves, just as it could limit other private property rights . . . Beginning in Brazil, it became the norm in Latin America for slaves to have their own plots of land . . . In North America slave-owners felt empowered to treat all their 'chattels' as they saw fit, regardless of whether they were human beings or plots of land . . . A Virginian law of 1669 declared it no felony if a master killed his slave. A South Carolinian law of 1726 explicitly stated that slaves were 'chattels' (later 'chattels personal').[91]

Mere article of property in the North, in the South the slave could even be a property-owner. Partial and contested in the South, the de-humanization of slaves was consummated in the North. Things did not change with the birth of the USA:

> Before we celebrate the long-run success of the British model of colonization in North America, we need to acknowledge that in one peculiar aspect it was in no way superior to Latin America. Especially after the American Revolution, the racial division between white and black hardened. The US constitution, for all its many virtues, institutionalized that division by accepting the legitimacy of slavery – the original sin of the new republic.[92]

---

90   Ibid., pp. 125–7.
91   Ibid., pp. 131–2.
92   Ibid., p. 129.

Once again, the flip side of American liberty is delineated with the utmost clarity. In addition to the expropriation, deportation and decimation of the natives, it comprised the advent of 'the vilest [slavery] that ever saw the sun' (to quote the English abolitionist John Wesley once again) and its consecration by the Constitution. This constituted the emergence of a veritable racial state.

There is no doubt that the line of demarcation between whites and races deemed inferior was much clearer in the North than the South. Not by chance, laws criminalizing 'miscegenation' were in force in the North and survived well beyond the abolition of black slavery: 'As late as 1913, twenty eight states retained such statutes, ten of them had gone so far as to make the prohibition on miscegenation constitutional. There was even an attempt, in December 1912, to amend the US constitution so as to prohibit miscegenation "for ever".'[93] In fact, in the southern USA the racial state survived the collapse of the Third Reich: 'as late as 1967 . . . sixteen states still had laws prohibiting racial intermarriage'.[94]

The empirical details recorded by the historian utterly contradict the conclusion stated by the theoretician of the absolute moral and political primacy of the North of the American continent (and the West as a whole). In the latter guise, Ferguson contrasts the 'inequality' obtaining in Latin America with equality in the British colonies and, subsequently, the USA.[95] But it is manifest that in the second case the relationship between whites and 'races' of colour was characterized by an extremely pronounced and tenacious inequality! In Ferguson's view, 'the constitution of 1787' (which laid the basis for the Civil War) is to be regarded as 'the most impressive piece of political institution-building in all history'.[96] For US abolitionists, by contrast, it was a tool of Satan. Sanctioning slavery in its most abject form, and establishing an absolute, insurmountable inequality between the different races, it destroyed the very unity of the human race asserted by Christianity.[97]

From the value of 'equality', let us pass to liberty. In this case too, the empirical details reported by the historian are eloquent:

> Slaves on Latin American plantations could more easily secure manumission than those on Virginian tobacco farms. In Bahia slaves themselves

---

93   Ibid., p. 135.
94   Ibid., p. 138.
95   See ibid., p. 119.
96   Ibid., p. 117.
97   See Losurdo, *Liberalism*, Chapter 5, §12.

purchased half of all manumissions. By 1872 three quarters of blacks and mulattos were free. In Cuba and Mexico a slave could even have his price declared and buy his freedom in instalments.[98]

Unlike in the North, then, the barrier separating the slave from the possession of liberty was not insurmountable. Thus far we have the historian's reconstruction. But now the ideologue intervenes, repeating that in any event it was North America (an integral part of the West – in fact, its contemporary vanguard) which embodied liberty.

This does not mean that every problem has been resolved: 'The most successful revolution ever made in the name of liberty was a revolution made in considerable measure by the owners of slaves, at a time when the movement for the abolition of slavery was already well under way on both sides of the Atlantic.' And so? We are dealing with a 'paradox'.[99] But resort to this category is certainly insufficient to dispel the major shadow cast over American liberty by the fate reserved for blacks (and Native Americans). All the more so because the 'paradox' might be differently, or conversely, formulated. Owners of slaves (and of land taken from the natives fraudulently and violently) were the authors of a rebellion against the London government who 'paradoxically' waved the banner of liberty! If, as emerges from Ferguson's formulation, the 'paradox' refers to the secondary aspect of a blatantly contradictory admixture, does it consist in the reality of the violence perpetrated against entire peoples or in the ideology whereby the reality and the violence were legitimized? Even if we agree to overlook the 'inferior races', and focus exclusively on the white community, it is not logical to identify a country which, sanctioning or tolerating bans on miscegenation, intervened in the most private individual sphere as an embodiment of liberty. Let us be clear: it is not a question of reversing the result of the comparison between the South and North of the American continent in favour of the former. It is a question of highlighting the fact that the empirical evidence adduced by the British historian utterly contradicts the aprioristic thesis stated by him. Above all, it is a question of challenging a comparison between different societies and cultures represented in essentialist fashion, arbitrarily smoothing out the contradictory aspects of each of them, and ignoring history and geopolitics.

Having celebrated the North by contrast with the South of the American continent, Ferguson compares 'the West' with 'the Rest', invariably to the

---

98   Ferguson, *Civilization*, p. 130.

99   Ibid., p. 129.

greater glory of the former and the eternal shame of the latter. We are already familiar with the methodology. In fact, it is even more arbitrary now. The 'West' is referred to in general, but no mention is made of the Third Reich. What is contrasted with 'the Rest' is the liberal West. But history and geopolitics remain absent for the most part. Let us seek to make good this lacuna.

From the late seventeenth century onwards, liberalism asserted itself in two countries (Britain and the USA), which could avail themselves of the 'outlet of colonisation' (to use Hegel's terminology) and were sheltered from the threats faced by the continental European states. It should be added that it was no accident if the Glorious Revolution followed Britain's victory first over Spain and then over France, while the revolt of the American colonies began only after France's defeat in the Seven Years' War. In other words, both liberal revolutions presupposed a marked improvement in the geopolitical situation. As regards continental Europe, we can distinguish two phases. After the defeat of the Turks at the gates of Vienna in 1683, and the fading of the Ottoman threat, the liberal order began to enjoy widespread support in continental Europe itself. The second phase was the so-called hundred years' peace, from the end of the Napoleonic Wars to the outbreak of the First World War. This was the period when liberalism also achieved victory politically in the most advanced countries of continental Europe. Further proof of the thesis just formulated is to hand. Just as the liberal institutions deriving from the turning-point of 1789 did not withstand the war in which revolutionary France became embroiled, so, with the explosion of the great historical crisis of the first half of the twentieth century, the liberal institutions that had flourished in continental Europe during the hundred years' peace were overwhelmed or experienced a dramatic crisis. Even countries enjoying a more or less insular position, like Britain and the USA, suffered a process of attrition at times, with an unprecedented intensification of executive power. War and states of emergency are not conducive to the maintenance of the principle of the limitation of power. And the more devastating and threatening to national sovereignty the war, the more acute is the state of emergency and the lower the chances of the rule of law surviving.

Hence to place the colonialist great powers and countries that suffered their aggression (or the threat of it) on the same footing evinces a colossal methodological naivety, when it does not derive from a calculation informed by cynical realpolitik. It was precisely the former countries that rendered the advent of liberal institutions, of which they claimed to be the champions, impossible in the latter. In the US Constitution itself, which Ferguson celebrates as an insuperable model, it is clearly written (Section 9) that 'the privilege of the Writ of Habeas Corpus' can be 'suspended' when 'in cases of Rebellion or Invasion the Public Safety may require it'.

Ferguson takes no account of any of this when he celebrates the West's secular primacy in every respect over China. However, in this case too, what refute him are the facts he records. Following the catastrophe of the Opium Wars and the punitive expedition against the Boxers, the great Asian country seemed in the early twentieth century to be one of those 'relatively decentralized entities' whose 'dissolution' was anticipated by 'many Westerners'.[100] The situation certainly did not improve with the collapse of the Manchu dynasty and the advent of a Republic that looked to the West as a model politically as well: 'The extent of China's disintegration in the 1920s is hard to overstate.' An objective, long-standing fact also has to be appreciated: with more than fifty 'ethnic groups', 'eleven or more language groups still identifiable today, inhabitants even of neighbouring villages could speak mutually incomprehensible dialects'.[101] This was a situation that could only be dealt with by a strong central government, whose emergence was made impossible by the clashes between feuding warlords. Did the West at least seek to encourage the advent of democracy? Nothing of the kind: 'Although British politicians seemed willing to make concessions on the issue of extra-territoriality, the proverbial men on the spot continued to act as if China were merely an extension of the Raj.'[102] In addition, the threat of a different imperialism began to emerge: 'The line that the Japanese now took was that China was on the verge of disintegration.'[103]

The foundation of the People's Republic of China, following an epic national liberation struggle, certainly did not result in an immediate end to the situation of danger. To end the Korean War and teach the country that had challenged US hegemony in Asia a memorable lesson, US General MacArthur proposed that 'up to fifty atomic bombs should be dropped on Chinese cities'; and the author of this proposal, far from being isolated, paraded in New York saluted and acclaimed by 'a crowd of up to seven million. It was a triumph worthy of a Caesar.'[104] What sense does it make to criticize a country threatened with nuclear destruction on this occasion, and again in subsequent years, for failure

---

100 Ferguson, *The War of the World*, pp. 10–11.
101 Ibid., p. 292.
102 Ibid., p. 293.
103 Ibid., p. 286.
104 Ferguson, *Colossus*, pp. 90–1.

to achieve the rule of law? The country whence the threat of nuclear destruction issued itself experienced a period not free of institutional unrest: 'The year 1951 was perhaps the only moment in its history that the American Republic came close to meeting the fate of the Roman Republic' and falling under the rule of a 'Caesar' played by General MacArthur.[105]

In reality, although protected by the Atlantic and the Pacific, every time it has rightly or wrongly felt itself imperilled, the North American republic has proceeded to a more or less drastic reinforcement of executive power and to more or less heavy restrictions on freedom of association and expression. This applies to the years immediately following the French Revolution (when its devotees on American soil were hit by the Alien and Sedition Acts), to the Civil War, the First World War, the Great Depression, the Second World War and the Cold War. Even in our day, the sequel to the attack of 11 September 2001 was the opening of a concentration camp at Guantánamo, where detainees have been imprisoned without trial, and without even being informed of a specific charge, regardless of age. However terrible, the threat of terrorism is minor compared with that of invasion and military occupation, not to mention nuclear destruction.

'Property', 'Liberty', 'Competition': An Unthinking Use of Categories

We can readily understand why, in depicting 'the Rest' in negative terms, Ferguson particularly targets China, whose rapid rise threatens the economic primacy of 'the West'. But here too the contrast between multifaceted empirical description and ideological conclusion (Manichaean in character) is arresting. Is there anything to be admired in the millenarian civilization of the great Asian country? Referring to the voyages of geographical exploration, the British historian compares the Portuguese (hence Western) Vasco da Gama with the Chinese Zheng He. 'A streak of ruthlessness – indeed, of downright brutality' can be detected in the former that is largely absent from the latter.[106] Hence it was the West's geographical explorations in particular that seem to have resulted in the annexation of continents and 'discovered' lands, and the subjugation and even enslavement and decimation of the peoples inhabiting them. Let us now see what happened after the

---

105   Ibid., pp. 88–9.
106   Ferguson, *Civilization*, p. 34.

emancipation (partial or sometimes only formal) of black slaves in the European colonies and the USA: 'comparable numbers of indentured labourers from India and China were also on the move in the 1900s, their condition only marginally better than slavery, to work in plantations and mines owned and managed by Europeans' (and, in fact, US citizens too).[107] Hence it was Westerners who enslaved Chinese (and Indians), not vice versa.

In the light of all this, anyone who sought to credit the West with some absolute moral and political supremacy would be demonstrating an incapacity for logical judgement and moral hypocrisy. However, Ferguson's conclusion is exactly the opposite. In his view, it would be absurd 'relativism' to cast doubt on the permanent moral and political primacy of Western civilization: 'No previous civilization had ever achieved such dominance as the West achieved over the Rest', largely controlling the planet militarily and economically.[108] That is to say, regardless of the terrible practices it often engaged in, colonial expansionism is regarded as proof of the intrinsic, permanent superiority of the West; and rejection of 'relativism' takes the form of prostration before the law of the jungle and Social Darwinism!

Even more problematic are the very categories in which the dominant ideology stages the comparison between the different civilizations. According to Ferguson, what explains the irresistible rise of the West, and its moral and political primacy, was, *inter alia*, its scrupulous respect for property rights. Yet we have seen the British historian acknowledging that the process of outright de-humanization of black slaves in the North of the American continent resulted from the disappearance of any checks on the exercise of 'private property rights', including property in human livestock. Security of property rights is not in fact synonymous with respect for individual freedom.

Far from being a site where all individuals met freely as sellers and buyers of commodities, the liberal market was for centuries a site of exclusion and de-humanization. In the past, the ancestors of today's black citizens were commodities, not autonomous buyers and sellers. And for centuries the market even functioned as an instrument of terror: rather than the whip, what imposed total obedience on slaves was the threat of their sale, as a commodity to be exchanged on the market, separately from other family members.[109] Indentured white servants were long sold and bought on the

---

107 Ferguson, *The War of the World*, p. 47.
108 Ferguson, *Civilization*, p. 5.
109 See Walter Johnson, *Soul by Soul: Life inside the Antebellum Slave Market*, Cambridge, MA, and London: Harvard University Press, 1999, pp. 19, 22–3.

market as well, and thereby condemned to a fate not very different from that of black slaves. And in the name of the market, workers' combinations were repressed and economic and social rights ignored and denied, with a consequent commodification of essential aspects of the human personality and human dignity (health, education, etc.). In extreme cases, the superstitious cult of the Market has sealed enormous tragedies, like that which saw the United Kingdom condemn an enormous mass of concrete (Irish) individuals to death by starvation in 1847.

On the other hand, has the West truly distinguished itself by scrupulous respect for property rights? Marx's opinion on this subject is interesting:

> They [the bourgeoisie and the West] are the defenders of property, but did any revolutionary party ever originate agrarian revolutions like those in Bengal, in Madras, and in Bombay? . . . While they prated in Europe about the inviolable sanctity of the national debt, did they not confiscate in India the dividends of the rayahs, who had invested their private savings in the Company's own funds?[110]

And it was not only a question of 'ownership of the soil'. Following the second Opium War, Anglo-French troops set fire to the Summer Palace in Beijing, acquiring priceless items which even today the looters refuse to return.

Let us now concentrate exclusively on the logical aspect of the nexus between property and liberty established by Ferguson. Having underscored the merits of the 1787 US Constitution for having promoted 'a single market', the rule of law, and so forth, he continues:

> At root it was all about property. And in these terms Washington was one of those hard-nosed men who did well out of the War of Independence [accumulating new land taken from the natives]. Nothing could better illustrate the tightness of the nexus between land and liberty in the early history of the United States. In South America the Indians worked the land. In North America they lost it.[111]

Is this observation proof of the thesis cherished by the British historian or its refutation? On the one hand, land (seized from the natives) allowed the white community to defuse social conflict and consolidate liberal institutions.

---

110   Marx and Engels, *Gesamtausgabe*, Part I, Vol. 12, p. 252.
111   Ferguson, *Civilization*, pp. 118–19.

On the other hand, the land originally possessed by the natives consigned them to a fate of expropriation, deportation and decimation – that is, a complete lack of liberty and rights.

Similarly un-thought-out is another group of categories ('competition', respect for individual dignity, individualism), utilized by the dominant ideology to celebrate the West.[112] It is right to emphasize with Ferguson that Europe achieved its economic and technological development thanks to competition not only between individuals, but also between the states into which, unlike China, it was divided. But there is another side to the coin: the furious 'competition' between different states provoked the catastrophe of two world wars; and it was in reaction to this that the process of European unification was subsequently promoted.

Even if we stick to competition between individuals within a country, the result of the comparison between the different civilizations is much more problematic than the British historian imagines. In the Europe of the *ancien régime*, where the hereditary aristocracy wielded power, supporters of Enlightenment looked to China with admiration and envy. In that 'Confucian society', where 'learning was the key to advancement',[113] public competitions were used to select public servants. Hence a preeminent role was played not by supposed nobility of blood, but by 'competition' and individual merit. If we do not confine ourselves to including only the white community, the result of the comparison proves quite unexpected. In the USA, racial affiliation was long – very long (in the South as late as the mid-twentieth century) – the decisive criterion determining the fate of the individual. Did 'competition' and individualism play a more important role in the North American republic or Confucian China? Rather than opting for one of the horns of the dilemma, and allowing ourselves to become imprisoned in a schema of the 'clash of civilizations' with tendencies to fundamentalism, it is better to apply the principle of the 'circulation of thought' between different cultures.[114] Once the global colonial system and, in the USA, the racial state and regime of white supremacy had been defeated (thanks to the anti-colonial revolutions and the struggles of peoples of colonial origin), it can be said that 'competition' and individualism came to fruition in the West. But the fact remains that, if by individualism is meant recognition of the dignity of individuals in their universality, it cannot be conceived without

---

112 See ibid., p. 19ff.

113 Henry Kissinger, *On China*, New York: Penguin, 2011, p. 14.

114 See Losurdo, *Il linguaggio dell'Impero*, Chapter 2, §13.

the contribution made by the challenge of cultures and peoples foreign to the West and often in conflict with it.

We arrive at the same complex conclusion if we compare areas situated within the same civilization. As regards the West, which demonstrated greater 'individualism'? The Europe that constructed the welfare state, or the USA which mostly condemned it as synonymous with insane collectivism? The answer to the question is quite the opposite of obvious, if 'individualism' means concern for the fate of the concrete individual. In any event, whatever the answer, it is important not to lose sight of significant material circumstances. In the late nineteenth century, Bismarck in Germany sought to avert the feared socialist revolution through a reform from above that introduced elements of the welfare state. In the same years, across the Atlantic, social conflict was defused differently, and the 'welfare state' assumed a peculiar form: government support for colonists settled in the Far West and realizing the American dream at the expense of the natives.

Transfiguration of the West and De-legitimation of the Anti-Colonial Revolutions

Bound up with transfiguration of the West is de-legitimation of the anti-colonial revolutions. What is the sense in rebelling against a superior civilization, whose expansion was the result of 'a conversion achieved ultimately more by the word than by the sword'?[115] In reality, on other occasions Ferguson is compelled to acknowledge a different, opposed truth: 'The *ultima ratio* of the Western empires was, of course, force'; even in the twentieth century, 'the Western powers had no desire to relinquish their mastery over Asia's peoples and resources'.[116] The contradictions accumulate. We have seen the British historian draw attention to the bestial speech in which Wilhelm II harangued the German soldiers about to embark on repressing the Boxer Rebellion. But now that undertaking becomes 'the expedition to relieve Beijing'.[117] When it prevails, the apologetic concern works miracles, to the point of converting a 'sword' into a 'word'.

Already stripped of historical legitimacy, the anti-colonial revolutions are marked by 'economic failure' – in fact, by failure *tout court*. To prove this

---

115 Ferguson, *Civilization*, p. 5.
116 Ferguson, *The War of the World*, pp. 16, lxix.
117 Ibid., p. 287.

thesis, statistical data is piled up and put on display.[118] But tables and percentages are of little use if the meaning of the categories of 'failure' and 'anti-colonial revolution' is not clarified first. This might seem to be a polemical remark, but let us start by reflecting on the second category. On the one hand, Ferguson stresses 'the imperial origins of the United States',[119] and (as we know) defines the Founding Fathers of the USA as 'self-confident imperialists'. On the other, he writes that 'of course, the American political system had also been the product of a revolt against imperial rule'.[120] Can these assertions be reconciled?

Were the second of Ferguson's contradictory assertions to be correct, history would contain at least one instance of a shiningly successful anti-imperial and anti-colonial revolution – namely, that resulting in the enactment of the 1787 Constitution ('the most impressive piece of political institution-building in all history'!) and the foundation of a country which subsequently became an economic, technological and military super-power. In reality, as emerges from Ferguson's own account, the colonial peoples on the American continent found their most determined and dangerous enemies precisely in the Founding Fathers of the North American republic. The latter wanted to rid themselves of the restrictions on the expropriation and deportation of the natives imposed by the London government. As regards the blacks, it was the colonists who came to power via the War of Independence who regarded and treated slaves as sheer 'chattels' and put a constitutional seal on this condition and, more generally, on the racial state.[121] In any event, the abolition of slavery in the USA occurred three decades later than it did in the British colonies: 'From the point of view of most African Americans, American independence postponed emancipation by at least a generation . . . Nor was independence good news for the native Americans.'[122] The rebellion by the British colonists in America in the late eighteenth century can be assimilated to the secessions, or attempts at secession, made shortly after the mid-twentieth century by French colonists in Algeria and British colonists in Rhodesia. In the first case, it was a question of sweeping away the obstacles to the process of colonization erected by central government; in the other two, of blocking at any price the de-colonization that central government felt compelled to initiate. All three instances involved

---

118   See Ferguson, *Colossus*, p. 175.
119   Ibid., p. 26.
120   Ferguson, *The War of the World*, p. 613.
121   Ferguson, *Civilization*, pp. 131, 129.
122   Ferguson, *Empire: How Britain Made the Modern World*, p. 101.

movements whose protagonists were the most fanatical supporters of colonial expansionism and rule.

Having clarified this point, we may now deal with the problem of the 'failure' for which Ferguson reproaches anti-colonial revolutions, and confront it in the case of genuine anti-colonial revolutions. It is appropriate to start with the major upheaval of which the blacks of San Domingo-Haiti were the protagonists between the late eighteenth century and the start of the nineteenth. This is a historical episode that can be directly contrasted with the one resulting in the foundation of the USA. The latter involved the consummate de-humanization of black slaves, who by contrast rebelled on San Domingo, giving birth to the first country (in the Western hemisphere) to be free of the infamy of slavery. While the North American republic accelerated and aggravated the on-going tragedy of the natives, the ex-slaves who had come to power changed San Domingo's name to Haiti, referring to the island's pre-Columban past and thereby paying tribute to the victims of the discovery-conquest of America. Is the anti-colonial revolution we are discussing to be regarded as a failure or success? There is no doubt that San Domingo-Haiti did not succeed either in achieving economic development, or in furnishing itself with a stable political set-up, and in this respect the failure is undeniable. Internationally, however, without the rebellion of the black slaves led by Toussaint L'Ouverture, we cannot understand the abolition of slavery either in Britain's colonies or in Latin America. Nor can we understand the second, definitive abolition of slavery in the French colonies following the 1848 revolution. In other words, we are dealing with an imposing process of emancipation, in which case it is decidedly problematic to speak of 'failure'. In any event, those who claim to cherish the cause of liberty should not simplistically liquidate an essential chapter in the history of freedom as a 'failure'.

Around a century and a half later, another great anti-colonial revolution developed in China. With its success in 1949, it imparted crucial impetus to the anti-colonialist dynamic globally. Subsequently, after a laborious learning process marked by tragic pages, the country deriving from this revolution achieved extraordinary economic success and thereby encouraged other countries with a colonial or semi-colonial past, after having liberated themselves from politico-military domination, to jettison economic dependency. This is such a great success that Ferguson himself is obliged to register the decline of the West and the American Empire, or the termination of the historical cycle that began with the discovery-conquest of the New World. It is such a great success that it neutralizes the success achieved by the West during the Cold War: 'Thus was the supposed triumph of the West in 1989 revealed to be an illusion.'[123]

But all this does not prevent the champion of philo-colonialist revisionism from drawing a caricature of the anti-colonial revolutions (and their leaders). Take the case of Cuba, 'informally an American dependency since the time of Theodore Roosevelt',[124] who has been characterized by an eminent US historian as a 'herald of modern American militarism and imperialism' and also 'a touch of racism', and even been compared to Hitler by other, no less prestigious US scholars.[125] In 1959, the independence movement, which had virtually a century of history behind it, achieved victory under the leadership of Fidel Castro. But a mere three years later, the old masters sought revenge: the invasion of the Bay of Pigs. Following the 'abject' failure of this endeavour, 'a smarting Kennedy had reverted to a policy of dirty tricks aimed at destabilizing and perhaps even assassinating Castro'. Is this a condemnation of US imperialism? Not a bit of it. Ferguson expresses his dismay that the invasion was 'inadequately supported from the air'. And to think that a few years earlier a coup d'état promoted and supported by the USA had successfully overthrown the democratic government of Jacobo Arbenz in Guatemala. So 'the Cuban revolution was a grave setback for the American anti-Communist strategy, undoing at a stroke the success of the Guatemalan coup. Despite repeated attempts, the CIA could not pull off the same trick in Havana.'[126]

Was the defeat suffered by a formidable super-power proof of the historical legitimacy and wide social base of support for the Cuban Revolution, or at least for its leader, who also proved to be independent of Moscow? Ferguson has nothing but contempt for the intended victim of Kennedy's 'dirty tricks'. During the Missile Crisis of 1962, Castro adopted his intransigent attitude 'fuelled by sausages and beer'; he 'was Pinocchio, a puppet without strings'. Far from being an isolated case, the Cuba leader represents the prototype of the leaders of anti-colonialist countries and movements. In the so-called Cold War, 'the real and bloody Third World War was in fact fought by the likes of Castro – in the Third World itself'.[127]

---

123   Ferguson, *The War of the World*, p. 638.
124   Ibid., p. 599.
125   See Richard Hofstadter, *The American Political Tradition and the Men Who Made it*, New York: A. Knopf, 1967, p. 206 (for the definition as a 'herald') and Losurdo, *Liberalism*, Chapter 10, §5 (for the comparison with Hitler made by P.L. van den Berghe among others).
126   Ferguson, *The War of the World*, pp. 600, 612.
127   Ibid., pp. 603, 612, 606.

As we can see, talk about the 'economic failure' of the anti-colonial revolutions is simply a smokescreen. In reality, what they are criticized for is their political orientation. Why, asks Ferguson, were such revolutions fascinated with the Communist model, drawing inspiration from 'Lenin, Stalin and Mao'?[128] The answer to this question is not far to seek. Asia and, above all, Africa were still largely dominated by countries like Britain and France, which, to bolster their rule, had no hesitation in resorting to indiscriminate repression and even genocidal practices. But why, presses Ferguson, were the anti-colonial revolutions not inspired by the American Revolution and by 'Washington, Jefferson and Madison'?[129] For a while President Arbenz in Guatemala did indeed refer to the North American republic, prior to being overthrown by the CIA to make way for a dictatorship that was later guilty of genocide against the Maya, suspected of being excessively inclined to subversion. At all events, it should not be difficult to answer Ferguson's question. He it is who characterizes the Founding Fathers as expansionist and imperialist; who stresses that at times they 'were about the wealthiest people in the world',[130] and that they derived their wealth from land taken from the natives and the reduction of blacks to human livestock. It is the British historian who records that, by dint of the Monroe Doctrine and its privileged geopolitical situation, the USA in the late nineteenth century regarded itself as 'practically sovereign on this continent', in the Western hemisphere, and acted accordingly.[131] In any case, it is all the more remarkable to criticize the anti-colonial revolutions for not looking to the West and, at the same time, call on the latter (and its leading country) to establish a planetary empire, trampling over the principle of equality between nations which underlay the anti-colonial revolutions. Yet Ferguson is in no doubt:

> Ambitious Third World 'freedom fighters' like the opportunities the distinctly unfree Soviet system had to offer them. In a one-party system, the first winner takes all; there is no danger of his being asked to hand over power to some rival within just a few years. And with a planned economy, the new political rulers can acquire any economic assets they like in the name of nationalization.[132]

---

128   Ibid., p. 613.
129   Ibid.
130   Ferguson, *Empire: How Britain Made the Modern World*, p. 85.
131   Ferguson, *Colossus*, p. 42.
132   Ferguson, *The War of the World*, pp. 613–14.

De-legitimation of anti-colonial revolutions thus ends up in personal abuse of their leaders, who are not conceded any genuine motives, but appear motivated exclusively by *libido dominandi* and material greed. It remains to be explained why they faced the severe sacrifices and dangers of a protracted revolutionary struggle, and how they succeeded in winning a mass following (composed of militants themselves imbued with a spirit of sacrifice) and, further, in resisting attempts at destabilization and invasion (often undertaken by the USA and the West). On the other hand, of course, this insulting, *ad personam* hermeneutic of suspicion could easily be applied to the American Revolution taken as a model by Ferguson. Its authors (as he acknowledges) were able to expand their landed property at the expense of the natives, and to increase and consolidate their property in human livestock at the expense of the blacks.

Ferguson's line of argument is all the more trifling for liquidating the anti-colonial revolution in the whole arc of its historical unfolding, well prior to the advent of Communism. He ignores Toussaint L'Ouverture (who could not identify with the North American republic because it identified with the slave-owners whom the 'black Jacobin' was fighting). He condemns Simón Bolívar as inherently dictatorial. He does not even spare an anti-colonial revolution that began in Europe one year before the October Revolution, involving a country that came to be celebrated as an economic tiger, at least until the onset of the global economic crisis in 2008.

In 1916, while the First World War was raging, a rebellion broke out in Ireland. The rebels sought to take advantage of the situation to win independence, rather than to fight and die in the service of an age-old oppressor who had not hesitated to employ genocidal practices on occasion. Here is how the events are narrated by Ferguson. The insurgents were 'a thousand or so extreme Irish nationalists'; theirs 'was plainly an act of treason'. Repression followed: 'The dying Connolly had to be propped up in a chair to be shot.' After the war, the independence movement, which had become powerful, was confronted without pity. The colonial power did not hesitate to open fire on an unarmed mass of civilians. Such evidence of firmness does not seem sufficient to Ferguson:

> But as would happen so often in the period, the British lacked the stomach for repression . . . By 1921, with British losses approaching 1,400, the will to fight had gone and a peace deal was hastily cobbled together . . . Time and again, in the inter-war period, this was a pattern that would repeat itself. A minor outbreak of dissent, a sharp military

response, followed by a collapse of British self-confidence, hand-wringing, second thoughts, a messy concession, another concession. But Ireland was the test case. In allowing their very first colony to be split in two, the British had sent a signal to the Empire at large.[133]

The rebellion of colonial peoples extended far beyond the island: 'Indians looked to Ireland and drew the obvious conclusion. It was no good just waiting to be given Home Rule.'[134] From the periphery of the Empire, the crisis reached its centre: 'By the 1930s many people in Britain had got the habit of rubbishing the Empire.'[135] It was the beginning of the end for the British Empire. But is that proof of the failure of the Irish revolution or of its success?

The USA, China and Ferguson's Sequence

Just as the denigration of the 'Rest' by contrast with the 'West' is conducted with particular reference to Chinese civilization, so the de-legitimation of the anti-colonial revolutions focuses on the chapter of history concluding with the foundation of the People's Republic of China and on the leaders and first decade of the new state, which was subjected to terrible diplomatic isolation and forced to struggle for its survival.

We are familiar with Ferguson's forceful description of the horror of the Japanese invasion: utter de-humanization of the people to be subjugated, explicitly reduced to 'pigs' who could be sacrificed at will and for sheer pleasure; competitions to see who was quickest at killing them; and mass rape of women often followed by savage sadism and murder. Consequently, it would seem logical to acknowledge those who dared to rebel against all this, in what was a seemingly desperate situation because of the asymmetry of forces. But who were they?

The Japanese invasion did not elicit national unity, as some Chinese Nationalists had hoped it might. It boosted support for the Communist Party, which under Mao Zedong's leadership now committed itself to a campaign of protracted guerrilla warfare. At the same time, Japanese

---

133 Ferguson, *Empire: The Rise and Demise of the British World Order*, pp. 275–6.
134 Ibid., p. 276.
135 Ibid., p. 284.

incursion tended to widen divisions within the Guomindang. The more recruits the Communists were able to find among impoverished and disillusioned peasants, the more tempted some nationalists were to compromise with the Japanese.[136]

Hence, along with the names of Toussaint L'Ouverture and those who fostered uprisings against the Nazi troops engaged in the enslavement and decimation of the peoples of Central-Eastern Europe and the Judeocide, the name of Mao Zedong – at least as regards the years of anti-Japanese resistance – should occupy a place of honour not only in the history books, but also in texts of civic education.

However, this is not the position of Ferguson, who in fact stages a bizarre comparison:

> Despite the painful interruption of the Great Depression, the United States suffered nothing so devastating as China's wretched twentieth-century ordeal of revolution, civil war, Japanese invasion, more revolution, man-made famine and yet more ('cultural') revolution. In 1968 the average American was thirty-three times richer than the average Chinese.[137]

Here we have an outright condemnation of the Chinese anti-colonial revolution, pronounced on the basis of a comparison between two countries whose prior history and material conditions could not be more different. From its foundation, sheltered from the danger of invasion, the USA enjoyed an uninterrupted process of expansion, first continental and then overseas. By contrast, from the Opium Wars onwards China endured successive invasions and financial blood-lettings, in a process that culminated in the Japanese invasion, whose watchword says it all ('Take all, kill all, burn all').[138] It would unquestionably have been more logical to compare China before and after the Opium Wars, or before and after the victory of the anti-colonial revolution; or countries like India and China in the years following the end of their colonial or semi-colonial status. But if one wants to stick with a comparison between China and the USA, then we can offer a different one from Ferguson's, which is certainly no less polemical but is rather less dubious. In the years immediately following the revolution led

---

136   Ferguson, *The War of the World*, p. 482.
137   Ferguson, *Civilization*, p. 304.
138   Ferguson, *The War of the World*, p. 483.

by the Founding Fathers, we witness in the USA a deterioration in the
condition of black slaves and an intensification in the process of the expropriation, deportation and decimation of the natives. By contrast, the victory
of the revolution led by Mao Zedong put an end to the Japanese Empire's
plans to reduce the Chinese to Indians to be decimated or blacks to be
enslaved.

But we must now examine the sequence in which Ferguson encapsulates
the history of twentieth-century China: the 'ordeal of revolution, civil war,
Japanese invasion, more revolution'. An epic anti-colonial revolution, putting
an end to unprecedented horrors, is alluded to almost peevishly. And the
'Japanese invasion', treated as something comparable to the 'Great
Depression', figures as one of many misfortunes – and not the most serious – marking the twentieth-century history of China, which emerges as
the sole real culprit for the enormous tragedies it endured. One thing is
clear. When he contrasts the British Empire positively with its Japanese
counterpart, Ferguson provides an apt description of the latter's infamy. But
when it comes to contrasting the misery of the Chinese anti-colonial revolution with the splendour of the American Empire, that infamy becomes an
anodyne 'Japanese invasion'.

Still dealing with Ferguson's sequence, 'more revolution' follows immediately upon 'man-made famine'. A whole chapter of history is thereby
repressed. Even before the foundation of the People's Republic, the
revolution led by the party that had distinguished itself in the struggle
against Japanese imperialism became an American target. Politically,
diplomatically and militarily, the US backed the party which, in order to
defend the privileges of the small ruling elite, had sought a compromise
with the barbaric invaders. Washington responded to the Communists'
arrival in power with 'economic warfare' and a 'naval blockade', while
Guomindang air raids on the industrial cities of mainland China, including
Shanghai, continued with US assistance.[139] Hence the sequence set out by
Ferguson ('Japanese invasion, more revolution, man-made famine') needs
to be altered or at least completed: 'Japanese invasion, more revolution,
new aggression' – this time perpetrated not by the Empire of the Rising
Sun, but by the American Empire. The latter refused to recognize the
People's Republic diplomatically and in fact did everything it could to
isolate and strangle it, while domestically it engaged in a revealing debate:

---

139 See Shu Guang Zhang, *Economic Cold War: America's Embargo against China and the Sino-
Soviet Alliance*, Stanford: Stanford University Press, 2001, pp. 24, 32, 71.

'who lost China?' Even after Deng Xiaoping's reforms, Washington could not resign itself to the loss of a massive potential market and reserve of cheap labour (as well as a crucial region for the conquest of global hegemony):

> Some analysts even predicted that the Special Economic Zones would become like American colonies in East Asia . . . Americans had thought China would become a giant economic subsidiary of the United States, in an approximate re-enactment of the 'Open Door' era of the early twentieth century. Instead, they now found themselves facing a new economic rival.[140]

But let us pursue our analysis of Ferguson's sequence: 'Japanese invasion, more revolution, man-made famine'. We may start by posing a question: was 'famine', which follows revolution, its consequence, or a much earlier phenomenon, which the revolution sought to combat? Let us cite some data: 'the great droughts in North China . . . of 1876–79 . . . caused the death of nine to thirteen million people'.[141] This was a tragedy that tended to recur periodically. In 1928, the death toll amounted to 'nearly three million deaths in the province of Shensi alone'.[142] There was no escaping hunger or cold: 'People burnt the lintels of houses to warm themselves.'[143] 'Famine in spring remained a perennial threat across much of China.' Death from starvation was such a common occurrence that the ruling classes had no problem sacrificing people en masse in a different way in war: 'When in 1938 it [the Guomindang] blew the dykes of the Yellow River to block the Japanese advance, the flooding killed almost 1 million peasants. It repeated the dyke-blowing tactics in 1945 when attacking Communist bases.'[144] In any event, contrary to Ferguson's insinuation, in China famine was not a consequence of the revolution. If we examine the years 1850–1950, from the first Opium War and the irruption of colonialism to the victory of the anti-colonial (and socialist) revolution, and bear in mind the catastrophes punctuating this major historical crisis (military invasions, insurrections, 'natural cataclysms'), a conclusion dictates itself: 'Almost certainly the

---

140   Ferguson, *The War of the World*, pp. 637–8.
141   Gernet, *A History of Chinese Civilization*, p. 617; Alain Roux, *La Chine au XXe siècle*, Paris: Colin, 2007, p. 40.
142   Gernet, *A History of Chinese Civilization*, p. 617.
143   Roux, *La Chine au XXe siècle*, p. 41.
144   Mann, *The Sources of Social Power*, Vol. 3, pp. 416–17.

number of victims involved had never been so high in the history of the world.'[145]

Having analysed the substantive in the phrase 'man-made famine', let us now turn to the adjective or the participle employed in an adjectival form: 'man-made'. It is worth noting that, when it comes to the famine which struck Ireland in the mid-nineteenth century, Ferguson prefers to speak of the 'calamity of Irish famine'.[146] Yet the latter was greeted by a prominent representative of the British government as a gift from heaven, as something intended by an 'omniscient Providence' (Chapter 5, §10). Nothing of the sort occurred in China's Great Leap Forward in the late 1950s. Why only refer to 'man-made famine' in this instance?

We may set Ireland to one side. Positioned immediately after 'more revolution', the phrase 'man-made famine' refers exclusively to the responsibility of China's leaders. But is this a balanced judgement? We have seen that, emerging devastated from the Japanese occupation and a civil war that was not quite over, China under Communist rule became the target of American military threats and economic warfare. The Truman administration pursued an objective clarified by a US author who sympathetically describes the prominent role played in the Cold War by Washington's policy of encirclement and economic strangulation of the People's Republic. The latter must be 'plagued' by 'a general standard of living around and below subsistence level'; a country in 'desperate need' must be induced into a 'catastrophic economic situation', 'towards disaster' and 'collapse'.[147] In the early 1960s, a collaborator in the Kennedy administration – W.W. Rostow – boasted of the victory secured by the USA, which had succeeded in retarding China's economic development by at least 'tens of years'.[148]

Responsibility for the 'man-made famine' is not to be sought in one direction. The causes of the catastrophe were twofold: on the one hand, the policy lucidly and ruthlessly planned in Washington as early as the autumn of 1949; and on the other, the inexperience and impatience of Mao, who wished to skip the stages of development in order to escape the dangerous situation in which his country found itself. Responsibility was not equally shared between the two parties – especially given that when US leaders imposed their embargo, they were aware that 'Communist inexperience with

---

145   Gernet, *A History of Chinese Civilization*, p. 616.
146   Ferguson, *Colossus*, p. 25.
147   Zhang, *Economic Cold War*, pp. 20–2, 25, 27.
148   Quoted in ibid., p. 250.

urban economics' would render it even more devastating.[149] Having moved beyond this phase, following a painful, utterly tragic learning process, the great Asian country succeeded in putting the phenomenon of recurrent mass famine, which was generated by colonialist and imperialist aggression in the first instance, definitively behind it.

Western Fundamentalism and the Ideology of War

With a long history behind them, celebration of the West as the privileged or exclusive site of civilization, and claims for white or Western supremacy on a global scale culminated in Nazi ideology. The collapse of the Third Reich and the worldwide flaring of anti-colonial revolution led to serious impairment, but not the disappearance, of the ethnological-racial paradigm for interpreting historical processes and of the exalted, exclusivist sense of the West as an island of civilization surrounded by an ocean of barbarism.

In 1953, Churchill called upon the West to support the presence of Britain in the Suez Canal 'in order to prevent a massacre of white people'.[150] Three years later, despite the disagreement that had arisen between Washington and London in the meantime, Eisenhower cautioned that, with the nationalization of the Suez Canal, Nasser was intent on 'slapping the white man down'.[151] Clearly, as far as the two statesmen were concerned, the Arabs belonged to the populations of colour and for that reason, regardless of their political conduct, were alien to civilization (and the West). On other occasions, we have seen Churchill stressing the vanguard role that the 'white English-speaking peoples', or the 'English-speaking world', were called upon to play in confronting the peril represented by Communism and rebellious colonial peoples. Here the reference to skin colour tends to be attenuated or to disappear: the stress is placed on language. Yet we must remember that the British statesman proceeded no differently from supporters of the Aryan mythology. What was inferred from the linguistic community was the unity of the race underlying it, and the cultural products of the Aryan languages or the English language were adduced as evidence of the excellence of that race.

---

149 Ibid., p. 22.

150 Boyle, *The Churchill-Eisenhower Correspondence*, p. 25 (letter to Eisenhower of 18 February 1953).

151 Quoted in Steven Z. Freiberger, *Dawn over Suez: The Rise of American Power in the Middle East, 1953–1957*, Chicago: Ivan R. Dee, 1992, p. 164.

Even in our day, a prominent British intellectual – Robert Conquest – has identified the true West as the 'English-speaking community' (to be distinguished not only from barbarians utterly foreign to the West, but also from 'continental Europe', which has invariably been 'a source of bureaucracy and bureaulatry, of rejection of the Anglo-American concept of law and liberty, of anti-Americanism'), and made it clear that the excellence of the 'English-speaking countries' possesses a specifically 'Anglo-Celtic' ethnic basis.[152] The Anglo-Celtic mythology outlined here recalls the Aryan mythology of ill repute. There is only one clarification to be made. Cherished by a long tradition that developed on both sides of the Atlantic and then issued into Nazism, Aryan mythology tended to be identified with the white mythology. At all events, it paid tribute to the Nordic peoples and all the peoples that had started out from German soil, hence including the British and Americans. By contrast, the 'Anglo-Celtic' community celebrates its superiority even over continental Europe. The club of genuinely civilized peoples dear to Conquest is even more exclusive than that celebrated by Aryan mythology.

The racial or ethnologico-racial paradigm can assume a more or less attenuated form. The most famous theoretician of the 'clash of civilizations' today poses a question: why, in addition to Europe, the USA and Canada, do Australia and New Zealand form part of 'western civilization', whereas Mexico and Brazil, which are located not in Asia but in the Western hemisphere, are excluded from it? How are we to explain such inclusions and exclusions? Samuel P. Huntington responds with great clarity: 'Latin American civilization incorporates indigenous cultures, which did not exist in Europe [and] were effectively wiped out in North America [and in Australia and New Zealand].' To be precise, what, in addition to cultures, were swept away were the peoples embodying them. The famous political scientist does not conceal the fact. The Puritan colonists who landed in North America worked on the assumption that 'expulsion and/or extermination [of the Indians] were the only policies to follow in the future'.[153]

Surprisingly, there is an undeniable similarity with Hitler's way of arguing, when he explained the infinite superiority of the USA (in his view an integral part of the West and the Germanic world) over Latin America (completely alien to the West). Let us read *Mein Kampf*:

---

152   See Robert Conquest, *Reflections on a Ravaged Century*, New York: Norton, 2000, Chapter 14.

153   Samuel P. Huntington, *The Clash of Civilizations and the Remaking of World Order*, New York: Simon & Schuster, 1996, p. 46; *Who are We? The Challenges to America's National Identity*, New York: Simon & Schuster, 2004, p. 54.

Historical experience offers countless proofs of this. It shows with terrifying clarity that in every mingling of Aryan blood with that of lower peoples the result was the end of the cultured people. North America, whose population consists in by far the largest part of Germanic elements who mixed but little with the lower coloured peoples, shows a different humanity and culture from Central and South America, where the predominantly Latin immigrants often mixed with the aborigines on a large scale. By this one example, we can clearly and distinctly recognise the effect of racial mixture.[154]

Naturally, there is no question of equating positions that should not be confounded. But we do want to signal the danger of sliding into the ethnologico-racial paradigm starting from a paradigm (the clash of civilizations) that intends to be, and is, different. Civilizations have a real existence, which does not refer to skin colour or 'race'. If, however, rather than being understood on the basis of determinate historical conflicts, they are regarded as the expression of a quasi-eternal spirit or soul, then 'civilization', like 'race', tends to refer to a mythical 'nature'. It is no accident that celebration of the 'western soul' (*abendländische Seele*) plays an essential role in Oswald Spengler,[155] and in the reactionary German culture that flowed into Nazism. And it is no accident if, in the view of Alfred Rosenburg – the Third Reich's main theoretician – the 'soul' is 'race seen from within', just as race is 'the external side of a soul'.[156] We can understand Toynbee's warning in the 1950s against persistent 'Western race-feeling'.[157]

An essentialist vision of civilization and Western fundamentalism are even more marked in Ferguson. In his work, the eternal moral and political primacy of the West becomes a dogma. True, he criticizes as 'nonsense' the thesis dear to American 'white supremacists' (subsequently adopted by the Nazis) that 'segregation was the key reason why the United States had prospered, while the "mongrel" peoples of Latin America were mired in poverty'.[158] However, completely ignoring history and geopolitics, he considers but one side of the coin of American liberty and arrives at this conclusion:

---

154   Hitler, *Mein Kampf*, p. 260.

155   See Oswald Spengler, *Der Untergang des Abendlandes*, Munich: Beck, 1980, p. 178.

156   Alfred Rosenberg, *The Myth of the Twentieth Century: An Evaluation of the Spiritual-Intellectual Confrontations of Our Age*, Newport Beach, CA: Noontide Press, 1993, p. i.

157   Arnold Toynbee, *A Study of History*, Oxford: Oxford University Press, 1934–54, Vol. I, pp. 210, 211 n.1.

158   Ferguson, *Civilization*, p. 137.

the difference in economic and political development between the North and South of the American continent can be explained by the fact that the revolution led by Washington was 'the most successful revolution ever made in the name of liberty', while 'Bolívar's dream turned out be not democracy but dictatorship'.[159] We are once again referred to nature, albeit that the indicated nature is not 'race' this time, but the sick psychology of the Latin American leader (and his followers).

We should not forget that the ethnologico-racial paradigm readily inter-mingled with the psychopathological paradigm in Nazism. The 'nature' of an order based on healthy racial hierarchy was to be defended against the assault of barbarians or inferior races (ethnologico-racial paradigm), on the one hand, and against mass subversion inside the citadel of civilization by those fostering insane ideas of equality and levelling (psychopathological paradigm), on the other. Not by chance, Hitler boasted of having detected the Judeo-Bolshevik virus as the source of the revolt of inferior races.

Ferguson is aware of the fact that anti-Semitism and rabid hatred of the Jewish 'race' in inter-war Poland and, above all, in Nazi (or incipiently Nazi) Germany was imbued with the conviction that salvation lay in eradicating a virus or bacillus lethal to society: 'As one Polish politician put it, the Jewish community was "a foreign body, dispersed in our organism so that it produces a pathological deformation".' And a sort of Polish poem expressed itself in similar terms in 1922: 'Jewry is contaminating Poland thoroughly . . . It poisons the spirit . . . A terrible gangrene has infiltrated our body.'[160] Yet not many pages prior to this the British historian writes:

> Two epidemics swept the world in 1918. One was Spanish influenza . . . As if to mock the efforts of men to kill one another, the virus spread rapidly across the United States and then crossed to Europe on the crowded American troopships . . . The other epidemic was Bolshevism, which for a time seemed almost as contagious and ultimately proved as lethal as the influenza.[161]

The Judeo-Bolshevik virus that fuelled the anti-Semitic and anti-Communist campaign in the inter-war years, and which was Hitler's particular obsession, is now configured as the Bolshevik 'influenza'! Once again, there is no question of equating very different political and ideological positions. Instead,

---

159   Ibid., pp. 129, 124.
160   Ferguson, *The War of the World*, p. 170.
161   Ibid., pp. 144–5.

it is a matter of cautioning against the naturalistic connotations peculiar to the psychopathological paradigm and the latter's tendency to cross over into the ethnologico-racial paradigm. Tocqueville identified the French and, in particular, the Jacobins as the carriers of 'a virus of a new and unknown kind', which allegedly underlay the incessant French revolutionary cycle. Having condemned *ressentiment* as the motive behind rebellion against the power exercised by the masters and the successful, Nietzsche pointed to the Jews as 'the people of *ressentiment* par excellence'. Finally, Hitler prided himself on having finally discovered the source of the disease and the revolutionary infection. It was Jews and Bolsheviks, who were regularly equated, in part on account of the Jewish origin of a significant number of leaders of the Russian revolutionary movement (Chapter 5, §8). The process of ethnicization of the revolutionary virus can assume very different forms. But what remains constant is the danger of slippage from the psychopathological paradigm, which refers to mental illness, to the naturalistic paradigm, which refers to the inferior or degenerate ethnicity and race.

Ferguson's positions are disturbing for another reason. Visiting the United States in the late nineteenth century, when the racial state was more robust than ever and the regime of white supremacy rampant in the South, Friedrich Ratzel, the first theoretician of the *Lebensraum* cherished by Nazism, drew attention to the complete failure of the project of constructing a society based on the principle of racial equality. Where was the emancipation of the blacks? Subject to lynching and interminable torture staged as a mass spectacle for applauding crowds, the fate of ex-slaves was perhaps even worse than in the past. On closer inspection, the situation created in the North American republic 'avoids the form of slavery, but retains the essence of subordination, of social hierarchy on a racial basis'; it continued to recognize the principle of 'racial aristocracy'. The conclusion was obvious: 'experience teaches us to recognize racial differences'; they had proved much more enduring than the 'abolition of slavery, which will one day seem a mere episode and abortive endeavour'. A 'reversal' had occurred vis-à-vis the fond illusions of abolitionists and fanatics for the idea of equality. The impact of all this would be felt far beyond the United States: 'We are only just beginning to see the results this reversal will produce in Europe even more than in Asia.'[162] This was a prediction (and wish) of deadly lucidity. The racial state

---

162   Friedrich Ratzel, *Politische Geographie der Vereinigten Staaten von Amerika unter besonderer Berücksichtung der natürlichen Bedingungen und wirtschaftlichen Verhältnisse*, Munich: Oldenburg, 1893, pp. 179–82, 283.

became a trend with the Third Reich (but also, to different degrees and in different ways, with the Empire of the Rising Sun and Mussolini's empire).

Today, it is not difficult to point to the tragic condition of a considerable number of newly independent countries and peoples. But what does this prove? Simply that the process of emancipation, in the case of slaves as in that of colonial peoples in general, is long and tortuous. After the American Civil War, no longer slaves and 'chattels' subject to sale and purchase like any other commodity, African Americans did not thereby become free. As regards colonial peoples, the conquest of political independence does not betoken liberation from the domination exercised by 'informal' empire.[163] Or, in Lenin's words, to put an end to 'economic "annexation"', it is not enough to shake off 'political annexation'.[164] But neither the former slaves, nor the former colonies, aspire to return to the *status quo ante* or feel nostalgia for slavery or colonial subjugation.

Ferguson tirelessly proclaims the failure, if not of the abolitionist revolution, then of the anti-colonialist revolution. Furthermore, he regards the principle of the equality of nations, if not that of 'racial equality', as utterly refuted by historical experience. For this reason he repeatedly stresses the need for a theoretical and political turn: 'I am fundamentally in favor of empire. Indeed, I believe that empire is more necessary in the twenty-first century than ever before.'[165] Thus, successive neo-colonial wars are legitimized and hallowed. Where will it all end? To achieve a new order based on explicit denial of the principle of the equality of nations, the British historian believes one must be prepared to pay an extremely high price. How many deaths did the war in Vietnam cause? In 2004, a conservative French newspaper calculated that, thirty years after the end of hostilities, there were still 'four million' victims whose bodies were suffering the ravages of the 'terrible agent orange' (named after the colour of the dioxin unsparingly sprayed by US planes on a whole people).[166] The same year, Ferguson criticized the USA for having capitulated: 'On balance, Americans preferred the irresponsibilities of weakness.'[167]

What provides particular food for thought is Ferguson's assessment of the Korean War. In 1951, Truman rejected MacArthur's proposal to drop fifty

---

163   See Ferguson, *The War of the World*, p. 610.

164   Lenin, *Collected Works*, Vol. 23, p. 44.

165   Ferguson, *Colossus*, p. 24.

166   See François Hauter, 'Le campagne contre l'"agent orange" des Américains', *Le Figaro*, 6 October 2004.

167   Ferguson, *Colossus*, p. 100.

atomic bombs on Chinese cities. However, stresses Ferguson, in January of the following year it was the president himself who entertained a similar plan. The USSR and China were to be sent an ultimatum and, in the absence of a positive response within ten days, 'all-out war' would have to be launched: 'It means that Moscow, St. Petersburg, Mukden, Vladivostok, Peking, Shanghai, Port Arthur, Dairen, Odessa, Stalingrad and every manufacturing plant in China and the Soviet Union will be eliminated.'[168] As we know, things turned out differently, and Ferguson does not seem altogether content with it:

> By overruling MacArthur, Truman and the Chiefs of Staff had unwittingly prolonged the war for more than two years. By the time the armistice was signed (on July 27, 1953), more than thirty thousand American servicemen had lost their lives . . . The United States in 1951 had both the military capability and the public support to strike a decisive military blow against Maoist China. Many another imperial power would have been unable to resist the window of opportunity afforded by America's huge lead in the atomic arms race.[169]

In his time, Gandhi referred to 'Hitlerism', or conversion to 'Hitler's method', a propos of Hiroshima and Nagasaki.[170] But the plans pressed by MacArthur and entertained by Truman, from which the revisionist historian is careful not to distance himself, went far beyond the two atomic bombs that sealed the end of the Second World War and possibly the start of the Cold War. Let us be quite clear: it is not a question of conjuring up the spectre of the Fourth Reich – the historical process is quite distinct from any eternal return of the same. But the extraordinary success enjoyed by Ferguson and his imperial mythology confirms the West's inability to engage in a genuine 'coming to terms with the past' (*Aufarbeitung der Vergangenheit*) and does not augur well for the future.

---

168   Quoted in ibid., p. 100.
169   Ibid., pp. 92–3.
170   Mohandas K. Gandhi, *The Collected Works of Mahatma Gandhi*, New Delhi: Government of India, 1969–2001, Vol. XCLVIII, p. 319.

CHAPTER SEVEN

The Black Book, *the Communist Movement and the Struggle Against the Three Major Forms of Discrimination*

The Statistics of Horror

What is immediately striking in *The Black Book of Communism*,[1] and the massive literature that takes the same line, is the statistics. Listed, added up, repeated in an obsessive crescendo, they seem intent on stunning readers, inducing them to regard any further argument as superfluous and forcing them to acknowledge a truth with the self-evidence of a mountain of corpses. In readers who are less naive, whether on account of historical memory or familiarity with historical literature, this is followed by a different, unanticipated reaction: how the climate has changed compared with the immediate post-war period! These were years when any calculus of horrors targeted colonialism, along with the artisans of the 'final solution'. Hannah Arendt reproved colonialism for having resorted to the 'extermination of the natives', which was 'virtually on the agenda' when 'new colonial settlements [were being constructed] in America, Australia and Africa'.[2] Norberto Bobbio highlighted the practice of 'extermination' (as well as 'economic exploitation' and 'enslavement') inherent in 'four centuries' of 'colonial expansion' by the West (often the liberal West).[3]

This negative judgement was not expressed exclusively as regards the past. With the development of the colonial liberation movement, calculations

---

1   Stéphane Courtois et al., *The Black Book of Communism: Crimes, Terror, Repression*, trans. Jonathan Murphy and Mark Kramer, Cambridge, MA, and London: Harvard University Press, 1999.

2   Hannah Arendt, *Essays & Kommentare*, ed. E. Geisel and K. Bittermann, Berlin: Tiamat, 1989, Vol. I, p. 9.

3   Norberto Bobbio, 'Invito al colloquio', in Bobbio, *Politica e cultura*, Turin: Einaudi, 1977, p. 23.

increasingly involved the present. Having recorded 'the 45,000 dead at Sétif' (1945), 'the 90,000 dead in Madagascar' (1947), 'the 200,000 victims of the repression in Kenya' (1952), Fanon gave the floor to the Algerian anti-colonial movement, which in 1957 accused the French authorities of conducting a policy 'verging on genocide' – in fact, of seeking to realize 'the most frightful work of extermination of modern times'. The memory of the crimes of Nazism and Fascism was still fresh, and what had they been 'if not colonialism when rooted in a traditionally colonialist country'? Such were the sentiments of militants of the Algerian independence movement, cited by Fanon, who reiterated the point: 'Not long ago Nazism transformed the whole of Europe into a veritable colony.'[4]

Arendt's opinion was not dissimilar. During the war, she defined Nazism as 'the most horrible imperialism the world has ever seen'.[5] It was from the tradition behind it that the Third Reich – a kind of highest stage of imperialism – had inherited belief in the '"natural law" of the rights of the strongest' and the tendency to 'exterminate "inferior races unworthy of survival"'.[6] The major historian Arnold Toynbee ultimately moved in the same direction, drawing attention to the fact that Fascism and Nazism involved countries which were 'members' of the 'family' of the West from birth.[7] The dark pages in its history had to be examined if one wanted to understand the infamy that had culminated in Auschwitz.

Now, by contrast, everything has changed: the horror of Hitler's regime is but an adversarial replica of the horror of Communism, which is the veritable original sin of the twentieth century. In addition to the dictates of historical rigour, this new assessment claims to be dictated by the agonizing moral exigency of rescuing from oblivion the innumerable, long forgotten victims of the sanguinary experience that began with the Bolshevik Revolution. However, the Nazism-Communism equation leads to the disappearance of colonialism, which for very different authors was previously the privileged reference-point for understanding the Third Reich. Perhaps, contrary to appearances, one calculus of horrors replacing another without further ado is not so immediately self-evident; perhaps it does not render arguments or questions superfluous.

---

4   Frantz Fanon, *The Wretched of the Earth*, trans. Constance Farrington, London: Penguin, 1990, pp. 62, 71 n., 80.

5   Arendt, *Essays und Kommentare*, Vol. II, p. 193.

6   Hannah Arendt, 'Organized Guilt and Universal Responsibility', *Jewish Frontier*, January 1945, p. 23.

7   Arnold Toynbee, *The World and the West*, New York: Oxford University Press, 1953, p. 29.

Can we find an explicit theorization of genocide in the annals of history? In 1883, the year Marx died, Gumplowicz counter-posed the reality of the 'race struggle' to Marx's thesis of the 'class struggle', which was adjudged ideological. So implacable was this reality that it sometimes permitted of no escape. In specific conditions, it became 'naturally necessary' for members of a different ethnic group to be de-humanized and destroyed. This had happened to the 'natives of America', the Hottentots of South Africa, and the 'natives of Australia', swept away by a 'war of annihilation'.[8] Across the Atlantic, Theodore Roosevelt remarked that 'the hard, energetic practical men' charged with terminating barbarism and extending civilization must not allow themselves to be 'prone to false sentimentality'.[9] For his part, the American statesman was utterly immune to any such attitude. On the contrary, he seemed almost amused by the spectacle of the 'redskins' being wiped off the face of the earth: were there really any 'good Indians' apart from 'dead ones' (or slaughtered ones)? (Chapter 5, §5)

In fact, genocide was not only theorized. Between 1904 and 1907, the Herero rebelled in Africa against imperial Germany. The repression was pitiless: 'Any Herero found within German borders [of the colonies subjugated by the Second Reich], with or without a carbine, with or without livestock, will be shot. I shall no longer accept women or children: I shall send them back to their people, or give orders to open fire on them. Such is my decision about the Herero people.' The motivation for this decision is significant. General von Trotha explained that 'the nation as such must be destroyed', because it could no longer be utilized even as 'raw material'.[10]

It would be foolish and misleading to seek to impute all this to an imaginary eternal Germany. The logic followed by the German general had been clarified some years earlier by Hobson, the anti-imperialist liberal appreciated by Lenin. Hobson observed that colonialism entailed 'forced labour' for the natives and the decimation and destruction of peoples who could not be subjected to, or could not survive, it, as had occurred 'in the case of Australian Bushmen, African Bushmen and Hottentots, Red

---

8 Ludwig Gumplowicz, *Der Rassenkampf. Soziologische Untersuchungen*, Innsbruck: Wagner'sche Universitätsbuchhandlung, 1883, pp. 249, 250 n.

9 Quoted in Richard Hofstadter, *The American Political Tradition and the Men Who Made It*, New York: A. Knopf, 1967, p. 209.

10 See Horst Drechsler, *Südwestafrika unter deutscher Kolonialherrschaft*, Vol. I, *Der Kampf der Herero und Nama gegen den deutschen Imperialismus (1884–1915)*, Berlin: Akademie, 1966, pp. 184, 189.

Indians, and Maoris'. All these peoples had become a dead weight for the 'superior white settlers'.[11]

We need only add that a deadly struggle began to develop among the latter. The Boers, demanding the right to use the natives of southern Africa as 'work tools', and laying claim to the land and resources extorted from them, came into conflict with imperial Britain and in their turn were overpowered. They were imprisoned en bloc, regardless of age or sex, in what began to be called 'camps' or 'concentration camps'. One author reports that such a system had been employed by Spain, in an attempt to deal with the Cuban people's independence struggle.[12] (In fact, the USA had already used camps to repress the independence struggle of the Filipino people.) But it was the fate of the Boers (a colonizing people of European origin) that prompted indignation in much of Western public opinion, which denounced the horror of the *univers concentrationnaire*, the 'annihilation of the Boer race' and, above all, 'the unending death toll of children' and their 'holocaust'.[13]

By contrast, massacres of colonial populations elicited no particular response. In fact, in this instance, putting even 'women and children' to death was explicitly provided for and recommended. A warning from Theodore Roosevelt (which the Herero, unfortunately, were unable to read) dates from the late nineteenth century: 'if any black or yellow people should really menace the whites', or merely 'jeopardize white control', the 'superior' race would be bound to wage a general 'war of extermination' and the 'clamor' of protests would soon be 'hushed' – and rightly so.[14]

All the great colonial powers of the time resorted to such practices. In the case of the USA, the campaign against the Native Americans afforded a model. And it was explicitly invoked and flaunted, as well as ruthlessly applied, when it came to restoring order (and colonial rule) in the Philippines.

---

11   J.A. Hobson, *Imperialism: A Study*, Ann Arbor: University of Michigan Press, 1983, pp. 252–3.

12   See Stephen Koss, *The Pro-Boers: The Anatomy of an Antiwar Movement*, Chicago and London: University of Chicago Press, 1973, pp. 215–16, 222.

13   Ibid., pp. 263, 229.

14   Theodore Roosevelt, *The Letters*, ed. E.E. Morison, J.M. Blum and J.J. Buckley, Cambridge, MA: Harvard University Press, 1951–, Vol. I, p. 377.

The Laboratory of the Third Reich

This was a model constantly borne in mind by Hitler, who sought his Far West in the East and identified the 'natives' of Eastern Europe and the Soviet Union as 'Indians' to be stripped of their land, decimated and, in the name of the march of civilization, pushed ever farther back beyond the Urals. The survivors were permitted to work like black slaves in the service of the white, Aryan race.

Mussolini likewise admired the 'harsh and fascinating' 'great conquest' of the Far West, which could serve as a model for colonial expansion,[15] except that, rather than to Eastern Europe, Italian Fascism initially looked to Ethiopia for territory to colonize and 'natives' to decimate or enslave. Leafing through the speeches in which the Duce sought to justify and transfigure his aggression, it is as if we are rereading texts from earlier decades. At the Berlin Conference in 1884–5, on the eve of the annexation of the Congo, Leopold II of Belgium had declared: 'To open to civilisation the only part of our globe which it has not yet penetrated, to pierce the darkness which hangs over entire peoples, is, I dare say, a crusade worthy of this century of progress.'[16] Here is Mussolini on 30 December 1934: 'This problem has existed since 1885. Ethiopia is the last corner of Africa that does not have European masters.' And in two subsequent speeches, of 18 October 1935 and 6 May 1936, Mussolini referred to terminating 'age-old slavery' and a 'barbaric, slave-driving pseudo-state', ruled by the 'Negus of the slave-drivers'.[17] As in the Congo, so in Ethiopia, the civilizing crusade actually proved to be a war of extermination. Fascist troops employed mustard gas and poison gas on a massive scale, engaged in large-scale massacres of the civilian population, used concentration camps, and resorted to the destruction of intellectuals and all those who could help preserve a people's sense of identity. 'Abolitionist' rhetoric was belied by the reality of large-scale enslavement of the natives.

For Italian Fascism, the latter not only represented a reserve of servile manpower, but a reserve reproducing itself through hereditary transmission. Consequently, mixed sexual relations and marriages seemed insane and criminal. Quite apart from the 'abnormality of the physiological deed',

---

15   Quoted in Enzo Santarelli, ed., *Scritti politici di Benito Mussolini*, Milan: Feltrinelli, 1979, p. 282 (speech of 14 November 1933).

16   Quoted in Carl Schmitt, *Donoso Cortés in gesamteuropäischer Interpretation*, Köln: Greven, 1950, p. 190.

17   Quoted in Santarelli, ed., *Scritti politici di Benito Mussolini*, pp. 292–6.

declared the Minister for Italian Africa, Alessandro Lessona, 'coupling with inferior creatures' would end up causing 'social promiscuity . . . in which our best qualities as ruling stock would be obliterated'.[18] In turn, in a circular dated September 1938, the Minister of State Education, Dino Alfieri, drew attention to the need for 'defence of the race in the territories of the empire, preventing any miscegenation with the natives and hence the dreadful scourge of mongrelism'.[19] 'For the empire to be retained', urged the Duce personally, 'the natives must have a very clear, overwhelming conception of our superiority'. Bidding a final farewell to 'vacuous' words like 'human race',[20] racial hierarchy must be visible and incontestable to all; the ban on miscegenation and racial bastardization must be respected and segregation imposed.

This takes us back to the decades between the nineteenth and twentieth centuries in the United States and South Africa. The brutality theorized, and practised, against colonial populations also left its mark in the capitalist metropolises. Segregated, subjected to semi-servile labour relations, and often victims of lynching and violence by assault squads, blacks were assimilated to beasts in the South of the USA. As we know, their acts of rebellion against white supremacy even led to temptations of a 'war of extermination' (to adopt Theodore Roosevelt's terminology). It was here that a watchword emerged which was to enjoy tragic success in the twentieth century. An 'ultimate solution of the American negro question' was required, in the context of a 'final and complete solution' of the problem posed by peoples who resisted being subjugated and enslaved by white, Western colonizers.[21]

The fate meted out to Native Americans and blacks over centuries furnished Fascism and Nazism with a self-proclaimed model. The colonial tradition seems to have exercised a certain influence even on the fate of the Jews. They were doubly guilty in Hitler's view. They pursued a policy of miscegenation and bastardization of races different from the Semitic one and thus, along with the Bolsheviks, could all the more easily incite the revolt

---

18   Quoted in Angelo Del Boca, *La guerra d'Abissinia 1935–1941*, Milan: Feltrinelli, 1965, p. 208.

19   Lutz Klinkhammer, *Zwischen Bündnis und Besatzung. Das nationalsozialistische Deutschland und die Republik von Salò 1943 bis 1945*, Tübingen: M. Niemeyer, 1993, p. 603 n. 113.

20   Quoted in Santarelli, ed., *Scritti politici di Benito Mussolini*, pp. 306, 308 (intervention in the National Council of the National Fascist Party, 20 October 1938).

21   See Domenico Losurdo, *Liberalism: A Counter-History*, trans. Gregory Elliott, London and New York: Verso, 2011, Chapter 10, §4.

of inferior races. In order for there to be no escape from the regime of racial segregation, Mussolini stated, echoing Hitler, that the 'dignity' and purity of the dominant race must be asserted not only 'against Hamites, or Africans', but also against Semites – that is, Jews. There was no room for any form of 'pietism': 'the racial laws of the empire will be strictly obeyed and all those who sin against them will be expelled, punished, imprisoned'.[22] After the enactment of the anti-Semitic legislation, the parabola of the racist delirium culminated in the Republic of Salò. An appeal to youth to enrol 'so that the blacks in the service of England do not contaminate the sacred soil' of the fatherland[23] went together with delivering Jews to the Nazis and collaborating with the Third Reich in the 'final solution'. Initially, at any rate, the Nazi ringleaders proposed to establish a *Judenreservat*, a 'reservation for Jews',[24] similar to that to which the Native Americans were confined.

We have seen Alfred Rosenberg express his pleasure at the 'deportation' not only of the 'blacks', but also of the 'yellow men' (Chapter 1, §5). In the USA, the Exclusion Act directed against the Chinese, who were the target of legal forms of discrimination and sometimes the victims of pogroms, was still in full force. From the late nineteenth century, in different ways and to varying degrees of intensity, the myth of race tended to impact on all those who were alien to the pure stock of the whites. This was a general phenomenon, but it assumed particular prominence in a country where the social and racial questions were inter-linked, on account not only of the presence of blacks and Native Americans, but also of successive waves of immigration, if not from the colonial or semi-colonial world, then from zones regarded as alien to civilization or on its margins. These immigrants came to occupy the bottom rungs of the labour market. Often, they were frozen out of it and oscillated between unemployment and criminality. They were life's failures, who tended to reproduce themselves from one generation to the next and therefore constituted a 'race' harmful to society.

Deriving from Britain, where it was first theorized by Darwin's cousin Galton, a new 'science' – eugenics – arrived in the USA and enjoyed extraordinary success. From the late nineteenth century and into the early twentieth century, a movement developed that was intent on preventing procreation by elements prone to crime or parasitism. Between 1907 and 1915, thirteen

---

22   Quoted in Santarelli, ed., *Scritti politici di Benito Mussolini*, pp. 307–8.
23   Quoted in Claudio Pavone, *Une guerra civile. Saggio storico sulla moralità nella Resistenza*, Turin: Bollati Boringhieri, 1991, p. 81.
24   See Götz Aly, *'Endlösung'. Völkerverschiebung und der Mord an den europäischen Juden*, Frankfurt am Main: Fischer, 1995, p. 11.

US states enacted laws for compulsory sterilization, covering, according to Indiana's legislation (the first state to move in this direction), 'habitual delinquents, idiots, imbeciles and rapists'. There were those who proposed extending such legislation to 'vagabonds' (for the most part members of an 'inferior race').[25]

With the emergence of the anti-colonial revolution in the wake of the October Revolution, new anxieties arose or old ones increased. What was happening in the colonies and why were the savages rebelling? Who was inciting them, challenging the healthy, natural racial hierarchy? One thing was certain: a new, deadly danger must be recognized and 'The Menace of the Under Man' confronted. Such was the subtitle of a book published in New York in 1922, whose author was Lothrop Stoddard. He spelt out the significance of the term coined by him. It referred to 'all those melancholy waste-products which each living species excretes', the mass of 'inferior' elements, 'the unadaptable and the incapable', 'savages and barbarians', who were often full of resentment and hatred for 'superior' personalities, who had now proved themselves 'unconvertible' and ready to declare 'war on civilization'. Such was the terrible threat, at once social and ethnic, which absolutely must be averted 'if our civilization is to be saved from decline and our race from decay'. The book we are referring to was rapidly translated into German: *Under Man* became *Untermensch* (in the singular) and *Untermenschen* (in the plural).[26] This was a keyword of Nazi ideology and Rosenberg acknowledged the US author for having coined it.[27]

Let us take stock. The terminology that began to emerge and become established between the late nineteenth and early twentieth centuries is symptomatic. The main categories and keywords of Nazi ideology – those giving radical expression to its destructive charge against the universal concept of man and its genocidal drive, or which in any event afford a glimpse of the horror of the Third Reich – all go back, directly or indirectly, to the colonial tradition. *Konzentratsionlager* is a calque of 'concentration camps'; *Untermensch* is the literal translation of 'Under Man'; the *Endlösung* of the Jewish question recalls the 'ultimate solution' of the black question,

25   See Arthur E. Fink, *Causes of Crime: Biological Theories in the United States 1800–1915*, New York: Perpetua, 1962, pp. 188–210.

26   Lothrop Stoddard, *The Revolt Against Civilization: The Menace of the Under Man*, New York: Scribner, 1984, pp. 22–4, 86–7; *Der Kulturumsturz. Die Drohung des Untermenschen*, Munich: Lehmanns, 1925.

27   Arthur Rosenberg, *The Myth of the Twentieth Century: An Evaluation of the Spiritual-Intellectual Confrontations of Our Age*, Newport Beach, CA: Noontide Press, 1993, p. 126.

or the 'final and complete solution' of the problem of colonial peoples; the *Blutschande* (against which Nazism endlessly warned) brings to mind 'miscegenation' (a cause for horror in the USA of the white supremacy); behind *Rassenhygiene* is clearly 'eugenics'. As regards 'war of extermination', 'destruction of the race' and 'holocaust', comment is superfluous. If the terms in italics presided over Hitler's attempt to build a racial state in Germany and the German Empire, those in quotation marks date back to the British Empire and, above all, the American one, or the regime of white supremacy that raged against Native Americans and blacks in particular, but which did not spare immigrants variously suspected of being alien to the pure white race.[28]

There is no doubt that the laboratory of the Third Reich and of the horrors of the twentieth century was in full swing; and it went back to the colonial tradition, or the history of the treatment inflicted on the 'barbarians' in the colonies and the metropolises themselves by those who proclaimed themselves the exclusive representatives of Civilization.

Accordingly, when historical revisionism and *The Black Book of Communism* date the start of the history of genocide and horror from Communism, they engage in a colossal repression. Solemnly proclaimed, the moral commitment to give voice to unjustly forgotten victims turns into its opposite – a deadly silence that buries the Native Americans, the Herero, the colonial populations, the 'barbarians' for a second time. This is a silence fraught with consequences on a specifically historiographical level as well, because it makes it impossible to understand Nazism and Fascism.

Does the bombardment of statistics on the crimes of Communism at least help us to grasp the significance of the experience that began with October 1917?

The History of the West as the History of a 'Master Race Democracy'

Let us take a glance at the world so positively transfigured by the yearnings and mystifications of the dominant ideology – the world devastated by the Bolshevik Revolution. In the early twentieth century, no clouds appeared on the horizon to disturb the enchanted climate of the *belle époque*. In 1910, a

---

28   See Domenico Losurdo, *Il linguaggio dell'Impero. Lessico dell'ideologia americana*, Rome and Bari: Laterza, 2007, Chapter 3, §5.

funeral – that of Edward VII, King of England – was the occasion for a splendid procession, which saw kings, hereditary princes and dukes, united by ties
of kinship and common mourning, parade on horseback. Time seemed not
to have made the least dent in the power and prestige of the European aristocracy. Nine monarchs, all descendants of William the Silent, occupied the
stage; the representatives of France and the USA took more of a back seat.
The West presented itself as homogeneous in another respect as well.
Although conflicts were becoming visible, the great powers felt themselves
infinitely superior to the 'inferior races' and gloried in belonging to a family –
in fact, an extremely exclusive race. Defined and celebrated by a wide variety
of names (European, White, Nordic, Western, Aryan, etc.), it stood for
Civilization as such, a small, happy island in a boundless ocean of barbarism.
At the time, Czarist Russia, whose civilizing role in Asia was acknowledged
by Theodore Roosevelt, also belonged to this family.

Having been crowned king in London, Edward VII's successor, George V,
participated in a ceremony in India the following year that elevated him to
the status of emperor. Among those paying tribute to him were Indian princes
and maharajahs who acted as pages, sumptuously attired but submissive and
docile.[29] Corresponding to this splendid ceremony and similar ones, with
which the conquerors sought to impress on the 'natives' an image of their
infinite superiority, was the reality of a rule which, as we know, did not
shrink from the most terrible forms of oppression and violence.

The history of the West confronts us with a paradox, which becomes
intelligible if we start with the history of its leading country today. Democracy
within the white community developed *pari passu* with the enslavement of
blacks and the deportation (and decimation) of Native Americans. For thir-
ty-two of the first thirty-six years of the USA's existence, the presidential
incumbents were slave-owners, as were the men who drafted the Declaration
of Independence and the Constitution. In the absence of slavery (and the
subsequent racial segregation), we shall understand nothing of 'American
liberty'. They developed together, the one sustaining the other. While the
'peculiar institution' ensured iron control of the 'dangerous' classes at the
point of production, the shifting frontier and progressive expansion to the
West defused social conflict, transforming a potential proletariat into a class
of landowners at the expense of populations condemned to be repressed or
swept away.

---

29   See Arno J. Mayer, *The Persistence of the Old Regime: Europe to the Great War*, London:
Verso, 2010, p. 139.

After the baptism of the War of Independence, American democracy underwent further development in the 1830s with the Jackson Presidency. The abolition, in large part, of censitary discrimination within the white community was accompanied by a strong impetus to the deportation of Indians and the rise of a climate of resentment and violence against blacks. A similar observation can be made about the so-called 'progressive era', from the 1890s to the 1910s. It was unquestionably characterized by numerous democratic reforms (direct election of the Senate, the secret vote, the introduction of primaries and referendums, etc.). At the same time, however, it was a particularly tragic period for blacks (target of the squaddist terror of the Ku Klux Klan) and Native Americans (stripped of their residual land and subjected to a process of remorseless homogenization that sought to deprive them even of their cultural identity).

In connection with this paradox in the history of their country, US scholars have spoken of a '*Herrenvolk* democracy' – that is, a democracy that applies exclusively to the 'master race' (to use the language beloved of Hitler). The clear line of demarcation between whites, on the one hand, and blacks and Native Americans, on the other, was conducive to the development of relations of relative equality within the white community. The members of an aristocracy of class or colour tended to celebrate themselves as 'peers'. The manifest inequality imposed on the excluded was the converse of the relationship of parity established between those with the power to exclude 'inferiors'.

The category of '*Herrenvolk* democracy' is also of use in explaining the history of the West in general. From the late nineteenth century to the early twentieth, the extension of the suffrage in Europe went hand-in-hand with the process of colonization and the imposition of servile or semi-servile labour relations on subjugated peoples. The rule of law in the metropolis was bound up with police violence and bureaucratic arbitrariness and with states of emergency in the colonies. In the final analysis, these are the same phenomena as occurred in the history of the USA, except that in the case of Europe they proved less obvious because the colonial populations, rather than residing in the metropolis, were separated from it by an ocean.

Lenin's Turn

It is very difficult to find a critique of such '*Herrenvolk* democracy' in liberal thought, which instead is often a theoretical expression of that regime. Thus, in a text devoted in its very title to liberty, we find a theorization of the 'absolute obedience' required of 'races' that are still in their 'nonage': 'Despotism is a legitimate form of government in dealing with barbarians.'[30] The author of these sentiments in the second half of the nineteenth century was John Stuart Mill, who on another occasion blended considerations on the excellence of representative government (which he saw embodied primarily in the Anglo-Saxons) with depiction of 'the great majority of the human race' as still 'in a savage or semi-savage state', and of some colonial peoples as barely above the level of higher animal species.[31]

The main target of Lenin's struggle was precisely *Herrenvolk* democracy based on 'the enslavement of hundreds of millions of working people in Asia, in the colonies in general, and in the small countries' by 'a few chosen nations'.[32] The Russian revolutionary leader meticulously highlighted the major clauses of exclusion from liberal freedom applying to '"coloured races"', as well as immigrants 'from the more backward countries'.[33] As in a game of mirrors, the West that gloried in the rule of law was faced with the truth of the colonies: 'The most Liberal and Radical personalities of free Britain . . . become regular Genghis Khans when appointed to govern India.'[34]

Well might Giolitti's Italy pride itself on extending citizenship to virtually the whole male population. But once again liberal self-celebration was answered by Lenin's counter-melody. He noted how extension of the suffrage aimed to enlarge the social base of support for the expedition to Libya, that 'typical colonial war, waged by a "civilised" twentieth-century nation'. Here we have 'a civilised, constitutional nation' performing its work of 'civilisation' 'by bayonet, bullet, noose, fire and rape', even by 'carnage'. It is a 'perfected, civilised blood-bath, the massacre of Arabs with the help of the "latest" weapons . . . By way of "retaliation", about 3,000 Arabs were butchered,

---

30   John Stuart Mill, 'On Liberty', in Mill, *Utilitarianism, Liberty, Representative Government*, ed. H.B. Acton, London: Dent, 1972, p. 73.

31   John Stuart Mill, 'Considerations on Representative Government', in Mill, *Utilitarianism, Liberty, Representative Government*, pp. 215, 197.

32   V.I. Lenin, *Collected Works*, London: Lawrence & Wishart, 1960–, Vol. 26, p. 424.

33   Ibid., Vol. 22, pp. 281–2.

34   Ibid., Vol. 15, p. 184.

whole families were plundered and done to death, with women and children massacred in cold blood.'[35]

Mill could celebrate the British Empire as a step towards 'universal peace, and general friendly co-operation among nations'.[36] However, even if we overlook the conflict between the great powers that subsequently issued in the First World War, this celebration involves a monstrous repression: the great powers' expeditions to the colonies are not regarded as wars. We are dealing with wars in which 'few Europeans died . . . whereas hundreds of thousands of people belonging to the nations they were subjugating died in them'. And so, continues Lenin in stinging fashion, 'can you call them wars? Strictly speaking, they were not wars at all, and you could forget about them.' The victims were not even granted the honours of war. Colonial wars were not deemed such because their victims were barbarians, who 'could not be regarded as nations at all (you couldn't very well call those Asians and Africans nations!)',[37] and who were ultimately excluded from the human community itself.

These were the grounds for the rupture with social-democracy. What caused it was not the reform/revolution dichotomy. That is a formulaic representation, which becomes no more credible for having been so frequently shared, albeit with opposite value judgements, by both sides to the dispute. In the decades preceding the outbreak of the First World War, Bernstein saluted imperial Germany's expansionism as a contribution to the cause of progress, civilization and world trade: 'If socialists prematurely proposed to aid savages and barbarians in their struggle against impending capitalist civilization, it would be a reflux of romanticism.'[38] Along with the West in general, Bernstein, like Theodore Roosevelt on the other side, granted Czarist Russia the role of 'guardian and dominant power' in Asia.[39]

The idea of mission sometimes seems to cede to that of living space. In fact, the German social-democratic leader verged on Social Darwinism. The representatives of the cause of 'progress' were the 'strong races', which inevitably 'tend to grow and expand with their civilization',[40] whereas a

35   Ibid., Vol. 18, pp. 337–8.

36   Mill, 'Considerations on Representative Government', p. 380.

37   Lenin, Collected Works, Vol. 24, p. 406.

38   Edouard Bernstein, 'Die deutsche Sozialdemokratie und die türkischen Wirren', Die Neue Zeit, 1896–7, p. 110.

39   Edouard Bernstein, 'Sozialdemokratie und Imperialismus', Sozialistische Monatshefte, 1900, p. 239.

40   Edouard Bernstein, 'Der Sozialismus und die Kolonialfrage', Sozialistische Monatshefte, 1900, p. 552.

vain, retrograde resistance was mounted by peoples who were uncivilized and even 'incapable of civilizing themselves'. When they 'rebelled against civilization', they must also be opposed by the working-class movement.[41] While he struggled for democratic reforms in Germany, Bernstein demanded an iron fist against barbarians. Such is the logic of '*Herrenvolk* democracy', which we have already analysed.

The subjugation of colonial peoples must not be hindered by sentimental scruples or abstract legal considerations. The strong, civilized races could not make themselves 'slaves of formal legality'. The social-democratic leader who subsequently expressed his horror at disrespect for the rules of the game in the October Revolution theorized a higher substantive legality, on the basis of the philosophy of history dear to the colonial tradition.

The October Revolution effected a radical turn vis-à-vis an ideological and political tradition in which colonial arrogance and racial prejudice were a self-evident, undisputed fact. In these conditions, appeals for a liberation struggle addressed to the slaves of the colonies, and to the 'barbarians' present in the capitalist metropolis itself, was bound to seem a deadly threat to the white race, the West, and civilization as such. Bolshevism was perceived by much of the European and US press as a sworn enemy not of democracy per se, but of *Herrenvolk* democracy and, above all, of the global white supremacy on which the latter rested. Communists were branded and treated as renegades from the white race. An eminent member of the exclusive club of civilized peoples and the West when ruled by the Czarist autocracy and *ancien régime*, Russia became barbaric following the October Revolution and (in Spengler's words) revealed itself to be 'Asiatic', a member of the colonial world and 'populations of colour' (Chapter 2, §8).

We can now understand what happened in the South of the USA. Even after Franklin Delano Roosevelt became president, the policy of segregation and lynching of blacks continued its ravages. Communists struggled against it and were branded as 'foreigners' and 'nigger lovers' by the dominant ideology. An American historian describes the courage they were forced to display: 'Their challenge to racism and to the status quo prompted a wave of repression one might think inconceivable in a democratic country.' To be a Communist (and challenge white supremacy) meant 'fac[ing] the possibility of imprisonment, beatings, kidnapping, and even death'.[42]

---

41 Bernstein, 'Die deutsche Sozialdemokratie und die türkischen Wirren', p. 109.

42 Robin D.G. Kelley, *Hammer and Hoe: Alabama Communists during the Great Repression*, Chapel Hill and London: University of North Carolina Press, 1990, pp. xii–xiii.

That the October Revolution and the Communist movement had a racial, rather than a political, origin was likewise the opinion of Henry Ford. For him, the authors of this barbaric upheaval were not the colonial peoples and Asians strictly speaking, but primarily the Jews, who were themselves to be regarded as alien to the West and Civilization on account of their Oriental origins. The myth of the 'Judeo-Bolshevik conspiracy' enjoyed particular success in Germany and solemnized its bloody splendours after Hitler's arrival in power. The Jewish philologist Victor Klemperer described the insults and humiliations involved in wearing the Star of David in harrowing terms. However,

> a removal man who is friendly towards me following two moves . . . is suddenly standing in front of me in the Freiberger Strasse, takes my hand in both of his paws and whispers in a tone which must be audible on the other side of the road: 'Well, Herr Professor, don't let it get you down! These wretched brothers of ours will soon have reached rock bottom!'

Klemperer comments with affectionate irony that those who thus challenged the regime at a time when the racist contagion seemed irresistible were 'good people with more than a whiff of the KPD [German Communists]'![43]

Branded as a direct or mediated expression of the barbarism of races that were inferior or extraneous to civilization, the Communist movement performed an extraordinary pedagogical role, as well as a political one, and not only in the colonies, but also in the advanced capitalist countries. A historiography that ignores all this ends up taking the form of a tool for ideologically transfiguring *Herrenvolk* democracy.

The October Revolution, the Liquidation of the Ancien Régime, and the Advent of the Social State

But let us now turn from the colonies, and the lot of 'races' deemed to be in their 'nonage', and focus our attention on the capitalist metropolis – in fact, exclusively on its 'civilized' population. The splendid ceremonies we have alluded to are but one index of the extraordinary vitality of the

---

43   Victor Klemperer, *The Language of the Third Reich: LTI, Lingua Tertii Imperii – A Philologist's Notebook*, trans. Martin Brady, New Brunswick, NJ, and London: Athlone Press, 2000, p. 156.

aristocracy and the *ancien régime*. Lenin highlighted the fact that, within the imperialist metropolis itself, exclusion clauses from citizenship and democracy remained in force. In Britain, the electoral law 'is still "sufficiently restricted to exclude the lower stratum proletariat proper"'.[44] Furthermore, we might add, some privileged people continued to enjoy a 'plural vote', which was only finally abolished in 1948.[45] The process leading to realization of the principle 'one person, one vote' in the classical country of the liberal tradition was particularly tortuous. And it cannot be envisaged without the challenge represented by the revolution in Russia and the development of the Communist movement.

Even where male suffrage had become universal or well-nigh universal, it was neutralized by the existence of an upper chamber that was the preserve of the nobility and privileged classes. In the Italian Senate, the princes of the House of Savoy sat as of right. The remaining members were nominated for life by the king, on the recommendation of the president of the council. Similar considerations apply to the other European upper chambers which, with the exception of the French, were not elected, but characterized by an admixture of heredity and royal nomination. Even in the case of the Senate in the French Third Republic, which had behind it an uninterrupted series of revolutionary upheavals culminating in the Commune, it should be noted that it derived from an indirect election and was so composed as to guarantee marked over-representation of the countryside (and politico-social conservatism) at the expense of Paris and large towns and cities. Once again, the situation in Britain is of particular interest. In addition to the Upper House (entirely hereditary, with the exception of a few bishops and judges), the landed aristocracy had control of public affairs: a situation not very different from that obtaining in Germany and Austria.

In the USA, the *ancien régime* presented itself in a highly peculiar form. The residues of censitary discrimination were not of much significance. More important was the fact that the aristocracy of class was configured here as an aristocracy of race. In the South of the country, power was in the hands of those who not by chance were branded Bourbons by their opponents. The roots of a regime sometimes celebrated by its supporters, and sometimes criticized by contemporary scholars, as a caste regime, in as much as it was

---

44   Lenin, *Collected Works*, Vol. 22, p. 282.
45   See Domenico Losurdo, *Democrazia o bonapartismo*, Turin: Bollati Boringhieri, 1993, Chapter 1, §12.

based on ethnic-social groups rendered impervious by the ban on miscegenation, were very strong.

The largest exclusion clause affected women. In Britain, the Pankhursts
(mother and daughter), who led the suffragette movement, were periodically
obliged to visit their country's prisons. The situation was not very different in
the other major Western countries. Denounced by Lenin (and the Bolshevik
Party), the 'exclusion of women' from political rights was ended in Russia after
the February Revolution, which was greeted as a 'proletarian revolution' (because
of the influence of the soviets and popular masses) by Gramsci, who warmly
stressed that it 'has destroyed authoritarianism and replaced it by universal
suffrage, extending the vote to women too'.[46] The same road was then taken by
the Weimar Republic (deriving from the revolution that broke out in Germany
a year after the October Revolution), and only subsequently in the USA.

Social and economic rights also form part of democracy as generally
understood today. And it is precisely the great patriarch of neo-liberalism,
Hayek, who denounces the fact that their theorization and presence in the
West date back to the lethal influence of the 'Russian Marxist revolution'
(Chapter 1, §2). Naturally, the subaltern classes did not wait until 1917 before
demanding recognition of such rights. Their conquest went through the same
stages as the triumph of universal suffrage. Robespierre, who denounced
censitary discrimination in the suffrage as an echo of ancient slavery, solemnized the 'right to life' as the first of the 'imprescriptible rights of man'.[47]
The 1848 revolution, which sanctioned the triumph of universal male suffrage,
also witnessed the emergence of demands for the right to work: this was the
start of the second stage, whose protagonist was the socialist movement. In
Germany, where the latter was especially strong, Bismarck sought to prevent
a revolution from below by means of a revolution from above, which introduced the first vague elements of social security. Finally, the third stage,
starting with the upheavals in Russia, has extended virtually down to the
present. During the Second World War, in a famous speech on the 'four
freedoms', Roosevelt declared that to destroy 'the seeds of Hitlerism' it was
necessary to achieve 'freedom from want', therewith impacting radically on
existing socio-economic relations. The US president's watchwords seem to
delineate a project of social-democracy which, as Kissinger correctly observes,

---

46   Antonio Gramsci, *Selections from Political Writings 1910–1920*, ed. Quintin Hoare and
trans. John Mathews, London: Lawrence & Wishart, 1977, p. 29.

47   Maximilien Robespierre, *Oeuvres*, Paris: Presses Universitaires de France, 1912–, Vol.
VII, pp. 167–8 and Vol. IX, p. 112.

went 'far beyond' the prior American political tradition[48] – in fact, maintains Hayek, went back to the infamous Bolshevik Revolution.

Each stage in this process was marked by extremely bitter struggles. Here it is appropriate only to mention the years preceding the Bolshevik Revolution. In Milan in 1898, General Bava Beccaris had a crowd protesting at an increase in bread prices fired on by cannons, killing 100 unarmed demonstrators and earning him high honours (awarded by Umberto I) in the process. In the USA, Theodore Roosevelt declared himself ready for a similar trial of strength. Order 'will be kept at whatever cost. If it comes to shooting we shall shoot to hit. No blank cartridges or firing over the head of anybody'; 'I like to see a mob handled by the regulars, or by good State-Guards, not over-scrupulous about bloodshed'; 'The sentiment now animating a large proportion of our people can only be suppressed as the Commune in Paris was suppressed, by taking ten or a dozen of their leaders out, standing them against a wall, and shooting them dead. I believe it will come to that.'[49]

The three stages in the conquest of universal suffrage (involving the radical and Jacobin phase of the French Revolution, the development of the socialist movement, and the October Revolution) coincided with the stages of demands for, and the construction of, the social state – and this for a very simple reason. At bottom, it was a single process, which saw the subaltern classes demand recognition of their full human dignity. If denial of the latter primarily affected colonial populations, it did not spare the wretches of the capitalist metropolis. It was a stance that the liberal tradition only succeeded in surmounting with difficulty. For Mandeville, the wage-labourer brought to mind a 'horse' whom it was absolutely inappropriate to teach to read and write ('should a Horse know as much as a Man, I should not desire to be his Rider') and was equated by Burke and Sieyès with an *instrumentum vocale* or 'human work tool', a 'bipedal machine' (thus were adopted categories employed in classical antiquity to define slaves).[50]

We can now appreciate why, focusing on the excluded in both the colonies and the capitalist metropolis, Gramsci regarded Communism as 'integral humanism', or a completion of the process of constructing the unity of the human race.[51]

---

48   Henry Kissinger, *Diplomacy*, Simon & Schuster, New York: 1994, pp. 389–90.
49   Quoted in Hofstadter, *The American Political Tradition*, pp. 215–17.
50   See Losurdo, *Liberalism*, Chapter 3, §10 and Chapter 6, §2.
51   Antonio Gramsci, *L'Ordine Nuovo 1919–1920*, ed. Valentino Gerratana and Antonio A. Santucci, Turin: Einaudi, 1987, p. 41.

Contemporary Democracy as the Overcoming of
the Three Major Forms of Discrimination

Demonization of the historical experience that began with the Bolshevik Revolution prevents us from understanding contemporary democracy. The latter is based on the principle that every individual is to be regarded as the bearer of inalienable rights, regardless of race, property and sex, and hence presupposes overcoming the three major forms of discrimination (racial, censitary, sexual) that were still alive and well on the eve of October 1917. Perhaps what Edgar Quinet affirmed of the French Revolution in his time also applies to the Bolshevik Revolution: 'The people who made it are not the people who derived most benefit from it.'[52]

It makes no sense to seek to place Communism on a par with Nazism – the force that most consistently and brutally opposed overcoming racial discrimination and hence the advent of democracy. Whereas the Third Reich represented an attempt in conditions of total war to realize a planetary regime of white supremacy under German hegemony, the Communist movement made a decisive contribution to overcoming racial discrimination and colonialism, whose legacy Nazism sought to inherit and radicalize. To seek to liquidate the epoch that began with the October Revolution as a period of crisis for democracy entails reverting to regarding colonial peoples (as well as other victims of the liberal tradition's exclusion clauses) as a *quantité négligeable*; it means re-colonizing history.

The pages in which Gramsci criticized 'white supermen'[53] and the 'reactionary attitudes' of 'defenders of the West', and ironized about the fact that even for a prestigious philosopher like Henri Bergson '"humanity" actually signifies West',[54] could – and should – form part of any text of civic education and education in democracy. A similar honour might be accorded to the pages we have already cited in which Lenin draws attention to the sanguinary arrogance of the 'chosen nations' towards 'red and black skins'. Undoubtedly, other pages by the Russian revolutionary leader are repulsive. But this is also true of authors habitually elevated into the empyrean of the classics of liberal democracy. No one would wish to include in a textbook of civic education the pages where Locke regards slavery in the colonies as self-evident or where

---

52   Edgar Quinet, *Le Christianisme et la Révolution française*, Paris: Fayard, 1984, p. 249.

53   Gramsci, *L'Ordine Nuovo*, p. 142.

54   Antonio Gramsci, *Quaderni del carcere*, ed. Valentino Gerratana, Turin: Einaudi, 1975, pp. 837, 2013, 567.

he invites readers to feel no 'compassion' for the Irish 'papists', who at the time were the target of ferocious persecution and a veritable policy of colonial extermination. And no one would wish to include the pages in which Jefferson theorizes the natural inferiority of blacks, or those in which Mill demands 'absolute obedience' of 'races' deemed to be in their 'nonage' (or semi-animal), or where he celebrates the Opium War as a crusade for liberty.

It remains the case that the October Revolution did not achieve the objectives pursued or proclaimed by it. One thinks of Lenin and the leaders of the Communist International who saw the world soviet republic already emerging, with the ultimate disappearance of classes, states, nations, the market and religion. Not only did Communism never come close to achieving this objective; it never succeeded in advancing towards it. Are we therefore dealing with a self-evident outright failure? In reality, the discrepancy between programmes and results is typical of every revolution. The French Jacobins did not realize or restore the ancient polis; the American revolutionaries did not create the society of small farmers and producers without a polarization between wealth and poverty, without a standing army and without a strong central power; the English revolutionaries did not revive the Biblical society mythically transfigured by them. The experience of Christopher Columbus, who set out in search of the Indies but discovered America, might serve as a metaphor for understanding the objective dialectic of revolutionary processes. It was precisely Marx and Engels who underscored this point. In analysing the French or English revolutions, they do not start with the subjective consciousness of their *dramatis personae*, or the ideologues who called and prepared the way for them, but with an examination of the objective contradictions that provoked them and the real characteristics of the politico-social continent exposed or revealed by the ensuing upheavals. The two theoreticians of historical materialism thus highlighted the discrepancy between subjective project and objective result, and ultimately explained the reasons for the creation – the inevitable creation – of such a discrepancy. Why should we proceed any differently when it comes to the October Revolution?

It is worth recalling an indication by Engels, who, when assessing the English and French revolutions, observed: 'In order to secure even those conquests of the bourgeoisie that were ripe for gathering at the time, the revolution had to be carried considerably further . . . This seems, in fact, to be one of the laws of evolution of bourgeois society.'[55] There are no grounds

---

55   Karl Marx and Frederick Engels, *Selected Works*, Vol. 3, Moscow: Progress Publishers, 1977, p. 105.

for exempting the revolution inspired by Marx and Engels from the materialist methodology developed by them. Such is the context in which we must situate expectations of the withering away of the state, religion, the market, and any form of division of labour. This utopia, in which hopes of destroying the roots of the horrors on display in the First World War found exalted expression, has not withstood the test of reality. But in the absence of the historical movement inspired by it, we shall understand nothing of contemporary democracy.

Future history will clarify whether this outcome exhausts the new politico-social continent in its entirety, or whether it constitutes but an initial, partial configuration of it. The fragile equilibrium on which contemporary democracy is based favours the latter hypothesis. Far from being affirmed without the contribution of the Communist movement, we may now ask if democracy will withstand the disappearance of its challenge. Although pure and simple restorations are unknown in history, we should note not only the dismantling of the social state, but also and above all the explicit deletion (in neo-liberalism) of economic and social rights from the catalogue of human rights. For Hayek, the three stages of demands for the social state (and universal suffrage) are the three stages of the advent of '"social" or totalitarian democracy'.[56]

Even more disturbing is the tendency of historians like Paul Johnson and Niall Ferguson, who have enjoyed great media success, to justify – in fact, transfigure – colonialism and even imperialism and make claims for its enduring validity. They are not isolated figures. Among the undisputed *maîtres à penser* of neo-liberalism and the dominant ideology is Ludwig von Mises. This is an author who in 1922 uncritically transfigured the history of colonialism. Even when they embarked on the Opium War, the West and Britain were doing nothing but pursuing their glorious 'vocation to elevate backward people to a state of civilization'. But Mises does not stop there. He expresses the opinion that, along with the 'anti-social' elements of every type resident in the West, the 'savage tribes' of the colonies should be treated as 'dangerous animal[s]'. This is a rather sinister declaration, which sounds like an indirect justification of the destruction of whole peoples denied their human dignity[57] – as in the golden age of colonialism and 'democracy' for the exclusive benefit of the master race.

---

56   F.A. Hayek, *The Constitution of Liberty*, ed. Ronald Hamowy, Chicago and London: University of Chicago Press, 2011, p. 109. Cf. Losurdo, *Democrazia o bonapartismo*, Chapter 7, §5.

57   Ludwig von Mises, *Socialism: An Economic and Sociological Analysis*, trans. J. Kahane, Indianapolis: Liberty Fund, 1981, pp. 207, 284.

The Second Thirty Years' War, Total War and Totalitarianism

If we do not appreciate its compound of horror and emancipation, we are ill-placed to understand anything of the twentieth century, and the dreadful pages of Communism likewise prove incomprehensible in abstraction from the terrible pages of the history behind it. We left the splendid family of the *ancien régime* and *belle époque* at the ceremonies in which it celebrated its power. The outbreak of war instantly created a gulf of mutual hatred and contempt between the crowned heads, even though they were variously bound by kinship ties. There is a detail that reveals the true brutality of the struggle. The various sovereigns and rulers had hitherto recognized one another as members of one family even racially. Now, for the Entente's ideologues the Germans became 'Huns' and 'Vandals', while Britain was branded as an 'Asiatic power' by Thomas Mann, and France — 'black France' — became a 'Euro-African' in Spengler's view.[58] This mutual excommunication was symptomatic: the brutality that had always been regarded as legitimate in the case of 'inferior races' now tended to irrupt in the West, in the course of a war against an enemy who was expelled from the civilized world proper. This is the context in which to situate Wilhelm II's interpretation of the war between the Second Reich and Czarist Russia as one between Slavs and Germans — a war that was 'racial' in kind and which consequently precluded any possibility of peace or compromise. Subsequently, following the October Revolution, the West as a whole was unanimous in including Soviet Russia among the savages of the colonial world, and Hitler felt legitimized and encouraged in constructing a continental German empire in a gigantic space mired in barbarism, while drawing the most drastic lessons from the colonial tradition and further radicalizing them.

Nineteen-fourteen was the beginning of what many historians characterize as the Second Thirty Years' War — a complex set of contradictions and conflicts of the most varied kinds which, having raged until 1945, were finally resolved only with the collapse of the USSR and the triumph of the 'American century'. During this massive crisis, independently of the Bolshevik Revolution and often prior to it, we witness the emergence of all those constitutive features of the totalitarian and concentration-camp universe that

---

58 Thomas Mann, *Betrachtungen eines Unpolitischen*, ed. H. Helbling, Frankfurt am Main: Fischer, 1988, p. 423; Oswald Spengler, 'Frankreich und Europa', in *Reden und Aufsätze*, ed. Hildegard Kornhardt, Munich: Beck, 1937, p. 88; and *The Hour of Decision*, trans. Charles Francis Atkinson, London: George Allen & Unwin, 1934, p. 229.

historical revisionism and *The Black Book* seek to deduce from the fateful October 1917.

A merciless struggle required iron discipline on both sides; the regimentation of society reached unprecedented levels. The principle of individual responsibility was abrogated. This is demonstrated, for example in Italy, by the practice of decimation, the punishment even of the guiltless relatives of deserters, or reprisals against the civilian population carried out by firing into crowds – a measure which the British government did not shrink from in its efforts to quash the Irish rebellion, from 1916 until the achievement of independence by part of the unfortunate island. Like the abrogation of the principle of individual responsibility, what are today regarded as other characteristic aspects of the totalitarian regime made their appearance during the First World War. Is the totalitarian state an all-devouring Moloch? We have seen Weber remarking in 1917 that 'the state is accorded "legitimate" power over life, death, and liberty' (Chapter 5, §2). And this also applies to countries with the oldest liberal traditions. In the USA, although safe on the other side of the Atlantic and sheltered from any danger of invasion, people could be sentenced to as much as twenty years in prison for having expressed an opinion liable to disturb the climate of sacred patriotic unity. Such patriotic unity was configured as a kind of single party: political, trade union or cultural organizations that challenged it were ruthlessly suppressed. A feature of the totalitarian phenomenon is the imposition of a strict state monopoly on information. This monopoly first appeared, and proved brilliantly effective, in the North American republic. Seven days after declaring war, Wilson established a Committee on Public Information that even regimented high culture. Another characteristic of the totalitarian regime is an admixture of control and violence by the state with control and violence from below, perpetrated by political organizations or militarized sectors of civil society. During the First World War, a very prominent role was played in the USA by vigilante groups unearthing, attacking and terrorizing possible or potential 'traitors'. Finally, according to Arendt, totalitarianism is not content to impose a passive consensus, but demands an active consensus and active participation in a unanimous national effort. As a student of the propaganda techniques employed during the war observes, the belligerent countries' objective, which was most effectively achieved in the United States, was 'to fuse the waywardness of individuals in the furnace of the war dance', 'to fuse thousands and millions of human beings into one amalgamated mass of hate and will and hope', as well as 'bellicose enthusiasm'.[59] Above all, the same slogans prevailed: 'total mobilization', 'total war', and even 'total politics'. This is where we must start to explain the genesis of the term and reality of 'totalism' (as it was initially dubbed), or totalitarianism proper.

The iron fist targeted entire ethnic groups, suspected of maintaining links with the enemy or harbouring sympathy for him. Hence resort to deportation. Among its victims were the Armenians, whom the Turkish government blamed for favouring collaboration with Christian and Czarist Russia, which in its turn deported Jews, who were suspected of looking to Wilhelmine and social-democratic Germany as a possible liberator from the yoke of anti-Semitism. The protagonist in the first chapter of the twentieth-century tragedy that ended in Auschwitz was a country allied with the liberal West and at war with Germany, which subsequently became the artisan of the 'final solution'. In turn, during the First World War, Germans suffered violence and persecution not only in Czarist Russia, but also in the USA. Sometimes they were marked out by a yellow symbol, and there were those who invoked the sterilization of a genetically tainted race.[60]

Along with the practice of deportation, concentration camps emerged. The institution regarded as typifying the totalitarian regime was also set up in countries with the most stable liberal traditions. Immediately after the October Revolution, in the USA, McKellar, a Tennessee senator, proposed establishing a penal colony for political detainees on the island of Guam. The *univers concentrationnaire* became a reality during the Second World War, when Roosevelt had American citizens of Japanese origin (including women and children) deported to concentration camps, even rounding them up from Latin America. In 1950, the McCarran Act was passed, 'set[ting] up six concentration camps across the country to hold political prisoners'. Among its promoters were representatives who subsequently became famous as presidents of the United States: Kennedy, Johnson and Nixon.[61]

The diffusion in the most diverse countries of institutions and features typical of totalitarianism clarifies a crucial point: rather than in a particular ideology, its genesis is to be sought in war. We may venture a definition: totalitarianism is the political regime corresponding to total war – war that tends towards total control of the conduct and ideas not only of the

59   Harold D. Lassell, *Propaganda Technique in the First World War*, Cambridge, MA: MIT Press, 1927, p. 221.

60   See Chapter 5, §2 and Losurdo, *Democrazia o bonapartismo*, Chapter 5, §2.

61   See Peter N. Carroll and David W. Noble, *The Free and the Unfree: A New History of the United States*, New York: Viking Press, 1988, pp. 331, 358.

combatant population (the quasi-totality of adult males), but also of the civilian population in the rear (itself an integral part of total mobilization in terms of production and ideology) and of civil society as such. It goes without saying that this new political regime assumes very different forms depending on the respective geopolitical situations, political traditions and ideologies.

As a result of its intimate connection with total war, totalitarianism received its first critical analysis from within the anti-war movement. As we know, it was above all Bukharin who warned against 'the new Leviathan, compared with which Thomas Hobbes' fantasy seems child's play'. The Russian revolutionary drew a precise, impressive picture of the super-Leviathan that also materialized in the state of which he was to become a leader and, subsequently, a victim.

Russia and Germany as the Epicentre of the Second Thirty Years' War

Totalitarianism culminated in the two countries at the centre of the Second Thirty Years' War. In this regard, a comparison between Bolshevism and Nazism is not merely appropriate, but mandatory. This does not mean sharing the approach of historians who describe the lives of Stalin and Hitler as parallel, as if everything could be explained by two power-crazy, utterly unscrupulous personalities. Instead, it involves analysing the answers ventured by two different, antagonistic movements to the challenges represented by two objective situations that were not without their similarities.

Let us focus first on Soviet Russia, obliged to confront a permanent state of emergency. If we examine the period from October 1917 to 1953 (the year of Stalin's death), we see that it was marked by at least four or five wars and two revolutions (both of them followed by civil wars). In the West, the aggression of Wilhelm II's Germany (until the Brest-Litovsk peace) was followed by that first of the Entente and then of Hitlerite Germany. Finally, we have the Cold War, punctuated by bloody local conflicts, which threatened at any moment to turn into a hot war of major proportions, involving the use of atomic weapons. In the East, with its invasion of Manchuria we find Japan (which only withdrew from Siberia in 1922 and Sakhalin in 1925) engaged in a menacing military deployment on the borders of the USSR, which was involved in large-scale border clashes in 1938 and 1939, prior to the official start of the Second World War. Moreover, the aforementioned were total wars, both because they did not proceed from a declaration of war (both the Entente and the Third Reich abstained from one), and because they were bound up with civil war and the invaders' stated intention of overthrowing the existing regime. Hitler's campaign explicitly aimed at the extermination of the Oriental *Untermenschen*.

To these wars must be added internal upheavals and civil wars. That is, in addition to October 1917, we must bear in mind the revolution from above that was the forced collectivization and industrialization of the countryside from 1929 onwards. Revolution and war were closely connected, given that collectivization and industrialization were – or, at any rate, were considered – necessary if the USSR was to be capable of facing the dreaded new aggression, already clearly heralded by Hitler in *Mein Kampf*.

The key moment was the 'revolution' from above and without imposed by Stalin from Moscow on a countryside inhabited by national minorities traditionally branded as barbarians. The 'white man's burden' now assumed a peculiar form, with the Russian city exporting (socialist) civilization into the Asian countryside by force of arms. Ethnic conflict inter-meshed with political and social conflict. The conflict between poor or landless peasants and more or less affluent peasants already existed. But it was exacerbated, and rendered fanatical, by an ideological approach to the tragedy of starvation rampant in urban areas, responsibility for which was exclusively laid at the door of the money-grubbing kulak, a kind of vampire. The slightest opposition and resistance was ruthlessly repressed. Not only was the Gulag greatly expanded, but large-scale forced labour now became an element of economic and war planning. In an irony of history, having waved the banner of the slaves' revolt in the colonies, Soviet Russia ended up reproducing some features of the colonial tradition. But these should not be exaggerated. De-specification was invariably politico-moral, not racial. Forced labour was not a hereditary condition. We have seen the Soviet leadership stress that 'the son is not answerable for the father'. At the same time, precisely because people were sentenced to forced labour not on account of their ethnic affiliation, but for the purposes of political repression, this also afforded a narrow escape route for 'counter-revolutionaries'. This became clear after the outbreak of the war: detainees could be released from the Gulag and were even offered the possibility of social mobility and promotion (Chapter 5, §9).

Let us now take a look at the other country at the epicentre of the Second Thirty Years' War. Bled white and defeated on the battle field, shaken by the November 1918 revolution at the close of the First World War (which offered chauvinists a pretext for diffusing the myth of the 'stab in the back'), humiliated by the Versailles Treaty, Germany subsequently experienced a devastating economic crisis that further accentuated its internal divisions. Having arrived in power, Nazism launched a preventive civil war to liquidate any potential opposition to its revanchist programme and to make surrender on the internal front, which had occurred in 1918, impossible. Yet despite initial triumphs, the country once again became embroiled in a hopeless war on two fronts, attacked not only by regular armies, but also by the partisan resistance that sprang up in all the territories occupied by the Third Reich.

To equate the Soviet Union and Hitler's Germany as quintessential expressions of totalitarianism is, in one respect, a banality. Where should we expect to find the basic characteristics of the political regime corresponding to total war, if not in the two countries at the centre of the Second Thirty Years' War? It is no surprise if the *univers concentrationnaire* assumed a markedly more brutal form there than, for example, in the USA, which was protected from the danger of invasion by the ocean and which, in the course of the massive war, suffered loses and devastation far inferior to those of the other main participants. Around a century and a half earlier, on the eve of the promulgation of the new federal constitution, we have seen Hamilton explaining that the limitation of power and establishment of the rule of law had succeeded in two countries of an insular kind, which were sheltered by the seas from the threats of rival powers. It is worth noting that during the Second Thirty Years' War all the countries of mainland Europe, located as they were in the epicentre (or immediate vicinity of the epicentre) of the great historical crisis, experienced the collapse of representative, liberal institutions at different times and in different ways. To a certain extent, totalitarianism also emerged in the USA when involved in two world wars. In the twentieth century, an insular position was no longer a completely insurmountable obstacle. But the degree of brutality displayed by the totalitarian regime continued to be bound up with different geopolitical contexts, as well as different ideological and political traditions.

Naturally, the permanent state of emergency was not only an objective fact. In Nazism it was also the result of a political programme which, in aspiring to world domination, ended up making the state of war permanent. Similar considerations apply to Communism. When it obsessively pursued the utopia of a society undefiled by contradictions or conflicts, it ended up generating a variety of permanent revolution and war (this is what occurred especially during the Chinese Cultural Revolution). From this standpoint too, the comparison is wholly legitimate.

In another respect, however, equation of the Soviet Union with Hitler's Germany is inane. In the former case, totalitarianism was the result of an admixture of total war (imposed from without) and permanent revolution and civil war (to which, by contrast, Communist ideology made a major contribution). It also goes without saying that the Third Reich is not reducible to a mere episode of common criminality, as Bertolt Brecht seemed to believe when he wrote *The Resistible Rise of Arturo Ui*. In it we find a convergence of three historical processes: the logic of total war, taken to extremes by inordinate imperialist ambition; the legacy of the colonial tradition, whose brutality was further radicalized by the attempt to return peoples of ancient civilization, situated in the very heart of Europe, to the state of primitive tribes; and the motif of revolution as conspiracy, which led Hitler to identify the Jews as the secret architects of the Bolshevik October and to seek Germany's and Europe's salvation from the Bolshevik and Asiatic threat in elimination of the Jewish virus. It hardly needs saying that, far from being attributable to the October Revolution, these historical processes and ideological motives derived from the world against which the latter rebelled.

The Choreography of Categories

In contrast, let us see how the authors of *The Black Book of Communism* proceed. Having asserted the temporal priority of the Communist genocide over the Nazi one, they do their utmost to demonstrate that the former was much more imposing in quantitative terms. Wholly absorbed in their efforts to pile statistic on statistic, under the illusion of rendering their calculus invulnerable, they do not even question the categories employed. It is important to make good this lacuna.

Let us start with genocide. Referring to the First World War, Bukharin and Luxemburg respectively spoke of a 'horrible corpse factory' and 'mass extermination' and 'genocide' (*Völkermord*). Why should this denunciation be less credible than that which today aims to demonize the history of the Communist movement as such? Why should the horror of an international war be assessed differently from the horror of a civil war? The soldiers who refused or hesitated to engage in military actions, in the knowledge that they entailed certain death, became targets for their own side: they were even bombarded by heavy artillery in a Russia determined, against Bolshevik opposition, to pursue the war at any cost.

Perhaps denunciations from the Communist side are to be regarded as irrelevant. Very well. There are US historians who refer to genocide in connection with Hiroshima and Nagasaki, as well as the carpet bombing of Dresden and Tokyo, which, although carried out with 'conventional' weapons, destroyed the civilian population of whole cities. Hence we possess all the relevant elements for a serious discussion of the category of genocide. But historical revisionism and *The Black Book* do not like unnecessary conceptual complications. For them everything is clear. There are two types of genocide: racial genocide, which was committed by the Nazis and them alone (the colonial tradition is repressed); and class genocide, which was committed by the Communists and came first in chronological order (all that aside, the Armenian tragedy is ignored). And thus one can ultimately demonstrate the equivalence of Nazism and Communism.

Obviously, the meaning of 'class genocide' is likewise assumed to be immediately clear and unequivocal.[62] Yet we find ourselves confronted with a kind of yellow algorithm. The second term refers to a *genos*, a 'race' defined in naturalistic terms, subsuming every individual member regardless of his or her subjective consciousness and concrete behaviour. The first term refers to history rather than nature, and is used to indicate a social group with labile, shifting boundaries. The *Communist Manifesto* is not the only text to highlight the revolutionary role of transfuges from the dominant class. The thesis is clearly present in Lenin's *What Is to Be Done?*, which in fact insists even more forcefully on the decisive contribution of intellectuals from the bourgeoisie to the development of revolutionary theory. In turn, the revolutionary militant, the tribune of the people, has the task of diffusing this theory not only within the proletariat, but among all classes. It should be added that membership of a class does not always possess the same significance. There is a bourgeoisie that plays a progressive role not only in colonial countries, but also (according to Lenin) in all those situations where imperialist oppression puts the national question back on the agenda.

On the other hand, it is precisely *The Black Book* that underscores the obsession with indoctrination in Communist concentration camps: in Maoist China, 'there certainly were studies involved'. But in as much as it aims to alter the victim's behaviour, indoctrination indicates an absence of genocidal intent, defined as the closure of any escape route for members of the targeted group – defined, that is, as the project of destroying a group regardless of the conduct of the individuals comprising it. Indoctrination, and the altered

---

62   Courtois et al., *The Black Book of Communism*, p. 9.

conduct it induces, also changes its victim's treatment. At least as regards China, *The Black Book* acknowledges this: 'penitentiaries were above all places to teach . . . "bad students" who had been unruly or slow to learn . . . The solution . . . was quite simple: change people's ideas.'[63] However horrible this *univers concentrationnaire*, it cannot be described as 'class genocide'.

Nor is an imprecise, unthinking use of categories conducive to historical or moral judgement. Writing of post-Communist Russia, Maurice Duverger, having criticized the 'collapse in average life expectancy' attributable to the privileged few who have succeeded in 'accumulating enormous wealth' that is speculative and parasitic in origin, when not openly illegal, pronounces a terrible verdict: it is 'a veritable genocide of the elderly'.[64]

Following the genocide of soldiers and the genocide of kulaks ('counter-revolutionaries'), we have the 'genocide of the [impoverished] elderly'. To this list we might add the genocide of political opponents (e.g. that which struck hundreds of thousands of Communists in Indonesia in 1965). In reality, in all these instances the relevant specification (which refers to a group with shifting, mutable boundaries) comes into contradiction with the general category, which refers to a naturalistically defined group with very precise, inviolable boundaries. The individual elderly poor person can seek to escape misery (e.g. through begging or thieving); the individual soldier can hope that his ability will get him through until peace arrives; individual kulaks or Communists can, if time permits, renounce the political positions that they have hitherto adopted. Members of an ethnic group whose destruction has been decided cannot alter their own identity and group affiliation by their conduct. And that is what defines genocide.

Hence certain episodes in the two world wars do approximate to genocide proper. The individual inhabitant of Hiroshima or Nagasaki could not escape the destruction (but this does not apply, obviously, to individual members of the Japanese people). As regards the First World War, we have seen an eminent British historian (Taylor) remarking that 'some 50 million Africans and 250 million Indians were involved, without consultation, in a war of which they understood nothing'. Colonial inhabitants were simply rounded up and deported thousands of miles to be inducted into the 'corpse factory' – and this not on account of behaviour deemed unacceptable, but simply because they were members of an 'inferior race', utilizable as cannon fodder

---

63   Ibid., p. 501.

64   Maurice Duverger, 'Mafia e inflazione uccidono la Russia', *Corriere della Sera*, 18 October 1993.

by a 'master race'. Such behaviour on the part of colonial powers in some ways resembles genocide. Although not rigorous, in the black book of capitalism foreshadowed by Bukharin and Luxemburg, the category of genocide (or 'horrible corpse factory' and 'mass extermination') is used more persuasively than in *The Black Book of Communism*.

But let us see how 'class genocide' was committed. It was primarily the result of 'man-made famine'. The one that occurred in China following the Great Leap Forward of 1958 caused 30 million deaths (almost a third of the total number of victims attributed to Communism). Once again, we encounter a category on whose history and meaning historians should reflect. Let us also seek to fill this lacuna, formulating a preliminary question: without going too far back, when in the twentieth century did starving an entire people become a weapon of war? We have seen Weber in the immediate aftermath of the First World War draw attention to the hundreds of thousands of German victims of the British naval blockade, which, much more than on combatants, impacted on the civilian population and the weakest and most defenceless. Obviously, the great sociologist was at the same time a fervent German chauvinist. So it is worth noting that Gramsci's verdict on the subject was even more severe. In an article of 1916, he indignantly condemned a measure that sought 'to lock up the German people to enfeeble it, to stamp it out'. An accusation repeated when the victors maintained the blockade long after the signature of the armistice (until the vanquished agreed to sign a humiliating, vengeful peace treaty): 'Vienna is decomposing; its human component is dissolving; children are dying, women are dying; the population is languishing and expiring in an economic prison with no possibility of escape.'[65]

With reference to the First World War, not only Luxemburg, but also Gramsci ultimately spoke of genocide – genocide which, in the Italian Communist's denunciation, found its most concentrated expression in the 'man-made starvation' of a whole people. Herbert Hoover likewise expressed 'horror' at the continuation of the blockade. Subsequently, however, it was Hoover – director of the American Relief Administration under Wilson and future president of the USA – who, to check the Bolshevik 'infection', formulated a brutal strategy: peoples inclined to let themselves be seduced by the example of Soviet Russia must know that they would thereby risk 'absolute famine' and 'starvation'.[66]

---

65   Antonio Gramsci, *Cronache Torinesi 1913–1917*, ed. Sergio Caprioglio, Turin: Einaudi, 1980, p. 497; *L'Ordine Nuovo*, p. 391.

66   Quoted in Murray N. Rothbard, 'Hoover's 1919 Food Diplomacy in Retrospect', in

Meanwhile, the food weapon was employed against those who had already succumbed to the 'infection'. In Italy, this elicited contempt not only from Gramsci, but also from Guido De Ruggiero: 'The Entente's blockade which was intended to destroy Bolshevism is instead killing Russian men, women and children.' While the liberal philosopher pointed the finger at the 'Entente's starvers' in 1922,[67] today's ideologues attribute 'man-made famine' exclusively to Communism. However, as its very name suggests, food diplomacy was openly theorized in the USA, which ruthlessly practices it to this day – for example, against Cuba – after having long practised it in the Cold War years, and no less ruthlessly, against the People's Republic of China and, more recently, Iraq. Men, women and children ('guilty' only of being Cubans, Chinese or Iraqis) have been condemned to the 'starvation' menacingly held out by Hoover.

The Black Book overlooks all this. Paradoxically, in employing the category of 'man-made famine' it seems to be inspired by Stalin.[68] On the eve of the forced collectivization of agriculture, to demonstrate its utter indispensability, he accused the kulaks of hoarding food supplies so as to increase prices and garner higher profits – and this regardless of the terrible consequences in the cities of this kind of 'man-made famine'. What remains unclear is the degree of intentionality of the action. This also applies to *The Black Book*. In fact, there is at least one instance where such intentionality is explicitly excluded. In China, the 'Great Leap' was a disaster of more colossal proportions than the famines, however catastrophic, which have punctuated the history of the great Asian country. But 'undoubtedly it was not Mao's intention to kill so many of his compatriots'.[69] Why, then, equate political responsibility and deliberate homicide? And does 'man-made famine' refer to the one or the other? Not only are two forms of behaviour confounded, but with its silences the charge of 'man-made famine' spares precisely those responsible for acts explicitly aimed at inflicting starvation on the enemy.

'Class genocide' and 'man-made famine' refer to a regime branded as totalitarian in all its various manifestations throughout its history. The category of totalitarianism is likewise deployed in merely ideological fashion. What is lacking is any attempt to reconstruct the history of total institutions. When did the concentration camp emerge and how did it spread? The reader

---

Lawrence E. Gelfand, ed., *Herbert Hoover, the Great War and Its Aftermath 1917–23*, Iowa City: Iowa University Press, 1974, pp. 91, 96–8.

67   Guido De Ruggiero, *Scritti politici 1912–1926*, ed. Renzo De Felice, Bologna: Cappelli, 1963, p. 437.

68   Courtois et al., *The Black Book of Communism*, p. 4.

69   Ibid., p. 487.

learns nothing about its use by Spain in the deadly struggle against the Cuban Revolution, or by Britain at war with the Boers, or by the USA engaged in repressing a rebellion in the Philippines and waging war on Japan. From such silence one infers that use of concentration camps was restricted to Communism and Nazism, which therefore can and must be equated. QED.

'Genocide', 'man-made famine', 'totalitarianism': in one way or another, these three categories date back to the denunciation of capitalism and imperialism, of 'bourgeois' society, made by Communism in its time. Now such accusations are turned against it, but without a minimum of historical and critical awareness.

According to The Black Book, Communism in all its forms and represent-atives is to be regarded as totalitarian: Lenin, Stalin, Mao, Ho Chi Minh, Castro, Ortega. And the chaos of the Cultural Revolution in China? Simple: an 'anarchic totalitarianism'.[70] But would the adjective not appear to negate the substantive? And what are we to understand when we read that Cuba is still dominated by 'totalitarianism in the tropics'?[71] Is it totalitarianism in a bathing suit danced to the beat of the samba? Here is the explanation: 'The regime continued to marginalize religious institutions and believers; though claiming that it would allow Cubans to profess their faith freely, it subjected those who did so to repressive measures, such as forbidding them access to university education or to jobs in the civil service.'[72] But if this is totalitar-ianism, then the German Federal Republic, which did not shrink from Berufsverbot against Communists, would have to be regarded as totalitarian! Above all, when accompanied by threats of, and attempts at, invasion, the embargo creates a de facto state of war. The Cuban Communist regime would not appear to have reacted to this situation with measures more drastic than those implemented in the USA during two world wars.

'Talmon's Sophism'

The fact is that in The Black Book, as in an immense literature, the deeds and misdeeds of Communism are compared not with the actual behaviour of the world it sought to challenge (about which the strictest silence reigns), but with liberalism's declarations of principle. In the light of these, the historical expe-rience that began with the Bolshevik Revolution emerges in all its abjectness.

---

70   Ibid., p. 513ff.
71   Ibid., p. 647ff.
72   Ibid., p. 651.

The sophistical character of comparison between such heterogeneous magnitudes is patent. It might be called 'Talmon's sophism', after the name of the distinguished scholar who in the aftermath of the Second World War condemned 'totalitarian democracy' from Rousseau to Stalin, contrasting it with a liberalism that supposedly abhorred 'coercion' and 'violence' (Chapter 2 §10).

This appraisal not only completely ignores real history, but also proceeds extremely selectively when it comes to declarations of principle by different exponents of liberalism. As we know, the latter did not hesitate to theorize slavery or despotism for barbarians (not to mention war) and, in states of emergency, made provision for dictatorship in the metropolis. All this is ignored by Talmon, who, when referring to the political tradition he cherishes, prefers to soar into the firmament of hagiography. This manner of argument has triumphed in our day.

The tragic history of Communism, denounced as the very embodiment of totalitarianism, is set against an idyllic portrait of Britain and the USA, or other countries governed by the liberal rules of the game. But what of such rules in the colonies and in relations with populations of colonial origin? And what of such rules in situations of acute crisis? Marx denounced a key aspect of 'Talmon's sophism' – silence about the colonies – in advance: 'The profound hypocrisy and inherent barbarism of bourgeois-civilization lies unveiled before our eyes, turning from its home, where it assumes respectable forms, to the colonies, where it goes naked.'[73] After the tragedies of the twentieth century, the other key aspect becomes clear: abstraction from states of emergency, starting with that prompted by total war.

Let us seek to trace the history of the last 150 years employing 'Talmon's sophism', but turning it against its usual beneficiaries. Let us start with the present. The Italian judiciary has given vent to suspicions of the CIA's complicity in the Piazza Fontana massacre, and it is now public knowledge that in the post-war period the USA was ready to intervene at any point to cancel an electoral result favourable to the Communists by force of arms. To this we may add the long list of military interventions in Latin America, often on behalf of ferocious military dictatorships. And now let us read Stalin, who in 1952 called on Communists to pick up 'the banner of bourgeois-democratic freedoms', and the 'banner of national independence', cast aside by the bourgeoisie.[74]

---

73   Karl Marx and Friedrich Engels, *Gesaumtausgabe*, Berlin: Dietz, 1975– and Amsterdam: IMES, 1990–, Part I, Vol. 12, p. 252.

74   J.V. Stalin, *The Essential Stalin: Major Theoretical Writings 1902–1952*, ed. Bruce Franklin, London: Croom Helm, 1973, pp. 510–11.

These were the years when the Communist movement was mobilized in a global campaign to collect signatures for peace and a ban on nuclear weapons. On the other side, by contrast, Truman entertained a radical idea for securing complete victory in Korea, which emerges from a diary entry from January 1952. An ultimatum could be issued to the enemy countries, spelling out in advance that a failure to comply would entail the destruction of the largest cities and 'every manufacturing plant in China and the Soviet Union' (see Chapter 6, §11). This was not a hypothetical private reflection. Even after the end of the Korean War, the atomic bomb was brandished against the People's Republic of China on several occasions, and the threat was all the more credible given the fresh, terrible memory of Hiroshima and Nagasaki.

Let us proceed backwards. During the Second World War, along with the two cities wiped out by the atom bomb, the Americans and British set numerous other Japanese and German towns and cities ablaze. The destruction of the civilian population was not coincidental. What lay behind it was a precise strategic design. Dresden was attacked because it was full of refugees (women, the elderly, children), using a particular technique. First of all, windows and roofs were destroyed with high explosives, which were followed by incendiary bombs that could thereby more easily penetrate the interior of houses and set fire to carpets, curtains, furniture and so forth. The distinction between combatants and non-combatants seems to have been abolished. Roosevelt explicitly asserted this when, as we saw earlier, he declared: 'We have got to be tough with Germany, and I mean the German people, not just the Nazis. We either have to castrate the German people, or you have got to treat them in such a manner that they can't just go on reproducing people who want to continue the way they have in the past.' And now let us read Stalin, who in August 1942, while Nazi barbarism was the rampaging in the USSR, was concerned to make a clear distinction: 'it would be ludicrous to identify Hitler's clique with the German people, with the German state. The experience of history indicates that Hitlers come and go, but the German people and the German state remain. The strength of the Red Army lies, finally, in the fact that it does not and cannot feel racial hatred for other peoples, including the German people.'

Let us take a further step back. During the struggle against the Bolsheviks, the Russian Whites, supported by the Entente, sparked pogroms of appalling proportions in which around 60,000 Jews lost their lives. Echoing the thesis of the Judeo-Bolshevik conspiracy, Churchill personally denounced Lenin as 'the high priest and head' of 'a formidable sect, the most formidable sect in the world'. Indeed, to counter anti-Semitic agitation, the Russian revolutionary leader, in addition to taking drastic measures, mounted a major propaganda campaign and had a speech recorded on disc so that it could reach the millions of illiterates.

As is well known, the October Revolution broke out in the wake of the struggle against the First World War. Wilson celebrated it as 'a holy war — the holiest in all history'; US soldiers were 'crusaders', protagonists of a transcendent enterprise whose sword shone with divine light. By contrast, in addition to 'genocide', Rosa Luxemburg referred to an 'atmosphere of ritual murder', while Lenin denounced the fact that in all belligerent countries even the home fronts had become 'military convict prisons'.[75] To stifle such protest, repression from above intersected with repression from below (this is a key characteristic of Fascism). Thus, in the USA the Ku Klux Klan staged a baleful return and, even after the war was over, targeted those suspected of insufficient patriotic loyalty and racial homogeneity — Jews, Communists and, above all, blacks. Corresponding to the anti-Jewish pogroms incited by White Russians were cases of lynching of blacks in the USA, which had been going on for decades.

In its turn, the oppression of blacks referred back to the lot of 'inferior races'. In 1890, the massacre at Wounded Knee, with the killing of defenceless women and children, sealed the conquest of the Far West and the well-nigh complete erasure of 'redskins' from the face of the earth. These were the years when Theodore Roosevelt thundered against 'sentimental humanitarians' who sympathized with the fate of the Native Americans, and who were to be regarded as worse than 'the professional criminal class'. These were the years when, in Stalin's ringing words, 'scores and hundreds of millions of Asiatic and African peoples . . . usually remained outside [the] field of vision . . . white and black, "civilized" and "uncivilized", [were not put] on the same plane'. Only 'Leninism laid bare this crying incongruity, broke down the wall between whites and blacks, between Europeans and Asiatics, between the "civilized" and "uncivilized" slaves of imperialism.'[76]

One more step backwards. While Europe witnessed the birth of the working-class movement inspired by Marxism, in the USA another wave of deportations removed the Native Americans ever farther West, confining

---

75 Lenin, *Collected Works*, Vol. 25, p. 383.
76 The positions quoted here have been cited previously: Chapter 4, §5 (for F.D. Roosevelt); Chapters 4, §2 and 2, §8 (for Stalin); Chapter 5, §8 (for Churchill); Chapter 4, §1 (for Wilson); Chapter 5, §2 (for Luxemburg); and Chapter 3, §3 (for T. Roosevelt).

them to reservations that resembled concentration camps, where it became increasingly difficult to counter hunger and the cold, and where bedclothes deliberately infected with smallpox were sometimes introduced. At the same time, in the South, blacks were slaves. In the event of rebellion, they were subjected to the most refined tortures, in accordance with an old tradition that involved roasting the victims over a slow fire, in an ordeal that could last up to eight or ten hours. Thus continued the 'idyllic proceedings' which, according to *Capital*, characterized 'the dawn of the era of capitalist production'.[77] The old slavery had not been abolished when a new form of it developed, destined to survive the Civil War: the trade in coolies imported from India and China. It was Engels who denounced this new disgrace.

The history sketched above invents absolutely nothing. But it is equally ideological, in as much as it contrasts the liberal West's concrete political conduct with the most noble aspects of the Communist movement's ideological platform, ignoring its concrete behaviour and the most terrible pages in its history. Yet this, in an inverted mirror-image (and in even more heavily ideological fashion), is how *The Black Book of Communism* proceeds. It is a literary genre that ill becomes historical research. Comprehension of massive conflicts presupposes analysis of the interacting behaviour of the antagonists. The presumption on the part of one of the interested parties – the one that emerged victorious – to erect itself into judge of the other, condemning it on the basis of criteria to which it declines to submit, is ridiculous. Rather than a work of history, *The Black Book of Communism* is a kind of historiographical caricature of the Nuremburg Trial.

Conflict of Happiness, Conflict of Liberty

We have seen that the twentieth century signalled the advent of democracy. We may now pose a further question: was the twentieth century the one in which the phenomena of deportation, concentration camps, genocide first made their appearance? Or was it the century when all these horrors irrupted into Europe? Unless we want to repress or transfigure the colonial tradition, the second answer manifestly dictates itself. Hence if the horror of the twentieth century is undeniable, escape into the past, to happier, less cruel centuries, is problematic. Where would it end? The nineteenth century? Among the innumerable massacres that marked it, it is enough to think of

---

77   Karl Marx, *Capital: Volume One*, trans. Ben Fowkes, Penguin: London, 1976, p. 915.

the decimation of the Congo's population, referred to by Arendt. Moreover, it was the century in whose wake Hitler situated himself, committed as he was to reviving the achievements of colonial expansionism. The eighteenth century? The fate reserved for the internal colonies of Scotland and Ireland by England was terrible, while between the two Atlantic coasts and in America the Black Holocaust (in the definition ventured by descendants of black slaves), or the American Holocaust (according descendants of the Native Americans), was consummated. These are tragedies that were already in full swing in the seventeenth century – the century which, with its Thirty Years' War proper, serves as a reference-point for numerous historians in interpreting the twentieth century. Must we go back even further, to the sixteenth or fifteenth centuries? We then encounter what an eminent intellectual (Tzvetan Todorov) has characterized as 'the greatest genocide in human history'. Moreover, it would be bizarre to seek to counter-pose the epoch of the Conquest to the century of Hitler's infamies, given that with his war of extermination against the 'natives' he might be regarded as the last of the *conquistadores*!

Escape from the twentieth century into the past secretes an implicit Eurocentric and 'negationist' logic (in this instance, of the Black Holocaust, the American Holocaust, and the innumerable massacres of the colonial tradition).

While escaping to happy times past and denying the emancipatory charge of the Communist movement prove fruitless, the latter's major contribution to the horror of the twentieth century cannot be denied. What historical victory could ever justify it? In fact, on closer inspection, did not the catastrophe precisely begin with Marx's presumption in sacrificing morality on the altar of the philosophy of history and the impending radiant future? This is the principal theme in the tendency, today extremely widespread, to search for a kind of philosophical original sin, reverting from the October Revolution to the philosopher with whom it identified.

This view results in a Manichaean contrast between a (liberal) political tradition attentive to the claims of morality and a political tradition incurably deaf to them. This is Talmon's sophism, with which we are familiar – only now, rather than in historiographical form, it is presented *sub specie philosophiae*. Yet in this version too it can easily be inverted.

Having painted a dreadful picture that fully accords with the reality of British colonial rule in Ireland, an eminent English liberal historian (Trevelyan) stressed what in his view was the essential aspect: the subjugation of the unhappy island 'saved Protestantism in Europe and enabled the British Empire to launch forth strongly on its career of prosperity, freedom and expansion overseas'.[78] Terrible human costs are justified in the name of a country's imperial mission: we are in 1942, in the midst of the catastrophe caused by the Third Reich or the Germanic Third Empire! And now let us compare the English historian's philosophy with Marx's. The latter recognized that, despite its arbitrary and brutal character, British colonial rule in India had a modernizing impact. In this sense, 'progress' had been realized, but progress resembling 'that hideous pagan idol, who would not drink the nectar but from the skulls of the slain'![79]

This is not an isolated point. Marx's main work can be read as a critical reflection on the bourgeois and Western philosophy of history. Having stressed that 'capital comes dripping from head to toe, from every pore, with blood and dirt' – 'conver[ting] Africa into a preserve for the commercial hunting of blackskins' and bringing about 'the extirpation, enslavement and entombment in mines of the indigenous population' in America – the chapter on 'original accumulation' in *Capital* ironically paraphrases the motto with which Virgil summarized the foundation of a city destined by the gods to rule the world: *Tantae molis erat*.[80] This denunciation remained operative in Lenin, who defended the claims of the 'red and black skins' against the arrogance of a 'few chosen nations'.

The search for the original philosophical sin that allegedly explains the horrors of our time does not stop at Marx. Behind the Bolsheviks we find the model of the Jacobin Terror, whose protagonists often referred to Rousseau. Such is the mandatory starting-point – the 'organicism' of the author of *The Social Contract*, who presumes to sacrifice individuals on the altar of the 'general will' and an omnivorous Whole. In reality, any such attitude was so alien to the philosopher that in a letter of 27 September 1766, written when the contradictions resulting in the French Revolution were already evident, he asserted: 'the blood of one man is more valuable than the liberty of the whole human race'.[81]

Yet Rousseau continues to be viewed as the father of the Terror (and grandfather of the Gulag). Set against him is once again the Anglo-American liberal tradition, replete (so we are assured) with sacred respect for the

---

78   G.M. Trevelyan, *History of England*, London: Longman, 1979, p. 575.

79   Karl Marx and Friedrich Engels, *Gesamtausgabe*, Berlin: Dietz, 1975– and Amsterdam: IMES, 1990–, Part I, Vol. 12, p. 253.

80   Marx, *Capital:Volume One*, pp. 925–6, 925.

81   Jean-Jacques Rousseau, *Correspondence complète*, ed. R.A. Leigh, Oxford: University of Oxford/Voltaire Foundation, 1977, Vol. XXX, p. 385.

claims of morality and the concrete individual. However, less than three decades after the letter we have just mentioned, we encounter another, no less eloquent one. It is the summer of 1792 and the Terror is already on the horizon in France. In seeking to justify it, the author of this letter declares that, rather than tolerating the triumph of the cause of despotism, 'I would have seen half the earth desolated.' More precisely: 'Were there but an Adam and an Eve left in every country, and left free, it would be better than it now is.' The author was Jefferson.[82] A direct line seems to lead from the view expressed here to a slogan that became widespread in the worst years of the Cold War, dominated by the spectre of nuclear holocaust: 'Better dead than red!' The 'liberty of the human race' seems to require much more than 'the blood of one man'.

This is a complete inversion of Rousseau's position. The Jacobins did indeed invoke him. At this point, we might be tempted to sigh: if only they had complied with the author they venerated, instead of providing the Bolsheviks with a model in the Terror! Unfortunately, the criterion formulated by the Genevan philosopher does not withstand the test of reality. On the one hand, it is too restrictive. Taken literally, it would require condemnation of any revolution and any war. Even an assassination attempt on Hitler would be difficult to justify, and it would be very hard to justify a police operation that involved shedding blood. The police, the army and the judiciary (at least in countries where the death penalty is provided for) operate on the basis of the presupposition that the blood of one or more human beings is worth less than the liberty, not of the human race, but of a particular political community. The state as such entails this principle. In Rousseau's letter, we can read a vague aspiration to the extinction of states – the anarchical utopia adopted by Marx and, subsequently, the Bolsheviks themselves. We are returned to the vicinity of a revolution which, at first blush, seems separated by an abyss from the criterion formulated by Rousseau.

What becomes clear is that such a criterion is, on the other hand, too broad. It is a pious illusion to believe that adhering to the absolute value of the individual is in and of itself an antidote to revolutionary upheavals and the ensuing shedding of blood. Rousseau reiterates that absolute value when, in the *Discourse on Political Economy*, he asserts that the social contract would risk being null 'if in the state there perished even a single citizen who could have been assisted, if even a single trial were to end with a

---

82   Thomas Jefferson, *Writings*, ed. Merrill D. Peterson, New York: Library of America, 1984, p. 1004 (letter to W. Short of 3 January 1793).

manifestly unjust sentence'. It would be imperative to remedy that eventuality, uninhibited by the 'pretext of the public good', or public order, that terrible 'curse'.[83] No society was, or is, in a position to meet the challenge contained in such a view.

This is where we must start from to understand the dialectic that developed in the French Revolution. In articulating the 'new idea' of 'happiness', Saint-Just formulated an extremely ambitious and pugnacious programme: 'Not a single poor, unhappy being in the state will be tolerated . . .: let Europe learn that you no longer wish to see either an unhappy being or an oppressor on French territory.'[84] We are a few months from the fateful Thermidor 1794, which saw Saint-Just go to the guillotine along with Robespierre. Two years later, this programme was adopted verbatim by Babeuf, in a speech to the judges of the tribunal that shortly afterwards likewise sentenced him to death.[85]

As well as invoking Saint-Just, Babeuf referred to the 1793 Constitution, article 34 of which states that 'there is oppression of the social body when there is oppression of a single one of its members'. But the politico-social order already tends to be impugned by poverty and unhappiness, which are no longer treated as a natural calamity or divine punishment, as in the ideology of the *ancien régime*. The misery and unhappiness of a single human being suffice for a condition of oppression to obtain, but then (continues the Jacobin Constitution) 'insurrection becomes the most sacred of rights and the most imperative of duties'. From a factor of potential conservatism in Rousseau's letter of 1766, the sentiment of the absolute value of the individual is converted into a tool of permanent revolution. In no instance is it permissible to sacrifice the concrete individual to society! Formulated with an eye to the future, highlighting the dangers contained in any project of social transformation, this categorical imperative can elicit resignation. Formulated with an eye to the present, with its suffering and sacrifices, it opens up a chasm of endless negation. The criterion stated by Rousseau is too narrow for any concrete political action and project to be capable of meeting it, and too broad to be capable, if not of blocking, then at least of containing and screening impulses to rebellion.

---

83 Jean-Jacques Rousseau, *Oeuvres complètes*, ed. B. Gagnebin and P. Raymond, Paris: Gallimard, 1955–, Vol. III, pp. 256, 258.

84 Louis Antoine Léon de Saint-Just, *Oeuvres complètes*, ed. Michèle Duval, Paris: G. Lebovici, 1984, pp. 707, 715.

85 See Gracchus Babeuf, *Écrits*, ed. Claude Mazauric, Paris: Messidor/Éditions Sociales, 1988, p. 316.

The unhappiness of a single human being is intolerable! Babeuf seems to realize the utopian character of such a demand and, in fact, sometimes prefers to speak of the 'happiness of the greatest number'. This is a formula subsequently found in Bentham. The idea of happiness thus becomes more 'realistic'. The unhappiness of a certain number of persons is now taken into account. The possible conflict between the happiness of some and that of others is now sometimes configured as a conflict between liberties. Focusing on the British colonists in America, where a kind of local self-government by white colonists who were often slave-owners obtained, Smith observed that slavery could more easily be suppressed under a 'despotic government' than a 'free' one, 'where every law is made by their masters, who will never pass anything prejudicial to themselves'. From this the *Lectures on Jurisprudence* draw an extraordinary conclusion: 'The freedom of the free was the cause of the great oppression of the slaves . . . And as they are the most numerous part of mankind, no human person will wish for liberty in a country where this institution is established.'[86] What a scandal from the standpoint of contemporary apologetic liberals is the preference indirectly expressed here for 'despotic government' as the only form that can eliminate the institution of slavery!

This anticipates the political and moral dilemmas of the American people either side of the Civil War. We can restate the political dilemma. Contrary to Smith, it involved choosing not between 'liberty' and 'despotic government', but between the freedom of blacks reduced to slavery and the freedom of their owners. Slavery was only abolished following a bloody war (conducted by Lincoln with remorseless Jacobin energy) and a subsequent military dictatorship over the secessionist states. When the Union abandoned the iron fist, whites were once again granted *habeas corpus* and local self-government, but blacks were deprived not only of political rights, but also, in large part, of civil rights.

The political dilemma was also a moral dilemma. Let us leave aside self-declared defenders of the institution of slavery. Those who hoped for a gradual, painless reform process accepted an albeit temporary reduction of black slaves to means and things; the more radical abolitionists, who first pressed for a confrontation and then supported the military dictatorship over the South, in effect accepted the reduction of the victims of the war and subsequent military dictatorship to means to an end. The situation was

---

86 Adam Smith, *Lectures on Jurisprudence*, Indianapolis: Liberty Classics, 1982, pp. 452–3, 182. Cf. Losurdo, *Liberalism*, Chapter 1, §1.

reversed with the return of the ex-slaves to semi-serfdom and the condition
of sacrificial victims, immolated on the altar of new-found harmony within
the white community and restored 'democracy' for the master race.

The Civil War achieved a lasting result (the abolition of slavery), but at
the cost of a terrible bloodbath: the number of casualties was higher than
that caused on the US side by two world wars put together. Was it worth
it? Might it not have been better, suggest revisionist historians, to await the
natural course of things, especially given that acceleration of the process of
emancipation did not have the anticipated effects? What has been called the
second American revolution evinces a disastrous balance sheet. It did not
achieve liberty for blacks; it abolished slavery only to make way for the
arbitrary violence of the regime of white supremacy.

Certainly, the international influence of the abolitionist revolution weighs
on the other side of the scale. It occurred in the same period as the abolition
of serfdom in Russia and at a time when the most odious aspects of what
not only Marx, but an abundant literature, denounced as wage slavery or
white slavery were being challenged in Western Europe. We should also not
lose sight of the fact that 1867 saw the passage in Britain of the Second
Reform Bill, which significantly extended the suffrage. At a time when
American blacks were conquering, or seemed to be conquering, political
rights along with civil rights, it was hard to deny the white working class
the former. Again in 1884, during demonstrations to secure the Third Reform
Act and a further extension of citizenship, British workers waved flags
invoking the Union's struggle to abolish slavery.[87]

That gesture might seem rather naive to contemporary historians: it
appears to ignore the white supremacy which had supervened in the interim.
Compared with the pre-Civil War years, the condition of blacks had in a
sense even deteriorated. They were now forced to endure a situation of
permanent isolation, intimidation and terror (cases of lynching multiplied).
The restoration of racial hierarchy, which had been experienced by its victims
as natural for so long, but which had then fallen into crisis, required a
surcharge of violence and brutality. Something similar occurred after the
October Revolution and the appeal addressed to the slaves in the colonies.
In Ethiopia and Eastern Europe, the reassertion of colonialism and the process
of re-colonization assumed forms that were all the more horrible given the
difficulties encountered in reversing the course of history.

---

87 See Philip S. Foner, *British Labor and the American Civil War*, New York and London:
Holmes & Meier, 1981, pp. 95–6.

The abolition of slavery, following a bloody war conducted as a Crusade for freedom, strengthened the North American republic's democratic good conscience and sense of mission. Colonial and imperial impulses received a strong impetus, as demonstrated by the war with Spain, the radicalization of the Monroe Doctrine (and theorization of a pedagogical 'big stick' for the recalcitrant peoples of Latin America), the annexation of the Philippines, and so forth. An analogous dialectic developed after the Bolshevik October. Issuing from a revolution that waved the banner of oppressed nations in Czarist Russia, the colonies and the world generally, the USSR in turn felt itself invested with a mission that pushed it to the point of theorizing a kind of Monroe Doctrine for the countries of Eastern Europe, to which it conceded only a 'limited sovereignty'. Thus, while they significantly advanced emancipatory processes, the ideas that governed the abolitionist revolution in the first instance, and the Bolshevik Revolution thereafter, functioned as an instrument for legitimizing imperial ambitions.

Once again, then, the crucial question emerges in the case of both revolutions: were they worth it? But the question is ill-formulated. When Lincoln decided to respond to the challenge of the secessionist states, violence was already in train – and not only because the enslavement of a people is in itself (as Rousseau stressed) an act of war. The bloody assault by rebel troops on Fort Sumter had already occurred, and was itself preceded by attempts on the part of abolitionists in the North to introduce weapons into the South and appeals to the slaves to rebel. The war had been brewing for decades.

This consideration applies *a fortiori* to the October Revolution, which erupted when the 'genocide' it wanted to prevent had been raging for years. In the view of youth who adhered to Communism, it was the war that seemed like a gigantic, inhuman experiment in social engineering. This 'furnace', 'smelting furnace', and instrument of 'regeneration of present social existence' was celebrated by Gaetano Salvemini and Benedetto Croce.[88] Across the Atlantic, even after the signature of the armistice, Herbert Hoover credited the war with 'purif[ying]' men and thereby preparing 'a new golden age'. His conclusion was a ringing one: 'We are proud to have taken part in this renaissance of humanity.'[89]

---

88   See Gaetano Salvemini, *Opere*, Milan: Feltrinelli, 1964–78, Vol. III, pt. 2, pp. 726–7; Benedetto Croce, *Storia d'Italia dal 1871 al 1915*, Bari: Laterza, 1967, p. 271, and *L'Italia dal 1914 al 1918. Pagine sulla guerra*, Bari: Laterza, 1950, p. 22.
89   Quoted in Rothbard, 'Hoover's 1919 Food Diplomacy in Retrospect', p. 89.

On the other side, Gramsci's irony about the enormous human and social costs of 'five years of purification, regeneration and martyrdom' was scathing.[90] The fact that they had been imposed from above confirmed that the subaltern classes were mere 'human material', 'raw material for the history of the privileged classes'.[91] In the young revolutionary's view, there was a direct line leading from the liberal tradition to interventionism. Regarded for centuries as lacking in human dignity in the full sense, the semi-bestial multitude could be calmly sacrificed in a war whose stake was also, or primarily, a division of colonies, or dominion over populations even more manifestly reduced to work tools and things.

Having arrived in power on the back of protests against this world, Communism in turn involved the sacrifice of millions of human beings, who were reduced to 'raw material' for building a new society. Rousseau's admonition not long before the outbreak of the revolution that he unquestionably helped induce comes to mind once again: 'the blood of one man is worth more than the freedom of the whole human race'. Albeit utopian, it contains an essential lesson that might be reformulated in Kantian terms: as an autonomous moral subject, every human being is an end in him- or herself and cannot be degraded into an instrument for the attainment of higher ends.

The Constant Moral Dilemmas of Our Time

This truth is often mobilized to liquidate the Jacobin-Bolshevik tradition that is also at work behind it. We have seen distinguished liberal thinkers equate wage-workers with horses or machines and work tools, thereby denying them the dignity of moral subjects as well as political subjects. Even more radically and persistently, such a denial has operated to the detriment of members of 'inferior races'. The decisive blows dealt to this world are key moments in conferring on every human being, regardless of race, property and sex, the dignity of a moral subject, of being an end in him- or herself. Making a major contribution to the attainment of this result, paradoxically, the French Revolution and the October Revolution helped develop the theoretical and moral tools that enable us to adopt an attitude of mature critical distance towards them, which has nothing to do with the

---

90   Gramsci, *L'Ordine Nuovo*, pp. 244–5.
91   Gramsci, *Cronache Torinesi*, p. 175; *L'Ordine Nuovo*, p. 520.

commonplace demonization beloved of 'Talmon's sophism'. When, focusing on their blameless victims – the autonomous moral subjects objectively reduced to means in the course of the many revolutions that marked the birth of today's world – people query their legitimacy and expediency, they are unaware of the fact that such questioning was precisely made possible by those revolutions.

On the other hand, it would be naive to think that with the new situation political and moral dilemmas have disappeared. Was it right to support the Gulf wars, and was it right to support the prolonged embargo imposed on Iraq? The consequences of the latter were described thus in an article in the *Washington Post* signed by the director of the Center for Economic and Social Rights: 'According to estimates by UN agencies, more than 500,000 Iraqi children have died from hunger and disease – roughly the combined toll of two atomic bombs on Japan and the recent scourge of ethnic cleansing.'[92] That calculation dates from 1996; thereafter the toll increased considerably.

We are dealing with a kind of postmodern version of the concentration camp. In the age of globalization, there is no need to deport a people: it is enough to block the flow of food and medicines – especially if one succeeds in destroying aqueducts, drainage systems and health infrastructure with 'intelligent' bombing, as happened in Iraq. What will future historians say about this 'man-made famine', this collective death sentence, pronounced not in the course of a ruthless civil war or a dramatic life-and-death struggle between great powers, but in 'peace' time, without even the justification of the Cold War?

Such criticisms are generally answered by pointing to the need to pursue the struggle against a dictatorial, criminal regime. But here is the reply of the article cited above: however grave the list of charges against Iraq's leaders, it cannot justify resort to a terrible 'collective punishment', a practice typical of totalitarianism.

If the 'collective punishment' inflicted on an already exhausted people had really aimed to defend the cause of democracy and peace (and it is possible to entertain the strongest doubts), a bitter conclusion would impose itself. We might formulate it by referring to a text by Marx that we have already cited. It invokes a 'great social revolution' bringing about a situation where 'human progress' ceases to 'resemble that hideous pagan

---

92   Roger Normand, 'Deal Won't End Iraqi Suffering', reported in *International Herald Tribune*, 7 June 1996.

idol, who would not drink the nectar but from the skulls of the slain'.[93] While faith in a 'great social revolution', definitively resolving things, has vanished, the tragedies to which it sought to put an end are still the order of the day.

---

93   Marx and Engels, *Gesamtausgabe*, Part I, Vol. 2, p. 253.

Bibliography

Accademia delle Scienze dell'URSS, *Storia universale*, Vol. VII, Italian trans., Milan: Teti, 1975.

Adams, Michael C.C., 'Retelling the Tale: Wars in Common Memory', in Gabor S. Boritt (ed.), *War Comes Again: Comparative Vistas on the Civil War and World War II*, New York and Oxford: Oxford University Press, 1995.

Agursky, Mikhail, *The Third Rome: National Bolshevism in the USSR*, Boulder, CO: Westview Press, 1987.

Alexander, Edward, *A Crime of Vengeance: An Armenian Struggle for Justice*, Free Press: New York and Toronto, 1991.

Alfieri, Vittorio Enzo, Introduction and notes to J.G. Fichte, *Sulla rivoluzione francesca*, Bari: Laterza, 1974.

Alperovitz, Gar, *The Decision to Use the Atomic Bomb and the Architecture of an American Myth*, New York: Knopf, 1995.

Aly, Götz, *'Endlösung'. Völkerverschiebung und der Mord an den europäischen Juden*, Frankfurt am Main: Fischer, 1995.

Ambrose, Stephen E., 'Ike and the Disappearing Atrocities', *New York Times Book Review*, 24 February 1991.

———— 'Eisenhower and the Germans', in Günter Bischof and Stephen E. Ambrose (eds), *Eisenhower and the German POWs: Facts against Falsehood*, Baton Rouge and London: Louisiana State University Press, 1992.

Anonymous, 'Per Nicola II si prepara una corona di santo. Parte la canonizzazione della famiglia dello zar', *Corriere della sera*, 8 April 1992.

Arendt, Hannah, 'Organized Guilt and Universal Responsibility', *Jewish Frontier*, January 1945.

———— *The Origins of Totalitarianism*, New York: Harcourt, Brace & World, 1951.

———— 'Reflections on Little Rock', *Dissent*, Winter 1959.

———— *On Revolution*, London: Faber & Faber, 1963.

———— *Crises of the Republic*, San Diego, New York and London: Harcourt Brace Jovanovich, 1972.

———— *Essays und Kommentare*, 2 vols, ed. E. Geisel and K. Bittermann, Berlin: Tiamat, 1989.

Ascherson, Neal, 'The Breaking of the Mau Mau', *New York Review of Books*, 7 April 2005.

Asseo, Henriette, 'La specifité de l'extermination des Tziganes', in Y. Thanassekos and H. Wismann (eds), *Révisions de l'histoire. Totalitarismes, crimes et génocides nazis*, Paris: Éditions du Cerf, 1990.

Babeuf, Gracchus, *Écrits*, ed. Claude Mazauric, Paris: Messidor/Éditions Sociales, 1988.

Bacon, Francis, *The Works*, reprint, Stuttgart and Bad Cannstatt: Frommann-Holzboog, 1963 [1859].

Bacque, James, *Other Losses: An Investigation into the Mass Deaths of German Prisoners at the Hands of the French and Americans after World War II*, Toronto: Stoddart, 1989.

Baechler, Jean, Introduction to Augustin Cochin, *L'esprit du jacobinisme*, Paris: Presses Universitaires de France, 1979.

Bailyn, Bernard, 'An American Tragedy', *New York Review of Books*, 5 October 1995.

Bairoch, Paul, *Economics and World History: Myths and Paradoxes*, Chicago: University of Chicago Press, 1995.

Barnes, Harry E. (ed.), *Perpetual War for Perpetual Peace*, Idaho: Caldwell, 1953.

———— Preface to *Entlarvete Heuchelei (Ewig Krieg um ewigen Frieden)*, Wiesbaden: Priester, 1961.

———— *Revisionism: A Key to Peace*, New York: Revisionist Press, 1973.

Bauman, Zygmunt, *Modernity and Holocaust*, Cambridge: Polity Press, 1991.

Beaumont, Gustave de, *L'Irlande sociale, politique et religieuse*, 2 vols, ed. Godelaine Charpentier, Villeneuve d'Ascq: CERIUL-Université Charles de Gaulle-Lille III, 1990 [1839].

Belissa, Marc, *Le Cosmopolitisme du droit des gens (1713–1795). Fraternité universelle et intérêt national au siècle des lumières et pendant la Révolution française*, doctoral thesis, Panthéon-Sorbonne, Paris I, 1996.

Bergson, Henri, *Mélanges*, ed. A. Robinet, Paris: Presses Universitaires de France, 1972.

Bernstein, Eduard, 'Die deutsche Sozialdemokratie und die türkischen Wirren', *Die Neue Zeit*, 1896–97.

———— 'Der Sozialismus und die Kolonialfrage', *Sozialistische Monatshefte*, 1900.

———— 'Sozialdemokratie und Imperialismus', *Sozialistische Monatshefte*, 1900.

———— *The Preconditions of Socialism*, ed. and trans. Henry Tudor, Cambridge: Cambridge University Press, 1993 [1899].

Beveridge, Albert J., *The Meaning of the Times and Other Speeches*, Freeport, NY: Books for Libraries Press, 1968 [1908].

Berresford-Ellis, Peter and Mac a' Globhaim, Seumas, *The Scottish Insurrection of 1820*, London: Pluto Press, 1989 [1970].

Bertaud, Jean-Paul, 'La presse royaliste parisienne, l'idée de guerre et la guerre, 1789–1792', in F. Lebrun and R. Dupuy (eds), *Les Résistances à la Révolution*, Paris: Imago, 1987.

Bieberstein, Johannes Rogalla von, *Die These von der Verschwörung 1776–1945*, Bern and Frankfurt am Main: Lang, 1976.

Bobbio, Norberto, 'Invito al colloquio', in Bobbio, *Politica e cultura*, Turin: Einaudi, 1977 [1951].

Boffa, Giuseppe, *Storia dell'Unione sovietica*, 2 vols, Milan: Mondadori, 1979.

Boutroux, Émile, *Études d'histoire de la philosophie allemande*, Paris: Vrin, 1926.

Boyle, Peter G. (ed.), *The Churchill–Eisenhower Correspondence 1953–1955*, Chapel Hill and London: University of North Carolina Press, 1990.

Breitman, Richard, *The Architect of Genocide: Himmler and the Final Solution*, New York: Knopf, 1991.

Bruce, Robert V., 'Toward Sumter and Pearl: Comparing the Origins of the Civil War and World War II', in Gabor S. Boritt (ed.), *War Comes Again*, New York and Oxford: Oxford University Press, 1995.

Buchner, Rudolf and Baumgart, Winfried (eds), *Quellen zum politischen Denken der Deutschen im 19. und 20. Jahrundert. Freiher vom Stein – Gedächtnisausgabe*, Darmstadt: Wissenschaftliche Buchgesellschaft, 1976–.

Bukharin, Nicolai, *Lo Stato Leviatano. Scritti sullo Stato e la guerra 1915–1917*, ed. A. Giasanti, Milan: Unicopoli, 1984.

—————— and Preobrazhensky, Evgeny, *L'accumulazione socialista*, ed. Lisa Foa, Rome: Riuniti, 1969.

Burckhardt, Jacob, *Reflections on History*, trans. M.D.H., London: George Allen & Unwin, 1943.

Burke, Edmund, *The Works: A New Edition*, 16 vols, London: Rivington, 1826.

—————— *Correspondence*, 10 vols, eds Thomas W. Copeland and John A. Woods, Cambridge: Cambridge University Press, 1958–.

—————— *Betrachtungen über die franzöische Revolution*, ed. Friedrich Gentz, reprint, Frankfurt am Main: Suhrkamp, 1967 [1794].

Calhoun, John C., *Union and Liberty: The Political Philosophy*, ed. R.M. Lence, Indianapolis: Liberty Classics, 1992.

Calloway, Colin G., *The American Revolution in Indian Country: Crisis and Diversity in Native American Communities*, Cambridge: Cambridge University Press, 1995.

Calvin, John, *The Institutes of the Christian Religion*, trans. Henry Beveridge, Edinburgh: Calvin Translation Society, 1846 [1537].

Canedy, Susan, *America's Nazis: A Democratic Dilemma*, Menlo Park: Markgraf, 1990.

Canfora, Luciano, *Marx vive a Calcutta*, Bari: Dedalo, 1992.

Cannadine, David, 'The Context, Performance and Meaning of Ritual: The British Monarchy and the "Invention of Tradition", c. 1820–1977', in Eric Hobsbawm and Terence Ranger (eds), *The Invention of Tradition*, Cambridge: Cambridge University Press, 1983.

—————— *The Decline and Fall of the British Aristocracy*, New Haven and London: Yale University Press, 1990.

Carroll, Peter N. and Noble, David W., *The Free and the Unfree: A New History of the United States*, New York: Viking Press, 1988 [1977].

Césaire, Aimé, *Toussaint Louverture. La révolution française et le problème colonial*, Paris: Présence Africaine, 1961.

Chamberlain, Houston, *Foundations of the Nineteenth Century*, 2 vols, New York: Howard Fertig, 2006.

Chamberlin, William H., *America's Second Crusade*, Chicago: Regnery, 1950.

Charmley, John, *Churchill: The End of Glory*, London: Hodder & Stoughton, 1993.

Chesneaux, Jean (ed.), *La Cina*, 2 vols, trans. Settimio Caruso and David Mamo, Turin: Einaudi, 1974 [1969–72].

Churchill, Winston, *Great Destiny*, ed. F.W. Heath, New York: Putnam, 1965.

———— *Complete Speeches 1897–1963*, 8 vols, ed. R.R. James, New York and London: Chelsea House, 1974.

Class, Heinrich (Daniel Frymann), *Wenn ich der Kaiser wär'. Politische Wahrheiten und Notwendigkeiten*, Leipzig: Dieterich'sche Verlagsbuchhandlung, 1912.

Cobban, Alfred, 'The Myth of the French Revolution', in *Aspects of the French Revolution*, London: Jonathan Cape, 1968 [1954].

———— *Dictatorship: Its History and Theory*, New York: Haskell, 1971 [1939].

Cochin, Augustin, *Les sociétés de pensée et la démocratie moderne. Études d'histoire révolutionnaire*, Paris: Copernic, 1978 [1921].

———— *La Révolution et la libre pensée*, Paris: Copernic, 1979 [1924].

Cohen, Warren I., *The American Revisionists: The Lessons of Intervention in World War I*, Chicago and London: University of Chicago Press, 1967.

Cohn, Norman, *Warrant for Genocide: The Myth of the Jewish World-Conspiracy and the Protocols of the Elders of Zion*, New York: Harper & Row, 1967.

Commager, Henry S. (ed.), *Documents of American History*, 2 vols, 7th edn, New York: Appleton-Century-Crofts, 1963 [1934].

Condorcet, Marie-Jean-Antoine, *Oeuvres*, 12 vols, ed. Arthur Condorcet O'Connor and François Arago, Stuttgart and Bad Cannstatt: Frommann-Holzboog, 1968 [1847–49].

Conquest, Robert, *Reflections on a Ravaged Century*, New York: Norton, 2000.

Constant, Benjamin, *Cours de politique constitutionelle*, 3rd edn, Brussels: Société belge de librairie, 1837.

———— *Journal intime*, précédé du *Le cahier rouge et de Adolpe (1767–1787)*, ed. Jean Mistler, Monaco: Éditions du Rocher, 1945.

———— *Oeuvres*, ed. Alfred Roulin, Paris: Gallimard, 1957.

Courtois, Stéphane et al., *The Black Book of Communism: Crimes, Terror, Repression*, trans. Jonathan Murphy and Mark Kramer, Cambridge, MA, and London: Harvard University Press, 1999.

Croce, Benedetto, *L'Italia dal 1914 al 1918. Pagine sulla guerra*, Bari: Laterza, 1950.

———— *A History of Italy, 1871–1915*, trans. Cecilia M. Ady, New York: Russell & Russell, 1963 [1928].

———— *Scitti e discorsi politici (1943–1947)*, ed. A. Carella, Vol. 1, Naples: Bibliopolis, 1993.

Dallek, Robert, *Franklin D. Roosevelt and American Foreign Policy 1932–1945*, New York and Oxford: Oxford University Press, 1995.

Davis, David B., *The Problem of Slavery in the Age of Revolution 1770–1823*, Ithaca, NY, and London: Cornell University Press, 1975.

———— *The Slave Power Conspiracy and the Paranoid Style*, Baton Rouge and London: Louisiana State University Press, 1982.

———— 'The Slave Trade and the Jews', *New York Review of Books*, 22 December 1994.

Davis, Jefferson, *The Rise and Fall of the Confederate Government*, 2 vols, ed. J.M. McPherson, New York: Da Capo Press, 1990 [1881].

Davis, Mike, *Late Victorian Holocausts: El Niño Famines and the Making of the Third World*, London and New York: Verso, 2001.

Del Boca, Angelo, *La Guerra d'Abissinia 1935–1941*, Milan: Feltrinelli, 1965.

———— *Il Negus. Vita e morte dell'ultimo Re dei Rei*, Rome and Bari: Laterza, 1995.

De Ruggiero, Guido, *Scritti politici 1912–1926*, ed. Renzo de Felice, Bologna: Cappelli, 1963.

Deutscher, Isaac, *Stalin: A Political Biography*, 2nd edn, New York and Oxford: Oxford University Press, 1967 [1949].

Drechsler, Horst, *Südwestafrika unter deutscher Kolonialherrschaft*, Vol. 1, *Der Kampf der Herero und Nama gegen den deutschen Imperialismus (1884–1915)*, Berlin: Akademie, 1966.

Du Bois, William E.B., *Black Reconstruction in America 1860–1880*, ed. D.L. Lewis, New York: Atheneum, 1992 [1935].

Duffy, Christopher, *Red Storm on the Reich: The Soviet March on Germany, 1945*, New York: Atheneum, 1991.

Duverger, Maurice, 'Mafia e inflazione uccidono la Russia', *Corriere della sera*, 18 October 1993.

Eisenhower, Dwight D., *Crusade in Europe*, New York: Doubleday, 1948.

Elkins, Stanley and McKitrick, Eric, *The Age of Federalism: The Early American Republic, 1788–1800*, New York and Oxford: Oxford University Press, 1993.

Ellsworth, Scott, *Death in a Promised Land: The Tulsa Race Riot of 1921*, Baton Rouge and London: Louisiana State University Press, 1992.

Encyclopédie, ou Dictionnaire raisonné des sciences, des arts et des metiers, new edn, Vol. XXXIII, Geneva: Pellet, 1778.

Erasmus, *The Complaint of Peace*, New York: Da Capo Press, 1973 [1517].

Fanon, Frantz, *The Wretched of the Earth*, trans. Constance Farrington, London: Penguin, 1990 [1961].

Fattorini, Emma, 'Il colpo di grazia sessuale. La violenza delle truppe nere in Renania negli anni venti', in A. Bravo (ed.), *Donne e uomini nelle guerre mondiali*, Rome and Bari: Laterza, 1991.

Fauré, Christine (ed.), *Les Déclarations des droits de l'homme de 1789*, Paris: Payot, 1988.

Fejtö, François, *Requiem pour un empire défunt. Histoire de la destruction de l'Autriche-Hongrie*, Paris: Le Lieu commun, 1988.

Ferguson, Niall, *The Cash Nexus: Money and Power in the Modern World*, London: Penguin, 2001.

────── *Empire: The Rise and Demise of the British World Order and the Lessons for Global Power*, New York: Basic Books, 2004 [2002].

────── *Empire: How Britain Made the Modern World*, London: Penguin, 2004 [2003].

────── *Colossus: The Rise and Fall of the American Empire*, London: Penguin, 2005.

────── *The War of the World: History's Age of Hatred*, London: Penguin, 2007 [2006].

────── *Civilization: The West and the Rest*, London: Penguin, 2011.

Ferro, Marc, *La Révolution russe de 1917*, Paris: Aubier, 1967.

────── *Nicholas II: Last of the Tsars*, trans. Brian Pearce, New York: Oxford University Press, 1993.

Fichte, Johann G., *Werke*, ed. I.H. Fichte, Berlin: de Gruyter, 1971.

Fink, Arthur E., *Causes of Crime: Biological Theories in the United States 1800–1915*, New York: Perpetua, 1962 [1938].

Fischer, Fritz, *Griff nach der Weltmacht. Die Kriegszielpolitik des kaiserlichen Deutschland 1914/18*, 4th edn, Düsseldorf: Droste Verlag, 1971 [1961].

Fitzpatrick, Sheila, *Stalin's Peasants: Resistance and Survival in the Russian Village after Collectivization*, New York and Oxford: Oxford University Press, 1994.

Foner, Eric, *Reconstruction: America's Unfinished Revolution 1863–1877*, New York: Harper & Row, 1989.

Foner, Philip S., *British Labor and the American Civil War*, New York and London: Holmes & Meier, 1981.

Forcella, Enzo, Preface ('Apologia della paura') to E. Forcella and A. Monticone (eds), *Plotone di esecuzione. I processi della prima guerra mondiale*, Bari: Laterza, 1972.

Ford, Henry, *The International Jew: The World's Foremost Problem*, Dearborn, MI: Dearborn Publishing Company, 1920.

Forrest, Alan, 'La guerre de l'Ouest vue par les soldats républicains', in J.-C. Martin (ed.), *La Guerre civile entre histoire et mémoire*, Nantes: Ouest Éditions, 1995.

Franklin, John Hope, *From Slavery to Freedom: A History of Negro Americans*, 8th edn, New York: Knopf, 2000.

────── *Race and History: Selected Essays 1938–1988*, Baton Rouge and London: Louisiana State University Press, 1989.

Frederickson, George M., *Racism: A Short History*, Princeton: Princeton University Press, 2002.

Freiberger, Steven Z., *Dawn over Suez: The Rise of American Power in the Middle East, 1953–1957*, Chicago: Ivan R. Dee, 1992.

Friedman, George and Meredith, Lebard, *The Coming War with Japan*, New York: St. Martin's Press, 1991.

Furet, François, *Interpreting the French Revolution*, trans. Elborg Forster, Cambridge and New York: Cambridge University Press, 1981 [1978].

———— *La Gauche e la révolution au milieu du XIX siècle. Edgar Quinet et la question du jacobinisme*, Paris: Hachette, 1986.

———— 'Burke ou la fin d'une seule histoire de l'Europe', in F. Lebrun and R. Dupuy (eds), *Les Résistances à la Révolution*, Paris: Imago, 1987.

———— 'Barnave', in Furet and Mona Ozouf (eds), *A Critical Dictionary of the French Revolution*, trans. Arthur Goldhammer, Cambridge, MA: Belknap Press of Harvard University Press, 1989 [1988].

———— 'Mirabeau', in Furet and Ozouf (eds), *A Critical Dictionary of the French Revolution*.

———— *Revolutionary France, 1770–1880*, trans. Antonia Nevill, Oxford and Cambridge, MA: Blackwell, 1992 [1988].

———— *The Passing of an Illusion: The Idea of Communism in the Twentieth Century*, trans. Deborah Furet, Chicago and London: University of Chicago Press, 1999 [1995].

———— and Richet, Denis, *La Révolution française*, new edn, Paris: Hachette, 1999 [1963].

Fussell, Paul, *Wartime: Understanding and Behavior in the Second World War*, New York: Oxford University Press, 1989.

Gabriel, Ralph H., *The Course of American Democratic Thought*, 3rd edn, New York and London: Greenwood Press, 1986.

Gandhi, Mohandas K., *The Collected Works of Mahatma Gandhi*, new edn in 100 vols, New Delhi: Publications Division, Ministry of Information and Broadcasting, Government of India: 1969–.

Gauthier, Florence, *Triomphe et mort du droit naturel en Révolution*, Paris: Presses Universitaires de France, 1992.

Geggus, David, 'British Opinion and the Emergence of Haiti, 1791–1805', in James Walvin (ed.), *Slavery and British Society 1776–1846*, London: Macmillan, 1982.

Genovese, Eugene D., *The Southern Front: History and Politics in the Cultural War*, Columbia, MO: University of Missouri Press, 1995.

———— *The Slaveholders' Dilemma: Freedom and Progress in Southern Conservative Thought, 1820–1860*, Columbia, SC: University of South Carolina Press, 1995 [1992].

Gentz, Friedrich von, *Ausgewählte Schriften*, ed. W. Weick, Stuttgart and Leipzig: Rieger, 1836–38.

Gernet, Jacques, *A History of Chinese Civilization*, 2nd edn, trans. J.R. Foster, Cambridge and New York: Cambridge University Press, 1996 [1972].

Gesensway, Deborah and Roseman, Mindy, *Beyond Words: Images from America's Concentration Camps*, Ithaca, NY, and London: Cornell University Press, 1987.

Gilbert, Martin, *The First World War: A Complete History*, New York: Henry Holt and Company, 1994.

Goldhagen, Daniel J., *Hitler's Willing Executioners: Ordinary Germans and the Holocaust*, London: Little, Brown and Company, 1996.

Goebbels, Joseph, *Reden 1932–1945*, ed. H. Heiber, Bindlach: Gondrom, 1991.

Gosset, Thomas F., *Race: The History of an Idea in America*, New York: Schocken Books, 1965.

Gramsci, Antonio, *Quaderni del carcere*, 4 vols, ed. Valentino Gerratana, Turin: Einaudi, 1975.

────── *Selections from Political Writings 1910–1920*, ed. Quintin Hoare and trans. John Mathews, London: Lawrence & Wishart, 1977.

────── *Cronache Torinesi 1913–1917*, ed. Sergio Caprioglio, Turin: Einaudi, 1980.

────── *La città future 1917–1918*, ed. Sergio Caprioglio, Turin: Einaudi, 1982.

────── *L'Ordine nuovo 1919–1920*, eds Valentino Gerratana and Antonio A. Santucci, Turin: Einaudi, 1987.

Graziosi, Andrea (ed.), *Lettere da Kharkov. La carestia in Ucraina e nel Caucaso del Nord nei rapport dei diplomatici italiani, 1932–33*, Turin: Einaudi, 1991.

Grimsley, Mark, *The Hard Hand of War: Union Military Policy toward Southern Civilians 1861–1865*, Cambridge and New York: Cambridge University Press.

Guillemin, Henri, *Benjamin Constant muscadin 1795–1799*, 6th edn, Paris: Gallimard, 1958.

Guizot, François, 'Avertissement de l'auteur pour la deuxième édition' (1841), in *Histoire de la révolution d'Angleterre*, Brussels: Société Typographique Belge, 1850.

Gumplowicz, Ludwig, *Der Rassenkampf. Soziologische Untersuchungen*, Innsbruck: Wagner'sche Universitätsbuchhandlung, 1883.

Guttmann, Bernhard, *Schattenriss einer Generation 1888–1919*, Stuttgart: Koehler, 1959.

Habermas, Jürgen, 'Nachspiel', Italian trans. in G.E. Rusconi (ed.), *Germania: un passato che non passa*, Turin: Einaudi, 1987.

Hamilton, Alexander, Madison, James and Jay, John, *The Federalist: A Commentary on the Constitution of the United States*, ed. Robert Scigliano, New York: Modern Library, 2000 [1787–88].

Handlin, Oscar and Handlin, Lilian, *Liberty in Peril 1850–1920*, New York: Harper Collins, 1986.

Harbutt, Fraser J., *The Iron Curtain: Churchill, America and the Origins of the Cold War*, New York and Oxford: Oxford University Press, 1986.

Harris, Sheldon H., *Factories of Death: Japanese Biological Warfare and the American Cover Up*, London and New York: Routledge, 1994.

Hauter, François, 'La campagne contre l'"agent orange" des Américains', *Le Figaro*, 6 October 2004.

Hayek, F.A., *The Road to Serfdom*, London: Ark Paperbacks, 1986 [1944].

———— *The Constitution of Liberty*, ed. Ronald Hamowy, Chicago and London: University of Chicago Press, 2011 [1960].

———— *Law, Legislation and Liberty: A New Statement of the Liberal Principles of Justice and Political Economy*, Abingdon: Routledge, 2013 [1973–79].

Hegel, G.W.F., *Vorlesungen über die Philosophie derWeltgeschichte*, ed. G. Lasson, Leipzig: Meiner, 1919–20.

———— *Werke in zwanzig Bänden*, eds E. Moldenhauer and K.M. Michel, Frankfurt am Main: Suhrkamp, 1969–79.

———— *Lectures on the Philosophy of World History: Introduction*, trans. H.B. Nisbet, Cambridge: Cambridge University Press, 1975.

Herder, Johann G., *Outlines of a Philosophy of the History of Man*, trans. T. Churchill, New York: Bergman Publishers, 1966 [1784–91].

Herzstein, Robert E., *Roosevelt and Hitler: Prelude to War*, New York: Paragon House, 1989.

Heydecker, Joe J. and Leeb, Johannes, *Der Nürnberger Prozess*, Köln: Kiepenheuer & Witsch, 1985 [1958].

Hilberg, Raul, *The Destruction of the European Jews*, Vol. 1, New York and London: Holms & Meier, 1985.

Hildebrand, Klaus, *Vom Reich zum Weltreich. Hitler, NSDAP und koloniale Frage 1919–1945*, Munich: Fink, 1969.

Hillgruber, Andreas, *Zweierlei Untergang. Die Zerschlagung des Deutschen Reiches und das Ende des europäischen Judentums*, Berlin: Wolf Jobst Siedler Verlag, 1986.

———— *Die Zerstörung Europas. Beiträge zur Weltkriegsepoche 1914 bis 1945*, Frankfurt am Main and Berlin: Ullstein/Propyläen, 1988.

Hitler, Adolph, *Hitlers Zweites Buch. Ein Dokument aus dem Jahre 1928*, ed. Gerhard L. Weinberg, Stuttgart: Deutsche Verlags/Anstalt, 1961.

———— *Hitler's Table Talk 1941–44*, London: Weidenfeld & Nicolson, 1973 [1953].

———— *Monologe im Führerhauptquartier 1941–1944. Die Aufzeichnungen Heinrich Heims*, ed. W. Jochmann, Hamburg: Albrecht Knaus, 1980.

———— *Mein Kampf*, trans. Ralph Mannheim, London: Pimlico, 1992 [1925/7].

Hobson, J.A., *Imperialism: A Study*, Ann Arbor: University of Michigan Press, 1983 [1902].

Hoffmann, Joachim, *Stalins Vernichtungskrieg 1941–1945*, Munich: Verlag für Wehrwissenschaften, 1995.

Hofstadter, Richard, *The American Political Tradition and the Men Who Made It*, New York: Alfred Knopf, 1967 [1948].

———— and Hofstadter, Beatrice K., *Great Issues in American History*, 3 vols, New York: Vintage Books, 1982 [1958].

Hunecke, Volker, 'Tendenze anticapitalistiche nella rivoluzione francese', *Società e storia*, Vol. 1, No. 1, 1978.

Huntington, Samuel P., *The Clash of Civilizations and the Remaking of World Order*, New York: Simon & Schuster, 1996.

———— *Who Are We? The Challenges to America's National Identity*, New York: Simon & Schuster, 2004.

Irons, Peter, *Justice at War: The Story of the Japanese American Internment Cases*, New York and Oxford: Oxford University Press, 1983.

Irving, David, *The Destruction of Dresden*, London: W. Kimber, 1963.

Isnenghi, Mario, *Il mito della grande guerra*, Bari: Laterza, 1970.

Jacobsen, Hans-Adolf, 'Kommissarbefehl und Massenexekutionen sowjetischer Kriegsgefangener', in *Anatomie des SS-Staates*, Vol. II, Munich: DTV, 1989 [1967].

Jefferson, Thomas, *Notes on the State of Virginia*, ed. W. Peden, Chapel Hill: University of North Carolina Press, 1955 [1787].

———— *Writings*, ed. Merrill D. Peterson, New York: Library of America, 1984.

Johnson, Paul, *A History of the Jews*, New York: Perennial Library, 1988 [1987].

———— *Modern Times: The World from the Twenties to the Nineties*, revised edn, New York: Harper Collins, 1991 [1983].

———— *Ireland: A Concise History from the Twelfth Century to the Present Day*, Chicago: Academy, 1993 [1980].

———— 'Colonialism's Back – and Not a Moment Too Soon', *New York Times Magazine*, 18 April 1993.

Johnson, Walter, *Soul by Soul: Life inside the Antebellum Slave Market*, Cambridge, MA, and London: Harvard University Press, 1999.

Jünger, Ernst, 'Total Mobilization', in Richard Wolin (ed.), *The Heidegger Controversy: A Critical Reader*, Cambridge, MA, and London: MIT Press, 1993.

Kant, Immanuel, *Gesammelte Schriften*, Berlin: Editions of the Academy of Sciences: Berlin, 1900–.

Karsten, Peter, 'Militarization and Rationalization in the United States, 1870–1914', in J.R. Gillis (ed.), *The Militarization of the Western World*, New Brunswick and London: Rutgers, 1989.

Katz, Steven T., *The Holocaust in Historical Contexts – Volume I: The Holocaust and Mass Death before the Modern Age*, New York and Oxford: Oxford University Press, 1994.

Kennedy, Paul M., *The Rise of the Anglo-German Antagonism 1860–1914*, London and New York: Ashfield Press, 1987 [1980].

Kerensky, Alexander F., *The Kerensky Memoirs: Russia and History's Turning Point*, London: Cassell, 1966.

Kelley, Robin D.G., *Hammer and Hoe: Alabama Communists during the Great Depression*, Chapel Hill and London: University of North Carolina Press, 1990.

Kesting, Hanno, *Geschichtsphilosophie und Weltbürgerkrieg*, Heidelberg: Winter, 1959.

Kilzer, Louis C., *Churchill's Deception: The Dark Secret that Destroyed Nazi Germany*, New York: Simon & Schuster, 1994.

Kirk, Russel, *John Randolph of Roanoke: A Study in American Politics*, Indianapolis: Liberty Press, 1978.

Kissinger, Henry, *Diplomacy*, New York: Simon & Schuster, 1994.

———— *On China*, New York: Penguin, 2011.

Klemperer, Victor, *The Language of the Third Reich: LTI, Lingua Tertii Imperii – A Philologist's Notebook*, trans. Martin Brady, London and New Brunswick, NJ: Athlone Press, 2000.

Klinkhammer, Lutz, *Zwischen Bündnis und Besatzung. Das nationalsozialistische Deutschland und die Republik von Salò 1943 bis 1945*, Tübingen: M. Niemeyer, 1993.

Koselleck, Reinhart, *Critique and Crisis: Enlightenment and the Pathogenesis of Modern Society*, Cambridge, MA: MIT Press, 1988.

Koss, Stephen, *The Pro-Boers: The Anatomy of an Antiwar Movement*, Chicago and London: University of Chicago Press, 1973.

Kotek, Joel and Rigoulot, Pierre, *Le Siècle des camps. Détention, concentration, extermination: cent ans de mal radical*, Paris: Lattès, 2000.

Kraditor, Aileen S., *Means and Ends in American Abolitionism: Garrison and His Critics on Strategy and Tactics, 1834–1850*, Chicago: I.R. Dee, 1989 [1967].

Krausnick, Helmut, *Hitlers Einsatzgruppen. Die Truppen des Weltanschauungskrieges 1938–1942*, Hamburg: Fischer, 1985.

Kühl, Stefan, *The Nazi Connection: Eugenics, American Racism and German National Socialism*, New York and Oxford: Oxford University Press, 1994.

La Forte, Robert S. and Marcello, Ronald E., *Building the Death Railway: The Ordeal of American POWs in Burma, 1942–1945*, Wilmington: SR Books, 1993.

Laqueur, Walter, *The Terrible Secret: Suppression of the Truth about Hitler's 'Final Solution'*, New York: Penguin, 1980.

Laski, Harold J., *The American Democracy: A Commentary and an Interpretation*, Fairfield: Kelley, 1977 [1948].

Leckie, Robert, *The Wars of America*, new edn, New York: Harper Collins, 1992 [1968].

Lecky, William E.H., *A History of England in the Eighteenth Century*, 3rd edn, 8 vols, London: Longmans, Green and Co., 1883–88.

Lence, Ross M., Foreword to J.C. Calhoun, *Union and Liberty*, Indianapolis: Liberty Press, 1992.

Lenin, V.I., *Collected Works*, 45 vols, London: Lawrence & Wishart, 1960–.

Lensch, Paul, *Drei Jahre Weltrevolution*, Berlin: Fischer, 1917.

Levin, Nora, *The Jews in the Soviet Union since 1917*, 2 vols, London and New York: I.B. Tauris, 1990.

Lincoln, W. Bruce, *Passage Through Armageddon: The Russians in War and Revolution 1914–1918*, New York and Oxford: Oxford University Press, 1994 [1986].

Lipstadt, Deborah E., *Denying the Holocaust: The Growing Assault on Truth and Memory*, New York and Toronto: The Free Press/Macmillan, 1993.

Losurdo, Domenico, *La catastrophe della Germania e l'immagine di Hegel*, Milan: Guerini, 1987.

———— *Democrazia o bonapartismo. Trionfo e decadenza del suffragio universale*, Turin: Bollati Boringhieri, 1993.

——— *Heidegger and the Ideology of War: Community, Death and the West*, trans. Marella and Jon Morris, Amherst, NY: Humanity Books, 2001 [1991].

——— *Hegel and the Freedom of the Moderns*, trans. Marella and Jon Morris, Durham, NC, and London: Duke University Press, 2004 [1992].

——— *Il linguaggio dell'Impero. Lessico dell'ideologia americana*, Rome and Bari: Laterza, 2007.

——— *La non-violenza. Una storia fuori dal mito*, Rome and Bari: Laterza, 2010.

——— *Liberalism: A Counter-History*, trans. Gregory Elliott, London and New York: Verso, 2011 [2005].

Löwith, Karl, *Mein Leben in Deutschland vor and nach 1933. Ein Bericht*, Suttgart: Metzler, 1986.

Ludendorff, Erich, *Der totale Krieg*, Munich: Ludendorff, 1935.

Lukács, Georg, *The Destruction of Reason*, trans. Peter Palmer, London: Merlin Press, 1980 [1954].

Lukas, Richard C., *Forgotten Holocaust: The Poles under German Occupation 1939–1944*, New York: Hippocrene Books, 1990 [1986].

Luraghi, Raimondo, Introduction to *La guerra civile americana*, Bologna: Il Mulino, 1978.

Luxemburg, Rosa, *Politische Schriften*, 2 vols, ed. O.K. Flechtheim, Frankfurt am Main: Europäische Verlagsanstalt, 1968.

McAllister Linn, Brian, *The US Army and Counterinsurgency in the Philippine War, 1899–1902*, Chapel Hill and London: University of North Carolina Press, 1989.

MacDougall, Hugh A., *Racial Myth in English History: Trojans, Teutons, and Anglo-Saxons*, Montreal and London: Harvest/University Press of New England, 1982.

Maistre, Joseph de, *Oeuvres complètes*, reprint, Hildesheim, Zurich and New York: Olms, 1984 [1884].

Malaparte, Curzio, *Viva Caporetto! La rivolta dei santi maledetti*, Milan: Mondadori, 1981 [1921].

Malcolm X, *Malcolm X Speaks: Selected Speeches and Statements*, ed. George Breitman, New York: Merit Publishers, 1965.

Mann, Michael, *The Sources of Social Power. Vol. 3: Global Empires and Revolution, 1890–1945*, Cambridge and New York: Cambridge University Press, 2012.

Mann, Thomas, *Betrachtungen eines Unpolitischen*, ed. H. Helbling, Frankfurt am Main: Fischer, 1988 [1918].

Mannheim, Karl, 'Das conservative Denken', in *Wissenssoziologie. Auswahl aus dem Werk*, ed. K.H. Wolff, Berlin and Neuwied: Luchterhand, 1964.

Mao Tse-Tung, 'On Protracted War' (1938), in *Selected Military Writings of Mao Tse-Tung*, Beijing: Foreign Languages Press, 1967.

Markov, Walter (ed.), *Revolution im Zeugenstand. Frankreich 1789–1799*, Leipzig: Reclam, 1982.

Markusen, Eric and Kopf, David, *The Holocaust and Strategic Bombing: Genocide and Total War in the Twentieth Century*, Boulder, CO, San Francisco and Oxford: Westview Press, 1995.

Martineau, Harriet, *British Rule in India: A Historical Sketch*, London: Smith, 1857.

Marx, Karl, *Capital: Volume One*, trans. Ben Fowkes, Harmondsworth: Penguin, 1976 [1867].

Marx, Karl and Engels, Friedrich, *Werke*, 38 vols, Berlin: Dietz, 1955–.

—— *Selected Works*, 3 vols, Moscow: Progress Publishers, 1977.

—— *Gesamtausgabe*, Berlin: Dietz, 1975– and Amsterdam: IMES, 1990–.

May, Christopher, N., *In the Name of War: Judicial Review and the War Powers since 1918*, Cambridge, MA, and London: Harvard University Press, 1989.

Mayer, Arno J., *Political Origins of the New Diplomacy, 1917–1918*, New York: Vintage Books, 1959.

—— *The Persistence of the Old Regime: Europe to the Great War*, London and New York: Verso, 2010.

—— *Why Did the Heavens Not Darken? The Final Solution in History*, London: Verso, 2012.

Meinecke, Friedrich, *Die Entstehung des Historismus*, Munich: Oldenbourg, 1965 [1936].

Mercier, Louis-Sébastien, *L'An deux mille quatre cent quarante. Rêve s'il en fut jamais*, ed. Raymond Trousson, Paris: Ducros, 1971 [1770].

Merl, Stefan, ' "Ausrottung" der Bourgeoisie und der Kulaken in Sowjetrussland?', *Geschichte und Gesellschaft*, Vol. 13, No. 3, 1987.

Merriam, Charles E., *A History of American Political Theories*, New York: Kelley, 1969 [1903].

Michaelis, Meir, *Mussolini and the Jews: German-Italian Relations and the Jewish Question in Italy 1922–1945*, New York: Oxford University Press, 1978.

Michelet, Jules, *Histoire de la Révolution française*, 2nd edn, Paris: Gallimard, 1961 [1847–53].

Mill, John Stuart, *Collected Works*, 33 vols, ed. F.E.L. Priestley, J.M. Robson et al., Toronto and London: University of Toronto Press/Routledge & Kegan Paul, 1963–.

—— *Utilitarianism, On Liberty, Representative Government*, ed. Harry B. Acton, London: Dent, 1972.

Millis, Walter, *The Martial Spirit*, Chicago: Elephant Paperbacks, 1989 [1931].

Mintz, Frank Paul, *Revisionism and the Origins of Pearl Harbor*, Boston and London: University Press of America, 1985.

Mises, Ludwig von, *Human Action: A Treatise on Economics*, 3rd edn, Chicago: Contemporary Books, 1966 [1949].

—— *Socialism: An Economic and Sociological Analysis*, trans. Jacques Kahane, Indianapolis: Liberty Fund, 1981 [1922].

—— *Omnipotent Government: The Rise of the Total State and Total War*, Spring Mills: Libertarian Press, 1985 [1944].

—— *Liberalism: The Classical Tradition*, ed. Bettina Bien Greaves and trans. Ralph Raico, Indianapolis: Liberty Fund, 2005 [1927].

Misra, Amaresh, *War of Civilizations: India AD 1857*, 2 vols, New Delhi: Rupa, 2008.

Mommsen, Wolfgang J., *Max Weber. Gesellschaft, Politik und Geschichte*, Frankfurt am Main: Suhrkamp, 1974.

———— *Max Weber und die deutsche Politik, 1890–1920*, Tübingen: Mohr (Siebeck), 1974.

Morgenstern, George, *Pearl Harbor: The Story of the Secret War*, Newport: Institute for Historical Review, 1991 [1947].

Möser, Justus, *Sämmtliche Werke*, ed. B.R. Abeken and J.W.J. von Voigts, Berlin: Nicolaische Buchhandlung, 1842.

Mosse, George L., *The Nationalization of the Masses: Political Symbolism and Mass Movements in Germany from the Napoleonic Wars through the Third Reich*, New York: Howard Fertig, 1974.

———— *Fallen Soldiers: Reshaping the Memory of the World Wars*, New York: Oxford University Press, 1994.

Mukerjee, Madhusree, *Churchill's Secret War: The British Empire and the Ravaging of India during World War II*, New York: Basic Books, 2010.

Nevis, Allan and Commager, Henry S., *America: Story of a Free People*, Oxford: Oxford University Press, 1943.

New York Times Book Review, 14 April 1991, Letters.

Nichanian, Marc, 'Le droit et le fait: la campagne de 1994', *Lignes*, No. 26, October 1995.

Nietzsche, Friedrich, *Sämtliche Werke, Kritische Studienausgabe*, ed. G. Colli and M. Montinari, Munich: DTV, 1980.

Nolte, Ernst, *Three Faces of Fascism: Action Françise, Italian Fascism, National Socialism*, trans. Leila Vennewitz, New York: Mentor, 1969 [1963].

———— *La crisi dei regime liberali e i movimenti fascisti*, trans. E. Gamaleri and A. Caiani, Bologna: Il Mulino, 1970 [1968].

———— *Marxismus und industrielle Revolution*, Stuttgart: Kletta-Cotta, 1983.

———— *Der europäische Bürgerkrieg 1917–1945. Nationalsozialismus und Bolschewismus*, Frankfurt am Main and Berlin: Ullstein, 1987.

———— *Nietzsche und der Nietzscheanismus*, Frankfurt am Main and Berlin: Propyläen, 1990.

———— *Dopo il comunismo. Contributi all'interpretazione della storia del XX secolo*, trans. P. Sorge, Florence: Sansoni, 1992.

———— 'The Past That Will Not Pass: A Speech That Could be Written but Not Delivered', in *Forever in the Shadow of Hitler? Original Documents of the Historikerstreit, The Controversy Concerning the Singularity of the Holocaust*, trans. James Knowlton and Truett Cates, New Jersey: Humanities Press, 1993 [1986].

———— 'Standing Things on Their Heads: Against Negative Nationalism in Interpreting History', in *Forever in the Shadow of Hitler?* [1986].

———— *Intervista sulla questione tedesca*, ed. Alberto Krali, Rome and Bari: Laterza, 1993.

———— *Dramma dialettico o tragedia? La guerra civile mondiale e altri saggi*, ed. F. Coppellotti, Perugia: Settimo Sigillo/Perugia University Press, 1994.

———— *Gli anni della violenza. Un secolo di guerra civile ideologica, europea e mondiale*, trans. P. Azzaro and S. Azzaro, Milan: Rizzoli, 1995.

Normand, Roger, 'Deal Won't End Iraqi Suffering', *International Herald Tribune*, 7 June 1996.

Pakenham, Thomas, *The Year of Liberty: The History of the Great Irish Rebellion of 1798*, New York: Random House, 1969.

Palmer, Robert R., *The Age of Democratic Revolution: A Political History of Europe and America, 1760–1800*, 2 vols, Princeton: Princeton University Press, 1959–64.

Paquet, Alfons, *Im Kommunistischen Russland. Briefe aus Moskau*, Jena: Diederichs, 1919.

Pareto, Vilfredo, 'Perche?' (1904), in *Scritti politici*, ed. G. Busino, Vol. 2, Turin: UTET, 1974.

Pavone, Claudio, *Una guerra civile. Saggio storico sulla moralità nella Resistenza*, Turin: Bollati Boringhieri, 1991.

Peterson, H.C. and Fite, Gilbert C., *Opponents of War 1917–1918*, Madison: University of Wisconsin Press, 1957.

Phelps, Reginald H., 'Hitler als Parteiredner im Jahre 1920', *Vierteljahreshefte für Zeitgeschichte*, Vol. XI, 1963.

Pick, Daniel, *War Machine: The Rationalisation of Slaughter in the Modern Age*, New Haven: Yale University Press, 1993.

Pipes, Richard, *The Russian Revolution*, New York: Vintage Books, 1990.

Pocock, J.G.A., *Virtue, Commerce and History*, Cambridge: Cambridge University Press, 1988.

Poliakov, Léon, *Le Mythe aryen. Essai sur les sources du racisme et des nationalismes*, new edn, Brussels: Complexe, 1987 [1971].

———— *The History of Anti-Semitism*, 4 vols, trans. Richard Howard et al., Philadelphia: University of Pennsylvania Press, 2003 [1955–68].

Post, C. Gordon, Introduction to John C. Calhoun, *A Disquisition on Government*, New York: Liberal Arts Press, 1953.

Procacci, Giuliano, *Dall parte dell'Etiopia. L'aggressione italiana vista dai movimenti anticolonialisti d'Asia, d'Africa, d'America*, Milan: Feltrinelli, 1984.

Quinet, Edgar, *Le Christianisme et la Révolution française*, Paris: Fayard, 1984 [1845].

Ranke, Leopold von, *Über die Epochen der neueren Geschichte*, Darmstadt: Wissenschaftliche Buchgesellschaft, 1980 [1854].

Ratzel, Friedrich, *Politische Geographie der Vereinigten Staaten von Amerika unter besonderer Berücksichtung der natürlichen Bedingungen und wirtschaftlichen Verhältnisse*, Munich: Oldenburg, 1893.

Rigoni Stern, Mario, Introduction to Leonardo Zanier, *Carnia, Kosakenland, Kazackaja, Zemlja*, Udine: Mittelcultura, 1996.

Ritter, Gerhard A. and Miller, Susanne (eds), *Die deutsche Revolution 1918–1919*, Frankfurt am Main: Fischer, 1968.

Robespierre, Maximilien, *Oeuvres*, Paris: Presses Universitaires de France, 1912–.

Rochester, Stuart I., *American Liberal Disillusionment in the Wake of World War I*, University Park: Pennsylvania State University Press, 1977.

Romein, Jan, *The Asian Century: A History of Modern Nationalism in Asia*, trans. R.T. Clark, Berkeley: University of California Press, 1962 [1956].

Roosevelt, Theodore, *The Strenuous Life: Essays and Addresses*, New York: The Century, 1901.

—— *Letters*, ed. Elting E. Morison and John M. Blum, 8 vols, Cambridge, MA: Harvard University Press, 1951–.

Rosdolsky, Roman, 'Friedrich Engels und das Problem der "geschichtlosen Völker"', *Archiv für Sozialgeschichte*, Vol. IV, 1964.

Rosenberg, Alfred, *The Myth of the Twentieth Century: An Evaluation of the Spiritual-Intellectual Confrontations of Our Age*, Newport Beach, CA: Noontide Press, 1993 [1930].

Rosenberg, Arthur, *A History of Bolshevism: From Marx to the First Five Years' Plan*, trans. Ian F.D. Morrow, New York: Anchor Books, 1967 [1932].

Rothbard, Murray N., 'Hoover's 1919 Food Diplomacy in Retrospect', in Lawrence E. Gelfand (ed.), *Herbert Hoover, the Great War and Its Aftermath 1917–23*, Iowa City: Iowa University Press, 1974.

—— and Trani, Eugene P., 'Herbert Hoover and the Russian Revolution 1917–20', in Gelfand (ed.), *Herbert Hoover, the Great War and Its Aftermath*.

Rousseau, Jean-Jacques, *Oeuvres complètes*, ed. Bernard Gagnebin and Marcel Raymond, Paris: Gallimard, 1959–.

—— *Correspondence complète*, ed. R.A. Leigh, Oxford: Voltaire Foundation, 1977.

Roux, Alain, *La Chine au XXe siècle*, 4th edn, Paris: Colin, 2007 [1998].

Ryerson, Egerton, *The Loyalists of America and Their Times: From 1620 to 1816*, 2 vols, New York: Haskell House, 1970 [1880].

Saint-Just, Louis Antoine Léon de, *Oeuvres complètes*, ed. Michèle Duval, Paris: G. Lebovici, 1984.

Salbstein, Michael C.N., *The Emancipation of the Jews in Britain: The Question of the Admission of the Jews to Parliament, 1828–1860*, London and Toronto: Associated University Presses, 1982.

Salvatorelli, Luigi and Mira, Giovanni, *Storia d'Italia nel periodo fascista*, Milan: Oscar Mondadori, 1972.

Salvemini, Gaetano, *Opere*, 9 vols, Milan: Feltrinelli, 1964–74.

Santarelli, Enzo (ed.), *Scritti politici di Benito Mussolini*, Milan: Feltrinelli, 1979.

Sartori, Giovanni, *Democrazia e definizioni*, 4th edn, Bologna: Il Mulino, 1976.

—— *The Theory of Democracy Revisited*, Chatham, NJ: Chatham House Publishers, 1976.

Sartre, Jean-Paul, 'The Political Thought of Patrice Lumumba', in Sartre, *Colonialism and Neocolonialism*, trans. Azzedine Hadour, Steve Brewer and Terry McWilliams, Abingdon and New York: Routledge, 2006 [1964].

Schlesinger, Arthur M. Jr. (ed.), *History of United States Political Parties*, New York and London: Chelsea House and Bawker, 1973.

Schmid, Alex P., *Churchills privater Krieg. Intervention und Konterrevolution im russischen Bürgerkrieg, November 1918–März 1920*, Zürich: Atlantis, 1974.

Schmidt, Martin and Stein, Dieter, *Im Gespräch mit Ernst Nolte*, Potsdam: Junge Freiheit, 1993.

Schmitt, Carl, 'Die deutsche Rechtswissenschaft im Kampf gegen den jüdischen Geist', *Deutsche Juristen-Zeitung*, 15 October 1936.

——— *Donoso Cortés in gesamteuropäischer Interpretation*, Köln: Greven, 1950.

——— *Verfassungsrechtliche Aufsätze*, 3rd edn, Berlin: Duncker & Humblot, 1985 [1958].

——— *The Crisis of Parliamentary Democracy*, trans. Ellen Kennedy, Cambridge, MA: MIT Press, 1985 [1926].

——— *Positionen und Begriffe im Kampf mit Weimar-Genf-Versailles 1932–1939*, Berlin: Duncker & Humblot, 1988 [1940].

——— *Glossarium. Aufzeichnungen der Jahre 1947–1951*, ed. E. Freiherr von Medem, Berlin: Duncker & Humblot, 1991.

——— *L'unità del mondo e altri saggi*, ed. A. Campi, Rome: Pellicani, 1994.

——— *The Nomos of the Earth in the International Law of the Jus Publicum Europaeum*, trans. G.L. Ulmen, New York: Telos Press, 2006 [1950].

——— *Theory of the Partisan: Intermediate Commentary on the Concept of the Political*, trans. G.L. Ulmen, New York: Telos, Press, 2007 [1963].

——— *Writings on War*, ed. and trans. Timothy Nunan, Cambridge: Polity Press, 2011.

——— *Dictatorship: From the Origin of the Modern Concept of Sovereignty to Proletarian Class Struggle*, trans. Michael Hoelzl and Graham Ward, Cambridge: Polity Press, 2014 [1921].

Schnur, Roman, *Revolution und Weltbürgerkrieg. Studien zur Ouvertüre nach 1789*, Berlin: Duncker & Humblot, 1983.

Schröder, Hans Christoph, *Die Revolutionen Englands im 17. Jahrhundert*, Frankfurt am Main: Suhrkamp, 1986.

Schumpeter, Joseph A., *Imperialism and Social Classes*, trans. Heinz Norden, New York: A.M. Kelly, 1951 [1919].

Secher, Reynald, *Le Génocide franco-français. La Vendée-Vengé*, Paris: Presses Universitaires de France, 1986.

Shirer, William L., *The Rise and Fall of the Third Reich: A History of Nazi Germany*, London: Pan, 1964.

Skidelsky, Robert, *John Maynard Keynes – A Biography. Hopes Betrayed: 1883–1920*, London and Basingstoke: Macmillan, 1983.

Slotkin, Richard, *Fatal Environment: The Myth of the Frontier in the Age of Industrialization 1800–1890*, New York: Harper Perennial, 1994 [1985].

Smith, Adam, *Lectures on Jurisprudence*, Indianapolis: Liberty Classics, 1982 [1762–63 and 1766].

Smith, James Morton (ed.), *The Republic of Letters: The Correspondence between Thomas Jefferson and James Madison 1776–1826*, New York and London: Norton, 1995.

Sombart, Werner, *Der proletarische Sozialismus*, 2 vols, Jena: Fischer, 1924.

Spengler, Oswald, *The Hour of Decision*, trans. Charles Francis Atkinson, London: George Allen & Unwin, 1934 [1933].

———— 'Frankreich und Europa' (1924), in *Reden und Aufsätze*, ed. Hildegard Kornhardt, Munich: Beck, 1937.

———— *Der Untergang des Abendlandes*, Munich: Beck, 1980 [1918–23].

Spini, Giorgio, *Disegno storico della civiltà*, 7th edn, Rome: Cremonese, 1963.

———— *Storia dell'età moderna*, 6th edn, Turin: Einaudi, 1982 [1965].

Stalin, J.V., *On the Great Patriotic War of the Soviet Union*, London, New York and Melbourne: Hutchinson, n.d. [1944].

———— *Works*, 13 vols, Moscow: Foreign Languages Publishing House, 1952–.

———— *Problems of Leninism*, Moscow: Foreign Languages Publishing House, 1953.

———— *Über den Grossen Vaterländischen Krieg der Sowjetunion*, Frankfurt am Main: Dokumente der Kommunistichen Weltbewegung, 1972.

———— *The Essential Stalin: Major Theoretical Writings 1902–52*, ed. Bruce Franklin, London: Croom Helm, 1973.

———— *Letters to Molotov*, ed. L.T. Lih, O.V. Naumov and O.V. Khlevniuk, New Haven and London: Yale University Press, 1995.

Stampp, Kenneth M. (ed.), *The Causes of the Civil War*, 3rd edn, New York: Simon & Schuster, 1991 [1959].

Stannard, David. E., *American Holocaust: The Conquest of the New World*, Oxford and New York: Oxford University Press, 1992.

Stimson, Henry L. and Bundy, McGeorge, *On Active Service in Peace and War*, New York: Octagon Books, 1971 [1947].

Stoddard, Lothrop, *The Rising Tide of Color against White World-Supremacy*, n.p.: 1920.

———— *The Revolt against Civilization: The Menace of the Under Man*, New York: C. Scribner's Sons, 1922.

Sun Yat-Sen, *The Three Principles of the People*, trans. Frank W. Price, Vancouver: Soul Care Publishingm 2011, [1924].

Taine, Hippolyte, *Les Origines de la France contemporaine*, Paris: Hachette, 1899 [1876–94].

Talmon, Jacob L., *The Origins of Totalitarian Democracy*, London: Secker & Warburg, 1952.

Tansill, Charles C., *Back Door to War: The Roosevelt Foreign Policy 1933–1941*, Chicago: Regnery, 1952.

Taylor, A.J.P., *The Struggle for Mastery in Europe, 1848–1918*, Oxford: Clarendon Press, 1954.

———— *English History 1914–1945*, Oxford: Oxford University Press, 1965.

———— *The Origins of the Second World War*, London: Penguin, 1991 [1961].

Thomas, Hugh, *Armed Truce: The Beginnings of the Cold War 1945–46*, London: Sceptre, 1988 [1986].

Tocqueville, Alexis de, *Oeuvres complètes*, ed. Jacob-Peter Mayer, Paris: Gallimard, 1951–.

———— *Democracy in America*, London: Everyman, 1994.

Todorov, Tzvetan, *The Conquest of America: The Question of the Other*, trans. Richard Howard, London: Harper Perennial, 1992 [1982].

Toynbee, Arnold, *A Study of History*, Oxford: Oxford University Press, 1951–54.

———— *The World and the Rest*, New York: Oxford University Press, 1953.

Trevelyan, G.M., *The English Revolution 1688–1689*, London, Oxford and New York: Oxford University Press, 1968 [1938].

———— *British History in the Nineteenth Century and After (1782–1919)*, Harmondsworth: Penguin, 1979 [1922].

———— *History of England*, new illustrated edn, London: Longman, 1979 [1926].

Trotsky, L.D., *Their Morals and Ours*, trans. Max Eastman, New York: Pioneer Publishers, 1942 [1938–9].

Tucholsky, Kurt, *Gesammelte Werke*, ed. M. Gerold Tucholsky and F.J. Raddatz, Hamburg: Rowohlt, 1985.

Tucker, Robert C., *Stalin in Power: The Revolution from Above, 1928–1941*, New York and London: 1990.

Vattel, Emer de, *Le Droit des gens ou principes de la loi naturelle*, ed. J. Brown Schott, Washington: Classics of International Law, 1916 [1758].

Veale, Frederick J.P., *Advance to Barbarism: The Development of Total Warfare*, Newport: Institute for Historical Review, 1979 [1948].

Venner, Dominique, *Le blanc soleil des vaincus. L'épopée sudiste et la guerre de Sécession, 1607–1865*, Paris: La Table Ronde, 1975.

Waite, Robert G.L., *Vanguard of Nazism: The Free Corps Movement in Postwar Germany 1918–1923*, Cambridge, MA: Harvard University Press, 1970 [1952].

Walter, Gérard, *La Rivoluzione russa*, Novara: De Agostini, 1990 [1972].

Walzer, Michael, *The Revolution of the Saints: A Study in the Origin of Radical Politics*, Cambridge, MA, and London: Harvard University Press, 1965.

Washington, George, *A Collection*, ed. W.B. Allen, Indianapolis: Liberty Classics, 1988.

Weaver, Richard, M., *The Southern Essays*, ed. G.M. Curtis III and J.J. Thompson Jr., Indianapolis: Liberty Press, 1987.

Weber, Max, *Gesammelte politische Schriften*, ed. J. Winckelmann, 3rd edn, Tübingen: Mohr (Siebeck), 1971 [1958].

———— *Zur Politik im Weltkrieg. Schriften und Reden 1914–1918*, ed. W.J. Mommsen in collaboration with G. Hübinger, Tübingen: Mohr, 1988.

———— 'The Meaning of "Ethical Neutrality" in Sociology and Economics' (1917), in Weber, *Methodology of the Social Sciences*, ed. and trans. Edward A. Shils and Henry A. Finch, New Brunswick, NJ: Transaction Publishers, 2011.

Wehler, Hans-Ulrich, *Le mani sulla storia*, trans. A. Missiroli, Florence: Ponte alle Grazie, 1989.

Wilberforce, Robert Isaac and Samuel, *Life of William Wilberforce by his Sons*, London: Murray, 1838.

Williams, Eric, *Capitalism and Slavery*, London: Deutsch, 1990 [1944].

Woodward, C. Vann, *Origins of the New South 1877–1913*, Baton Rouge: Louisiana State University Press, 1951.

Zawodny, J.K., *Death in the Forest: The Story of the Katyn Forest Massacre*, London and Basingstoke: Macmillan, 1971 [1962].

Zayas, Alfred M. de (ed.), *Die Wehrmachtuntersuchungsstelle. Deutsche Ermittlungen über alliierte Völkerrechtsverletzungen im zweiten Weltkrieg*, 4th edn, Munich: Universitas, 1984.

Zhang, Shu Guang, *Economic Cold War: America's Embargo against China and the Sino-Soviet Alliance*, Stanford: Stanford University Press, 2001.

Index